TRIGGERNOMETRY

A GALLERY OF GUNFIGHTERS

with Technical Notes, too, on
Leather Slapping as a Fine Art,
gathered from many a Loose
Holstered Expert over the years

A Gallery of Gunfighters

WITH

TECHNICAL NOTES
on Leather Slapping *as a* Fine Art,
gathered from many a Loose Holstered
Expert *over the* Years

By
Eugene Cunningham

Foreword by
Eugene Manlove Rhodes

Illustrations from the
Rose Collection, *San Antonio*

Introduction by
Joseph G. Rosa

University of Oklahoma Press
Norman

Library of Congress Cataloging-in-Publication Data

Cunningham, Eugene, 1896–1957.
    Triggernometry : a gallery of gunfighters : with technical
notes on leather slapping as a fine art, gathered from many a
loose holstered expert over the years / by Eugene
Cunningham ; foreword by Eugene Manlove
Rhodes ; illustrations from the Rose Collection, San
Antonio ; introduction by Joseph G. Rosa.
        p.   cm.
    Includes bibliographical references.
    ISBN 978-0-8061-2837-5 (paper)
        1. West (U.S.)—Biography.   2. Frontier and pioneer life—
West (U.S.)   3. Outlaws—West (U.S.)—Biography.   I. Title.
F591.C85   1996
364.1'552'092278—dc20
[B]   95-38776
                                                                        CIP

The paper in this book meets the guidelines for permanence and durability of the Committee on Production Guidelines for Book Longevity of the Council on Library Resources, Inc.♾

Copyright ©1934 by Eugene Cunningham. Copyright ©1941 by The Caxton Printers. Copyright © 1969 renewed by Mary Carolyn Cunningham Call, Jean Cunningham Weakley, and Cleve Cunningham. Oklahoma Paperback Edition published 1996 by the University of Oklahoma Press, Norman, Publishing Division of the University by special arrangement with Golden West Literary Agency. Introduction to the Oklahoma Edition © 1996 by the University of Oklahoma Press. Manufactured in the U.S.A.

Affectionately and Appreciatively
Dedicated To
JOHN R. HUGHES · JAMES B. GILLETT
Two Great Horseback Rangers
friends of mine

"*Those were frontier towns, ol' pardner;*
'T was a game o' take an' give,
An' the one who could draw the fastest
Was the only one who'd live!"

—(N. HOWARD) "JACK" THORP.

CONTENTS

ILLUSTRATIONS

TRIGGERNOMETRY · *Foreword*

Stories of oldtime gunfighters are apt to be highly colored, and to vary with the square of the distance.

As you read Eugene Cunningham's tales of a few of the gunfighters of The West that Was, it is well to remember that 'Gene writes for the most part from first-hand knowledge and, at worst, from accounts given by participants or eye-witnesses. Moreover, these stories were gathered on the scenes of the events narrated. That meant prompt denial and confutation, if a narrator stretched his story beyond the expected and accepted variations of the partisan. No way has been invented to eliminate partisanship and the historian must allow for these variations, as the engineer allows for heat and cold in laying a pipe line.

Gunfighters. . . . In the old days we said "gunman" —a word exactly comparable with "swordsman." Because of the modern gangster, the word gunman now carries the implication of coward, of baby-killer. It brings up the idea of seven against one; of helpless victims "taken for a ride" or "put on the spot"; of time-fuse bombs and steel vests, armored cars and machine guns; the safe and shameless!

When you read these stories of the oldtime gunmen, you will see that for even the worst of them, such deeds were unthinkable. If they were criminals—and some of them were—at least they were present at the scenes of their crimes, at their own proper peril. . . They set no dynamite to kill an enemy as he opened his garden gate. They killed armed men—not men unarmed and bound. . . . . It is impossible to imagine the worst and lowest of them, even if he were crazy-drunk, killing children or women. Some of them were pretty poor specimens. But to compare the vilest of them with such monsters as Leopold and Loeb would be infamous.

And the thought will occur to you that if some of these oldtimers could come to life now, Chicago and New York could use their courage and skill, thanking God!

Eugene Manlove Rhodes

TRIGGERNOMETRY · *Introduction*

SOME YEARS ago I was browsing in London's largest bookstore when my attention was drawn to the section devoted to mathematics. There, next to a book about slide-rule practice, was a copy of *Triggernometry*. To this day I do not know if it was put there in error or by someone who shared my own sometimes perverse sense of humor. Certainly it is not the first time that people have confused the book's title with trigonometry. There are those who have criticized the title for being flippant, whereas others think it inspired. But whatever one's view, it is a title one never forgets!

Eugene Cunningham's *Triggernometry: A Gallery of Gunfighters, with Technical Notes on Leather Slapping as a Fine Art, Gathered from Many a Loose Holstered Expert Over the Years* was first published in 1934 by the Press of the Pioneers, New York. Its success led to a 1941 edition and numerous reprints by Caxton Printers. An abridged paperback edition, which omitted the chapters on Wild Bill Hickok and General Lee Christmas, was published in Great Britain in the mid-1950s. Another British paperback edition appeared in 1978, this time in two volumes—an unpopular move because potential readers complained that they rarely found both volumes together. Now, however, the University of Oklahoma Press has reproduced the original text—with an updated bibliography—in a one-volume paperback.

The original illustrations from the Rose Collection (now owned by the University of Oklahoma) have been retained, including their captions. Therefore, the following comments concerning several of them may be appreciated. The photograph of Bass Outlaw originally formed a part of a group pose of Texas Rangers photographed at Camp Leona. Similarly, the photograph of Ben Thompson

dressed in his uniform as Austin's city marshal also came
from a group pose. The caption to the photograph of Wild
Bill Hickok states that it was taken at Deadwood. It was
taken ca. 1873–74 when Hickok toured with Buffalo
Bill's Combination.

Despite a constant updating of materials and information on the gunfighting elite, *Triggernometry* remains a
classic work. This I think is due largely to the author's
enthusiasm for his subject. I first read the book in the
1950s and was greatly impressed by it. Even now, forty
years later, with hindsight and a wider knowledge of the
subject, I still find the book of interest, and the grim-
faced, steely-eyed characters who populate its pages fascinating. And what a colorful crowd they were! Some were
heroic, others cruel and cowardly. But their appeal is
timeless.

Vying for attention are such diverse characters as Wild
Bill Hickok, Bat Masterson, John Wesley Hardin, Bass
Outlaw, Butch Cassidy, Billy the Kid, and—to a lesser
extent—Wyatt Earp. Each of these men contributed something toward the now legendary part-man part-myth we
call the gunfighter.

In hindsight I can understand why I was so taken with
the book. One section in particular appealed to me, the one
devoted to the expertise of the gunfighters that inspired the
book's title. At that time I was researching my own book
on the subject of gunfighters, so I was most interested
in Cunningham's comments on the skill of the various
"pistoleers" under discussion. In most respects he came
close to reality.

Ignoring the speed factor, many purists might well
argue that Cunningham's comments on the gunfighters'
dexterity with pistols were unbalanced, because he was
concerned only with the merits of the Colt Single-Action
Army Revolver, Model of 1873, which was a metallic
cartridge weapon, rather than examining the many reputations made or broken during the earlier era of the percussion or "cap and ball" pistols. This was a time when it
was necessary to load each chamber with either loose pow-

der and ball or a prepared paper or metallic foil cartridge, and then place a percussion cap on the nipple or cone at the rear of each chamber. This period lasted from the 1830s until well into the 1870s. It was the era of Wild Bill Hickok, and to a lesser extent John Wesley Hardin.

During the percussion-revolver era, body-belt "scabbards" (known today as "holsters") were introduced. At that time pistols were generally carried butts forward. This enabled the wearer to use a cross-body draw or the plains "reverse" or "twist" draw—a method adopted by the United States Cavalry. It allowed the trooper access both to his saber and to his pistol, leaving his left hand free to control his horse. It worked as follows: as the hand dropped to the butt, it was turned so that the palm faced away from the body. At the same time the thumb curled around the hammer spur and the index finger entered the trigger guard. With a firm grip the pistol was pulled out, and the momentum both spun the barrel forward to line up on its target and also cocked the hammer. The shooter could either hold the weapon at full cock or fire it as it came level. Because the thumb was locked over the hammer spur, releasing the spur was impossible until the barrel was clear of the body, making the cross-body or "reverse" draw much safer than the hip draw. The later so-called "conventional" hip-draw holsters did and do sometimes lead to accidents: when the barrel snags, jerking the trigger finger, the result can be a bad leg wound or, perhaps, a dead horse!

Many people who have studied the era of the gunfighters, but who have little knowledge of firearms (or indeed have ever handled one), cynically declare that few gunfighters could "hit a barn door from the inside" simply because their pistols were too cumbersome and hopelessly inaccurate. Nothing could be further from the truth! If we ignore the "miraculous" shooting attributed to such gunfighters as Wild Bill and concentrate upon facts, the situation is entirely different. Personal practice with various Colt's percussion and metallic cartridge revolvers has convinced me that with perseverance one can become a reasonable shot, bearing in mind that one has to aim and take one's time. I have witnessed some excellent shooting at ranges from twenty to one hundred yards. If that sounds like a tall tale, then I can cite the records of both the British and the American Ordnance Departments, who in the 1850s and 1860s both conducted exhaustive tests of Colt's and other makes of revolvers at such distances. Indeed, in 1854 the British government tested the Colt Dragoon pistol by firing it at a six-foot iron target 400 yards away with excellent results. But it was officially noted that its close range accuracy and penetration was of far greater importance, for the weapon's performance depended very much upon the individual using it. Few gunfighters cared for long-range accuracy—the results of shoot-outs within five to fifteen feet were what counted.

The weapons available to the gunfighting fraternity in the middle and later years of the nineteenth century were impressive. The most popular (and most plentiful) were those revolvers made by Samuel Colt. Among the early models, the Navy was a great favorite. First produced in 1850, this six-shot, .36 caliber "cap and ball" revolver rapidly achieved a reputation for accuracy and reliability. Unloaded, it weighed about two pounds ten ounces. (The big Dragoon in .44 caliber weighed four pounds two ounces.) The Navy revolver (immortalized as the Model 1851 to distinguish it from the version introduced in 1861) was the most frequently copied Colt pistol. In 1853, following his success at the Great Exhibition of 1851 held in London's Hyde Park, Colt opened a factory in London and sold several thousand Navy pistols to the British government for naval and military use during the Crimean War.

In company with many of its rivals and successors, the Navy pistol was a single-action weapon—that is, the hammer was thumb-cocked for each shot. Double-action pistols (cocked and fired by pressure on the trigger) also existed but were not very reliable. In fact, even with improved mechanisms by the 1880s, few gunfighters, cowboys, or other frontier types relied upon double-action weapons, preferring instead the single-actions.

"Gunfighter" as a word to define a gun-toting individual is not as modern as some might think. On July 19, 1874, the *Topeka Daily Commonwealth* carried a story about one "Cemetery Sam" who hailed from Eureka, California, where he announced that he was a "gunfighter" from Pioche, Nevada. Someone promptly knocked him down. Later, in his series of articles for *Human Life* on "Famous Gun Fighters of the Western Frontier," published in 1907, Bat Masterson also referred to them more aptly as "man-killers." Some also described the gun-toting fraternity as "shootists." Clay Allison was reported by the *St. Louis Republican* of July 25, 1878, to have declared: "I am a shootist."

The subtle distinction between gunfighters and gunmen was touched upon by Eugene Manlove Rhodes when he wrote in the original foreword to this book that *gunfighter* was comparable with the old-time *swordsman,* but because "of the modern gangster, the word gunman now carries the implication of coward, of baby-killer. It brings up the idea of seven against one; of helpless victims 'taken for a ride' or 'put on the spot'; of time-fuse bombs and steel vests, armored cars and machine guns; the safe and shameless!" Today, perhaps, he might have included terrorists and hijackers. But the point is made: the hero was a gunfighter and the villain a gunman—in Hollywood terms, white hats and black hats!

During the heyday of the so-called Wild West, the gun, or more correctly the revolver or pistol, was as much a part of a man's clothing as his hat and coat—but not everyone expected to use it. The exceptions were the men of reputation—those who had passed the acid test of gunfighting: shooting while being shot at. Prepared as they were to kill or risk being killed, few of them spent much time worrying about speed on the draw. Rather, they concentrated upon ensuring that their weapons were easily accessible and ready for use. Accuracy and the "drop" counted much more than "speed." Wild Bill Hickok, who remains the archetypal gunfighter, was under no illusion when confronted by his own mortality. "Whenever you get into a row be sure and not to shoot too quick," he is alleged to have told Colonel George Ward Nichols in 1865, adding, "I've known many a feller to slip up for shootin' in a hurry." He gave similar advice to his friend Charles Gross in 1871: "Charlie[,] I hope you never have to shoot any man, but if you do[,] shoot him in the Guts near the Navel. *you* may not make a fatal shot, but *he* will get a shock that will paralize [*sic*] his brain and arm so much that the fight is all over." Gross was also intrigued when he watched Hickok fire and reload his pistols, carefully checking each chamber, the flash hole in the nipple, and the fulminate in each cap. When asked if his pistols were damp, Hickok remarked: "I ain't ready to go yet & I am not taking any chances, *when I draw & pull I must be sure.*" His reaction was understandable: dampness affected the salt-laden black powder, prompting men like Hickok to carry two pistols and thus inspiring yet another legend—the "two-gun" man.

The emphasis upon "taking one's time" in a gunfight pinpoints the individual's reflex reaction rather than the speed at which he operated. The true gunfighter was already confident of the result when he drew and fired. The mistake so many fast-draw fanatics make is to believe that speed is of essence, whereas a cool, cold-blooded, and determined approach, backed by the killer instinct, invariably wins.

If asked who was the quickest and most deadly gunfighter, many historians might cite Hickok or Hardin, while others would turn to lesser-publicized individuals who, despite a lack of reputation, were their equals. No one knows, however, who was the quickest or truly deadliest gunfighter. The only guide might be in the number of men he killed, assuming that they were all face-to-face shoot-outs. As far as we know, Hickok's tally did not exceed about ten men, even though the press avidly recounted his "man-killing" exploits, which incurred Wild

Bill's wrath. On the other hand, John Wesley Hardin was credited with "forty notches" (not that there is any evidence that anyone really notched pistols), and by his own statements, he enjoyed killing. If that sort of mental approach justifies the term "deadliest," then he would win hands down. But I would prefer "deadliest" to mean skillful. In that respect, the answer will never be known.

Wyatt Earp is among several legendary heroes who get scant mention in this book. Some suggest that this was because Cunningham himself detested the man, or perhaps knew little about him. In fact, he was quite scathing when it came to judging the efforts of Stuart N. Lake, whose book *Wyatt Earp: Frontier Marshal* made Wyatt the hero he had not been during his own lifetime: "I have always figured that Friend Lake suffered from a bad attack of hero-worship while in Earp's company, nor is it any secret that I hold this conviction. My own opinion of the Earps is not very high, nor can I get enthusiastic about any of the crowd the brothers ran with." He concluded that the Earps and most of the other cowtown peace officers were best described as "Fighting Pimps" because of the time they spent in bordellos. Cunningham may well have learned more about the Earps in later years, but he never changed his text. As for Wyatt Earp, he is as controversial today as he was when he died, despite a reputation enhanced by being elevated to sainthood via 1950s television.

Readers will quickly appreciate how pro-Texas the author was. Nevertheless, he did include material on famous non-Texas gunfighters, many of them the subject of biographical studies. Others, such as Bass Outlaw, General Lee Christmas, and a number of prominent Texas Rangers, are scarcely known outside the state. Since the time *Triggernometry* first was published, additional research has uncovered much new information not available to Cunningham during the course of his research. Therefore, the following comments, which are based upon recent scholarship, are not meant to be criticisms of Cunningham's text.

The first character to come under scrutiny is William P. Longley. Today he is the subject of some considerable research and interest. In his time he was a contemporary and arch rival of John Wesley Hardin, whom he disliked. Justice, when it eventually caught up with Longley, decreed that he should hang for his sins, whereas Hardin, in many ways far worse, was sentenced to jail. This infuriated Longley: "It is rather hard to kill me for my sins," he wrote, "and give Wes Hardin only twenty-five years for the crimes he has committed." On October 11, 1878, the day of his execution, Longley stood on the trap and declared, "I see a good many enemies around, and mighty few friends." Even his hanging was bungled—the rope slipped on the beam, and his feet touched the floor. The sheriff then had to support him until the rope could be resecured. Eleven minutes later he was declared dead. After his death someone suggested that he was known as "Wild Bill" Longley, a nickname furiously denied by his family when I put that question to them some years ago. Certainly, it was a term unknown to Eugene Cunningham.

John Wesley Hardin, who looms large in the gallery of Texas gunfighters, has aroused considerable controversy since his murder in 1895. His autobiography, *The Life of John Wesley Hardin As Written by Himself*, published posthumously, is rife with statements justifying his frequent killings, and in his voluminous correspondence with his wife written from jail, he displays a character that needs expert analysis. In this respect, a book published by a psychiatrist, Richard Marohn, entitled *The Last Gunfighter* (1995), goes far toward understanding what it was that drove Hardin to claim or create "forty notches" on his pistol. Certainly, any individual who callously shoots six Mexicans on the trail to Abilene, Kansas, in 1871; another one for the alleged murder of a fellow Texan; and then an innocent boss herder named Charles Couger, killed when Hardin fired through his bedroom wall as he sat on his bed reading a newspaper, demands some explanation. His tenure in Abilene was brought to an abrupt halt after the Couger killing. He fled, one jump ahead of Marshal Hickok and the posse.

Also available are many versions of the confrontation between Hickok and Hardin, when the young Texan, known for some reason as "Little Arkansaw," is reputed to have pulled the "road agents' spin" on Wild Bill when Hickok demanded that he hand over his weapons. According to Hardin, Hickok had two cocked pistols pointed at him. Hardin offered his pistols to the marshal butts first, and then he jumped back and spun them into his hands as Hickok reached for them. We must assume that Hickok holstered his own pistols—a move that does not make sense! No contemporary evidence has been found for this story, and Cunningham expressed the opinion that the tale should be taken "with salt" (p. 46). Others believe that Wes invented it for his autobiography to boost a fading ego. In a letter written to his wife in 1888, he claimed that "no braver man" than Hickok "ever drew breath," which is a far cry from the "scoundrel" he describes in his book!

An obvious favorite of the author's is Ben Thompson, the English-born Texas gunfighter whose reputation in many respects outshines that of Hardin, for despite his sometimes unsavory exploits, Ben did serve a period as an efficient, highly respected peace officer. Cunningham wrote that Ben's birthplace was in doubt, that it was either in England or in Lockhart, Texas. Fortunately, that has now been resolved. According to the records of the local Registrar, he was born on the "Second of November 1843 [at] 25 minutes to 5 a.m." at Knottingley, Yorkshire. His father, William, was described as a "mariner" (some sources have assumed that he was in fact an officer in Her Majesty's Royal Navy), and his mother was Mary Ann, formerly Baker. His brother William was also born at Knottingley. The family later emigrated to the United States.

Thompson shared the jaundiced view of the "Yankee Peace officers" held by most Texans. He was reputed to have held Hickok in spite, but there is no real evidence of a confrontation. Hardin claimed that Thompson tried to get him to force a showdown with Hickok, but Hardin told him to do it himself. Reports that Ben was a dead shot with a pistol may be true, but his expertise with a rifle apparently was inferior. According to the *Austin Daily Statesman* of December 10, 1879, Buffalo Bill Cody, using Ben's rifle, struck six of seven half dollars that were tossed into the air. Ben was impressed. In its June 15, 1881 issue, the paper reported that Ben had received a gift from Cody, a "costly target pistol manufactured by Stevens & Co. of Chicopee Falls, Massachusetts." Cody's association with Ben was further cemented when, in July 1880, Ben's homicidal brother Billy was in trouble at Ogallala, Nebraska. He had shot and wounded a bartender, who in turn had wounded him. Ben telegraphed Bat Masterson and asked him to rescue Billy, and on their way back to Dodge City, the pair stopped at Cody's ranch at North Platte.

Cunningham was not convinced by Lake's claim that in August 1873 Wyatt Earp arrested Ben Thompson when he "treed" Ellsworth, Kansas, after his brother, Billy, while drunk, had shot sheriff Chauncey B. Whitney on the 15th. The controversy surrounding Lake's disclosure that Wyatt, not Deputy Sheriff Edward O. Hogue, had arrested Ben was not resolved until the original newspapers and court records were checked some years later, when Hogue received proper recognition. As for Billy, he fled with Ben's help. Sometime later he was arrested and brought back for trial, but then he was acquitted on a technicality.

Billy the Kid, variously described as juvenile delinquent, psychotic killer, or simply rebel without a cause, is also featured. Although Cunningham makes a brave stab at it, he was engulfed by the then-current welter of fact and fiction surrounding not only the Kid but also many of the other luminaries he featured. Fortunately, recent scholarship has revealed a great deal about the activities of the Kid, especially during his early years. We now know that his real name was Henry McCarty, and current research suggests that he was born on September 17, 1859, in New York City, the son of Patrick and Catherine Devine McCarty. His father died when he was quite young, and his widowed mother, accompanied by Henry and his older brother, Joseph (there is evidence of a sister Bridget, but she disappeared early on), moved eventually to Wichita, Kansas. There young Henry first became acquainted with cowboys and cattle. Later the family moved to Silver City, New Mexico, where his mother married William Antrim, an alias sometimes adopted by his soon-to-be notorious stepson. By most accounts, Billy is reputed to have killed twenty-one men (one for each year of his life), but according to Frederick Nolan (*The Lincoln County War*) the "tally" was closer to six. The more up-to-date sources on Billy and his remarkable career are listed in the bibliography.

Dallas Stoudenmire, the "Two-Gun Marshal" of El Paso, also receives much attention. The ex-Texas Ranger who almost single-handedly "cleaned up" El Paso, took to the bottle, and eventually was killed in a brawl, has long been a favorite of gunfighter enthusiasts. Considering the lack of material available to him at the time, Cunningham did well. Later, Leon Metz elaborated on the character in his book, *Dallas Stoudenmire: El Paso Marshal*, but Stoudenmire's law-enforcement reputation was dramatically revised with Fred Egloff's discovery—and publication in *El Paso Lawman*—of letters and other material relative to the exploits of former city marshal George Campbell. Campbell was a shadowy character, respected by many of his contemporaries but disliked by those in power. His period as marshal of El Paso in 1880 was controversial, but new evidence indicates that he was an honest man fighting against corruption. He eventually resigned and was replaced by the town drunk, Bill Johnson, who was himself succeeded on April 11, 1881, by Stoudenmire.

Although Cunningham gives an interesting account of the events that led to Campbell's death, he was never

able to obtain reliable statements from surviving witnesses. However, when George's brother Abe arrived in
El Paso to determine what had happened, he was told by
the townfolk that just before his death, George stated
that in the confusion of the fight, it was Dallas who shot
him. One theory put forward by Egloff was that no charges
were made because the mayor and council were anxious
to be rid of Campbell, and so they backed their own man,
Stoudenmire. Whatever the reason, students will find
much to mull over.

The information in Cunningham's chapter on Long-
Haired Jim Courtright was supplemented in later years
by Oliver Knight in his *Fort Worth: Outpost on the Trinity.*
Knight uncovered a wealth of material on Jim's period as
marshal of Fort Worth as well as on some of his other
activities. Knight had relied upon the contemporary press
when discussing Jim's final gunfight with Luke Short
on February 8, 1887. Cunningham, however, repeated
hearsay. He describes how a wild shot from Luke tore off
Jim's thumb as it was cocking the hammer of his pistol.
Jim then tried to toss the pistol to his left hand in a classic
"border shift," but by then Short had put three bullets
into him. Knight discovered instead that when both men
went for their pistols, Jim was the quicker, but his cylinder
jammed. Short then shot him five times.

Wild Bill Hickok, whom Cunningham describes as
"The Magnificent," was, at the time this book first was
published, the most popular of the Old West's characters.
His exploits have provoked much controversy among historians. My own explorations into the Hickok saga have
confirmed many facts and revealed a great deal of fiction.
Cunningham, faced by an enigma, admits that Hickok
had "one of the greatest reputations of the frontier. He
has become a figure gigantic and omnipotent as one of
the mythical creatures of the Norse sagas—credited with
Homeric battles and incredible slaughters." Rather than
play up the legend, however, he preferred to seek the
"living, breathing human being" behind the legend.

In describing Hickok's performance at Rock Creek,

Nebraska Territory (where on July 12, 1861, he reputedly
wiped out ten of the "McCanles gang" single-handedly),
Cunningham relied heavily on the account published in
1927 by the Nebraska State Historical Society, which was
updated in William E. Connelley's version that appeared
in the Kansas State Historical Society's *Collections* a year
later. Both writers reduced the death toll to three men.
Cunningham accepts that Hickok shot David McCanles,
and later had a hand in murdering his two employees,
James Woods and James Gordon.

We may never know the truth of that affair, but I
remain unconvinced that Hickok murdered McCanles. I
suspect that Horace Wellman, the stationkeeper, who had
reason to fear McCanles, fired the fatal shot (both he and
Hickok were in the house at the time). Jane Wellman,
whose father had been thrashed by McCanles for allegedly
stealing from him, did not disguise her hatred of the
man. And then there is the enigmatic Sarah Shull, who
accompanied McCanles from North Carolina when he left
in a hurry with monies belonging to the county. Her
relationship with him has been the subject of much speculation, but only recently was it disclosed that back in
1856 she bore him a child, who died a year later (Mark
Dugan, *Tales Never Told Around the Campfire*). Perhaps it
was the shame of that birth, along with other problems,
that prompted McCanles to steal county funds and flee
west. When he later sent for his family, he only added
to his difficulties. Finally, shortly before she died, Sarah
denied having a love affair with Hickok, although she
admitted it would have been easy. She also stated that he
was not the sort of man to back away from anyone. The
most frustrating part of her recollections, however, is her
disclosure that she was in the house when McCanles was
shot. She and another woman (Sarah Kelsey) were pushed
into the root cellar and only heard the shot. Sarah never
disclosed who actually fired it.

In reviewing Hickok's career, Cunningham tried to
verify the facts, although in some areas he simply relied
upon hearsay. Nevertheless, he was right to criticize the

attempts to elevate Wild Bill to a sainthood he neither
sought nor deserved.

Butch Cassidy, still a topical character thanks mainly
to the movie *Butch Cassidy and the Sundance Kid,* starring
Paul Newman and Robert Redford, is given a lot of space
in this volume. His real name was Robert LeRoy Parker,
but he adopted his more bizarre moniker in honor of an
individual who led him to the path of crime. Despite
mixing with the "Wild Bunch," which boasted some of
the most dangerous characters then at large in the West,
Cassidy is reported never to have killed anyone. He and
Sundance finally quit the United States and fled to South
America, where it was later reported that they had been
killed in a fight with Bolivian troops. This was refuted
by Cassidy's sister, Lula Parker Betenson, who died in
her nineties adamant that he had returned, visited his
home several times, and lived to die of old age. According
to Larry Pointer's book, *In Search of Butch Cassidy,* Butch
changed his name to William T. Phillips and died under
that name in 1937.

Cunningham's opinion is quite obvious from the title
of his chapter on Tom Horn, "Railroaded?" Subsequent
events have proved him right. Tom Horn was one of the
truly legendary figures of the Old West, yet mention of
his name in certain parts of Wyoming can still lead one
into trouble. A highly respected scout in the Apache wars,
bronco buster, and first-class shot, he was much in demand
by Wyoming cattlemen in their fight against "rustlers"—
also called "Nesters" and "Sodbusters"—because the
cattlemen objected to people taking advantage of the
Homestead Act to build a home on what was considered
open range.

Whether Tom really shot such people from ambush
or simply confined his expertise to eradicating wanted
criminals is a moot point. But the murder of a fourteen-
year-old boy named Willie Nickell, and Tom's alleged
boasting of the deed when drunk, led to his trial and
hanging in 1903. Then, as now, opinion was divided on
his guilt. In September 1993, however, a mock retrial

was held in Cheyenne, Wyoming, during which evidence
inadmissible (or concealed) at the first trial was allowed.
The trial, initially covered by the *Wyoming State Tribune,*
received much publicity worldwide. Even Amnesty International took an interest. Both the defense and prosecuting
attorneys worked hard to overturn or uphold the original
verdict, and the evidence of Joe LaFors, the deputy U.S.
marshal who coerced a drunken Tom Horn into admitting
his guilt, was torn apart. Predictably, the verdict was "Not
Guilty!" Perhaps now someone will write the definitive
biography of Tom Horn and include a full account of all
the evidence and details of those involved, despite threats
from relatives and other "interested parties" who would
rather let the affair rest.

The last—but by no means the least—man in the
book is General Lee Christmas. Christmas is unknown to
most Western fans, probably because he made his name
and reputation in South America. Cunningham describes
him as "worth an army corps," and gives us a most enter-
taining resume of his many adventures. Such discussion
also focuses our attention on the fact that when the North
American gunfighter was creating his own myth, "gunfighter" types existed in Australia, South and Central
America, and parts of South Africa. Australia's bush-
rangers were every bit as tough as the James Gang, and
some of their police "troopers" proved equally as tenacious
as the Texas Rangers or the U.S. Marshals. But no other
place had the terrain, or the colorful ingredients that made
the "Wild West" so fascinating.

As a student of firearms, I was naturally drawn to the
final chapter, "Triggernometry." As I noted earlier, I was
much impressed with it, and despite its emphasis upon
cartridge weapons and the period post-1870, it makes a
great contribution to what we know about the men and
their weapons. Cunningham does not pull his punches
when describing the awful effect of a soft lead .45 caliber
bullet, backed by forty grains of black powder and fired
at close range. The impact could knock a man down, he
wrote, and the ".45 burned terribly at close range. It was

impossible to face it—as I once discovered for myself! It will even set your clothes on fire. So, the man who got to shooting first when only a few feet away, he had a big advantage even if he missed his first shot."

The impact of soft lead bullets also prompted Cunningham to suggest that Hickok shot Phil Coe at Abilene with a pair of .41 caliber deringers (I use the original spelling from Henry Deringer's name). But the evidence is that both men were armed with revolvers when they stood eight feet apart and opened fire. Coe fired twice and missed, one shot going through Hickok's coat and the other hitting the sidewalk between his legs. Wild Bill shot him twice in the stomach, and then turned in a flash and fired twice more at a man waving a pistol, who he assumed was another Texan. This was Michael Williams, an ex-bartender from Kansas City, and for a short period a jailer in Abilene. Hickok supposedly carried a pair of .41 caliber dual-ignition Williamson deringers (capable of firing a .41 caliber rim-fire cartridge or loose powder and ball in an insert) as "backup" weapons, although there is no proof that he ever used them in a gunfight.

Cunningham gives good coverage to the amazing number of tricks credited to old-time gunfighters. Some unique means of carrying pistols might appear bizarre, such as plates on belts to hang a pistol by means of an extended hammer-screw. Other topics discussed pertain to hide-out pistols, shoulder holsters, and other items of equipment devoted to the well-being of the up-to-date gunfighter. One of the "tricks" suggested by one old-timer to Cunningham for those eager to learn the state of their reflexes was this:

"For practice, there's nothing better than the so-called poker chip draw. Hang your gun to fit your arm. Now, take a poker chip and put it on the back of your gun-hand. Hold the gun-hand out at shoulder-level. Turn the wrist deliberately, to let the poker chip drop—and go for your gun as if somebody was pulling to kill you! See if you can get it out, cocked, up to horizontal, and pointed—

as you'd point your forefinger—at the target, and a shot loosed, all before the chip hits the floor.

"It will be some time before you can loose one shot ahead of the rap of the chip on the floor. But practice will make you amazingly fast and accurate."

Back in the far-off days of my own misspent youth, I, too, fell under the spell of the "fast draw," and spent more time than I now care to admit trying to beat a coin to a tin lid laid on the floor. I used a Colt's Navy revolver worn butt forward in the approved Plains manner with percussion caps on the nipples. My youthful reflexes eventually enabled me to "burst a cap" before the coin rapped against the lid. I soon realized, however, that proving a good reflex action was one thing, but finding just cause to put it into practice was something else. I promptly abandoned the "fast draw." Others, however, have fallen for the "speed" factor and think of it as the be-all of gunfighting. One hopes they never learn the truth.

Meanwhile, I recommend *Triggernometry* to all who are fascinated by the myriad characters who once populated the Old West and continue to survive as a part of its myths and legends.

Joseph G. Rosa

IF—AS IS often claimed—history is no more than biography, then the sum-total of this book must amount to history. History of the Old West. History of the New West—in those places where Old West men and Old West habits persist in this stereotyped twentieth century. But history which is a fast-moving, vividly-colored pageant, dappled now and again with the orange flashes of gunfire. History which is a record of men who were at once grimly determined, incredibly reckless and fearless—and quite unconscious of being that same. History of an era as extinct as wild buffalo. Finally, history which is as fair to all the characters concerned as I can make it.

For those who say: "This is all of the long ago. What does it matter?" there can be but one answer:

It doesn't matter—to them. They will not be interested in this or any similar book. But there are many of us—readers and writers alike—who are interested in seeing honor given where honor is due; in pushing the braggarts from the stage they have preëmpted overlong; in—just for instance—assuring a hearing to a man who was scout for Crook and Miles and Spanish War veteran of unquestioned ability, honesty and service (TOM HORN), and who was hanged in a hostile region for the alleged murder of a boy, a crime of a character fitting in with nothing in *his* character and for which no motive was ever shown.

The Dime Novel and the Press Agent were abroad in the land, even in the day of "Wild Bill" Hickok and "Buffalo Bill" Cody. Just for instance—during all the years since the Civil War, Hickok has been credited by virtually every writer of western pages and by almost

every writer since that marvel of the craft, Colonel
George Ward Nichols (*Harper's Magazine*, February,
1867), represented him as having heroically defended
Stage Company property against "the terrible McCanles
Gang," with resultant deaths of "six of the scoundrels."
Hence the name "Wild Bill."

As a matter of dull fact and truth, three respectable
citizens were shot down, without warning, while they
stood unarmed, by Stableman—not Agent—"Duck
Bill" Hickok and his boss, one Wellman.

But the original lie told by some drawer of the long
bow to the incredibly guileless and imaginative and hero-
worshipping Nichols still persists. It was current even in
the West, during my own childhood. It was believed in
fact by some of Hickok's contemporaries.

As for Buffalo Bill—one of the tall yarns he has been
famous for telling, a tale polished for him by such as
Buntline, was *All About My Terrible Duel With the Great
Chief Yellow Hand*. Actually—according to men who were
on the spot—Cody didn't arrive on the ground until the
day after Yellow Hand's killing! So the press-agented
figures grow taller, at the expense of the real heroes who
did the work.

There are many of us who would like to see the actors
of the Old West drama clearly-portrayed; taken out of
the distorted proportions so long hazing their true stature; made human, understandable; made figures in
which an adult can believe!

There is but one way to arrive at even an approxima-
tion of the truth. That is by the most patient and careful
sifting, balancing, weighing, study, not only of the
books, but of the first-hand accounts of witnesses contemporary to the actor, the play and the stage-setting.

This digging after facts—and their study after discovery—has been one of the pleasantest of my occupa-
tions for years. In the course of the process, I have yarned
with countless old-timers. Talked of the Old Days, the
Old Ways, in the sandy plazas of sleepy little Spanish-
colored towns of the Southwest; or while lazing beneath

some gnarled, gigantic cottonwood of sinisterly horizontal limb that once bore "cottonwood blossoms" on short, hempen stems; or standing on the gallery of the old Lincoln County courthouse in the very tracks of Billy the Kid, where he leaned with shotgun in small, deadly hands, awaiting Bob Ollinger; or hunkered beside a loading corral in the cow-country; even while sitting in a Central American café with ancient expatriates who "took it on the run" out of Old Texas.

In such places, with men such as were there, a half-dozen words have often been as a searchlight's ray, to make clear a murky, a smudged or shadowed, corner of the character or "psychology" of some famous old-timer, to make ride again on phantom *caballo*, across yellow sand and rugged *malpais* and greasewood and mesquite and buffalo grass, some lightning-fast gunfighter long dead beneath the wreathing gray smoke of Colt or Winchester.

The effort has been made to bring history accurately down to date in each biographical sketch in this Gallery. For that reason, my analyses and evaluations may have some interest for the student of Things Western, even for the authority on the subject. As for the casual reader—

There is, I hope, an hour or two or three of interesting reading. Interesting, because brave men and adventure-seeking are interesting to most of us. And all of the figures in this Gallery were possessed of at least a bulldog quality of courage. Some, indeed, owned (or own today) an intelligent, imaginative sort of bravery, which hurled them against odds that would daunt most of us.

Eugene Cunningham

TRIGGERNOMETRY
A GALLERY OF GUNFIGHTERS

The Gunman

ENVIRONMENT made him—this composite figure we have come to call The Gunman. Lineal descendant of every venturesome, fiercely individualistic pioneer of the Leather-stocking days, in the Gunman's veins ran the wild blood of Boone and Kenton—and Simon Girty.

His birthplace hardly concerns us. In choosing a cradle for our composite character, we could draw upon Iowa farms, the slums of New York, log cabins in the bottom lands of the Brazos and the Trinity Rivers, quiet communities of Missouri or Wisconsin, sprawling 'dobe ranch-houses of the Southwest. . . .

But where he was born is immaterial. There was in him the urge to look over the next hill. Nothing could halt him. Like water, he found his own level. Circumstances had decreed that he should be born within a period covering the westward sweep of settlement. So he must be born at a time which would set him functioning within the years 1860 to 1900. That span of forty years roughly limits the Gunfighter.

As for his stage—approximately it was the vast, wild region between Milk River and the Rio Grande, between the Mississippi and the Pacific Ocean. Wherever the Gunman might first see the light, inevitably he would catch the spotlight somewhere in this frontier region.

The cattle-trail knew him, whooping behind the longhorns and looking through the dust toward blazing nights in Abilene, Caldwell, Dodge, Hays City. He dug gold or he preyed on those who dug it in a hundred now-forgotten camps. He sat with the green eye-shade low over his steady, inscrutable eyes, at the faro and stud poker tables. He stood behind a star, The Law of frontier communities. He stood *before* the star—and thumbed his belligerent nose at the symbol. In short, wherever there were vast spaces unpopulated save by wild animals and wilder men—there he was, The Gunman.

His story is the story of the frontier. Not all of it, of course! But if we add the record of the men with whom he brushed elbows, and his women and their women, The Gunman's story is pretty much the Story of the West, within those limits of time and space mentioned as his stage.

What, then, *was* a Gunman?

The most apparent, the most basic, interpretation of the term would be no more than "a man possessed of a gun." To the early settlers, lying up behind the walls of their crude forts, fearing the onslaught of the red men during "the light of the moon," and attempting to compute the armed strength of the Indians, any boy or man possessed of rifle or smoothbore and capable of taking the war-trail, was counted "a gunman."

But as what we are pleased to call The Frontier marched westward across the Rockies, the word took on a narrower, a greatly specialized, a more technical, meaning:

When a Gunman was mentioned, the speaker did not intend to designate a man possessed of a rifle. Paradoxically, the smoothbore musket, the rifle, the shotgun—the only *guns*, in strictest technical use of the term—were eliminated from consideration.

By "*gunman*" was really meant "*pistolman*."

In the heyday of the Genus Gunman the term took on an implication still narrower. When you said of a man that he was a gunman, you meant not only a pistolman—a man bearing one or more pistols. You meant to designate (and were understood to designate) a man specially skilled in the use of a pistol—and much more than normally ready to demonstrate that ability in blazing, homicidal gunplay. The word gunman had flexed to neatly take into account, not only the weapon, but the character, of the man you were discussing.

It was apt to be synonymous with "killer" in the stories written by the oldtime newspaper men. Not always! For there were also many men like some of the figures in this *Gallery*—upstanding, outstanding, peace officers; grim men who held the fort against the killer-type of gunman; gunfighters who could match speed at "leather slapping" and deadly accuracy of marksmanship with any of the other variety, but, withal, men who shot only when they had it to do.

Perhaps this development of the gunman, the gun-fighter, was no more unnatural than the backwoodsmen's development of uncanny skill at rifle-shooting, which so amazed and discomfited the British during the American Revolution.

The Civil War was raging, at the beginning of the Gunfighter Era. On the frontier every able-bodied man wore weapons and if unable to use them—so much the worse for him! A man of the other side, or an Indian warrior, would the more quickly and easily take his scalp. Police protection there was none, either in the community or the surrounding country.

The War ended. Back to civil life came young men spoiled by four years of camp-life and killing for quiet existence. As they flocked to the West they brought with them the weapons, and the skill in their use, the readiness to practise that skill, gained from army experience. Their new life was a hard life, a man's life. They learned pugnacity—if it were necessary to *acquire* the quality!—by fierce battle with the pioneers' natural foes, the country itself and its copper-skinned natives. This belligerence could not easily be laid aside in their contacts with their own kind and color.

Killing, it seems indisputable, would be natural with such men. An old resident of Abilene, watching that famous marshal Tom Smith perform, commented that the Texas cowboys were like wild men; that they did not understand (nor appreciate!) Tom Smith's ability with his big, hard fists. To me, this observer's accent of surprise has a good deal of *naivete* about it!

A Texas cowboy, riding into Abilene in the drag of a longhorn herd, was not an ordinary man in any sense of the word. Born, perhaps, in a frontier cabin, he was used to seeing Comanche or Lipan or Kickapoo or other hard-hitting horse-Indian descend upon his section with the light of the moon. He had perhaps seen his mother kill a warrior who was trying to kill or capture one of her children.

He had from earliest childhood learned to depend upon himself in the fierce battle for survival. His associates in cow-camp or little cow-town were of the same hard, self-sufficient breed. When they disagreed among themselves and came to fighting, they brought into play the methods learned in Indian-fighting. Fist-fighting was not developed because it was not efficient in the removal of an enemy. But the six-shooter was a natural weapon. Olmstead, an early traveler through Texas, wrote that an inventory of the Colt revolvers owned in the state would approximate in numbers the census of the male adults of the state.

When W. W. Mills, brother of Brigadier General Anson Mills of cartridge-belt fame, came to El Paso in '58, every male citizen regardless of age or vocation took his six-shooter from beneath his pillow the first thing in the morning, and blew upon it gently. He might possibly omit washing his face. He might probably skimp his oral hygiene, confining efforts in that direction to a bite on his plug of Horseshoe. But he would never slight the really vital ceremonies of life on the frontier.

As he finished buttoning his shirt, he would never forget to slide Colt or Remington or Smith-and-Wesson into the holster on his thigh; nor fail to adjust it so that his hand dropped in easy, natural fashion to grip its butt.

The green Indianan, Mills, who still regarded a neck-tie as a more important part of his costume than the product of Colonel Colt, once burst forth upon the public

street in what was—for the day and place—semi-
nakedness. An acquaintance jerked him frantically to a
halt.

"Buckle it on, Mills! Go back and buckle it on!"
cried this experienced citizen. "We don't often need
'em, but when we do need 'em, we *need* 'em—oh, God!"

But there was a difference, even on the frontier, between being a man who owned and could "sling" a six-
shooter, and being a gunman. Already, the term was
taking on a somewhat sinister implication. Pains were
taken to distinguish between a gunfighter and a gunman.

"Yonder's John Wesley Hardin, the notorious gunman," a man might say to a stranger, indicating one of
the "sights".

But Hardin was not an officer; his forty-odd killings
were on the Law's left hand. He was a dangerous man, a
killer, belligerent as a gunpowder-dieted bulldog. So—

"That's Jim Gillett! City Marshal!" the same
stranger's guide might have put it, indicating still
another of the sights. "Man! but he's a lightning gunfighter!"

IN EVEN the outland, the frontier, community, the
gunman might conceivably be an individual troublesome, dangerous, only to his own kind. But however
professional his outlook in the matter of taking on competition, he was not, could not be, entirely normal. He
must be different from the average inhabitant, who
wished only to work and play, make money and enjoy
himself.

The Typical Gunman is hard to create. Personal
acquaintance with a few furnishes evidence that they
varied as widely in size and coloring and disposition as
do other men. But certain traits they did own in common.

Some were men of blind, bulldogged courage—men
who seemed to have been born with no idea of fear; who
could not be convinced (short of killing them) that they
could be mastered by anything that walked on legs.

Others were almost arrant cowards. They depended on prestidigital skill at weapon-work to give them an advantage over the ordinary man. Their notches often represented the deaths of mere amateurs in the ancient craft of bloodletting. They—to borrow the expressive modern phrase—"never gave a sucker a break." They preferred to take no chances whatever, if that were possible.

Give *them* a nice armor-plated ambush and their victim coming unsuspiciously toward it—as Sheriff Brady walked toward the 'dobe wall that sheltered Billy the Kid.

Give them a chance to tamper with the six-shooter of the other fellow, so that they could seem to be pulling and shooting on equal terms, while actually throwing loaded dice—as Billy the Kid twirled the cylinder of Bad Man Joe Grant at Fort Sumner, so that the hammer would click first on an empty chamber.

Others, still, would calmly "take their foot in their hand" and withdraw from a situation where the advantage was not with them—as Wild Bill Hickok is said to have done, when he met that little Texican fire-eater, John Wesley Hardin, in Abilene. They were not considered cowardly for such strategic withdrawal—merely careful. Which reminds me!

There used to be an old hawk-faced, snowy-haired man around Fort Worth, who had in his younger days policed various little towns on the fringe of Things Tremendously Texan. He had been a good town marshal, yet he always said that he was not much of a shot, not fast on the draw. These paradoxical statements were puzzling until the time when he was moved to discuss the psychology of the Gunman breed. He mentioned a certain bad man hardly remembered by one so technically-informed as Captain Bill McDonald, even, who was of the listeners.

"He was callin' hisself The Terror o' the Prairies, or some such foolishness. He was a-ridin' across Texas an' folks was bustin' down the timber, hightailin' out o' his

sight. He'd always send word ahead that he was comin'
like a blue norther an' he took plenty o' room. Folks
better be gittin' back, else he'd crowd 'em clean to the
bone-yard.

"Well . . . he was headin' our way an' his reputation
was gittin' bigger all time. I was town marshal an' our
folks was kind o' wonderin' what I'd do when this
lightnin' gunman got to us. They knowed I was not fast
on the draw or a special good shot. I never told 'em what
I aimed to do.

"But when the Terror come lopin' his big bay hawse
into our one main street an' let out a yell, I dropped
down behind a rain water bar'l on the street, about as
sudden as my knees'd bend. For this Terror, he had a
gun in each hand an' like I said, I was no gunman.

"He come ridin' on, lookin' one way an' another like
a mad bull crossin' a pasture—a big, fine-lookin' darkish
man with long mustaches. When he come up even with
me, I riz up from behind that bar'l with a sawed-off ten-
gauge shotgun lookin' him mean in both eyes. Quick as
lightnin', he flipped them six-shooters around to cover
me.

"Well, sir! The' we was! He could kill me easy. But
not quick enough to keep me from blowin' him in two
pocket-high. We looked at one another. Then I says to
him: 'Y' drop them plow-handles, Mister, or I'll *about*
cut y' in two!'

"He never wanted to do it. I could see his thumbs
a-quiverin' on the pistol-hammers. But the trouble was,
he was just wantin' to kill me. He never wanted to kill
me so bad he was willin' to sure git killed, hisself, a-doin'
it. So he let the Colts drop an' he rode on, right out o'
our town, leavin' them fancy six-shooters lie in the dust.

"Huh? Coward? No-o-o! I reckon not . . . He stood
up an' shot it out with the town marshal down the line
from us. He plugged that marshal before he got killed.
But that was not the same thing. He was buckin' a six-
shooter, that time. Six-shooter ain't like a sawed-off
ten-gauge loaded with Blue Whistlers. Y' got a chance o'

bein' missed by the .45 slug that's comin' at y'. N-o-o
. . . he wasn't no coward. He'd take a chance on gittin'
killed, to kill the other fella. But he would not face
certain death for the pleasure o' killin' him. Mighty,
mighty few would ever buck a sure thing!''

There were members of the gunman's fraternity who
had more than average intelligence, more than ordi-
narily-sensitive nervous systems. They faced the odds
knowingly and unflinchingly. But, whether a gunman
were unthinkingly brave, or a coward, or a man afraid
but driven on by will, he was never a normal individual.
He could not be!

Very rarely did the killing of a man settle anything—
for the killer. There were the friends and relatives of the
late deceased. The killer had to consider them; had to
watch for and guard against them. Even if the gunman's
string of Boot Hill tickets brought no aftermath of
vendettas by brothers or cousins or close friends, there
was another penalty—

By virtue of his record, the gunman had set himself
up as shining target for rivals' lead. Night or day, sick or
well, generally it made no difference in the life of the
gunman. He must think of the time sure to come, when
some such belligerent, confident, gentleman as that Wolf
Killer of the Washita, Clay Allison, would ride into
town to inquire of the nearest bystander:

''Where-all's that dam' This an' That, that 'lows he's
so handy with a gun? I come to see him try slappin'
leather with *me*!''

The consequence of this was to make the average
gunman what the oldtimers so expressively called ''cat-
eyed.'' The more noted he was, the more his life must
resemble that of some scarred old hunted lobo; the more
cautious he must be in his every action; the more analy-
tical he must become, before every tiny, ordinary detail
of living.

Some almost imperceptible alteration in the location
of a familiar rain water barrel on the street might mean a
man with a gun behind it.

A man walking upon the street with bandaged hand might not be injured—the bandage might merely conceal a derringer or "bulldogged" pistol—what was known in the trade as "a stingy gun."

Walking into saloon, store, poolroom, or other gathering place of a frontier community, hardly more than a glance around was necessary to locate the gunmen present. The observer had only to note how many sat with backs against something solid! It was Wild Bill Hickok's lapse from this elementary precaution of the gunfighter which cost him his life to a rank amateur and cowardly murderer, Jack McCall.

A cautious man . . . a suspicious man . . . the gunfighter was bound to be both. He must be the original "touch-me-not," eschewing the friendly slap on the back, the rough, goodhumored horseplay of the frontier. Cocked and primed for trouble, ready in case of slightest doubt to shoot first and inquire afterward, he was a prickly customer!

Wild Bill Hickok, in Abilene, killed his friend Mike Williams, because Williams ran up on him unexpectedly with a pistol drawn. He was not the gentleman—our gunfighter of any place—upon whom to close unceremoniously, from the rear.

J. Marvin Hunter, of Bandera, who collects frontier history for that invaluable little monthly *The Frontier Times*, was the brother-in-law of George Scarborough, the famous deputy United States Marshal who killed Old John Selman and was himself killed by Bill Carver out of the Wild Bunch.

Marvin tells of an evening in El Paso, during the '90s, when he was sent by his sister to meet Scarborough at the station and tell him of their new address, to which she had moved during his absence from town on a case.

He was late going about his errand. He fairly trotted down San Francisco Street toward the station. But the train had come in and Scarborough had been seen heading toward the center of El Paso. Marvin, only a youngster, ran that way to overtake his brother-in-law. Presently,

he saw the tall figure ahead of him. Without considering
anything but his errand, he quickened his pace.

"Well, I finally caught you!" he panted.

The physical response was as flashing, as automatic—
and as explosive as the jump of a sleeping wolf touched
by a rolling stone. Scarborough whirled with a blurred
twinkling of his hands. Two Colts were trained upon a
much frightened young man's anatomy before he could
more than gasp. When identification was complete,
Scarborough reholstered the pistols and began to speak
slowly, with tremendous earnestness:

"Boy! Don't you ever, *ever* run up behind a man like
me, again, yelling that you've finally caught him! There
are entirely too many men looking for a chance to catch
me—with a gun poked in my back—for me to take
chances. The wonder is, that I didn't find out who you
were after you were dead!"

Scarborough, incidentally, belongs to the category of
peace officer-gunfighters who used their amazing skill
with pistols on the side of law and order. Gillett,
Stoudenmire, Hughes, Tom Threepersons, Billy Breakenridge, Jim Courtright, "John L." Sullivan, Bill Mc-
Donald, Tom Horn, were others of this bracket. They
were as quick on the draw, as deadly-accurate after
drawing, as any of the swaggering and lawless killers
whom they kept in check. But the killers had one advantage of them—the peace officer was not inclined to
shoot unless forced into it. The killer was under no such
restraint.

Because of the sinister implication the word so often
owned, none of these Star-Wearers would call himself a
"gunman"—regardless of the fact that their records
show ability at "slinging the guns" bordering upon the
magical, equal if not superior to that of any gun-toter
who ever stood on The Law's left hand. In the mechanical
sense, at least, they must be classed as gunfighters in any
such Gallery as this.

In other qualities, too, they shared—bravery, cold
nerve—efficiency in time of stress. No wearer of the

sixes, whether he stood before or behind an officer's star, could make his mark without most of these characteristics.

So much for the Gunfighter in general. The records of particular outstanding figures which follow will show in some degree the forces which shaped these frontiersmen, the circumstances which moved them this way and that upon their stage, something of the color of that stage-setting, better than much talk and philosophizing about it all.

"The ethical philosopher may base his judgment on such criteria as he will," says that shrewd and genial connoisseur of life, Charley Finger, "but the man of action in the wild lands holds fast to his long line of heroes and to them is applied one test and one test only —the test of daring."

Most of my "subjects" will, I believe, pass this test.

CHAPTER I · *Breed of the Border*

BILL LONGLEY

H E WAS A man before he was done being a boy. That was at once Bill Longley's fate and the explanation of this "big old He" of the long line of Texas gunmen, for —even more than Cullen Baker—Longley was Number One of the modern gunslingers.

He was a child of the Texas frontier. Upon him environment cut like a lathe-tool. Born October 6, 1851, on Mill Creek in Austin County, at the age of two he was taken by that God-fearing veteran of Houston's army, Campbell Longley his father, to Old Evergreen in Washington (now Lee) County.

He was ten when the Civil War got fully underway. Old enough to understand the bitter feeling between the two factions which, in Lee County as elsewhere in Texas, were local typifications of the North and the South. Old enough to understand the fury of the secessionists when Campbell Longley voted the Union ticket, a rage checked before it reached the stage of killing only by the San Jacinto record of young Bill's quiet, determined father.

Bill Longley was always large for his age. Six feet tall from his fifteenth year, his weight at maturity was to be two hundred pounds so magnificently proportioned as to make him look slender. He was the idol of the boys at Evergreen's field schoolhouse. Dark-eyed, dark-haired, his Indian-like face could smile or lower in the same minute. He rode like a Comanche. He could not remember when the "hogleg" shaped butt of the Colt's pistol was not familiar to his hard big palm.

Behind him was the background of the Texas pioneer who had asked no odds of anything that ran or walked or crept or flew. The Texan of incredible deeds—of the Alamo, of San Jacinto. This young gamecock being bred by quiet old Campbell Longley had in him the fiery independence of habit in thought and action which made the Texan of the '30s onward an adventurer, a hell-for-leather fighting man, whose superior has never been seen.

He was raw material at fourteen, but destined to be graved into what he became without much more delay, for the South's second war began with ending of its first, a savage guerilla war, fought never on a formal battlefield, but in a thousand desperate, bloody skirmishes, marked by bloody cruelty on both sides.

In Evergreen, the tiny community flanking the Austin-Brenham road, Bill Longley was a leading spirit among the younger generation. His size, his courage, his amazing skill with twin Colts, a certain fierce *elan* which was never to desert him, made him a marked figure among the gatherings at the crossroads blacksmith shop and store, under the wide shade of the court house oak—which had served both as justice court and gallows, in its day, and which still stands a brooding giant over that quiet land.

The carpetbaggers and the negroes were the problems discussed at these gatherings of the disfranchised whites. The older negroes were giving no trouble. But the younger freed men were drunk with liberty and license. Incited to swaggering insolence by the riffraff whites in power, protected by troops against prosecution for any crime, they were intolerable to the intensely proud people who were being stupidly affronted by the worst element among their conquerors.

When a week's tale of outrages major and minor was told, with the sullenly hopeless reflection added, that no legal process, no orderly method, of recourse was available to the outraged, then the human, the natural, reaction among a people of unbroken iron temper was the impulse to hit back.

The stage was set. Bill Longley, standing under the court house oak, with unwavering dark stare going from one face to another, was in the grip of shaping events which—he proved later by his letters—he understood not at all. All he knew was that conditions were such that no white man of any pride of race or history could endure them. He was no philosopher, no thinker. His brain was director of that magnificent body of his, no tool for abstract thought.

Bill Longley. . . There are old men yet alive who squint across the mists of a long half-century and see him as he was in his heyday. Hunkering in the sun with back to some corral, they mutter his name in their beards and recount the Longley legends. He rides again, gigantic on phantom *caballo*, across the blue-bonneted prairie, smoke wreathing from the muzzles of his Colts, the elfin echo of his fierce yell carrying to us, as once it carried thunderously into the cabins of the negroes and sent them cowering and mumbling to the shadowed corners. . .

He belongs to Texan folklore. Upon his shoulders—wide, now, as even those of the towering "Pecos Bill" of the Southwestern range's legend—are hung apocryphal tales borrowed from the Dick Turpin legend, from Robin Hood. Disregarding these incidents charged to him, he stands at the head of a long procession of Texas gunmen, slingers of the sixes who were to set style and pace for the Genus Gunfighter elsewhere on the frontier that stretched from Montana to Mexico, from Mississippi to California.

He is the major figure of the beginning of the Gunman Cycle that roughly embraced the span of years between 1860 and 1900, the period in which amazing skill in the mechanics of pistol-handling was developed, when gunplay became a be-all, end-all, an art separate from the business of mere promiscuous killing.

A LOUD-VOICED negro sat his horse on the Camino Real, the ancient Royal Highway of the Spanish, which ran from Bastrop to Nacogdoches. He was cursing certain white men of the Evergreen neighborhood. Beyond him

Bill Longley lounged in his saddle, hands held loosely on the great horn, listening.

"And Campbell Longley," the negro took up another name.

He cursed Bill Longley's father—but only for a sentence. The huge sixteen-year-old had moved. Down to the curving butts of the Colts sagging on his thighs his hands flashed. The negro saw and loud in the silence his hands slapped the stock of the rifle across his lap.

"Don't you move that gun!" Bill Longley snarled at him.

But the rifle lifted. Bill Longley spurred his horse and it leaped forward, turned sideway with knee-pressure and slight body-swaying of its rider. The rifle *whanged!* but the whirling horse had carried Bill Longley clear. Back it spun and as it straightened out into a gallop, Longley fired. The negro came sideway, sliding out of the saddle with a bullet hole through his head.

Sure that no second shot was needed, Bill Longley pushed the Colts back into their holsters. He took down the lariat from his saddle and shook out a loop. He tossed it deftly, to encircle the dead man's neck. He dragged the body off the road and to a shallow ditch. Here he buried it. His first. . .

He formed a partnership with Johnson McKowen, to race fast ponies. The Longley-McKowen quarter-horses had a reputation. They went to one race-meeting and found the negroes outnumbering the whites. The dangerous partnership ponies had to be withdrawn. To the partners, that evening, came the word that the negroes were celebrating at Lexington. Longley's dark stare narrowed as he looked at McKowen. His partner nodded. That was all.

When Lexington with good dark had become a bedlam of singing, shouting, drunken blacks, the two grim-faced boys pulled in at the edge of the milling crowd. Longley stared at the saturnalia for a little while. Then, without warning to McKowen, he dropped knotted bridle reins on his horse's neck. Out came the matched six-shooters. With a yell so high and fierce that it over-bore even the howlings of the celebrants, Longley rammed in the spurs. He charged into the crowd before Mc-Kowen could move.

It seemed pure madness—suicide. Above the bobbing heads Longley reared gigantic, deadly. But pistols began to flame, the reports so swift that they had the sound of a stick rattled upon a picket-fence. It was incredible that still the lone white face should rear above that dark sea. But Longley's guns were roaring. He roweled the rearing, maddened horse against the crowd, shooting down those who reached to pull him from the saddle. Miraculously, he plowed on, to emerge from the mass of frenzied negroes. Not a wound was on him, but two men lay dead in his wake and a half-dozen were wounded.

Thereafter, Bill Longley was held in superstitious fear by the negroes. From mouth to mouth his name was passed, the tales of his exploits swelling. He was invulnerable to lead or steel. The very horse he rode was not the same as other horses. A witch-horse, a devil-horse.

There was a porter on the Houston and Texas Central Railroad who made it a point to show his authority to white passengers. Upon a certain trip he was much annoyed by the pair of booted feet projecting into the aisle as he moved back and forth. Twice, three times, even a fourth time, he told that passenger to keep his feet out of the aisle. But the fifth time, he kicked them violently out of the way.

He went on, then, to the day-coach. Here he told the conductor all about it and finished on the triumphant note of the kicking. The conductor nodded carelessly:

"He always puts his feet in the aisle when he's riding the train," he told the porter. "Bill Longley does."

The porter made a low, agonized, moaning sound and leaped for the rear of the coach. His face, the color of cold wood ashes, hung upon his shoulder as he raced for the rear platform. He leaped for the ground, rolled over, got up and went at stumbling run for the brush. It made no difference that the passenger was not Longley

A few months after the Lexington episode, or in Mid-December 1866, Bill Longley was taking his alert ease in Evergreen. To him, where he sat talking with several young men, came one of the boys of the place. He was excited. Longley eyed him curiously.

"Three bad niggers down at the saloon, Bill," the boy gasped. "They're drinkin'. They're huntin' trouble. They're talkin' mighty big about hearin' that Evergreen's a bad place for niggers an' they'd like to see somebody make it bad for them!"

Bill Longley got up and mechanically looked to the hang of the six-shooters that sagged on his thighs. The others got up. Like Bill, they twitched the six-shooters they wore to positions more convenient for the draw. But the negroes were already mounted, turning away from the door of the saloon there by the motte of live oaks.

"Get your horses, boys," said Longley. "We'll just follow 'em and take those guns off 'em."

But the negroes had a good lead. They were across the line in Burleson County, more than seven miles away, when the young Evergreen men overhauled them. They whirled with the sound of the drumming hoofbeats. They turned their weapons on the galloping riders. The boys yelled fiercely and bent a little forward, spurring hard.

"Drop those guns!" Bill Longley's yell crossed the distance between the two parties.

One negro, bolder or drunker than the rest, answered with a shot. But the heat of the liquor in his companions had given way to the chill of that December day—and the chill of sure death that came from the pistol-muzzles that menaced them. The man who had fired grunted and pitched slantingly forward out of the saddle, stone-dead. Longley and his fellows took the other negroes' pistols and turned back.

Christmas Day dawned. To Bill Longley came the word that a deputy sheriff and posse were coming fast and quietly into Evergreen, to arrest him for the negro's death. He went out and saddled his horse. He was gone when the posse arrived.

FOR THE MOMENT, Washington County was inconveniently warm for Longley. Early in '68 he drifted west to punch cows in Karnes County. Riding through Yorktown, a bunch of Federal soldiers mistook him for a friend of his, Charley Taylor. They chased Longley but he was splendidly mounted and the lead from his six-shooter buzzed close enough to the Federal heads to weigh down their bridle-reins and blunt their spurs.

The sergeant in charge of the detachment was as well-mounted as Longley. And a bold man. He overhauled the fugitive steadily. Five miles, six miles, they raced. Longley had one shot left. He watched the sergeant coming up. When the soldier came stirrup-to-stirrup with him, Longley lunged out with the pistol. The hammer caught in the sergeant's coat. Longley jerked it back, to free it. There was an explosion and the sergeant fell dead from the saddle.

That ended the pursuit. Longley jogged into Evergreen, but left quickly for Arkansas, for the word was out against him. It was almost fatal for a white man to kill a negro, but when he had also killed a soldier, he had no chance at all, in the Texas of that day.

On the road he met a pleasant young fellow named Johnson and after some talk, they decided to ride together for a while. Longley went home with this personable young fellow—and that night the cabin was surrounded by vigilantes. Johnson was a horse-thief and those frontiersmen in the posse were firm believers in the adage covering birds of a feather. Longley's protests availed nothing. He was taken with Johnson out into the woods. Behind them, unobserved, a boy came creeping, the small brother of Johnson.

The grim business of noosed ropes and led horses was soon arranged. Young horse-thief, young rebel, they sat beneath one limb with ropes about their necks. Not yet seventeen, but with five notches on his pistols, Bill Longley was face-to-face with Fate.

At a brief word from the leader, the horses were led out from under the prisoners, the condemned. There was a jerk and two bodies, one smallish, one big-limbed, heavy, kicked at the ends of the ropes. Then the vigilantes, turning away, gave the "salute" that was so often farewell to just such writhing forms, over all the frontier. They fired a ragged volley in the general direction of the condemned.

They were hardly out of sight in the brush when a strand of the rope that held up Longley snapped and curled loosely. He weighed over two hundred pounds and in the convulsions of strangulation that great weight became dynamic, jerking on the bullet-weakened manila. Another strand cracked—and another. Bill Longley dropped heavily to the ground, to twitch and writhe against the still-tight noose.

Out of the bushes came the boy who had followed and watched horror-stricken while his brother and Longley were being hanged. He raced to Longley's side and loosened the strangling noose. He cut the lashings from Longley's wrists. The world came back to Bill Longley. Fate had struck but glancingly, that time. But only for him. When he cut Johnson down, the horse-thief was dead.

For days Longley hid near the Johnson cabin, fed by the family. Then he joined the desperate band of Cullen M. Baker, robbers, killers, in what they called guerilla warfare against carpet-baggers, negroes and Northern sympathizers. He rode on various raids with the Baker gang.

There came a day in the Spring of '68 when the Bakers rounded up some of those vigilantes who had hung Longley and Johnson. One witless prisoner bragged about it and told of firing the final shots at the swinging bodies. Up into the forefront of the captors pushed a huge figure, with a grim dark face and glare that must have stricken the boaster dumb.

"I want this fellow!" Longley told Cullen Baker. "I want him right where he did this shooting at us. . . ."

The prisoner was taken to the tree on which Longley and young Johnson had dangled. That night's business

was reenacted, but this time it was the vigilante who
was dragged from the saddle under that sinister limb.
And when Bill Longley, vindictively bent on revenging
himself for the night when he, casual acquaintance of
Johnson, was made to share the criminal's fate, emptied
his six-shooter, he took very good care not to hit that
rope with a bullet.

Sixteen and a half, now, but a veteran warrior. . . A
savage youngster, shaped by a savage environment. A
tooth for a tooth was the border-code—or, better still,
two teeth for one! Riding that summer with Cullen
Baker and his mates, he must have shared in their killings of eight to ten men whom they called enemies. But
heavy rewards were posted by the Federal troops for
Cullen Baker. Longley slipped away and back to Old
Evergreen.

IF THIS GRIM, deadly youngster, marvelously adept at
weapon-play, had any notion of settling quietly down,
he gave it up speedily. Sheridan had been removed from
his command of Louisiana and Texas. But his successor,
the humane and sensible Hancock, could not satisfy the
rabid bloody shirt element in Congress. Apathy on the
part of Texans greeted the attempts at forming a constitution. The military still ruled; Governor Pease was con-
trolled by army officers. Soldiers were police, everywhere.

They chivvied Bill Longley and his brother-in-law,
John Wilson, back and forth. The negroes, who trembled
at the mere name "Longley," set soldiers on the pair's
trail. Seven or eight negroes died that summer, when
Longley and Wilson struck back. But Bill tired of this
life of the hunted wolf. He started for Salt Lake City.

There was one Rector, a trail-driver from Bee County,
heading for Kansas. Perhaps Longley would not have
joined that outfit had he known of Rector's violent
temper and overbearing habit. But it was a chance to
lose himself in the identity of a cowboy and he had to
get out of Texas.

The herd rolled on, with Rector ranting at his riders, finding fault with their handling of the cattle, straining already strained tempers to the snapping-point. But he had the name of a dangerous man to cross and he seemed to be the hardest man with his herd. Nobody "called" him until the day when, turning from abuse of a cowboy, he overheard the youngest member of his outfit remarking blandly that he would like to have Rector address *him* in that manner.

The cowman stood gaping. Resistance from this quarter was the last thing he expected. He was handicapped, standing there in his trail-camp, by ignorance of this level-eyed boy. Asked to name the three most dangerous men in Texas at that time, it is highly doubtful if his list would have included even Ben Thompson of Austin. Certainly, Bill Longley's name would not have been mentioned. Which was his error. There was no more deadly gunman, none with more of the bulldog's belligerent readiness to fight, than this huge youngster who faced him now with dark stare. The born fighting-machine—that was Longley.

Rector exploded. Longley replied calmly in kind. Finally, they agreed to rather more of formality than was usual. They went out from the herd, each Colt-armed. One might sympathize with Rector, but for his willingness, a grown man, to kill a cocky boy. For he walked to certain death. Longley's six-shooter came flashing from the holster, hammer back, hammer dropping, hammer lifting-falling-lifting. Six shots he threw at the cowman and the oldtimers tell of it with slow-shaking heads. For they say that Rector had not begun to fall before the sixth bullet had struck him.

Longley left the herd with one of the cowboys. The two encountered a pair of horse-thieves (one wonders if Longley thought of luckless Johnson, swinging in the moonlight. . .) Longley killed one and delivered the other in Abilene. He stayed only a short while in what was becoming the wildest of towns, the cattle capital of America. He had a brother-in-law in Salt Lake and he

wanted to visit him. But before he could get out of
Kansas, he had trouble in a Leavenworth saloon.

Trouble! He was magnetized for it. . . a bulldog in a
world of bulldogs. A big, competent, touchy gunfighter,
moving over that frontier where the bulk of the population was comprised of seeded men of action—men with
something Jovian about them, in that they owned the
power to take life, could swagger unafraid with their
Colt thunderbolts in each hand. The marvel is that more
fatalities are not of record, when such as the Longleys,
the Hickoks, the Thompsons, the Hardins, were constantly colliding one with another!

It was a soldier, in the Leavenworth saloon. He
looked at the huge youngster, and Longley, product of
"reconstructed" Texas, returned the stare darkly with
nothing of favor.

"Texas, huh?" the soldier remarked. "From Texas..."

"Yes, Texas! And what about it?" Longley demanded.

"Hell of a country!" the soldier informed him.
"Every man's a thief and every woman's a whore!"

There was the expected, the inevitable, slap of Longley's hands upon the butts of his ever-loose six-shooters.
The soldier slid down the front of the bar with the roar
of the right-hand Colt. Longley looked down at him,
head on one side. Then he slid, step by step, backward to
the door. He ran to his horse and swung up. At the hotel
he got his saddlebags.

But this was not Texas, where he knew every foot of
the ground, every trick of the pursuing Law. The telegraph wires hummed. He was caught at St. Joseph,
taken back to Leavenworth and thrown into the guardhouse awaiting trial for murder. There was a sergeant
whose confidence Longley won. He had money to pay
for what he wanted. The two were not long in understanding each other. Longley escaped.

Speed! Speed! He was like a phantom horseman riding
hellbent. Every day was sufficient unto itself. Every day
might be the last. Fate was riding on the saddle-cantle

and perhaps even the wild youth felt the disturbing presence. The restlessness that spurred him on to constant journeying, wild ventures, could be read as chafings against his destiny.

Cheyenne saw him. He joined a party of miners and, when they were turned back from the Big Horn Mountains by the soldiers, he teamed for the government. He opened a saloon in a settlement rejoicing in the name of Miner's Delight. He became a corral-boss for the army quartermaster. The quartermaster, one Gregory, is alleged to have initiated Longley into the mysteries of tangled and crooked red tape. But they quarreled over a division of spoils when the pupil became so apt that he would rob, not only the Government, but his accomplice. Gregory, like the luckless Rector, misjudged his foe. He came hunting Longley, armed. He died without knowing what had killed him. For Longley "dry gulched him."

LONGLEY, riding a Government mule, did not wait to see if Gregory would recover consciousness long enough to tell the tale of the shooting. He headed for Salt Lake City and was overtaken by cavalrymen. For nine months he was under guard. Once he escaped but was recaptured after a long pursuit.

At last, he was tried and convicted of the killing and sentenced to imprisonment for thirty years. While awaiting transfer to the Iowa State Prison, he made a daring escape and for a year lived as one of the Snake Indians. It was a wild, free life. One might have expected it to so suit the untamable Longley that he would have ended his days with the tribe. But there is an itching to Texas feet. . . It drives the Texan out to wander over every land beneath the sun. But, also, it brings him back or, if return be impossible, breaks his heart.

Longley pictured Old Evergreen, the green grove of live oaks and their patriarch, the Court House Oak, with the little stores about them. He saw with the eye of his mind the green sod of the prairies, carpeted by the acre with vivid blue bonnets. He was homesick as a child. Back he came, but he dared not come directly. Too much blood lay on the straight trail now. He worked circuitously—the Southwest, where a Mexican girl saved his life, then Kansas—homeward. In Parkersburg, Kansas, he and a young man named Stuart sat down to a card-game. A quarrel developed and Stuart went for his gun. Longley's speed on the draw came once more into play. Stuart fell across the table with gun unfired, a bullet in his heart, another in his head.

Whatever might have been Bill Longley's lot, in another environment, different circumstances, he was now definitely on the trail that the James brothers, the Youngers, the Daltons, followed—the trail into other than political outlawry, into criminality.

Killing meant nothing much to such as Longley. He had seen too much of it, done too much of it. Self-preservation was strong in his huge body and deadly skill with six-shooter or rifle made it easy. Every man who looked askance at him might be a seeker for that thousand dollars of reward, word of which had trickled to Longley. Any man who put so much as a straw in his path was an enemy—and he knew of but one way to meet an enemy. But from homicide, he was now to turn to its natural corollary—the taking of subsistence from the world in any way that offered.

This Stuart killing—perfectly justifiable in the day and place—brought evidence of the new Longley, who had made his beginning in thievery at the Government corral in Wyoming. For young Stuart's father offered a reward of fifteen hundred dollars, for the capture of his son's killer.

They called Longley "Tom Jones" these days. And when the news of the reward came to him, he went out and found two men to help him in a plan he had conceived. They listened to instructions and grinned. Then they tied up "Tom Jones" and delivered him to the sheriff, claiming the reward. Stuart, senior, came down to look at the slayer of his boy. He handed over the money. The sheriff paid it to the "captors."

"And that's that!" he said. They nodded.

"We'll be saying goodbye to Jones," one of them suggested. "Where he's headed, we won't be seeing him again."

That was understandable to the sheriff. He led them up to Longley's cell, to watch this parting. But the grin faded abruptly from his face. Something was poking into his back.

"We'll just have to cut you off, pocket-high, if you make any noise," one of the men drawled. "Don't do it!"

They tied him up and gagged him. They opened up the cell and Longley came out, grinning, with hand out-thrust for the reward. They stood there, with the help-less sheriff in the cell watching, and divided the fifteen hundred. Then they drifted out of town.

Longley and a partner embarked in a counterfeit scheme and were captured by a Federal Marshal in the Indian Territory. Longley always claimed that it took two thousand in real money to paralyze that officer long enough to let them go. He said that he was dead-broke when he continued toward Texas. But home lay ahead, now. He was not worried about money.

Campbell Longley, most tragic figure of the Longley Saga, had found life too hard in Evergreen. He had moved to Bell County to escape if he could the persecu-tion of those who hunted his wolfish son. But whatever peace he found in the new locality was destroyed by Bill's return.

Word of Bill's presence on the farm drifted back to Evergreen. A posse came hunting the thousand dollars the state had offered for the young gunfighter. Bill waited only long enough to get a new model Colt six-shooter, then "lit a shuck" for Comanche County.

There was a bad negro in that neighborhood, who made a practise of riding up to lonely ranch-houses and ordering white women about. He encountered Longley in a store and pulled his hat down over his eyes.

"Who the hell are you?" he demanded.

"Bill Longley!" replied the young man, with the twinkle of hand-motion that none had ever matched. The new Colt roared twice in the confined space of the little store. Two bullets went through the black desperado's head.

"These certainly are fine guns!" said Longley, looking at the newly-christened weapon, rather than at the dead man. "They shoot right where you hold 'em!"

He had plenty of friends, who kept him informed of the various movements against him. Word came to him to move west. He made Coleman County, then pushed farther into West Texas. With two companions, he headed for the Colorado River country. Five men overtook the trio, near the Santa Anna Mountains. Longley killed one and the others left that dangerous neighborhood.

Longley, for some reason known to himself only, if to himself, even, went back to the farm in Bell County. But even he could see the impossibility of long escaping capture in that country. He rested a few days and drifted toward Mason County, on the real frontier, where still the Comanches and Kiowas raided every light moon.

SHERIFF FINLEY had a printed description of William P. Longley. He had studied that "flier" until he walked and rode with before his eyes a picture of a sinewy, quick-moving six-footer, dark of hair and eyes and soft youthful mustache, "going heavily-armed," who "must be approached with caution," because he was "a very dangerous man always ready to fight."

Bill Longley could only guess that the sheriff recognized him through the thin mask of his alias—William Henry. Perhaps he did not even guess, at first, for Finley was "smooth people." But as he and the sheriff became the closest of companions, drinking together, yarning by the hour of this and that, sitting down together to play seven-up, he proceeded on the basis that the sheriff did know him and was only trying to put him off his guard.

When Finley brought in two strangers and suggested a game of cards between them all, that night, Longley agreed. But he had a suspicion about the kind of game Finley intended. He went out and got on his horse. He made no stop until he reached the quaint German town of Fredericksburg.

Finley showed up in Fredericksburg. He still wanted a game of cards, it seemed. Once more Longley made and broke an engagement. He rode to Kerrville but left quickly, heading out for Edwards County. Sheriff Finley and a large posse followed, rounded up Bill's camp and at dawn Finley hailed Longley, who jumped out of his blankets with a six-shooter in each hand. There was parleying, but it was death or surrender. And he had escaped the authorities before. He handed over his Colts to Finley.

This was late in '73. Edmund J. Davis, last of the reconstruction governors, famous for his "nigger police" which had replaced the Texas Rangers, had troubles of his own. He was fighting bitterly the accession of Richard Coke to the governor's chair. When Finley brought Longley into Austin, he was informed that no reward would be paid.

Sympathize for a moment with a shrewd, brave officer! The most dangerous man in Texas in his custody, captured after a long period of working up the case and after three attempts. Now, the thousand dollars he had expected was nonexistent. It was a sad day for Sheriff Finley! But when a relative of Longley's came along and paid over five hundred dollars to Finley, to secure Bill's release, the sun came out again. He could hardly be blamed for turning Longley loose, when the state's chief executive refused to take him.

Longley went home—to Evergreen, not to Bell County. He moved on, once more the Fate-ridden outlaw. There were warrants out for him, for negroes killed at Old Evergreen. He had enemies interested in seeing him prosecuted. He says that he discussed with his father giving himself up and the old man shook his head drearily:

"It would bankrupt me even to try to clear you," he told his son.

Longley put faith only in his six-shooters, after that. He was twenty-three—or in his twenty-third year. The huge-limbed boy had become a magnificent physical specimen, towering over six feet, weighing over two hundred pounds, but looking almost lean. A figure to take a man's eye—or a woman's. . . .

He drifted into Frio County. A Mexican argued with him over a horse-trade and the argument ended with the roar of the Longley six-shooters punctuating, setting period to, the Longley objections. He was not above a grim sort of jest—as he proved when he rode up to the farm of William Baker, on Walnut Creek in Bastrop County.

"Mr. Baker," said Bill innocently, "my name's Baker, too. I reckon we're kinfolks and I'd like to work for you."

He got a job but when word came by the grapevine telegraph that Lee County had been cut off old Washington County and a brand-new sheriff named Jim Brown was on his trail, he called Baker to one side.

"Mr. Baker, I've got a confession to make," he told the farmer. "I'm not really kinfolks of yours. I'm that hell-roaring Bill Longley you've heard so much about. I like a warm climate as much as the next man. But this weather is more than warm—it's getting hot! I'll be leaving you!"

November of 1875, by his own record of dates, found him working north of Waco at a gin. The big, dark laborer was known as Jim Patterson around McLennan County. He was not considered a bad egg, but George Thomas was. George was known to have killed some men. So when the gin-laborer had a ferocious fist-fight with the gunman and Thomas rode off the field promising to "smoke it" at their next meeting, public sentiment regarded "Patterson" as a walking dead man.

Longley rode up to Thomas that same night, where he sat his horse outside of a little store. He had waked the storekeeper and they were talking, plain in the moonlight.

"Well, Thomas," said Longley, "this is our first meeting and I'm ready to settle our trouble."

"All right!" Thomas grunted and whipped out his pistol.

It was doubtless a fast McLennan County draw. But, somehow, the amazed storekeeper noted, "Patterson" had beat the gun-fighter to the draw. His gun barked in the quiet night. Thomas' pistol fired only as he tumbled from the saddle. Three more bullets Longley sent into him. Then he apologized very courteously indeed, to the storekeeper, and rode out of that neighborhood.

At a Mexican ranch on the Medina near San Antonio, his horse was stolen and he killed the man who had taken it. He went on to Frio Cañon in Bandera County and the natural beauty of this lovely region affected even his fierce, restless heart. He was ready to settle down there for life.

But there was a hard case going by the name of Sawyer, with whom Longley grew quite intimate. When he found that Sawyer was cultivating him to learn if a reward were offered for him, with the idea of capturing him to earn it, he decided to turn the tables on the traitor. He got himself deputized to capture Sawyer, whom he knew to be a fugitive. He and Sawyer fought a fierce duel in the cedar brakes, Sawyer's shotgun and pistol against Longley's Colts.

Four bullets, Longley put into him, but Sawyer was a fighting man! He killed Longley's horse and they continued the battle through the brush. Longley killed him, at last, when he had lodged thirteen balls in his body!

AGAIN HE MOVED on. He found a couple of men on the Castroville road who wanted to free a prisoner in Castroville jail. Longley still had some warrants given him by the sheriff at Uvalde. Warrants for King Fisher,

John Wesley Hardin, and other notorious gunfighters. He posed as an officer, in Castroville, threw the sheriff offguard, captured him and released the prisoner. Then he rode eastward.

A deputy sheriff stopped him near Lockhart. He wanted to know by what authority Longley wore a pistol. Longley produced his sheaf of warrants. But the deputy could not show authority for his pistol. So Longley took it away from him.

He went through Lee County, under Sheriff Jim Brown's very nose. In April of that year, Longley had taken furlough from Jim Baker's Walnut Creek farm, to come back to Evergreen and interview Wilson Anderson. Word had come to Bill that Anderson and Cale Longley—Bill's cousin—had ridden out together but Anderson had come home to report Cale killed by his horse.

Longley and Anderson met in an Anderson field. For once Bill had abandoned the sixes with which he was so deadly. He killed Anderson with a shotgun.

Now, he rode calmly through Lee County. Jim Brown must have been furious when he learned that Texas' most notorious wanted man had shown him so little respect. But he could afford to let Longley have the laugh on him—his complete triumph was coming.

So was the one real love of Longley's hunted life. A Madison County girl had once softened him, but Louvenia Jack, slender, pretty sixteen-year-old *Desdemona* to Longley's dark, saturnine *Othello*, made him regret his wasted life, when he caught his first glimpse of her at her father's farm house in Delta County.

He introduced himself to the Jacks as William Black, a Missourian and a roving man. When he said that he wanted work, old Jack was reminded that Parson Lay had a farm a mile beyond, and wanted someone to raise a crop on shares. That suited Longley. It suited Parson Lay, when they approached him. Longley did not precisely lay aside his Colts, beat his reddened blade into a plowshare, but he did farm.

His love-affair with Louvenia Jack ran into snags. . . There are two sides to this story. The Lays claimed that Longley, a hard case, grew unreasonably angry over a mere joke and murdered Lay. Longley insisted that the Lays objected to his attentions to the girl—favoring a man of the neighborhood—and also wanted to drive him away from the crop he had made. He quit the Lay farm, but the trouble was not over. Lay had him arrested, charged with threatening his life. Longley burned out of the little plank jail, rode to the Jack place. There he secured a double-barreled shotgun, went over to Lay's and found the preacher milking cows. He killed him there with a load of turkey-shot.

He ran for the Red River and crossed into the Indian Territory. He had trouble with the Indians and was shot. A half-breed Cherokee girl nursed him until he could make his way to the house of a friend in Arkansas.

He went back to Evergreen, taking a couple of friends out of the custody of a deputy sheriff enroute. It needed only the magic of the Longley name behind the Longley six-shooter to jerk that deputy's hands aloft. He rode on to Delta County to see Louvenia. Delta County knew, now, that the William Black who had killed Lay was really the desperado, Bill Longley. He could not stay there, with the country alive with officers searching for him. Back to Bell County he went, to that quiet, puzzled old man, who had hatched this fierce chick to amaze and discomfit him.

There was a reward of five hundred dollars on his head, for Lay's killing. Sheriffs everywhere were poring over the famous description:

". . . Six feet high; tolerably spare built; black hair, eyes and whiskers; slightly stooped in shoulders. . . . can be recognized in a crowd of 100 by the keenness and blackness of his eyes . . . $250 being offered in Lee County"

Always wandering . . . De Soto Parish, ten miles over the Louisiana line from Texas, knew him in early '77. A farm-hand again, known as William Jackson, and a great friend of young Constable Courtney, whom he often assisted in making arrests around Keatchie.

Courtney was a shrewd young officer. He was forever picking up the "fliers" describing famous criminals and studying them until his head was a very file of descriptive lists. There came a day when he received one on the "most desperate criminal in the Southwest" who was not—unfortunately!—just then in the Southwest, but a fugitive.

"Why, that fits Bill Jackson to a T!" Courtney said amazedly. But it seemed impossible that the quiet, fiddling, likable Jackson could be this lightning gunfighter, this killer of thirty-odd notches, the hell-roaring Bill Longley.

He began to investigate. At Nacogdoches, Texas, Sheriff Milt Mast was also thinking of Longley. He and Courtney exchanged some letters and Mast with Deputy Bill Burrows slipped across the Louisiana line one night in May, 1877. Mast could hardly believe that he was so close to an unsuspecting Longley. He looked up Courtney, who was expecting him.

"He's hoeing in a piece of corn, about half a mile from the Gamble house," Courtney told the Texas sheriff. "He may or may not have his pistol on. That's something to risk. We'll go out and you men wait in the house-yard. I'll go into the field and tell Bill I want him to come help me arrest a bad negro. He's done that so often, he probably won't suspicion a thing. When we get into the yard, you'll have to step out and cover him."

Longley saw nothing strange about Courtney's request. He had done the same thing many times. He walked into the Gamble yard and as they entered, Courtney dropped back a step. Captain Mast and Bill Burrows stepped out, pistols drawn. At the same moment Courtney rammed the muzzle of his pistol in Longley's back.

Courtney, unloading his pistol, stepped up and tied Longley's hands behind him, to the tune of Longley's cursing. Mast and Burrows loaded the prisoner into a wagon. It was no time to hesitate. They wanted no fight over extradition. They ran Longley back into Texas and took him to Giddings. The *Austin Statesman* on June 21, 1877, recorded the capture and added that "he is credited with killing thirty-two men."

HE WAS TRIED for the murder of Wilson Anderson and pleaded self-defense. The trial began September 3, 1877. Longley claimed that he had no attorney and was given no chance to procure witnesses for the defense. The jury got the case the next day, deliberated for an hour and a half, and then brought in a verdict of guilty with sentence of hanging.

Appeals and other legal technicalities delayed execution of the sentence, but after a long wait in the Giddings and Galveston jails, on October 11, 1878, at 1:30 in the afternoon, Sheriff Jim Brown and his group of guards brought Longley out of his cell. He was quite cheerful as he got into the ambulance that was to convey him to the gallows.

Giddings was packed. The negroes who had feared him so were there by hundreds. It seemed impossible that their bogie-man was about to die. The ambulance came through the crowd and stopped at the gallows-steps. Longley got out and looked up at the scaffold. Nearly a hundred guards were massed about it, for Longley had many friends, even more sympathizers. There had been rumors of a rescue and those keen black eyes the reward-fliers had so often noted roved over the sea of faces surrounding him. But no movement came from the spectators.

He shifted the cigar in his mouth and climbed the steps. They swayed a trifle and Longley grinned at Brown:

"Look out! The steps are falling!" he called. "I don't want to get crippled!"

Sheriff Jim Brown was ill at ease. He had bought the old Longley homestead. He was living there, where this prisoner had lived. He looked down at the crowd from the gallows.

"This is Lee County's first legal hanging," he said—then added fervently: "And I hope it will be the last!"

Longley was much calmer. He spoke briefly, without any of the rancor he had shown in letters written from Giddings jail. He had seen none of his family. In one letter he had remarked that his father had been forbidden under penalty of death to defend his son; claimed that Wilson Anderson was heavily-armed at the time of his killing and had made the first movement toward a weapon. In that letter he accused the authorities of admitting the testimony of "a sworn gang of cutthroats and murderers." None of this was evident as he faced a noosed rope for the second time in his twenty-seven years.

The black cap was drawn over his face and the noose placed. The drop was great—about twelve feet. With the twang of the tautened rope, it slipped on the crossbeam. Longley landed on his feet, with the rope slack. The sheriff and a deputy lifted him while a man tightened the rope. Eleven minutes later three doctors pronounced him dead.

Perhaps it was this circumstance which roused speculation in certain minds. The rumor had gone abroad that Longley would be rescued by desperate allies. It had been hinted that the rescue would not be the crude, if spectacular, dash of armed horsemen against the sheriff's party at the gallows-foot.

As the tale came to be repeated in the months that followed the digging of "the Longley grave" outside of the cemetery fence at Giddings, friends had persuaded the not-unwilling Jim Brown to clothe Longley in a sort of harness, which came up to protect the neck and permitted him to take that long drop, give a few realistic groans and kicks and be cut down, to vanish with darkness, after an empty coffin had been interred.

In the years since then, the story has lost nothing in the telling. Veraciously, men and descendants of men who knew Longley have described meetings with him, years after that murky October day of 1878 in Giddings.

Against these stories (which are told of Billy the Kid and Jesse James, also) must be set the evidence of three doctors, who examined the dangling body. One doctor, we may concede, might have been persuaded. But when the almost incredible happens, when any three doctors of the same community are unanimous in their opinions about anything, it must be so. And there was no minority report concerning Bill Longley's condition, after his drop from the gallows.

Except in the manner of his meeting it, there is nothing heroic about Bill Longley's death. There was nothing heroic about his life, for that matter. But there was much that was tragic! Not even John Wesley Hardin was so much a creature of his times.

Longley met Hardin once and there was a card-game in which the younger man came off winner. Longley has left no record of that encounter and Hardin was never a man to give himself the worst of any report that he made.

But, whether or not Hardin's account is correct, there is no doubt that Longley disliked Hardin, his rival in the Smoky Seventies for top-honors at gun-slinging. He went to his death bitter because he had received the death-sentence for killing Wilson Anderson, while Hardin escaped with a penitentiary-sentence for killing Charley Webb, the Brown County deputy sheriff. In Giddings Jail, October 29, 1877, he wrote Sheriff Milton Mast of Nacogdoches:

"You know what I told you about John Wesley Hardin, and myself, and all such cases. When the right ones jump a fellow they always take him in out of the wet. I told you that John Wesley Hardin would get picked up some time, for all that he and his friends have told it everywhere that he would never be captured alive.

"There never was a man so fast but what he found a man just a little faster than he was. But, then, Captain, you know that you and Bill Burrows got the dead-drop on me, and so did Lieutenant Armstrong get it on John Wesley Hardin. But, drop or no drop, John Wesley

Hardin and myself now inhale the gentle breezes that flow through prison windows.

"Did you see the interview that was given out by John Wesley Hardin when he was first brought to Austin? He said that he had never had anything to do with Bill Longley, nor any such characters, and that he never had anything to do with anybody except gentlemen of honor.

"Now, as a matter of information, I would like to know where these gentlemen of honor friends of his are now! They certainly are not in jail where the Honorable John Wesley is himself. I wonder if it is King Fisher, Brown Bowen, Bill Taylor, Gladden Ringer, Scott Cooley, Grisson and two or three dozen others whom I might name?"

He recounts the killings of Hardin and his clan, calling them cowardly murders by a gang, and continues:

"Hardin was afraid of Webb and when he killed him he took every cowardly advantage that it was possible to take. It seems that it was death by their law—the law of Hardin and his gang—for a man just simply to say that he was not afraid of Wesley Hardin, and poor Charley could not help saying that, for he was a man that was never known to tell a lie, and so one day when somebody asked him if he would tackle John Wesley Hardin, he said he would certainly do so if he had the necessary papers for his arrest . . .

"Now, I do not mean to say that Wes Hardin is not brave, but the woods in Texas are full of brave men, and I suspect that Hardin remembers at least one—and that is old Reagan, who captured him near Palestine several years ago. I heard that when Hardin got back to his crowd in the brush, he said:

" 'Boys, don't ever let Old Man Reagan get after you, for he is hell! I tell you!' . . .

"Captain Mast, I suspect that they will hang me. It is just as I have told you in previous letters and in course of conversation. I cannot and do not think hard of you for arresting me, but don't you think it is rather hard to kill me for my sins, and give Wes Hardin only twenty-five years for the crimes he has committed?

"But I guess he would say it was none of my business."

They were touchy about their reputations, the old gunfighters. And Longley, Hardin, Ben Thompson and King Fisher were the outstanding quartette in Texas of the '70s, with little love lost between them.

Each was doomed to a tragic death but Bill Longley —the only one who met his Fate coming to him behind a badge of the Law, was perhaps least deserving of that end. For destiny made him the creature he was—one of the fierce, undisciplined Border Breed.

CHAPTER II · *Forty Notches*

JOHN WESLEY HARDIN

"Y OU WON'T come along?
Won't even skip with me,
if I hold up the jailor when he opens the door?"

Wes' Hardin's blue eyes shuttled contemptuously
from face to face of his cellmates, in the gloom of Longview jail. He twirled an ancient Colt on his forefinger by
the trigger-guard. He stared those older jailbirds down.

"Hell! There's nothing *to* it! I've been in plenty
tighter places," he told them persuasively.

"I—reckon," a loutish farmer-boy sneered. "Like
the time in that Waco barber-shop when you took an'
murdered Huffman. But they landed you here in jail, I
notice!"

"You're a dam' liar," Wes said calmly. "Seems that I
don't know half as much about that Waco murder I'm
locked up for, as some of you! If I'd killed Huffman, I
wouldn't lie about it! But all your talk's not covering up
your yellow streaks! You haven't got nerve enough to
make a break, even when I take all the risk."

The other prisoners—all older than Wes Hardin—
did not openly resent his manner. He was only seventeen, but he was the best man in that jail. They knew it!
Had they known of certain grim incidents of the past
two years, in which this preacher's son had been chief
actor, they would have been more respectful still. But
they understood him well enough . . .

"All right, then," he drawled. "I'll buy Old Peacemaker, here, from Rufe. I'll buy John's new overcoat,
too. Forty, gold, for the hogleg. Twenty-five to you,
John, for the coat."

He was counting out the gold when the cell-door
rattled. Gold won earlier in that month of January **at**

poker. Won, too, from a man notorious as a flaming daredevil, a gunman of gunmen, famous throughout Texas in 1871—Bill Longley.

Wes' cellmates popped the money into their pockets. The old Colt Wes had bought—loaded with four .45 cartridges—vanished into his waistband like a sleight-of-hand trick. But it was only the old negro woman who served as jail cook. She waddled in through the murk of the winter evening.

"Boss-man say we goin' lose a boarder, white folks," she grinned. "Reckon it's you he means," she told Wes.

He nodded. Blue eyes narrowed a shade, hardened. That would be better than a jail-break. Nobody took him seriously—at first. His face was too smooth, too boyish. He looked too completely the inexperienced youngster of good family. When the old woman was gone, he made his preparations quickly.

He had two undershirts—he put on both. He pulled on his dress-shirt. Then, by a cord, he suspended the Colt under his left arm. He had a second dress-shirt. He put it on over the weapon. His sack coat and the fur overcoat he had just bought covered the "cutter's" bulge. So he took off both coats and lay down on his cot. Presently, the door rattled again. It was dark inside the cell.

Stokes was the officer who was to take young Wes Hardin to Waco, to stand trial on the charge of murdering a man named Huffman in a barber-shop. He was a smallish man of forty-five, and the prisoners knew him as a good deal of a bully. He had a lamp. He set it down and crossed to Wes' cot to shake the boy.

"Up y' come!" he snapped. "Y're Waco-bound to git hung. An' if y' try any funny business on the road, y'll wish y'd got hung here! I got a man with me that's plumb killer!"

Wes trembled artistically as he donned his coats and stuffed the pockets with food. Stokes laughed. So did the other prisoners. But there was a difference—for Stokes was laughing at Wes Hardin and the prisoners were *not*. . .

Outside the jail, the earth was heavily blanketed with snow. Stamping there, in the bitter cold, were a big bay gelding, a pretty sorrel mare and a runty black pony wearing only a folded blanket. A wide-shouldered, swarthy man stood at their heads, snarling to himself.

"Say!" Wes Hardin cried, with sight of the black pony. "You can't come that one on me! Where's my horse and saddle? The horse I had when you arrested me?"

"Sonny!" Stokes told him sinisterly. "Where y' goin', they don't *ride* hawses. No, sir! They flap their wings an' fly! Git onto that pony. Y' ride it to Waco!"

And the only concession he would make was the getting of one more blanket, for the ride of two hundred twenty-five miles to Waco. Wes' hands were tied in front of him. His ankles were hobbled under the pony's belly. The swarthy man, Jim Smolly—quarter-Mex', quarter-nigger, half-white and all bad—cursed Wes venomously for causing him a trip in weather like this. He suggested to Stokes that they go a mile out, shoot the boy and save trouble.

Wes hunched his shoulders and listened. He was almost enjoying himself! They were so sure that they dealt with only a frightened kid. And in this blue-eyed son of Brenham's old circuit-rider, there ran a streak of bulldog dare-devilry that could not be tamed. He grinned to himself.

He would not be eighteen until May 26. But already he had notches on his guns—*eight of them!* Billy the Kid came close to amateur status, when compared to John Wesley Hardin, either in number of tallies or in trigger-nometry!

At fifteen, Hardin had killed a "bad nigger" and, going on the dodge with Yankee troops after him, tallied one white and two black soldiers, ambushing them when they thought to dry-gulch him. For this was "Reconstruction" when nobody but a carpetbagger or a nigger had any rights in the South.

With Simp Dixon, his cold-nerved cousin, Wes had run into another squad of Yankees, down in the tangles of Richland Bottoms. He and Simp each downed one. His sixth man had been a long-haired Arkansas desperado named Bradley, who almost got Wes during a gambling quarrel, but made the fatal mistake of missing.

The seventh man was a roaring big canvasman of the John Robinson show, who "chose" Wes at Horn Hill. Wes was already developing that amazing speed on the draw which was to make his name the all-time symbol of gunplay. He "slapped leather" with the canvasman and left him dead.

Leaving Horn Hill on the jump, Wes had continued his journey homeward, toward Brenham. And wherever young Wes Hardin went, he went "on the prod." In Texas of 1870, liberally salted with two-fisted, two-gunned gentlemen, he was never long out of hot water. He was already a professional gambler. The saloon and the crib were his hangouts.

At Kosse, the gentleman-friend of a Cyprian beauty of the town tried the ancient badger-game on Wes. The boy pretended to be scared to death. He dropped some money on the floor. The "badgerer," gun in hand, grinned and stooped to pick it up. There was a twinkle of the boy's hand, a scream from the woman. The man jerked but before his gun could lift there sounded, hollow in that little room, the roar of a .45. The man fell with a bullet-hole in his forehead.

It was Wes' boast now, as it remained for many a year, that he took "no sass but sassparilla!"

And *this* was the smooth-faced, frightened, helpless boy, whom those two thickwitted, bullying officers were carrying to Waco!

THEY HUDDLED close together, leaving Longview, bitten by that still, ferocious cold. The Sabine River they found "on a high lonesome," as the punchers say. They had to swim it. Wes revised his opinion of that runty black he rode. He had told Stokes furiously that he could own a dozen like the pony and still be afoot. But the little brute swam like an alligator-gar. They came out into the bitter January night, wet from the waist down, numbed and shivering. Two miles beyond the Sabine they made camp and slept until day.

On the second day of the trip they were ferried over the Trinity River and made camp on a dry ridge. Stokes went for corn-horse feed. The surly, bullying Smolly was left to guard the prisoner. Wes slipped behind his pony. It was now or never! He got his old Colt out.

"Stick 'em up, you dam' mongrel!" he yelled.

Smolly whirled with an oath. His hand slapped pistolbutt. *That* was suicide. The old Colt roared. Wes shot Smolly dead. He looked down grimly at him for a space, then resaddled the breed's fine sorrel mare. He headed for his father's house in Mount Calm.

There were to be several turning-points—points of hesitation, anyway—in the life of this preacher's son who had been named for the great Methodist John Wesley. Wes Hardin—tales of his doings—Texas has talked over for nearly sixty years. Men yet alive (like Captain Jim Gillett, that old Ranger and splendid peace officer, Jeff Milton, Captain John R. Hughes, to name but three) knew him more or less intimately. I have listened to talk of him virtually all my life. He was the Individualist, born. What he wanted to do, he would do —and "God be on the side of the heaviest artillery!"

This was one of those crossroads in his life, this moment when a fine old frontier preacher sent his son running for Mexico. Texas, in the grip of carpet-baggers, of Davis' scalawag State Police (largely negroes), was only the execution chamber for Wes Hardin.

Wes for once listened to his father. He left Mount Calm for San Antonio, on the first leg of his journey. But he ran head-on into three men of the State Police, between Belton and Waco. One travels that road, today, at 45 miles an hour, in a car. It was "horseback country" in '71—and travelers made camp where they could. These three State Policemen, having captured Wes, made camp at nightfall. It seems more than passing strange, the way men treated the youngster!

They wanted him for murder—or for nothing. They had him. But no special precautions seem to have been taken against him. That boyish, handsome face must have fooled them, as it had fooled nine others. Too, they had been drinking. One Smith took the first watch while Jones and Davis slept. From his blanket, Wes watched calmly. He saw them take off their guns. He marked exactly where the guns were put. He listened to their snoring while he kept an eye on Smith.

The sentry's head began to nod. Wes looked once more at the weapons, then settled like a panther on a limb, to wait for his moment. Smith began to breathe deeply. His head fell farther forward. Wes' hands slid out. He got Davis' shotgun, then Jones' six-shooter.

He wasted no time on formalities. The average Texan of that day hated not even the carpetbagger as he hated one of Davis' State Police (which were to be supplanted by the Texas Rangers as soon as Texas rid herself of Davis). Wes Hardin had seen too much bloodshed to be worried about killing enemies. This was the keynote, the explanation, of his whole career. It was the dominating impulse, that night, as he lifted himself with the shotgun, to aim at Smith.

He might have got out of that camp without firing a shot, but that would not have been like Wes Hardin. He killed Smith, then turned the second barrel upon Jones. Davis jumped up, yelling. Wes dropped the shotgun and snatched up Jones' six-shooter. He slammed .45s at Davis until certain the policeman was dead.

Back, then, he turned to his father. He made an oath that never would he surrender, again, merely because the drop was on him. He kept that oath, too. It was one which was to add materially to the mortality-rate among those who came in contact with John Wesley Hardin. For he would take a chance at drawing and beating a shot from a gun pointed at him—a cocked gun. And to make his chance better, he practised incessantly at the draw; he invented a "holster vest"—of which more later.

He got no nearer Mexico than Gonzales, where the Clements, his relatives, were gathering cattle for a drive up the trail. He went with them—with Manning, Gyp, Jim and Joe. He argued with a Mexican monte-dealer— and killed him, here. In February the trail-herd started for Kansas, moving up through Williamson County to cross Red River north of Montague County.

The Indians were levying a tax of ten cents a head on all cattle crossing The Nation. Wes was in charge of the herd and he conferred with other trail-bosses. It was decided to tell the feather-dusters where to go. This naturally caused trouble. One Indian had a bowstring to his ear, the arrow pointed at Wes, when he dropped with a bullet through his head.

The herd crossed into Kansas near Bluff Creek. Here the Osages bothered the herd, riding boldly into it to cut out fifteen or twenty head for the camp-kettles. One bunch of warriors loped into camp while Wes was out. They carried off everything that was not buried—including a fine silver-mounted bridle of the young trail-boss. They came raiding the herd again and this time Wes was very much present. He saw a big buck with his bridle. He told that buck to hand it over—and told all the Indians that no more cattle would be taken from this herd.

The buck from whom Wes had recovered his bridle showed fight. Wes hit him over the head with the barrel of his Colt. The other Osages were riding into the herd, beginning to cut out steers they fancied. Wes rammed in the hooks and shot the nearest one dead. The others hightailed. There was no more trouble on the trail until he got to Newton Prairie.

A Mexican trail-boss had a herd behind Wes. The Mex' herd kept crowding and Wes' remarks to the Mex' boss were pointed. The Mex' galloped back to his wagon, got a "sharp shooter" rifle and knelt on the ground. He took deliberate aim and the bullet grazed

Wes' hat. Something went wrong with the rifle, then. The Mex' jerked his six-shooter and rode toward Wes, whose old cap-and-ball six-shooter had a rocking cylinder. By holding the cylinder, Wes managed to hit his opponent in the thigh. They came together later and in a horseback duel Wes killed the other. José was his name. The battle was general with the *vaqueros*. Wes dropped four.

On to Abilene! Abilene, surrounded this Spring of '71 by seething masses of long-horned cattle; Abilene crowded by swaggering young men from the southern ranges, wide-hatted, bespurred and booted, the fringe of their leggings slapping as they rocked along the noisy length of Texas-"Hell"-Street; Abilene bossed by Wild Bill Hickok; Abilene the hell-roaring, twenty-four-hours-a-day shipping-point for wild cattle. stopping-point for wilder men.

And who—not excepting the famous Wild Bill—was wilder than this eighteen-year-old Texan who could handle the six-shooter as a stage-magician handles his "props!" Swaggering into the Alamo where Wild Bill hung out, he was quickly a marked man. The Clements brothers indicated him to drinkers with jerk of head or thumb. "Twenty men, that kid's downed. Chain-lightnin' an' eleven claps o' thunder, with the six-shooters. Fight at the drop of a hat—an' drop the hat hisself!"

IN ABILENE, he met an older man—Texan, also whose name was to be bracketed with his own. But neither this devil-may-care youngster nor the grimmer, more calculating gambler thought of that. John Wesley Hardin and Ben Thompson—with Bill Longley they form a trio of killers whose names will always be associated with amazing gunplay.

Ben Thompson and a friend from Austin—Phil Coe—ran the Bull's Head Saloon and gambling house on Texas Street. They had a picture of a bull painted on the false front of the building. The city council objected to the picture. The solemn members declared that the painter had too realistically, too minutely, detailed the bull's anatomy. Wild Bill was deputed to order Thompson and Coe to either make the place the Steer Saloon or hide the bull behind a bush.

I have written elsewhere the story of Ben Thompson, drawing the man as Texas, in general, understands and recalls him. Nothing about him pointed to tendency to knuckle under to anybody on earth. He was finally persuaded to alter his sign. But he never forgave Wild Bill his part in the argument. When young Wes Hardin came toting twenty notches into Abilene. Thompson had an idea.

He told Wes that Wild Bill, a Northerner, always picked Southern men to kill. He suggested that Wes kill Hickok.

"I keep busy doing my own killings," Wes told him. "If you want him killed, why don't you do it yourself?"

"Oh, I'd rather get somebody else to do it," Thompson said—doubtless with truth.

But Wes on his own account soon ran foul of Wild Bill. Hickok had a tremendous job on his hands, in Abilene. He has been variously described as a racketeering, cowardly, officer, and as a very paragon of chivalrous bravery. The truth, of course, lies between these two opinions. It seems certain that he was not a particularly good shot. But he was always ready to shoot, always looking for a suspicious move, and amazingly fast on the draw.

Such fire-eaters as Wes Hardin did nothing to make life easy for him. A kid will take a chance where a grown man hesitates. And a kid's bullet is just as deadly as anyone's. Hickok seems to have been rather friendly to Wes, who promptly swaggered the more. Wes' accounts of making Wild Bill back water; of catching Wild Bill with the "road agents' spin" and disarming him—these, I think, have to be taken like the tails of the little birds in the proverb—with salt.

But Wes did clash with a bad man of not-too-heavy caliber. He killed the fellow rather easily. But Wild Bill, he thought, would now be on his trail. He jumped on his horse and rode furiously to Cottonwood. Here he stopped to think. Wild Bill, he knew, had Texas requisitions for him. Would the marshal decide to rid himself of Wes by ramming those requisitions down his famous Colt-muzzles?

A Texas cowman got killed by a Mex' named Bideno and temporarily solved the problem. Wes and some others chased Bideno down to Bluff. Wes killed him and rode triumphantly back to Abilene, hero of the cowboys who were friends of Bill Coran, the murdered cowman.

Wild Bill let him alone. But when on the night of July seventh, Wes waked to find a robber with a dirk bending over him, he first killed the fellow, then looked out the window. Wild Bill and four men came galloping up in a hack. They had heard the shooting. Wes looked at them as they jumped out. Three years, now, he had lived the life of the hunted lobo. He suspected everybody. At this moment, he particularly suspected Wild Bill. He believed that Hickok would kill him before yelling "hands up." And here he stood with empty six-shooter.

The robber had run out into the hall to die—and he had carried Wes' trousers with him. There was no time to recover them. Wes locked the room-door, then ran back to the window. The hack came under it, moving off from the rooming house door. Wes dropped lightly out upon its roof. He lay flat upon it. Presently, he dropped to the ground and went cautiously out of Abilene. He came to some farmer's haystack beside the road. Into it he burrowed, watching that road.

A cowboy came along and Wes jumped out, waving his empty Colt menacingly. Down swung the cowboy from his saddle. From the direction of town came the sound of yelling, the thunder of pounding hoofs. Wes went into the saddle of the confiscated horse in a catlike jump.

"Give Wild Bill my love," he told the cowboy. "My name is Wes Hardin. Wild Bill will recognize the name!"

And off he went. When the posse reached the cowboy their louder yells told Wes that the message had been delivered. He quirted the horse with rein-ends and grinned as he headed for Solomon River, three miles ahead. He kept in front and splashed across with a defiant yell. His herd-camp was just beyond. As he raced toward it, he looked back and saw three riders burning up the prairie. He quirted the "borrowed" horse a little harder. Into his camp he came and flung himself out of the saddle. Snatching up a Winchester that belonged to one of the Clements brothers, he went back to meet the three possemen.

"Get down, gentlemen!" he invited them. "Boot's on the other hoof, now. No funny motions—no motions but what you have to make, taking off your clothes. You're going back to Abilene the way you sent me out of it—without pants!"

And presently they marched off, afoot, pants-less and without boots. Wes Hardin watched them out of sight. Then he saddled up a horse, got a pair of pants and a six-shooter and went back to Texas.

Gonzales County was the battleground of a war of factions—natural aftermath of reconstruction days. Surely, I have shown enough of the young bulldog, who had to red pepper his diet with excitement, to make it very plain that he could not remain in Gonzales where he had many relatives, without becoming a violent partizan. And to the natural violence of this internecine warfare was added the inflammatory bluster and swagger of negro State Police.

A couple of negro policemen decided to capture Wes. They found him in a grocery store with his back to the door. One covered him while the other waited outside. Wes held out his Colt with handle foremost—*and with forefinger hooked in the trigger-guard.* . .

The negro reached for it and the Colt did the "road-agents' spin" to come into Wes' hand and explode. The negro fell with his own pistol still cocked in his hand. Wes jumped to the door and whanged away at the negro sitting a white mule outside. That one yelled and sent the mule at a 2.40 gait for the river-bottom.

His next encounter was with a posse of negroes. They had thought to surprise this young wolf. Instead, they were surprised. He killed three of them. Twenty-seven tallies. . .

HE MARRIED, but not for him any settling down to the role of peaceful, hardworking husband. In fairness to him, he could hardly do that. The locality was simmering, ready for an explosion. He was a marked man. Your gunfighter is always that. Someone is always scheming to kill him and prove himself the better man.

He went from Gonzales toward the King ranch and killed a Mexican highwayman on the road. The next year, while driving a horse-herd, Wes again fell foul of the law. He remarked of this encounter:

"At Willis some fellows tried to arrest me for carrying a pistol. They got the contents thereof, instead."

There were old warrants by the sheaf, out against him. But Gonzales County was pretty evenly divided between a secret vigilance committee of carpetbaggers and negroes and the citizens of the county who termed themselves law-abiding. These last were Wes Hardin's allies. They were strong enough to prevent his arrest. But always there was the possibility of private brawls.

One Sublett quarreled with Wes over a tenpin game. The two swapped lead and Sublett got a bullet in the shoulder, while Wes was almost fatally wounded. His friends nursed him and with the State Police sniffing frantically for his hideout, he was shifted from place to place. At last he surrendered to an officer for whom he had complete respect—Sheriff Dick Reagan. He surrendered because two policemen had stumbled on his hiding-place. From his bed, he had battled these, killing

one, wounding the other, and himself receiving a new
bullet-hole in his thigh. When Reagan came with a
posse, to receive Wes' surrender, an excited posseman
shot at Wes and hit him in the knee.

From the jail at Austin where Reagan first took him,
Wes was returned to Gonzales. Here he was permitted to
escape custody. He got up and about and celebrated the
recovery by a saloon-row with one Morgan. He killed
Morgan. The carpetbaggers' committee was hand-in-
glove with Sheriff Jack Helms. Wes heartily disliked
Helms and after some quarreling, the trouble ended in
the smoke—with Helms dead.

Wes was credited now with at least thirty-nine men.
I have mentioned the thirty-one killings of which he
ever talked with any detail. There is nothing to show
that his notches troubled Wes' sleep. He felt that every
killing was justified—each man he had killed had been
attempting to kill him—or at least willing to kill him.
It was a bulldog's existence, that of the frontier, of
Texas, in the '70s. But the charmed life he had led could
not preserve its invulnerability forever. The 26th of May,
1874, Wes' came of age. Twenty-one years old and he
had crammed into what is, for most men, merely the
beginning of life, the preparation for life, battle, murder,
and sudden death. Thirty-nine men. . .

He went to the races at Comanche that day. The
Hardin clan horses took first, second and third. Wes had
$3,000 in winnings. He set many a man afoot, then
loaned him the horse won on a bet, to ride home again.

Deputy Sheriff Charles Webb, of Brown County, came
over to Comanche to capture or kill Wes—or so the news
ran—and to kill Wes' good friend Jim Taylor, for whom
a reward was offered. Wes drank steadily. When word
came to him that Webb was looking at the sun and remarking that it would go down upon Wes Hardin and
Jim Taylor, dead or captured, he laughed.

"Oh, I hope he'll put it off till dark, or altogether!"
he told the men in the saloon.

Webb came in. Hardin pushed up to him, looking at the two six-shooters Webb wore. Hardin's own pistol was out of sight, in the slanting holster sewed to his vest. (His invention, that holster-vest. Jim Gillett wore one in El Paso.) Webb claimed that he had no reason to want John Wesley Hardin. Wes invited him to have a drink and turned slightly away. Bud Dixon. Wes' cousin, suddenly yelled: "*Look out!*"

Webb had drawn his six-shooter. He fired and the bullet struck Hardin in the side. Wes jerked out his gun and with the roar of its explosion Charley Webb died, a bullet through his head.

Somewhat later, a mob captured Wes' brother Joe and his cousins Tom and Bud Dixon, lynched them and went on to shoot two friends of Hardin.

It looked wise to take it on the run. Hardin went to New Orleans, then to Florida. His career in the South was turbulent. He operated saloons in various places. He dealt in cattle and horses and timber. But he was never too busy to gamble and in the natural course of things there were shooting affrays and killings rising out of the young bulldog's way of living.

Brown Bowen, his wife's brother, also found Texas too hot for him. There were murder indictments running against Bowen and he found it desirable to slip out of Gonzales County and pay a visit to relatives in Polland, Alabama.

The Rangers were watching Hardin's relatives, looking for a lead to the wanted gunman. Special Ranger Jack Duncan intercepted a letter addressed to "J. H. Swain, Polland, Alabama" through correspondence Brown Bowen carried on with his father in Gonzales. He and his superior, Lieutenant Armstrong, having conferred with Governor Hubbard in Austin, set out for Polland on Hardin's trail.

At Pensacola Junction, August 23, 1877, Armstrong and Duncan found Hardin in the smoking car of a train. Several boon companions were with Hardin.

Armstrong had been a sergeant in the company of that famous McNelly who cleaned up the Border country. He was a man fearless to the point of rashness. Duncan was of a different sort, cool, level-headed, calculating. The Rangers had the help of the local sheriff and a posse in making their arrest. Only one of Hardin's companions showed fight, a boy named Mann, who was shot dead. Hardin was seized before he could draw his pistol. But even with Armstrong's Colt at his head, he would not surrender. He struggled desperately until overpowered and tied. The posse was all for killing him.

"He's too brave to kill," Armstrong told them. "The first man who shoots him—I'll kill!"

NUMEROUS attempts were made to get Hardin out of the Rangers' hands, on the trip back to Texas. Some were made by legal authorities enlisted by Mrs. Hardin and her friends. Others were merely gatherings of men resolved to rescue Hardin from Armstrong and Duncan. But the Special Ranger was—in Hardin's own term— "the wily Jack Duncan." He foresaw everything; he turned up in court in Mobile in time to quash a *habeas corpus* hearing; he would not leave the city from the railroad station, but insisted that Hardin be driven out of town several miles to a little siding where the train for Texas might be boarded—and thus avoided collision with Hardin's friends.

Hardin had now changed his tactics. He played hail-fellow with Armstrong and Duncan. They treated him with the utmost kindness, but not for a moment did Duncan—at least—forget that, with Bill Longley behind the bars, here sat Texas' most dangerous outlaw, with $4,000 reward on his head.

At Decatur a change of trains was made. The Rangers took Hardin to a hotel room and sent out for meals. Let Hardin tell what happened:

"Jack and Armstrong were now getting intimate with me and when dinner came I suggested the necessity of removing my cuffs and they agreed. Armstrong un-

locked the jewelry and started to turn around, exposing
his six-shooter to me. Jack jerked him around and
pulled his pistol at the same time.

" 'Look out!' he said. 'John will kill us and escape.'

"Of course I laughed at him and ridiculed the idea.
It was really the chance I had been looking for . . . I intended to jerk Armstrong's pistol, kill Jack Duncan or
make him throw up his hands. I could have made him
unlock my shackles, or got the key from his dead body. .
. . That time never came again. . ."

He must have cursed "wily Jack Duncan" a good
many times as the train rolled on toward Texas! He must
have thought many a time of those other occasions when
the hand of the Law had held him, but had relaxed
enough to let him jerk free—thought of the surly,
swarthy Smolly, dying on the snowy ridge above the
Trinity six years before; of the three State troopers who
had gone to sleep in camp and waked only to die. . .

He had no reason to look ahead with optimism. The
factions were at war in Gonzales County. He might well
be dragged from jail and lynched as his brother and other
relatives had been, at Comanche three years before. If he
had to stand trial, it would be in a community bitterly
hostile to him.

Nor was he wrong! People flocked to the way-
stations to see the famous desperado. Some were sympathetic—particularly when they found a handsome
young man of pleasant manners and smooth speech—
others were hostile, more were merely curious.

Bill Longley—as recorded elsewhere—thought it
hard that Hardin should be sentenced to twenty-five
years in the penitentiary while he was condemned to
death. His complaint seems just. Nobody concerned with
Longley's prosecution has anything to remember with
pride. There seems small doubt that Longley was "railroaded" to the gallows without a fair trial.

But Hardin, who complained that he, like Longley,
was not permitted to call witnesses because the opposing
faction had frightened his witnesses out of the country,

was more fortunate in one respect than his rival for gun-slinging honors: The State's own testimony proved that Charley Webb drew his pistol and wounded Hardin before the latter put hand to gun. It could not be charged that Hardin was guilty of murder in the first degree.

But he drew a stiff enough sentence! Twenty-five years in a gun-toting Texas, for killing a man who has already shot you, seems to an unprejudiced observer pretty close to the limit.

While he was held prisoner in Austin jail, his associates were eighty men as desperate, perhaps, as any similar number who could be got together. The Austin *Statesman* remarks under date of August 29, 1877:

"Some of them are from De Witt and many are considered as desperate characters as Hardin, characterized as 'the notorious murderer', though he has not been tried."

Hardin himself makes much the same remark. He lists as fellow-prisoners Bill Taylor of his own bunch, his brother-in-law, Brown Bowen, John Ringo who was to make six-shooter history in Tombstone and back down the Earps, Manning Clements, John Collins, Jeff Ake, and Pipes and Herndon of the Sam Bass gang.

Certainly, it was a company to make uneasy the jailor! But Lieutenant Reynolds' Rangers were guarding the neighborhood and he was not an officer whose charges got away.

Hardin was tried for Charley Webb's killing and, as I have said, suffered the penalities of his turbulent reputation. He was convicted and his enemies were partially satisfied.

He was taken to the penitentiary and it was like his journey from Pensacola Junction—the people thronged to see Wes Hardin. "From the hoary-headed farmer to the little maid hardly in her teens"—all crowded about the wagon where three other prisoners were chained and guarded by a company of Rangers.

He had never before known confinement of more than brief duration. He had been used to good clothing, to boots that fitted. He had been a person of importance in his own community and of notoriety the length and breadth of Texas.

When the prison gates slammed behind him and he was stripped for examination, his hair cropped, his first breakfast of watery coffee, corn bread, fat bacon and molasses put before him, he looked around furiously. It was October 5, 1878. He would be 26 years old the following May. If the State of Texas kept him behind bars for the full sentence prescribed, he would be 50 years old when released—an old man!

He set about his schemes for escape almost at once. But his theory that "in jail even a coward is a brave man" altered with experience to a belief that "convict" and "traitor" were words synonymous. His every plan was reported by stool pigeons. He was beaten unmercifully. He went for long periods to the dungeon. Perhaps he almost envied Brown Bowen, his brother-in-law, who was hanged in Cuero for the murder of Thomas Handleman while Hardin lay in Austin Jail.

Months became years. Hardin's spirit was subdued, if not broken, by confinement and harsh treatment. He gave over attempts to escape, began to study. First it was theology! But soon he decided to take up law.

On February 17, 1894, he was released from Huntsville, and stepped into the open after more than 15 years of convict-life. Just a month later Governor Jim Hogg granted him full pardon and restoration of citizenship.

Prominent men over the state were interested in Hardin. They wrote him friendly letters; they offered him help in establishing himself for a new beginning; they were uniformly cordial and they pointed out to him that, with his intelligence, his courage, he might well be hopeful of the future.

He went home to Gonzales, to his family. He hung out his shingle and began to practise law. But he was too naturally belligerent, too full of strong convictions, ever to keep to the middle of the road. It was a bitter election contest that embroiled him once more in Gonzales politics, factional warfare. He backed one candidate for sheriff and in the course of the struggle bloodshed was very narrowly averted. His man lost and Hardin left Gonzales. He moved to Karnes County.

His wife died shortly after his release. In London, Texas, Hardin married a young girl—hardly more than a child, so the old-timers tell me. He was restless. He lived with his second wife only the briefest time.

J. MARVIN HUNTER, historian, editor, who publishes at Bandera a quaint little magazine called *The Frontier Times*, was setting type in his father's newspaper office at Mason, in those days. He recalls how a tall, mustached man of middle age came into the office one morning, bearing a thick manuscript. It was a book he wanted published.

"I'm sorry that our press isn't large enough to handle that sort of work," Judge Hunter told the stranger. "Whom have I the honor of addressing?"

"John Wesley Hardin," the other said—with equal courtesy. "This is the story of my life."

Young Marvin stared open-eyed at the famous gunman who had forty-odd notches on his weapons. He recalls particularly how little Hardin resembled the desperado.

About this time a call came to Hardin, from Pecos City. It was from Jim Miller and, whatever we may think of Miller today, to Hardin it was a clan-call, for Miller was a brother-in-law of Manning Clements and the Hardins and Clementses were cousins.

Jim Miller stands well up at the head of list, among Texas' cold-eyed killers. His trail across West Texas and New Mexico is a crimson trail. Sometimes he served as a deputy sheriff or deputy marshal. More often he merely rode with quiet tongue across a given scope of range— and his silence would be broken by the sound of his rifle or pistol. Someone would fall dead and there would be the sound of a horse galloping fast away and Jim Miller would report to his paymaster that he had "collected

the tail feathers" of such and such a one and—"please
send the amount agreed upon."

In Pecos, he had "tangled ropes" with Bud Frazer,
the sheriff. They had a good deal of trouble and finally
met on the street and Frazer got into action first. But
his shot merely crippled Miller. As the old boys tell
it, Frazer upon learning that he had not killed the formidable gunman, left the country in a cloud of dust. He
went over to Eddy and ran a livery business. But he had
been indicted for assault with intent to kill and the case
was transferred to El Paso. Hardin came down to assist
in the prosecution.

One of the abiding traditions of El Paso has to
do with Mayor Johnson's receipt of the news of Hardin's
coming to town. According to this story, the mayor and
a delegation of leading citizens, including Chief of Police
Jeff Milton, went down to the train to meet the famous
gunman. But not to do him honor. On the contrary, they
are said to have warned Hardin that El Paso wanted no
desperadoes and his first wild and woolly play would be
his last.

Perhaps this occurred. But if so, there is no reflection
in the local papers of any such sentiment—none that I
can discover, at least—unless a little news-note in the
Around Town column, in the *Times* of April 2, 1895, was
directed at John Wesley:

"It is understood that a lot of the people interested in
the Frazer-Miller case from Pecos come to El Paso armed
to the teeth and they will no doubt be taught the lesson
that El Paso has her own peace officers. The day for man
killers in this town has passed."

But Juan Hart, publisher of the *Times*, no less than
"Uncle Jimmy" Smith of the *Herald*, was a doughty ex-
ponent of Personal Journalism and the *Times* seems to
have indirectly championed Bud Frazer in his trouble. At
least, under date of March 24, one reads that "Bud
Frazer is still very much alive, despite the efforts of the
Miller gang at Pecos to exterminate him. He is now in
the city from Eddy, where he is conducting a livery
business."

Apparently, John Wesley Hardin did not stand out unfavorably in an El Paso which needed a peace officer like Jeff Milton to preserve order, and which elected a curly wolf like Old John Selman a constable. Indeed, he seems to have produced a very favorable impression, somewhere in the *Times* office! One has to recall that this was the day of the "Paid Personal." But, whether he made a call upon the editor and spellbound him, or merely wrote and paid for insertion of the following, the "notice" is nothing if not commendatory:

"Among the leading citizens of Pecos City now in El Paso is John Wesley Hardin, Esq., a leading member of the Pecos City bar. In his younger days Mr. Hardin was as wild as the broad western plains upon which he was raised. But he was a generous, brave-hearted youth, and got into no small amount of trouble for the sake of his friends, and soon gained the reputation for being quick-tempered and a dead shot.

"In those days, when one man insulted another, one of the two died then and there. Young Hardin, having a reputation for being a man who never took water, was picked out by every bad man who wanted to make a reputation, and that was where the 'bad men' made a mistake, for the young westerner still survives many warm and tragic encounters.

"Forty-one years has steadied the impetuous cowboy down to a quiet, dignified, peaceable man of business. Mr. Hardin is a modest gentleman of pleasant address. But underneath the dignity is a firmness that never yields, except to reason and to law. He is a man who makes friends of all who come in close contact with him.

"He is here as associate attorney for the prosecution in the case of The State vs. Bud Frazer, charged with assault with intent to kill. Mr. Hardin is known all over Texas. He was born and raised in this state."

Certainly, he could have asked little more in the way of a "write-up!" Not a word about his penitentiary record; nothing but florid recital of his virtues. If he had been running for office as Juan Hart's candidate, the *Times* could not have done much more for him!

The jury in the Frazer trial could not agree and Judge Buckler at last discharged them on April 14, 1895. (At a second trial in Colorado City, Frazer was acquitted. Jim Miller later killed Bud in Toyah, Texas, emptying a shotgun into his enemy as Frazer sat at a poker table.)

Hardin looked El Paso over, during those days of the Frazer trial. Apparently, the border suited him. He had already discovered that Texas had not forgotten him. Wherever he went, heads turned and eyes came to him. After fifteen years of repression, small wonder that Hardin began to strut and swell in such an atmosphere.

Even though Mayor Johnson did not warn Hardin to be careful of his conduct in El Paso, any gunfighter with a grain of discretion would have been thoughtful in the Pass City, one thinks!

Jeff Milton, veteran badge wearer, as chief of police rode the town with a firm, if light, hand. Milton is one of the really great old-time officers and as a gun-expert need touch his hat to very, very few!

Old John Selman was of entirely different type. Although he wore the badge at this time, of Constable, Precinct One, and had the backing of prominent citizens, he was of the killer type and there were mysterious blind spots on his backtrail. As a gunman he stood as one of the experts.

Deputy U. S. Marshal George Scarborough, ex-sheriff of Jones County, was another peace officer of the day who did not back water in the face of any sort of gun-competition.

There were other belligerent gentlemen on the stage, men who simply could not understand that anyone might be their superiors at any sort of fighting.

Hardin began the practice of law in El Paso. And out of his very first case came lines that were to tangle his feet and bring about his fall a few months later.

Two cowboys of the period had been "using the sticky loop" in Texas and New Mexico. Vic Queen was a

tall, straight, vividly brunette man. His partner, Martin
M'Rose, was not so much of a figure, being of middle
height and possessed of light brown hair and eyes that
did not impress anyone enough to permit memory of
their exact color.

The pair were unusual in one respect: They got themselves arrested and so irritated stockmen that, when
they jumped bond the Live Stock Protective Association
of southeastern New Mexico posted $1,000 reward for
the arrest of each, to which their bondsmen added $250.

They crossed into Mexico and rode along the safe side
of the Rio Grande toward Juarez, El Paso's neighbor
city in the Mexican state of Chihuahua. Now enters the
picture a dashing blonde lady calling herself Mrs.
M'Rose. She followed her consort and Vic Queen and
stopped in El Paso. Apparently, she was here before
John Wesley Hardin arrived from Pecos.

She had statuesque beauty and she had money. Presently, she was to attract Hardin's eye. But before this, on
March 26, 1895, Jeff Milton had secured the arrest in
Juarez of Vic Queen. On April 6, M'Rose was arrested at
Magdalena by Beauregard Lee, of Raton, New Mexico.
Both men were lodged in the Juarez *calaboza* and a bitter
legal fight began. The New Mexico authorities were
trying to extradite the pair. M'Rose and Queen were
fighting extradition and attempting to secure their release from jail. In El Paso and Juarez were grim men of
two factions, watching each other steadily—friends of
the two cow-thieves, and officers from New Mexico who
included the redoubtable ex-Texas Ranger captain,
George Baylor.

Moving about the town, John Wesley Hardin soon
crossed the trail of the blonde lady. And he was retained
in the case pending between the New Mexican authorities and the jailed men. Feeling ran higher and became
more bitter.

Apparently, Hardin had lost little of either his
belligerence or his magic with the Colts. Nor did his
weakness for Mrs. M'Rose extend to those whose money

was in her custody—$3,000 of it, according to old-time officers who were in position to know. He and his clients had decided to resort to a writ of *habeas corpus*, in an effort to get M'Rose and Queen back on the Texas side of the Rio Grande. M'Rose's friends sent Hardin word that if he continued to interfere with the defense plans, he could expect trouble.

The *Times* of April 23, 1895, carries the following item:

"The toughs who rallied around the imprisoned M'Rose and Queen in Juarez gave it out that they would bulldoze Attorney John Wesley Hardin if he tried professionally to defeat their schemes to defeat extradition. Last night Mr. Hardin met the gang in Juarez and slapped their faces one after another."

And if Jeff Milton had not been one of Hardin's companions that evening, one of the men slapped would have died in that saloon backroom where the encounter took place. The arguments pro and con between Hardin and M'Rose's friends had got to the face-slapping stage. Hardin struck one Fenessy of the other side and, whipping out his pistol, rammed it into Fenessy's belly. Jeff Milton yelled at him, then argued him out of his intention to kill Fenessy, who had been loudest of the M'Rose faction from the beginning.

I SAID THAT Hardin had lost little of his belligerence or his magic with the Colts. . . But, studying him in the light of his recorded actions, and the varying testimony of those who knew him well before and after his imprisonment, it seems to me that he was a shell of the young fire-eater who went to Huntsville prison in '78. I cannot explain him otherwise—the contradictions of his last days.

He drank heavily, drank steadily. He was quarrel some, given to braggadocio and ferocious glaring. In and around El Paso he swaggered it in the role of *The Famous Wes Hardin*. He lost at faro—but put hand on six-shooter and snarled at the house-men and snatched the money. He scooped in poker-pots without showing his hand, overbearing the other players. But—not always! There were some who refused to be bulldozed by Hardin or anyone else. . . And herein lies one of the contradictions noted in his conduct! He who had made a joke of the saying that he "took no sass but sassparilla!" did not whip out his lethal Colts when he was crossed.

Jeff Milton denies it, but there are several in El Paso who recall the time when Milton (no longer chief of police) and Hardin had an argument which ended by Milton slapping Hardin's face—without any return.

And there was "Colonel" Eakins (the title was complimentary, for Eakins was a pioneer real estate man of El Paso). . . Eakins was no respecter of persons and when Hardin picked a quarrel with him, Eakins promptly knocked him down and then, to add insult to injury, sat comfortably upon Hardin and was pounding away when old Judge Coldwell rushed up and in a very panic tried to intervene.

"My God!" he cried, to Eakins. "Don't you know what you are doing? Hardin will kill you for this!"

"So far as I'm concerned," the doughty Eakins replied, "this is the man who called me a liar!"

M'ROSE WAS DEAD, now. Hardin had been successful in his campaign to attach Mrs. M'Rose and the M'Rose-Queen bankroll. So much so that in his last days, M'Rose in Juarez could not get in touch with the lady. He enlisted Deputy U. S. Marshal George Scarborough and Scarborough tried to persuade the dashing blonde to cross to Juarez and talk to her consort. He returned to M'Rose and reported that the only way M'Rose could talk to Mrs. M'Rose was to come to El Paso.

With $1,250 reward on his head, M'Rose was naturally unwilling to come into the jurisdiction of Texas officers. But thought of the money, or memory of the lady's charms, got him to mid-river on the Mexican Central trestle one night. Here he stopped. There are conflicting stories concerning what occurred here. I do not profess to know what actually took place, or what circumstances led up to M'Rose's death. But there were shots and M'Rose was dead.

Jeff Milton, now a Special Ranger, Deputy U. S. Marshal Frank McMahan and Scarborough were indicted for the killing—rather as a technicality, I think—and promptly acquitted.

The result was to make Hardin's attachment for Mrs. M'Rose almost a regular union. She was addicted to the bottle and the bright lights and given to staging Wild West exhibitions on the street when in her cups. Which brings us to mid-August, 1895. . .

Hardin was away from town when his mistress created a disturbance and was arrested and fined for carrying a pistol. Young John Selman—so called to distinguish him from his father the constable—was a city policeman and a belligerent soul in his own right. He made the arrest and Hardin was furious when he came back and heard the story.

IN MY OWN mind there is no doubt that Selman was perfectly willing to kill Hardin, given opportunity, if not actually "laying for" him. There was much jealousy among the killer-type of gunmen. Each wanted to be cock of the walk. When one killed another, automatically he inherited the dead man's list of notches.

And the informed had no doubt that someone was going to kill Hardin. He could not strut and brag indefinitely, in such company as El Paso offered. It simply was not on the cards. He would make trouble with some quiet and efficient gentleman and get himself killed, or he would be shot by some glory-hunter.

On the evening of August 19, 1895, Hardin encountered Old John Selman near the Acme Saloon of R. B. Stevens, on San Antonio Street. Hardin was reminded of his grievance against Young John, with sight of the constable. By Selman's testimony, Hardin remarked that Young John was a cowardly This-and-That. They had words and Hardin claimed that he was unarmed.

This assertion is far from convincing. Hardin was always armed. Nor could he had much hope of making Selman believe the contrary. But, by testimony of Selman, the only witness to the encounter, Hardin went on into the Acme and began shaking dice.

Selman met his son and Captain Carr of the police and told them that he expected trouble—and that the police were to keep out of it, it was a personal matter between Hardin and himself. He sat down on a beer keg outside the Acme. He says that he was seated there when a friend came by and persuaded him to go inside for a drink. But the friend's testimony conflicts. . . . He says that he found Selman in the saloon and having heard of Hardin's threats against Selman, warned the constable *not* to drink! By his testimony, he and Selman walked outside, talking, then returned, he walking ahead of Selman. And he heard shots behind him, as he walked toward the back of the saloon.

He was a cautious man, this grocer-friend of Selman's. He kept his eyes straight front and walked on out through a cloud of pistol smoke. He saw nothing.

But Hardin, standing at the bar with Henry Brown, fell dead, a bullet through his head, another through his body, a third through the right arm.

Wes' Hardin, most notorious of Texas' Six-Shooter Experts, was dead, last of the trio which had summed up Triggernometry in the '70s, gone at last to join Bill Longley and Ben Thompson.

Selman was tried for the killing and to his counsel insisted that he had not shot Hardin in the back; that Hardin was looking him in the eye and apparently about to draw a pistol when he—Selman—fired.

Ex-Senator A. B. Fall assisted in the defense and he tells me an interesting story in connection with this assertion of Selman's. He says that he came to town after the killing and agreed to help defend Selman. But he insisted on going over all the case for himself. Examination of Hardin's hat showed that he had been shot

from behind, just as the examining physicians had said—
and contrary to Selman's dogged story.

"I couldn't help being impressed by Selman's appearance when he assured me that he had been looking
Hardin in the eye," Fall says. "I knew Selman well and
I felt that he wouldn't lie to me and he had all the appearance of a man telling what he firmly believed. It
puzzled me, so I went down to look over the scene of the
killing. I stopped at the Acme's door and looked inside.
There was a man standing at the bar and he lifted his
head. Then I had the explanation of Selman's statement.
For as that man stared into the mirror, I had the illusion
for an instant of looking him straight in the eyes."

But, be that as it may, Selman was easily acquitted of
a charge of murder. Hardin's reputation, his actions,
helped free Selman. John Wesley Hardin was buried in
old Concordia Cemetery and the tale of forty-odd notches
was told.

CHAPTER III · *One Night in San Anton'*
BEN THOMPSON

IN THE GREAT gallery of American gunmen, there stand all sorts of men. Long-haired, buckskin-clad frontiersmen walk arm in arm with booted and Stetsoned cowboys. Frock-coated, pallid and still-faced gamblers jostle others who are hardly to be distinguished from those ordinary citizens who walked the streets in their day.

In this last bracket fell that square-jawed, thickset Wizard of the Pistol; that black-haired, blue-eyed Typical Gunman of the great, inky mustache—Ben Thompson, who was variously printer, Confederate soldier, professional gambler, peace officer, and a gunslinger second to none that Texas has ever produced.

Anything like a correct tabulation of Ben Thompson's killings is impossible to compile. For he was charged in some quarters with many murders that he, or his friends for him, vehemently denied; and like most gunmen of the '80s, he doubtless committed several killings of which few but himself had knowledge, and of which he preferred not to talk.

By his own statement, he was born in 1843. Whether he was born in Yorkshire, England, or near Lockhart, Texas, has long been a disputed point, but that he began life as a printer seems well authenticated. He drifted about from place to place, following his trade, until eventually he reached New Orleans. His account of his adventures at this time are the only statements handed down to us. There is no substantiation possible, for much that he said. Today, just as during his lifetime, one must either believe, or decline to believe, Ben Thompson. It is merely a matter of deciding for oneself his credibility in any given instance. I have tried to weigh all evidence impartially—and I have known several men who knew Thompson; who were familiar with his record as he was making it.

He was fond of telling of how a young Frenchman in New Orleans was upon a time insulting a girl; and of how he, Thompson, full of Southern chivalric ideas, interfered, with the result that a duel was arranged between himself and the Frenchman. By Thompson's account he demanded that the Frenchman fight with pistols at ten paces, the shooting to continue until one man or the other was dead or incapable of continuing. This mode was rejected as "barbarous."

In these negotiations, Ben says that he refused to fight with swords, but countered with the suggestion that the two of them go alone into a dark room, armed with daggers, there to fight until the death. This was accepted.

Well, he killed the Frenchman, but it seems that the *code duello* operated in the romantic Crescent City at this time only for the aristocrats and, to these proud Creoles, Ben was, of course, hardly more than a street arab. When he came alive out of the room, the friends of the dead challenger raised a hue and cry against Ben as a murderer, but he found sanctuary in the Sicilian quarter and eventually—disguised as a Sicilian—escaped from the city and made his way to Houston, Texas, and then home to Austin.

After this return to Austin, he began the career that he followed the rest of his life, that which he preferred— the career of a professional gambler. At the beginning of the Civil War, he enlisted in Baylor's regiment, but he was not designed for a soldier. His whole army experience was one fierce round of brawling with his superiors. He shot a sergeant at Fort Clark, in a row over rations he had stolen and the return of which the non-com' demanded. Lieutenant Haigler then crossed him, according to Ben's account, and received a fatal wound in the neck.

Ben escaped the guardhouse and stayed out of sight until the expiration of his enlistment term. Apparently the lawlessness of the State of Texas of those days governed the Confederate Army also. For Ben appeared again at Fort Clark and calmly reënlisted, nor was he ever tried for shooting the sergeant and murdering the lieutenant. His time in the army was, more or less, mere indicator of his life to come. He was naturally of the chip-on-the-shoulder type; naturally a "sporting man." He ran gambling games for the soldiers; he smuggled liquor into camp. He obeyed his officers only when that could not be avoided.

He served on the border, always managing to be in hot water of some sort. He killed two Mexicans in a gambling row in Nuevo Laredo. He was hotly chased by the aroused Mexicans and had many wild adventures in escaping. Finally, he was detailed by his superiors to raise a company of soldiers in Austin. That was a touchy town in Civil War times. Ben proceeded promptly to get into a row with a desperado named Coombs, who chanced to be a member of the Home Guards. He killed Coombs, and for once this combative bulldog seems to have been at least no more at fault than his adversary.

After the war, he was arrested by the Union military authorities, then scourging Texas in the tragic mess of "Reconstruction." Ben escaped and joined the Emperor Maximilian in Mexico. When Maximilian was executed, he returned to Texas and stood trial for the killing of Coombs. The jury acquitted him without leaving the box. But he was immediately rearrested, charged with assault to kill one Brown. For this assault, he served two cruel years in the penitentiary.

But they couldn't break the spirit of a man with the jaw of Ben Thompson! After his release, he plunged into gambling and drinking and drifting. The wild trail-herd towns knew him—knew the roar of his pistols and the whir of his cards. He hit Abilene, Kansas when that "cattle capital" was in the blazing heyday of her brief glory, with Wild Bill Hickok for city marshal. Here Thompson found an old friend from Austin.

Phil Coe, as the oldtimers recall him, was a handsome six-footer, of splendid brown mustaches and beard, who was the very fashion plate of the successful gambler. After the Civil War he and a partner, Bowes, ran a saloon on Congress Avenue in Austin, Ben Thompson conducting the games in the Coe-Bowes place. He and Thompson opened the Bull's Head Saloon in Abilene and for a time got on well with Wild Bill.

Then these two, Coe and Wild Bill, fell out. Thompson says they quarreled over the favors of one of the fair Cyprians of the town, Jessie Hazel—so her name comes down to us. They were both mangificent bull-elk, but Coe won the lady and left the famous Wild Bill gnawing his golden mustache and plotting dire revenge.

Somewhat later, Phil Coe went out with a bunch of fellow-Texans, cowboys, to celebrate. He did something that nobody in Texas had ever known him to do—he brandished a pistol. Men who saw him every day in Austin "reckon he must have carried a gun," but cannot recollect seeing him with one. He was *not* a gunman. But on this occasion, he "shot off his gun." This was a violation of the ordinances of Abilene.

Wild Bill appeared instantly on the scene, ready for action—as he had a habit of appearing. What occurred, then, exactly, has been much disputed. But there is no doubt that Coe was no match for Hickok; and that he died with two bullets from Wild Bill's derringer in him, having bungled his own shots.

When word came to Ben Thompson that his old friend and partner, Coe, had been killed, he was furious. But at the moment he was bedridden as the result of an accident. It was months before he recovered and when he left the country to return to Texas the account with Wild Bill was still unsettled. I think that there can be no doubt that Thompson would have liked an encounter with Hickok. To his dying day, Thompson expressed the greatest contempt for Wild Bill and his like and the old Texans—many of whom had no liking for Thompson—still tell of the way he crossed Abilene's marshal at every opportunity.

He was a human bulldog, a human gamecock, this squatty man with the prognathous jaw. I hold no brief for him, but as a matter of judgment, one must see the man as he really was. Perhaps we can see him more clearly, today, than would have been possible fifty years ago. Much of the heat of those controversial times has vanished; we can evaluate the Thompsons and the Hickoks fairly, judging them by their records. We need not be apologists nor partisans.

Every word that I have ever heard of Thompson strengthens my belief that he belonged to that pugnacious breed of which the frontier has always produced a plenty—men owning, not courage in the real sense of the word, but an instinctive belligerence like that of a wild animal. In the old Texas phrase they "didn't know enough to be scared!"

Thompson was of this breed. His every action shows a senseless disregard of the most elementary caution, discretion, common-sense. And so I find partizan accounts of his backing down before this man or that utterly at variance with everything I know about Thompson. It is not that he was too brave to give way, it is that no believable record has come to me, of Thompson giving way even when he should have stepped back, when it was the sensible thing to do.

And so I find the account of Wyatt Earp backing down a shotgun-armed Thompson in Ellsworth—particularly a Thompson backed by wild-eyed Texas cowboys! —highly unconvincing, to use no stronger term. Stuart Lake had the tale of this from Wyatt Earp and others of the Earp faction. All my life I have heard the story of the killing of Sheriff Whitney by Billy Thompson, and the subsequent rioting, in very different fashion. Granted that my informants were Texas men who were in Ellsworth with trail herds at the time, it must be remarked that they were many of them men who did not drink, did

not gamble, had no good word to say of the brothers
Thompson.

You will find Lake's account of the Ellsworth business on pages 88-96, in his *Wyatt Earp*. I have always
figured that Friend Lake suffered from a bad attack of
hero-worship while in Earp's company, nor is it any
secret that I hold this conviction. My own opinion of
the Earps is not very high, nor can I get enthusiastic
about any of the crowd the brothers ran with. Since the
anti-Texans have been so free with their nasturtiums
directed at the men who brought cattle up the trail,
it seems no more than fair to recall that the Texas men
were wont to describe Wild Bill Hickok, the Earps, Bat
Masterson, Doc Holliday, Charley Bassett, Luke Short,
Mysterious Dave Mather and the rest of those cow-town
marshals, as "The Fighting Pimps"—an appellation
doubtless suggested by the fact that most of them hung
out in the bordellos of the towns.

Ben Thompson's stay in Austin was brief. His money
was almost gone and the business in which he had part-
nered with Coe had been "settled" by the authorities in
his absence. He accused Hickok of profiting most by the
settlement. He came north to try for another stake in
Kansas. A visit to Abilene (Wild Bill was no longer
there) recovered nothing of the Coe-Thompson property.
He went back to Ellsworth where Billy Thompson was
working for cowmen and gambling on the side.

By pawning jewelry and borrowing money, Ben got
enough to open up gambling rooms. Neill Cain dealt
monte for him and Cad Pierce and other cowboys bucked
the games. A good deal has been said about the animosity of the Texas men for the Northerners, a dislike
explained by the Texans' "unreconstructed Confederate
sympathies." Perhaps there were other reasons for the
cowboys' dislike of the authorities. . .

The "fighting marshals" were apt to ensconce themselves behind convenient shelter, when "quieting" the
Texans. From this cover they emptied their shotguns
into the cowboys' ranks. And the men who hired the

Bat Mastersons and Earps were only too often hardly the type to inspire confidence in an unprejudiced observer. So, in Ellsworth, the cowboys accused the officers of city and county of fake arrests, shake-downs of drunken cowboys, petty graft of every description. And Ben Thompson was their natural champion and the natural enemy of Deputy Sheriff Hogue and his fellows of the city force.

The Ellsworth papers were inspired by partizanship—naturally! And are in consequence hardly to be depended upon for unbiased reporting. There were too many axes to grind!

A row broke out in Thompson's place August 18,1873. Primarily, it was between Thompson and a gambler named Martin. But events crowded so fast upon each other that the truth was hard to get at, afterward. The result of the argument was that Martin slapped Ben Thompson in the face and Thompson promptly whipped out his pistol. "Happy Jack" Morco, one of Marshal Norton's deputies, interfered in time to save Martin's life.

Morco—himself a gunman with a record and one of Ben Thompson's bitterest enemies, Deputy Hogue being the other—hustled Martin out into the street. But he returned with a bunch of friends and began to yell at those in Thompson's to come out.

"Come out, you Texas fighting ———!" Martin yelled.

THOMPSON WAS NOT the man to invite to a row, unless one really wanted him to appear. He snatched up a Henry rifle, brother Billy grabbed a shotgun. They ran to the door and here Billy, who was about half-drunk, managed to let his shotgun go off at nothing. But the party outside took the will for the deed and left there. The Thompsons then came out into the street and took shelter behind a fire engine. The alarm sounded up and down the town. It was made out a clean-cut issue between Ellsworth citizens and Texas cowboys. Armed men began to swarm about the streets. Violent threats were hurled back and forth across the street where the townsmen faced Ben Thompson—but not too closely. Deputy Hogue, with Happy Jack Morco, the deputy marshal, were attempting to work up the townsmen to make a dash at the Thompsons' position. Ben and Billy were still alone in the street, but behind them in the hotel the cowboys were "forted," waiting for trouble.

Hogue worked closer, trying for a shot at the Thompsons. Almost in range of Ben's rifle, he stuck his head out of a window of a building. Ben whipped up his rifle and took a snapshot at the enemy, but Hogue jerked in his head quickly. Thompson then tried to shoot through the plank wall that sheltered Hogue. The bullet missed but it waked in Hogue a burning desire to emigrate. He left town and ran across the river, to stay there until the war was over.

Happy Jack Morco was another who profited that day by the poorest shooting Ben Thompson has ever been charged with. And he, too, decided that he wanted no more of this battle.

Sheriff Whitney was, to all intents and purposes, a friend of Ben Thompson's. Ben always insisted that he was and I have never heard anything which would lead me to believe that his death that day was anything but the accident it was claimed. The sheriff appeared during the shooting. He held a conference with Ben Thompson. The retreat of the two officers, Hogue and Morco, had left the mob with time for thought. Hostilities were slackened. It was at this time that Whitney appeared and persuaded Ben not to look for further trouble.

There are two conflicting accounts about the manner in which Whitney met his death. If we take the version of the Ellsworth ring or certain present-day chroniclers, Billy Thompson saw Whitney on the street and calmly walked to the door and emptied a shotgun, "to get him a sheriff." The other account, which I have heard all my life, seems to me more plausible, if nothing else.

By the latter account Thompson, with his brother Billy and Sheriff Whitney, were walking toward the Grand Central Hotel when Ben—keeping watch in the rear for enemies—saw Happy Jack some fifty yards away, at the corner of a building. Happy Jack ducked back as Ben let go a fast shot at him. With sound of the shooting Whitney and Billy both whirled about. Billy lifted his shotgun and fired and, being still under the influence of liquor, did both things clumsily. The load struck Whitney. Billy was shaken by this accident. He told Ben and told others that he had stumbled while trying to get a quick shot at Happy Jack Morco.

Ben knew that Billy was in trouble, now. He insisted that his brother get out of town, get clear out of the country. With the help of friends, Billy was at last armed and mounted and started off. Ben and several Texas men were armed and waiting for trouble when Deputy Sheriff, now Acting Sheriff, Hogue appeared with a posse. Hogue informed Thompson that he was ordered to arrest him for the killing of Sheriff Whitney. Thompson absolutely refused to be disarmed or to submit to arrest.

It seems a reasonable assumption that, if Thompson had put down his gun, in the presence of officers with the killing reputation of Hogue, Charlie Brown and Ed Crawford, he would have been murdered instantly. That was the Texas opinion of these men.

Thompson informed Hogue that while he would not submit to arrest in those circumstances, he would surrender to some official in whom he had confidence, one who could make and keep reasonable guaranties. Mayor Jim Miller now appeared on the scene and promptly discharged the whole police force. To Miller Thompson made his proposition: If the Mayor would disarm Happy Jack Morco and keep him disarmed, he, Thompson, would surrender to the mayor. Larkin, proprietor of the Grand Central Hotel, stood sponsor for Thompson's good faith. So Jim Miller then disarmed Happy Jack. To the mayor then, Ben Thompson surrendered, and was released in the sum of $10,000 cash bond.

Ben was eventually acquitted of complicity in the killing of Sheriff Whitney. But scapegrace Brother Billy was indicted, and though he stayed on the dodge was finally captured, extradited from Texas and put on trial. He was then acquitted.

Ben "*took a pasear*," as the old-timers say, over to Leadville, Colorado. His reputation and the manner in which he conducted himself there and everywhere, is rather vividly shown by this "dispatch" taken from an Austin newspaper:

"Ben Thompson, who is well known around Austin as a professional gambler, has been doing Leadville in his old familiar style. But he does not seem to have played it quite so successfully as he sometimes did in Texas.

"Ben was never known to labor very industriously— except with his thumb and forefinger when pulling cards from the box behind the faro table, or sitting in front of it wrestling with the tiger. A gentleman now in Leadville, who knows him, writes that some time ago Ben tried the faro table and lost two thousand in money, a diamond stud worth eight hundred, and a watch and chain worth three hundred, in one sitting. He had to borrow some money to start for home. But he did not start soon enough. He got drunk and turned over gambling tables, shot out lights, ran the crowd out of the house, pounded one man up with a six shooter and wound up by cleaning up the street with a Winchester."

BROKE, AND possessed of no abilities except his skill as a gambler, and his proficiency in Six-shooterology, he was glad to enlist as a gunman under the banner of the A.T. & S.F. Railway. A good deal has been gossiped and written about Ben's connection with this fight between the Santa Fe and D. & R.G., but my old friend, Major A. B. Ostrander, of Seattle, writes of the row as he, a veteran railroad man and actual participant, witnessed it:

"The A.T. & S.F. had completed their line to Pueblo. They wanted entrance to Denver, and to get it, they leased the D. & R.G. Road, supposing that this lease included the proposed building of their extension to the Royal Gorge. This, the D. & R.G. stubbornly denied, and attempted then to break the lease. So a genuine war followed.

"The Santa Fe put armed guards on all their trains and, to protect their roundhouse at Pueblo, they employed the noted Ben Thompson. They brought him up from Texas with ten 'good men,' to protect the roundhouse.

"When Governor Hunt and Pat Desmond (who was the city marshal of Pueblo) went over the road turning out all employes (I was 'captured' at Fort Garland) the officers and prisoners returned toward Pueblo. When our train was within four miles of that place, we were met by a handcar filled with D. & R.G. men, who informed us that the roundhouse had been turned over to them without the firing of a shot. This amazed everyone who knew Thompson's reputation. Upon arrival at Pueblo, we learned the facts:

"Ben and his men had held the house until exactly five minutes before twelve o'clock noon, the hour when the Santa Fe eastbound express was scheduled to leave. Ben and his men came out at 11:55, delivered their Winchesters to the D. & R.G. forces, boarded the express and went calmly on their way back to Texas. It was stated then and there that an emissary had got word to Ben that twenty thousand dollars awaited him at the door if he would come out peacefully. Well, he did! Thereby—incidentally—he saved lots of bloodshed. I was all through that fight and knew all the circumstances at the time."

Major Ostrander's version of this episode is one which has long been related in the West. Thompson (rather naturally) always denied that he received a cent for coming out and giving up the property which he had been paid five thousand dollars to hold to the death. He always claimed that he had been "relieved by proper authority." However that may have been, certainly he got back to Austin, as usual, and—as usual—went back to gambling.

As he grew older he "went oftener to the bottle and stayed longer." When drunk, he was apt to let his very primitive sense of humor range beyond the limits favored even by cowboy wits, in the matter of horseplay. He once shot up his own gambling house because of a falling out with one Loraine, his partner. The police walked clear of Ben and made no bones about it, because of his long, red record as a gunman.

So, Ben was permitted to sober up from his sprees and apologize—if he chanced to feel apologetic at that time—for whatever promiscuous shooting he might have done. He and his friends always explained deprecatively that he *was* a bit wild when drinking, but, when sober he was the best of men, the fondest of husbands and fathers, and very, very kind to his aged mother.

The marvel is that he was not quickly killed in some of his drunken brawls. Shakespeare has something to say about wine's tendency to "increase desire and defeat performance." This is as true in pistol-play as in the field the Bard meant. Men knew it, too. But nobody "took advantage" of his times of fuddlement.

The greater marvel is that Ben Thompson could have been made city marshal—chief of police—of a town like Austin, capital of Texas. But he had a large following among the sporting crowd and the denizens of the half-world and, like many of his kind, he was a queer mixture of intense loyalty to those he liked—so long as they didn't irritate him—and hair-trigger suspicion of everyone on earth.

He was twice a candidate for marshal. The first time, he was soundly defeated and, before making his winning campaign, he engaged in a gun battle with Mark Wilson, owner of the Senate Saloon and Variety Theatre. Thompson went into the Senate on a Christmas Eve, gently bent on raising a row and busting up the performance in his usual humorous fashion. It was not the first time he had bothered the Senate. Mark Wilson had word of Ben's intentions; he had been made a special policeman; was armed and waiting and a trifle more than willing.

The row began as Thompson planned it. With the first sound of disturbance, Wilson rushed out, hunting for the disturber.

Thompson interfered and slapped Wilson in the face, cutting the saloon keeper with a heavy ring he wore. He was armed, of course. Nobody ever saw him otherwise. According to reports, he wanted only the shadow of an excuse to kill Wilson. There is no doubt that he was ready to shoot, then as always, on slightest provocation. Certainly when Wilson went back to arm himself, Thompson watched him; watched him like a hawk.

Wilson came out with a shotgun, fired blindly at Thompson, missed and fell with the ready Thompson bullet in him. The bartender was afraid that Ben Thompson would kill him next. He fired at Ben but without much accuracy. Then he ducked back behind the bar. But Ben drive a bullet through the wood panel of the bar and into the back of the luckless drink-dispenser's neck.

Wilson had been shot four times and was dead before the bartender fell; the latter lingered a few weeks before dying.

Now,—having been duly acquitted for this pair of killings—Thompson became Austin's city marshal. Blinking back through the mist of the years, Ben Thompson's friends say that he was a good marshal. But those citizens who fought bitterly against the appointment of the most notorious gunman of Texas as chief of police, remarked that he was merely less humorous—in the manner that "humor" took him when drinking.

At any rate, we can be sure of one thing—that no longer was the Austin police afraid of anything or anyone on earth!

In San Antonio, at this time, the Vaudeville Variety Theatre on the main plaza was run by an unusual one-armed man, Jack Harris. He had served in the Confederate Army with Thompson. Before that, he had been scout and guide for General Albert Sidney Johnston, during the campaign of 1857, against the rebellious Mormons in Utah. He was "nobody's soft spot!"

There was, of course, a drinking and gambling saloon in connection with the "theatre." Joe Foster and a one-time Austin boy named Billy Sims were interested financially in "The Vaudeville" which was, at the time, one of the most notorious joints in the state.

If Thompson and Jack Harris were at the moment quite friendly (and "it do seem", to one unbiased observer, that they were birds very, very much of a feather!), between Thompson and Sims there existed enmity from times past, in Austin. Sims' father had been a stone mason and afterward a policeman, in the capital city. Billy Sims became a gambler and Ben Thompson, disliking his competition in the matter of keno, shot up the Sims game and ran Billy Sims out of town, to San Antonio.

Prior to his election as city marshal of Austin, Thompson had often gambled in the Harris place. On one occasion, he and Joe Foster, the dealer, rowed over the game. Ben had seesawed. At first, he had lost heavily, then won back a part of his losings. But when Joe Foster asked for the balance owed to the game, Ben called him thief and cheat and threatened to kill him. He stalked out, without settling.

Jack Harris' friendship for Ben Thompson died right there. He said that nobody could come into his place and question the honesty of his dealers. It would have been a fatal weakness for any gambling house proprietor to condone conduct of this sort. Every tinhorn and would-be gunman in the country would be trying the Thompson method of avoiding losses. This marked the breaking up of the intimacy—however deep it may, or may not, have been, between two men of this kind—which had on the surface existed between Ben Thompson and Jack Harris. In its place, came the bitterest of enmity. Jack Harris proclaimed loudly that he unqualifiedly backed up Joe Foster.

After he became marshal of Austin, Thompson heard threats that Harris was supposed to have made. He concluded that he must eventually go down to San Antonio and interview Harris. While the saloon keeper was one-armed, he was noted as an expert shot. Also he seems to have had plenty of the same sort of bulldog bravery that Ben Thompson owned. Certainly, he was in no wise awed by Thompson's record as a gunman. To the friends who told him just what to do and how and when to do it, he only remarked that he could kill a bird on the wing so, he thought he could "kill a man standing."

Occasion came for Ben to go down to San Antonio and, since he was not one to hide his light under a bushel, his presence was doubtless well-known. While there, he was informed that Harris was on the street "looking for him," and armed with a double-barreled shotgun. Through the influence of friends, Thompson was kept from the street that day; he remained in his room in the hotel. The next morning, however, he met Harris and asked if he were looking for him the night before.

"No," said Harris. "I was not *looking* for you, but I was *waiting* for you; and if you had come about my place I would have filled you full of shot!"

There would have been a fierce encounter then but a deputy sheriff intervened. Later, Thompson went down to the variety house bar and inquired of the bartender where Harris' famous "Shotgun Brigade" was. He had heard that they were "forted up" for him. He sent several insulting messages to Foster and Harris—or, rather, he asked the bartender to deliver them. But, apparently, this man of drinks was no more intimidated by the famous Ben Thompson than was his employer, Jack Harris. He told Ben shortly and grimly that if he had any messages to deliver, he could deliver them himself!

Later the same day, Thompson reappeared in the bar with a friend. Again, he asked about the Shotgun Brigade. Was it still "forted" for him? Harris came into his place and was told of Thompson's visits; of his drinking and of his threats. Harris armed himself with a shotgun and was standing at the door leading upstairs into a ticket room when Thompson caught sight of him through a Venetian blind.

"What are you going to do with that shotgun?" Thompson says he called.

Harris—according to the account given by Thompson's personal attorney—replied that he was going to shoot Thompson with it. Ben's pistol was out. He fired three times instantly; the first shot knocking Harris over, the second striking him as he fell, the third being to frighten off employes of the place who might have an idea of interfering.

For this killing he was indicted and acquitted. It was the ancient way of Texas; of the frontier. These two men were armed; they were bitter enemies; and each had made threats against the other. No other verdict was possible in a fair court. Certainly not in any Texas court of that day; nor, for that matter, in any Texas court of today!

As soon as he was indicted Thompson was brought to see the propriety of resigning his office as marshal. Thereafter, he had no official station whatever. After this acquittal, he had to busy himself on behalf of that restless young man, Billy Thompson, who seems to have been second only to Ben in his sheer genius for getting into trouble. This time it was a murder charge in Refugio County; a business of several years' standing. Ben had plenty of money and the expert array of lawyers he hired soon brought an acquittal for Billy.

Parenthetically, Billy was of course in no wise to blame for this murder. For this assertion, we have the assurance of no less than the Honorable Major Walton. And who should speak with more authority than Major Buck? (A really famous lawyer.) Was he not Ben's attorney for pay; his staunch admirer and unpaid press agent in and out of court; his biographer?

IN THE PERIOD now beginning, Ben drank more heavily than ever. He became a common nuisance to both his friends and his enemies; particularly perhaps, to his friends. Even his most indulgent apologist, the aforesaid Buck Walton, must admit that, when drinking, Ben became overbearing to a degree that made his company highly disagreeable.

His escapades were legion, but all had the similar factor of being irritating. Once, he swaggered into a saloon and, under the influence of continued drinks, conceived the brilliant idea of having the bartenders serve all negro customers at that end of the bar reserved for whites. He brandished a pistol and threatened the saloon's owner.

Only the coming-between of soberer, cooler heads, prevented bloodshed. The saloon keeper refused point-blank to have negroes among the whites and Ben swore that his command would be obeyed. Not even Ben's warmest—and blindest—partizans could defend this outburst. Not in a southern state where Reconstruction's savage scenes had been so recently ended! Not in the Texas of today, for that matter. Take a negro out of the "Jim Crow" section and try to put him among the whites and the only question will be how *large* the riot!

On another occasion, he loaded his pistol with blank cartridges and descended on a variety theatre which, he later explained with some humor, had been drawing trade away from his gambling rooms. He fired the blanks into the crowd with a wild yell and confessed to huge enjoyment at seeing the frightened people fairly wreck the place in their frantic efforts to escape.

This evokes a picture superficially funny. Almost funny, when it is examined. But as a Texas man, growing up in an era when "packing a gun" was the common thing, and as one who has worn belt-hardware a good deal, I fail to see the genuine humor of the situation. Some veteran gunmen—vastly better qualified than I to pass judgment from a gun-handler's viewpoint—sneer more bitterly even than I, at silly exhibitions such as this.

How many times have I heard the twin admonitions
—"don't pull your gun unless you're ready to go the
whole hog down to the last teency bristle on his tail!"
and "don't point a gun at nobody you ain't plumb
willin' to shoot, if that's necessary!"

It amused Ben to watch that panic-stricken crowd
mill and stampede like thunder-frightened cattle. But
one may inquire why they should not, most logically,
have believed that he was aiming lead-tipped cartridges
their way? They saw him standing there in the door;
saw the puffs of smoke, the red flashes, come from his
pistol-muzzles; heard the bellow of the shots. There was
Ben Thompson! The killer! The fellow who had shot a
poor dago organ-grinder's instrument to pieces. The man
who got drunk and cowed the police force and thereby
sniffed as he pleased at the law, in the capital of the
state. The "bad man," whose actions, when drunk, nobody could forecast.

No, it is not even *almost* funny, to some Texas men.

He broke up a stockmen's convention banquet in
similar fashion. Appearing in a doorway, he knocked
over a great castor of condiments. The stockmen looked
around. There stood Ben Thompson the Killer in the
doorway, pistol in hand. It is plain that his record was
lurid, for such as those two-fisted, capable men, accustomed to dangers and the handling of weapons, left the
hall without ceremony.

Incidentally, here was manifestation of a phe-
nomenon more than once commented in my hearing—·
the submissiveness in the face of firearms of men them-·
selves used to firearms. Familiarity, with such, does *not*
breed contempt! On the contrary, they know so well the
power of the gun that they do not trifle with one.

Raymond Spears, some time ago, had a most veri-
similitudinous yarn in *Adventure Magazine*, about the
ease with which some robbers stuck up a crowd of gun-
experts sitting in the back-end of a sporting goods store.
I know that many an outland, outdoors man, reading
that tale, nodded his head in complete agreement. The

easiest gang in the world to hold up. For they knew, each of them, just what were the chances, the odds, against their making unpunctured resistance. Be that as it may, there is no denying that Ben Thompson stampeded the stockmen's convention.

Another time he raided the office of the Austin *Statesman*. Fortunately, neither of his intended victims, the owner or the editor, was present, so bloodshed was avoided. Six charges were brought against Ben for this raid, but only two were ever tried.

The Thompson Luck . . . The question was, how long now could it continue? His best friends dodged him on the street, for a half-hour in Ben Thompson's company was sure to mean entanglement in at least a violent misdemeanor. The police (and many of them were ex-soldiers) had a holy horror of coming into conflict with Ben Thompson. Perhaps they could hardly be blamed for their lack of eagerness to enter into a contest with so skilful and merciless a killer. Even Buck Walton admits that the staccato bellow of Ben's pistol was almost a nightly sound on Austin streets. Men coming out of their houses in the morning, first asked acquaintances they met:

"What did Ben Thompson do, last night?"

For everyone anticipated a grave brawl or a blazing tragedy.

On a March day in 1884, Ben met in Austin an old acquaintance and sometime enemy, King Fisher, who was a figure of scarcely less note in the ranks of gunmen than Thompson himself. King Fisher's life had been spent on the border; a daring life, a reckless, a defiant; for some years actually criminal. So much so that a whole company of Rangers had been busy breaking up "The King Fisher Gang."

At this time, however, he was a deputy sheriff of Uvalde County. These kindred spirits wandered about Austin together that day and finally King Fisher suggested that Ben go to San Antonio with him.

Ben, it is said, was up to his usual tricks on board the train. Finally King Fisher had to threaten to kill him to prevent Ben from beating a negro porter and a German passenger.

The pair got to San Antonio around eight o'clock in the evening. After supper, they attended *East Lynne*, playing at a local theatre. When the show was over, they went together to the old Harris place—the Vaudeville—on the plaza, where, just twenty months before, Ben had killed Jack Harris. From this moment on there is no accurate charting of the course of events. Perhaps no other gunplay in the history of Texas was witnessed by so many persons, yet has been the subject of so many conflicting accounts.

They went into the Vaudeville together—that much, we know at least, with certainty. We know too, that they stopped on the way and asked some friends to go with them. These men, knowing Joe Foster and Billy Sims to be at the Vaudeville, energetically declined the invitation. They "had a hunch" and stayed away. What the reason was for a visit by Ben to this place, we do not know.

King Fisher was very fond of Joe Foster, who had supplied him with meals and tobacco and other comforts during Fisher's nine months in a San Antonio jail, some years before. Whatever Thompson may have intended doing, of completing a wiping-out of the Vaudeville owners, it seems hardly reasonable that Fisher, who was always openly contemptuous of Thompson, would have entered into the plan merely because it was the redoubtable Ben Thompson who proposed it. King Fisher's vices, so far as I have ever been able to learn, did not include ingratitude. He would not have been even a passive performer in a blow which included Joe Foster.

In the barroom, Thompson asked that Billy Sims be sent to him. Sims was administrator of the Harris estate. He and Foster were now operating the Vaudeville. It casts some little light on a situation sufficiently murky, to remember that Sims was not precisely a weakling. When somewhat later, he was operating the famous White Elephant Saloon in San Antonio, a certain well-known West Texan gambled there.

He was quite a gunman himself, this West Texan. He had notches for around a half-dozen men. Some there were who quite openly called him "hard case." He gambled frequently in the Coney Island at El Paso and was in the habit of writing checks to cover his gambling losses. Usually, afterward, he would stop payment on the checks on the pretense that he had been drunk and irresponsible when making them.

But when he wrote his first check in Billy Sims' White Elephant, Sims came quietly to him and without any show of being impressed by the West Texan's notched six-shooter:

"Reliable parties," he said, "tell me that you have a way of writing checks—like this one—and reneging on them. Now, I'm going to cash this check—and collect on it tomorrow!"

They do say—with broad grins—that Billy collected on every check thus given. Without any trouble whatsoever.

This, then, was the man who came into the barroom to Ben Thompson and King Fisher. A man with a good deal of iron in his backbone and one whose hatred of Thompson, born of that deal in Austin when Thompson had run him out of town, had been increased by the killing of his friend, Jack Harris. Somewhat nervously, Sims made the two men welcome.

Nothing is clear, thereafter. But, averaging the testimony given at the coroner's inquest, one gets a sort of picture—the more accurate, perhaps, if one reflects upon the hair-trigger atmosphere that must have gripped the Vaudeville with appearance of Ben Thompson and the noted King Fisher.

Thompson bought tickets for the variety performance. He and Fisher went upstairs where, in the balcony, spectators might sit comfortably and watch the tawdry performance while being served with drinks.

There were Thompson and Fisher, Billy Sims and a big Mexican policeman, Coy, together. They talked—according to Coy—about the killing of Jack Harris. By the same testimony, King Fisher said that he had come to be amused. Killings, as a topic of conversation, were entirely too commonplace to entertain him. He suggested adjournment to the bar. The party rose; started downstairs. But Thompson, looking about, chanced to see Joe Foster. He called to the spectacled little gambler to have a drink with him.

Foster refused; refused, also, to shake hands with the man who had killed his friend Jack Harris. He wanted no trouble with Thompson, he said. He wanted only to be let alone by him.

Coy and Sims testified to practically the same effect, concerning the subsequent events. Thompson was furious at Joe Foster. He whipped out a pistol and Sims says rammed it into Foster's mouth. Coy says that he slapped Foster with left hand and drew his pistol with his right hand. Coy was onto him like a terrier. He snatched at the pistol, holding the cylinder as best he could. He says a bullet went by his ear. King Fisher and Thompson both were yelling to Coy to turn loose of the pistol.

Coy, Thompson and Fisher fell in a heap, Thompson's pistol roaring all the time. Coy did not admit having shot anybody; Sims testified that "the shooting then began on both sides." All we know is that when the smoke went lifting to canopy the ceiling, Ben Thompson and King Fisher lay together on the floor, dead; that Constable Casanovas had helped Joe Foster downstairs with a bullet through his leg (a wound that killed him shortly); and that Coy turned over to Marshal Shardein a pistol which he said was Ben Thompson's. It was a six-shooter and—contrary to the usual practice of gunmen then and now—had been fully loaded. Five shots had been fired and one loaded cartridge remained.

A coroner's inquest found that Coy and Foster had killed the two and that it was a justifiable act done to save their own lives. But the old-timers call it an ambush. Captain Jim Gillett heard it talked about at the time. Everyone believed, he tells me, that Thompson was the pitcher that went too often to the well. Austin papers raged indignantly. An autopsy performed in the capital city showed that eight shots had struck Thompson, five of these entering his head in such manner as to *prove* that they had been fired from above him—which does seem to bear out the old-timers' story about a bunch of men armed with rifles and shotguns being posted in boxes above Thompson and Fisher.

Much was made of the fact that the coroner's jury had found only three bullets that had struck Thompson. It was said that the jury's verdict was made in fear of Sims and his potent crowd.

However, as one who remembers keenly the rivalry that often exists between two adjacent cities, not only in Texas, the attitude of the Austin papers toward the killing of Ben Thompson takes on a sort of patriotic color. As has been pointed out it was well known that Thompson's race was almost run; it was merely a question of who would kill him, of how many he might kill before he died, and of when the actual event would occur.

He was a nuisance in the capital city; he was more than a nuisance! He was as much a menace as a mad dog. But the tone of the Austin papers of that day might lead an uninformed stranger to believe that the Sacred Cow of the capital had been purely and wantonly slaughtered. But—whatever Austin newspapers said—so died Ben Thompson, March 11, 1884, in the forty-first year of his life.

Even more than John Wesley Hardin or Bill Longley, Ben Thompson seems to have been a very typical product of his times. He had the good traits that men demanded in their friends—courage and loyalty and good humor (when sober). But he outlived the time when his habits could be tolerated. The frontier has ever bred the individualist. There he thrives; for there is room to let him follow (pretty much) his impulses; there, also, is the state of mind that tolerates independence.

Texas, toward '84, was growing too "civilized" to bear with the individualist as the open range, the frontier, had done. Too civilized to endure being shot up and run by gunmen (and Thompson takes rank—as gunman—second to none that Texas has ever known).

It is indeed a marvel that he could die there in the Vaudeville Variety Theatre without a ring around him of dead men who had gone first. A greater marvel, when one considers the caliber of that dark, lean, swaggering, Uvalde County deputy sheriff, King Fisher, who in the wild, border country along the Rio Grande had a name for desperate gunplay, greater even than Thompson's own.

Ben Thompson was buried on March 13, 1884, in the city of Austin. The funeral attracted "a vast concourse of people," says the *Daily Dispatch* of that day, to witness the burial of a victim of assassination, according to the same authority. One fears there is little reason for doubting the truth of this. But it would have been sheer luck if Thompson had died with boots off. Gunmen of his caliber rarely died "sock-footed."

CHAPTER IV · *Tombstone's Deputy*

"BILLY" BREAKENRIDGE

Tombstone in December of 1879 was "wild and woolly." But William Milton Breakenridge, riding into the boom camp from Phoenix, found the "uncurried" aspect of the town very familiar, merely normal. He had celebrated his thirty-third birthday on Christmas Day by resigning as deputy sheriff of Maricopa County in order to try his luck at prospecting.

Behind him were sixteen years of freighting on the plains, of Indian-fighting, cowpunching, surveying for new railroads—sixteen years of life as a frontiersman, in short. So, to one who had seen Sidney, Nebraska, seen Julesburg and Denver and Bannock, Ogden and Cheyenne and the Kit Carson of Tom Smith's day as marshal, Tombstone's "uncurriedness" was just usual.

He prospected diligently that winter of 1879-1880— diligently and unsuccessfully. He looked over the neighboring camps of Charleston, where the industrious stock-rustlers headquartered under the leadership of John Ringo and "Curly Bill" Brocius, of Contention and Fairbank. On Tombstone streets he brushed shoulders with the notorious Earps—Wyatt and Virgil and James and Morgan—and with the cold-blooded dentist-killer who was their close companion, Doc Holliday, with Old Man Clanton the king-rustler, and his friends, prominent among whom were the McLowerys, Frank and Tom.*

The stocky, powerful, blue-eyed Breakenridge had a genius for making friends. Utterly fearless, no swaggering fire-eater like the Earps and their shady Kansas

*There are two spellings of this name. The one I use was current in Tombstone but present day members of the family spell it McLaury.

crew, quick-tempered, yet quick to smile, "Breck" was soon a very familiar and well-liked figure in Tombstone. In 1880 Tombstone was at the height of her boom. She was a rooting-tooting all-night town where the wealth jerked from the earth was shared by enough free spenders to support shops and saloons and bordellos and shows that would have been more in keeping with the larger population of important cities. The boom continued. The camp had a population of something under six thousand.

In January, 1881 John P. Clum, militant editor of the *Epitaph*, was elected mayor. Ben Sippy became city marshal, or chief of police, and Tombstone began to wonder who would receive the lucrative offices to be created with the formation by the Territorial Legislature of the new county of Cochise from a strip of Pima County some eighty-four by eighty-four miles.

Tombstone was a Republican stronghold although Arizona, generally, was Democratic. It was naturally expected that the office of sheriff-tax assessor-and-collector would go to some "deserving" Republican, put in by Governor Frémont.

It is impossible to study the history of any man prominent in the Tombstone of that day without understanding the background against which he stood, the political and personal desirabilities and necessities which moved him—and moved those with whom he contacted.

It is equally impossible to write of the Tombstone of that day without seeming to speak as a partizan of one faction or the other. Wyatt Earp (with his brothers and his followers) moved in the glare of the spotlight during all his days in Arizona. Being prominent, Wyatt has naturally caught the eye of most historians and his side of the controversy which split Tombstone has been given, times without number. It is not my purpose to belittle Wyatt Earp, a deadly gunfighter and an efficient peace officer. But the majority of histories, and a recent biography of Earp, have attempted to prove—in the classic phrase of Nye—that in Tombstone there were only two sides to any question: Wyatt Earp's and the wrong side.

His biographer, indeed, paints a picture of a superman, an incredibly perfect creature who never had a selfish thought, was a sort of *St. George* tilting against the dragon that was Johnny Behan. The very perfection of the figure painted would make me suspicious, if I knew nothing at all of Earp and his doings and the records of his contemporaries. And, as it happens, I have been fortunate in numbering among my acquaintances men intimately familiar, not only with the Earps and all that Kansas crew, but with the others—both friends and enemies of them—who made up the cast of characters in the Tombstone pageant.

In telling this story of Billy Breakenridge, who was a Behan-man in the sense that he was one of the sheriff's staff when Behan held the office, I have studiously hunted for the proper valuation of all the evidence appearing in the various controversies which, totalled, made up the major controversy between the Earp faction and the Behan side. I have not been able to find (as other historians and biographers seem to have discovered so easily!) any saintly figures who were always and completely right. Still, study of that particular section of the frontier *has* disclosed any number of rough, gentle, brave, cowardly, honest, dishonest, men, who by their very humanness are intensely interesting to me. And one of these is William Milton Breakenridge, who in his later years was my very good friend. No hero, in the sense of possessing incredible virtues, but one of the highest type of frontiersman.

I am trying now to show Breakenridge as he was when he lived in Tombstone, going calmly about the details of a day's work which often included the dodging of hostile Apaches while engaged in so prosaic a job as serving a writ of attachment on ranch or mine. And if, in showing Breakenridge as a very human (and to me most worthy) person, I have to knock somewhat askew the halo with which Walter Noble Burns and my esteemed fellow-craftsman Stuart Lake have amazingly supplied that efficient killer, Wyatt Earp—well, that halo has seemed, to many an old-timer better acquainted than Burns and Lake with Earp, an odd substitution for the unsanctified Stetson he wore when they knew him!

THE MAN who was fortunate enough to receive appointment as sheriff of Cochise County could count on about forty thousand dollars a year, in fees of office. Wyatt Earp had come to Tombstone with the thought of establishing a stage line and getting rich. But he found that field already filled. So he served as deputy of Sheriff Shibell of Pima County and, eventually, was appointed deputy U. S. marshal and also formed a connection with the Wells-Fargo Express Company. In later years he denied that he wanted the office of sheriff. He said that his friends wanted him to be Cochise County's first sheriff and that he was willing to accept it merely because they insisted. This may be true. But in Tombstone it was understood that the issue was very clear between John Behan—who had been the deputy sheriff of Pima County serving in Tombstone—and Wyatt Earp.

It was also Earp's statement that John Behan took him to one side and made a proposition—Earp was not to contend for the sheriff's office, which would leave Behan a clear field. If and when Behan received appointment he was to make Earp under-sheriff, or chief deputy. We have nothing but Earp's assertion for this. Breakenridge scoffs at the story.

"Johnny Behan had his faults and plenty of them," he told me. "But breaking his word was not one of them. And, if Behan had made this arrangement with Earp, there was no good reason for his not keeping it. It sounds like a typical Earp tale."

At any rate, Governor Frémont appointed Behan, a Democrat, to the combined office of sheriff, tax assessor and collector. Behan had, for natural opponents in Tombstone, the more belligerent Republicans, who felt that the office should have gone to them since Frémont was also a Republican.

Looking back upon that time and place with an attempt at impartiality, there seems no good reason for Wyatt Earp to have expected appointment to the office—except on the score of politics. Behan had served as Sheriff Shibell's deputy in Tombstone—had served quite satisfactorily. He seems to me always to have been a good, if never a dashing, officer. Too, on the score of residence in the Territory, Behan had the advantage, being the senior Arizonan. And Behan was appointed.

Breakenridge—like other old-timers—claims that Earp very bitterly resented the appointment, and that from that day and that incident dated the hatred that Wyatt Earp had for Behan, an enmity which had many tragic, if sometimes obscure, results. Even though Earp, as Fargo man and deputy U. S. marshal and partner in the Oriental gambling joint where those two famous Kansas killers, Bat Masterson and Luke Short, were dealing, made money, a great deal of money, he never forgave Behan. In many ways he managed to make life difficult, not only for the sheriff, but for the several members of Behan's staff.

John Behan appointed Harry Woods under-sheriff and Frank Stillwell and Breakenridge as deputies. There seems to have been no reason for making Breakenridge a deputy except the common knowledge that this square-jawed and likable man was efficient. He was comparatively a newcomer and there were plenty of politicians who would have been glad to get the place. I have been amused to read, a time or two, that Breakenridge was "half a tenderfoot" when he came to Tombstone; that the camp wondered how "so young" a man would conduct himself, as deputy sheriff in one of the wildest counties this country ever saw. I do not know what "half a tenderfoot" may be, but it seems to me that a man who had been half his life on the frontier, fighting Indians, surveying, freighting through Indian country, associating for sixteen years with frontier characters, can hardly be termed any part of a tenderfoot!

It may be that Tombstone wondered what sort of officer Breakenridge would make—even though I have never heard that assertion from any of the men who knew him in his day. It could not have been because of his age, for he was thirty-three when he took a badge from Behan. And on the frontier thirty-three was virtually middle aged! At any rate, Breakenridge had no apparent doubt of himself. He took up his duties in the office. I have heard from certain pro-Earp men that Breakenridge "was nothing but a process server," "just an office deputy." In reply to this charge—for the pro-Earp men make it sound like a charge—I can only say that, for a mere clerk, he was given a great many warrants to serve on men in the hardest, roughest company of Cochise County.

Actually, the truth is that Breakenridge did whatever was to be done, from assessing taxable property and collecting taxes to bringing in murderers and thieves of various sorts. Nor is it of record that he stepped aside for the toughest of the gun-toting population of Cochise County. Nobody walked on his toes—not the Earps, Masterson, Short, Doc Holliday and the rest of the train of town-gunmen, nor the rustler faction headquartering in Galeyville and Charleston.

He never had trouble, to amount to anything, with the Earp faction in Tombstone, and with the rustlers he was to get on very well. The Clantons and McLowerys, John Ringo and Curly Bill Brocius—most of the dealing of the sheriff's office with this faction was done through Breakenridge. He always attributed his ability to deal with them with a minimum of powder smoke to a stroke of luck that he had very early in his work under Behan.

CIRCUMSTANCES seem to prove that this particular "luck" of which Breakenridge speaks was merely an entering wedge; that his forthright character and unassuming bravery earned him the respect of the hard cases.

But the introduction to the outlaw element came when Behan, seeing the excellent job that Breakenridge had performed in assessing all the taxable property in Tombstone, ordered the deputy to go out into the country east of the county seat and assess, and collect taxes upon all property found.

Tombstone was highly amused, when word went around that Behan's deputy was to go into the very heart of the rustler country to collect taxes. Pima County had never received any tax money in that region and it seemed that Behan was unduly optimistic in expecting to do better. But Breakenridge accepted the task quietly. He had his own plan. And it hinged upon his opinion of one of the outstanding characters of Cochise—called, because of his crisp and kinky black hair, "Curly Bill" Brocius.

Breakenridge recalled that not long before, he had seen Curly Bill in a saloon in San Simon. The outlaw had been sprawling upon a table in the saloon when a cowboy lifted a tin cup of water to his mouth. Rolling over almost lazily upon an elbow, Curly had whipped out a six-shooter and with a single snapshot had knocked the cup from the cowboy's hand. Then, grinning like a schoolboy, Curly Bill invited the startled one up to the bar, to drink something more fitting to man's estate.

Starting out upon his assessment trip, Breakenridge had Curly Bill very much in mind. He recalled the efficiency of that shooting, and the respect shown Curly Bill by all the hard cases in that saloon. He recalled, too, the rough good humor of the man as evidenced by his quick smile, the cowboy horseplay with which he was always enlivening life for himself. His plan depended upon these two qualities of the outlaw.

Personal property constituted most of the taxable wealth of the eastern side of the county. Very few of the cowmen over there could show titles to their land. But there was much freighting going on—supplies moving back and forth, and lumber coming from Chiricahua sawmills to the towns of Bisbee and Tombstone. There was a good deal of stock on the ranches, Breakenridge went alone. The Apaches were raiding back and forth, but he was a veteran at the job of keeping his scalp in Indian country. He got through, and worked the Sulphur Springs Valley up to Wilcox.

He collected a large sum in taxes and moved toward Galeyville, next on his itinerary. Now, Galeyville, even more than Charleston, was the headquarters of the rustlers. Hard-faced men, lounging about saloon and store, stared curiously at the neat man on the good black horse coming into camp. Breakenridge nodded to them colorlessly and went on to a man named Turner, whom he knew to be the agent, the moneyed go-between for the rustlers.

"I want to meet Curly Bill," Breakenridge told Turner. "I've got some business I want to put before him."

Turner nodded. Breakenridge was known as a quiet, unassuming man, and one who said only what he meant, and meant every word he said. It was the finest sort of reputation, in Galeyville.

"He's probably down at Babcock's saloon. Let's go down there and see him."

They went down the street; rounded Babcock's corral. Turner, standing in the doorway of the saloon, nodded.

"There he is. I'll call him out."

Curly Bill came lounging out at Turner's call. He looked curiously at Breakenridge. He had not been much in Tombstone since the death of Fred White, and had never met Breakenridge. They shook hands when Turner introduced them. Then, without preface, Breakenridge plunged into his proposition.

"Johnny Behan sent me out to collect taxes in this part of the country. I've done pretty well in the Sulphur Springs Valley, but now I've got to assess and collect around Galeyville."

"Well?" Curly Bill grunted. "What's that to do with me?"

"I've got a good deal of money with me. I don't want to risk being held up and robbed. I want to hire you as deputy assessor, to go along with me and see that I get through all right."

For a moment, the kingpin of the Cochise County rustlers stared incredulously at this calm young man. Then he burst into a roar of laughter.

"Curly Bill collecting taxes for the sheriff! By God! I'll take you up on that!"

And he went into another paroxysm of bellowing amusement. But, once he had assumed the duty, he showed himself energetic—even enthusiastic. He led Breakenridge into the secret fastnesses of the rustlers and showed Mexican cattle—"wet cattle" —which were being held in lonely cañons, on high mountain meadows. Many times, as the pair rode on these expeditions, grim figures rode up fast, hands on weapons, to investigate the intruders on rustler territory. Recognizing that outstanding member of their craft, Curly Bill, they were surprised to be introduced by him to a deputy sheriff of the county:

"Boys, this here's Breakenridge, the tax assessor. He's come up to see what you fellas have got that he can tax. An' me—I'm his deputy. I come along to see that you give him a fair tally."

And, then and there, Breakenridge would assess the property and figure the amount of tax due the county. Without exception the rancher or rustler—and sometimes there was very little difference!—paid his taxes. Either he paid in cash, or he gave an order on Turner down in Galeyville, who banked the rustlers' money.

AS THEY rode back and forth on the tax collection the two men—deputy sheriff and outlaw—came to understand each other very well. It was not a friendship, in the precise sense of the word, that they knew. Rather, it was a sense of trust—limited, by reason of their divergent paths in life, but none the less very real. Breakenridge discovered that Curly Bill would not lie to him. And

Curly Bill came to understand that Breakenridge would not break his word once given. Neither had any thought of changing his ways, or of changing the other. Breakenridge knew that Curly Bill could never pass unguarded stock, and Curly Bill knew that Breakenridge, given a warrant for him, would serve it. On that basis then, they parted at Galeyville when the tax collecting was done. And the understanding was to bear fruit in other days. They said brief goodbyes and Curly Bill went about his quiet business, while Breakenridge rode back triumphantly to Tombstone—having performed the impossible. And when the story of his trick—for trick the Territory regarded it—was told, men slapped their thighs and laughed—and looked with new interest at John Behan's deputy.

When he had turned over nearly a thousand dollars of tax money to Behan, Breakenridge went about the regular routine of the sheriff's office. And his next job brought him in contact with one of the most interesting figures in that day's Arizona. . . .

John Ringo, even more than Curly Bill, was a leading spirit among the rustlers of Galeyville and Charleston. Curly Bill more often led rustlers than did Ringo, but that was because of Ringo's frequent withdrawals from his kind. John Ringo—Ringgold was the family name in California, Breakenridge learned in later years—was the black sheep of an aristocratic family and well educated. Liquor was his weakness. Or, perhaps—like many another of his wild kind—he found in the flaming whiskey of cowland a sort of anodyne for black memories. Men who knew him observed that he was more likely to go upon one of his wild sprees after receiving a letter from California addressed to him in feminine handwriting. But what the rustlers knew of him—besides his amazing dexterity with Colt or Winchester—was that no man could safely forecast John Ringo's next movement. One hour he was the best of boon companions, the next saw him in a black, sullen mood, quick to take offense, to kill. But erratic as he was, John Ringo was a man with whom everyone in that part of Arizona must reckon, the fastest gunfighter and the deadliest, a man who courted trouble, with the thoughtless courage of a bulldog. This was the man Breakenridge was to meet.

One night, during a poker game in Galeyville, Ringo lost all his money to the miners with whom he was gambling. He wanted to go on playing, but the miners refused to loan him a hundred dollars on his watch and chain. He was drinking heavily, becoming more and more ugly in his manner, and they wanted nothing more than to break up that poker game before shooting ensued.

Ringo went out angrily. But he did not go far. Quickly, he came back. He stood just inside the door, a big, darkly-handsome figure in his cowboy rig. He had a gun in his hand and he covered the poker players. They sat stiff and watchful, for John Ringo was ever an uncertain quantity.

"You had it your way, before," Ringo told them. "Now, I'll have it my way. Shell out!"

He came across the room, holding the men under his gun muzzle. He scooped up all the cash on both poker tables. Then he backed out and got on his horse. It seemed to the liquored Ringo that the episode was very funny. As he rode on toward San Simon Cienaga he laughed at memory of the stiff-set faces of the players. He rode up to Joe Hill's place and to Hill recounted with much effect the details of the robbery.

"Of course, sober, I wouldn't have done it. All those men are friends of mine. I'll tell you, Joe—you take the money and give it back to them."

Most of the players regarded the holdup as Ringo had seen it. But some of them came to Tombstone later and made complaint. The grand jury indicted Ringo for armed robbery and Breakenridge was given the warrant to serve.

"You'd better get up a good fighting posse before you go out after him," Breakenridge was advised in the sheriff's office.

"No, I'll try it by myself," Breakenridge disagreed. "Ringo's got fifty or sixty good fighters over there behind him. They'll back him up. If I can't serve that warrant by myself, it would take a calvary regiment to do it."

Breakenridge rode out of town and that night he slept at Prue's Ranch. Next morning early he saddled his horse and crossed the mountains into Galeyville. He came quietly into town before daylight and knocked at Ringo's door. Ringo opened at the knock and stood there with a six-shooter in his hand. He knew Breakenridge by sight.

"Come in," he invited the deputy, and Breakenridge stepped inside.

"Ringo, you remember that night you held up the poker game? Well, somebody kicked to the grand jury. So I've got a warrant for you."

"Hell!" Ringo said disgustedly. "Why, that's been settled for ages. I gave back the money right away. It was nothing but a joke."

"Well, I've got a warrant for you, anyway. You'd better come into Tombstone and settle it."

Ringo scowled but he dressed and invited Breakenridge to breakfast with him. While they were eating he looked across at the deputy sheriff.

"I'll go in, all right," he said slowly. "But I'd rather the boys didn't know that I'm under arrest. They might make trouble. I'll tell you—you go back to Prue's and wait there. I haven't any money with me and I don't want to go into Tombstone broke. Turner will be back this afternoon and I'll get enough from him to see me through. I'll meet you at Prue's."

Breakenridge nodded. He rode back to Prue's ranch and turned in there that night. The next morning Ringo appeared at the door, with hay upon his clothing.

"I got in last night," Ringo told Breakenridge. "But I didn't see the sense of waking everybody, so I slept in the haystack."

Outlaw and deputy, they rode together toward Tombstone. They rode in perfect amity. As a matter of fact, until they neared Tombstone, they would have more important things to consider than the charge that lay against Ringo, or their official relative positions. For the Apaches were out in force, killing and raiding. Both men were heavily armed and they rode most alertly. They made Tombstone by dark and Breakenridge bought supper for them. At the jail Breakenridge got the jailor to give Ringo a room in his house.

"You sleep there tonight," he told Ringo. "Keep your gun. I'll be down early tomorrow and we'll see about your bond."

The next morning Ringo waived examination and bond was fixed. The county treasurer, the county recorder and a gambler of Ringo's acquaintance agreed to sign it. It seemed a matter of common-place detail but Ringo chafed as he waited. For he knew a "Law and Order Party" had been formed in Tombstone. It sided with the Earps and was opposed to Behan's administration. The Law and Order men had gone out to try to arrest Curly Bill and a bunch of his rustler allies at Charleston. This was common talk on the streets. Ringo was impatient to have his bond approved and be gone to Charleston to side with Curly Bill.

Breakenridge and Ringo and the others sat in the sheriff's office. Judge Stillwell had yet to approve the bond as made and signed. Ringo's attorney appeared in the office door.

"All right, Johnny," he said. "Bond's approved."

"Fine!" Ringo grunted and stood up quickly. "See you later, Breck!"

He went fast out of the office, swung up and rode for Charleston.

MUCH HAS been made, by some present-day commentators upon the Tombstone canvas, of the "alliance" between Johnny Behan and the outlaws. The Earps were leading figures in the "Law and Order Party" and it is true that one can hardly be a champion of the Earps without being equally an attacker of Johnny Behan and all his men. Actually—and oddly, when one knows Breakenridge's history—it was the smiling deputy's ability to ride into rustler strongholds and bring back stolen stock or wanted men that was the real base of much of this criticism.

Politics, of course, was rampant in Cochise County—and especially in Tombstone. Wyatt Earp bitterly resented Behan winning the sheriff's fat-salaried position. He always claimed that he didn't want the job, but the evidence is to the contrary. Anything that would tend to hurt Behan would be good strategy for the Earps. For Wyatt still hoped that, come election time, he could defeat Behan and wipe out the blow he had suffered through Governor Frémont's appointment of the little man. And this was the background of the play that Tombstone saw, as John Ringo rode fast for Charleston to help Curly Bill send the "Law and Order Party" howling back home with drooping crests.

After Ringo's going, the day wore on quietly and monotonously. In early evening Johnny Behan—who had been informed by Breakenridge of the making of bond in the Ringo case—met Judge Stillwell on the street.

"I'll be ready to consider the matter of that Ringo bond tomorrow morning," the judge told Behan.

"But you approved it this morning!" Behan cried amazedly.

"I did no such thing!" the judge snapped.

"Why, his attorney came into the office and said you had approved the bond. Why—Ringo's gone."

"That is nothing whatever to me," the Judge told him flatly. "I did not approve the bond, but tomorrow morning I'll be ready to consider the matter. It is the sheriff's duty to produce the prisoner in court at that time."

Behan, furious, came hurrying to Breakenridge.

"It's some sort of dirty trick, on the part of that Law and Order gang and the Earps. What can we do?"

Breakenridge also was furious. Then two members of the Law and Order Committee appeared in the sheriff's office. They had warrants. Judge Stillwell had decided to take the matter out of Behan's hands. He had ordered these two vigilantes to bring in John Ringo.

The two men started for Charleston, but that camp was very much alert. The Law and Order attacking party had not appeared. Curly Bill and John Ringo were ready and waiting for the attack. At the bridge leading into Charleston, the two warrant bearers were surprised and surrounded by a bunch of cowboys. Their guns were taken from them. Then they were herded down the street and pushed into a saloon. Someone went to find Ringo. When Ringo came into the saloon Johnny Behan and Breakenridge were no more angry than he.

"Arrest me? Why there's not enough of the whole dirty Law and Order gang in Tombstone to arrest me! This is nothing but a trick you're trying to put up on the sheriff."

He turned to the cowboys guarding the two men.

"Hold them for a while. I'm going back to Tombstone."

And so Breakenridge was awakened by a pounding on the door of his room. He got up and opened the door and Ringo greeted him curtly.

"I just found out what they're trying to slip over on Behan and you. So I came back to square things."

It was nearly dawn now. Breakenridge and Ringo went down to the sheriff's office and Ringo made himself a bed on the lounge there. The cowboys in Charleston had taken John Ringo at his word. They had kept the Law and Order men there—as a matter of fact, did not let them come back until afternoon. So Judge Stillwell opened court with no knowledge of what had happened. And triumphant Law and Order men were in the courtroom, waiting for the moment of Johnny

Behan's discomfiture. Court opened. Judge Stillwell turned to Johnny Behan.

"Bring in John Ringo," he said formally.

"Breakenridge," Behan said calmly, "bring in John Ringo."

And, to the amazement of the judge and the Law and Order faction, John Ringo appeared. The bond was placed before the judge and he, looking at those names appearing upon it, had no alternative. He approved the bond with bad grace and Ringo rode out. And when he came to trial for the robbery of the poker game, no complaining witness could be found. The case was dismissed.

FOR A WHILE after their arrival in Arizona, the Earps got on well enough with the so-called "cowboy" element—which was really the rustler element—headquartering at Charleston and Galeyville. As a matter of fact, they had been quite friendly with the McLowerys and Clantons. Then, Wyatt Earp had gone out to look for stolen mules at McLowery's. After that, the McLowery-Clanton faction made threats against the Earps and the Earp faction replied in kind. Some sort of explosion seemed inevitable and, in the meanwhile, the Earps made life as miserable as possible for the Clantons and McLowerys. This was the situation when, in September, 1881, the Tombstone-Bisbee stage was held up by two masked men. The highwaymen robbed the passengers of money and jewelry and took the U.S. mail and the express shipment. John Behan deputed Breakenridge and Dave Nagle to try to cut the robbers' trail.

The two deputies found a clear, plain trail leading toward Bisbee. But, before they reached the mining camp the horse tracks vanished—wiped out by the passing of a herd of cattle. Coming into Bisbee, the officers found several of the passengers from the robbed stage. From these they tried to get descriptions of the robbers.

"They were masked, of course," a passenger told Breakenridge and Nagle. "But the smaller man kept asking each of us if we had any 'sugar'!"

Breakenridge and Nagle looked at each other. They knew that bit of slang—knew it well. It was Frank Stillwell's habit to call money "sugar." And they knew Stillwell, for he had been a deputy of Behan's

They looked around town. Stillwell was there with a man named Spence. And Stillwell—they discovered—had just had the high heels of his boots taken off and low heels put on. When they came to check the discarded heels from Stillwell's boots with tracks found at the scene of the robbery, they found a perfect match.

Meanwhile, Wyatt Earp and a posse rode into Bisbee, coming straight from Tombstone. Breakenridge and Nagle told Earp of the evidence they had, pointing to Stillwell and Spence. Earp was reluctant to act. The Wells-Fargo agent, also, refused to swear out a warrant.

"And, meanwhile, they may decide to leave town!" Breakenridge said disgustedly. "Dave, if you'll go down to the justice and get a warrant I'll arrest them."

While Dave Nagle went on this errand, Breakenridge hurried to the corral where Stillwell and Spence were staying. He arrested them with no difficulty. Then, when Wyatt Earp saw that Stillwell and Spence were in custody, he prevailed upon the Wells-Fargo agent to get out a warrant charging them with robbing the express. Earp's posse and Breakenridge and Nagle went back to Tombstone together. Justice Spicer conducted the examination and bound over Stillwell and Spence in the sum of $2,000, which they posted. They walked out.

But Wyatt Earp re-arrested them as they came out of justice court. They were bound over to the grand jury in the sum of $5,000, for robbing U.S. mail.

Spence and Stillwell were very close to the rustler element in Charleston. The bitter tension between the Earp faction and the Clanton-McLowery side was increasing. Apparently, Virgil Earp saw a chance to be clever. He came to Breakenridge and informed him that the Clantons and McLowerys were very much worked up about the arrest of Stillwell and Spence.

"They're threatening to kill every man who had a hand in the arrest," Virgil told Breakenridge. "The thing for you to do is to shoot the first time you see 'em. If you don't—they'll get you, sure!"

Breakenridge laughed.

"If I didn't know about the feud between you and the Clantons and McLowerys, I could take that a lot more seriously," he told Virgil Earp. "If you want the McLowerys killed, you kill 'em yourself!"

And proof of the correctness of Breakenridge's shrewd conjecture came only a few days later, when he saw ahead of him Tom McLowery. Breakenridge hurried a little to catch up with the rancher.

"McLowery," he said with his customary directness, "you know I helped arrest Stillwell and Spence for the stage robbery. I've heard some talk you're supposed to have made. So I want to ask you how you feel about it."

"Well, they're in hard luck," McLowery said with apparent sincerity. "I feel sorry for the boys, but I've got troubles of my own. I haven't anything to do with their being arrested. And I'm not buyin' into the trouble."

And then he invited Breakenridge to ride out and spend the night at the ranch. Breakenridge went with him and they talked further about the arrest of the two cowboys, McLowery reiterating his neutrality in the matter.

"The Earp side has always made a great to-do about what terrible fellows the McLowerys were," Breakenridge said in later years. "They *were* rough. And they did have dealings with the rustler element. But you have to understand the position of a rancher in those days, before you can really understand that, when shady cases came to the McLowery place, it was pretty hard for Tom and Frank to stand on their honesty and refuse to have anything to do with the armed, desperate men. Anyway, if there was ever a warrant for the McLowerys or the Clantons, *I* never heard about it—and I would have heard about it. For my particular job was the serving of warrants for men outside of Tombstone. For that matter, the Clantons and McLowerys were in and out of Tombstone all the time. Anyone who wanted them could have found them on the streets."

Bob Paul, who had been a Fargo shotgun guard, was also a deputy U.S. marshal. In Tucson he arrested a well-known gentleman, Pony Deal, who with Sherman Mc-Masters was suspected of the robbery of a stage near Globe. McMasters got away before Paul's arrival and came on to Tombstone. Virgil Earp recognized him. He telegraphed Bob Paul, asking if he wanted McMasters. But before an answer came, McMasters vanished. There disappeared at the same time—so simultaneously that reports connected the two—a fine saddle horse belonging to Gage, the general manager of the Contention Mine. It was rumored around Tombstone that, after sending his wire, Virgil Earp had hurried to McMasters and warned him to get out of Tombstone. (Later, McMasters returned to Tombstone, as one of the Earp henchmen.)

The sheriff's office made diligent search for Gage's vanished horse, and Breakenridge traced it to the San Simon Valley. He learned that McMasters had really stolen the horse and traded it to Milt Hicks. It seemed that the Contention manager would permanently mourn his valued saddler. Then, coming in one afternoon from a long trip, Breakenridge met Ike Clanton—the weak member of the Clanton tribe. Ike looked hesitantly at Breakenridge. Perhaps he wanted to curry favor in the sheriff's office; perhaps he merely had a grudge against someone. It was hard to tell, when dealing with Ike, what moved him.

"Lookin' for that Contention horse?" he asked Breakenridge, who nodded. "Well, if you was to hit McLowery's before dark, you'd find him there."

Then, as if frightened because of what he had said, Ike hurried on.

Breakenridge rode over to a livery corral and got stiffly down. His horse was too tired to ride farther and the best substitute he could hire was a fat, slow pony. He shifted to the pony and then rode out of town. But, because of his poor mount he did not make Mc-

Lowery's—as Ike had told him to do—before dark.
When he neared the house, he could see a bunch of cowboys at the front. Between him and them the yard was a
shallow lake. The McLowerys were irrigating. It was
not etiquette, to ride up to an Arizona house of that day,
that neighborhood, without warning. Breakenridge
pulled in at the edge of the water.

"All right to ride through the water?" he yelled
diplomatically. Frank McLowery appeared.

"Who is it?"

"Breakenridge. I want to come in."

McLowery told him to come on and Breakenridge
pushed the pony ahead. He rode splashing through the
water, to pull up in front of the door. He got down and
went inside. Curly Bill was there, and sullenness had replaced the usual good humor, on the outlaw's heavy
face. There were a dozen of hard-faced men—rustlers,
Breakenridge knew very well, even though they were
strangers to him—and they looked curiously or bel-
ligerently from Breakenridge to Curly Bill. The latter
greeted Breakenridge curtly, then the deputy and Frank
McLowery went to the corral to put away the pony.

"Frank," Breakenridge told McLowery, "I've come
to get that Contention horse. And I had better *get* him.
Everybody knows he's here and if you don't see that I
start back to town with him—good night, Frank Mc-
Lowery! You've always played yourself up as an honest
rancher who can't help himself when the rustlers come
around. But everybody knows that hard cases headquarter here, the same as they do at Clantons', and that
you do a big trade in stolen cattle. So far, nobody has
hung the deadwood on you. But, if I go back to town
now, and say the horse was here, but you and a big gang
wouldn't give him up—you'll have to clear out of here,
quick! You'll have to go over to the rustlers openly.
Think it over!"

McLowery watched sullenly while Breakenridge
took saddle and bridle from the pony and turned it into
the corral. At last, he seemed to make up his mind.

"Well, the horse ain't here, now. But—it'll *be* here before mornin'. Come on in and stay the night."

They went back into the crowded room. Curly Bill seemed now to have recovered his normal rough good humor.

"It's goin' be crowded, Breck," he grinned. "But we'll let you pick out a nice soft place on the floor. I reckon we can find enough blankets among us to fit you out."

That night Breakenridge slept on the floor with the others. Several times he was wakened by whisperings, and men quietly coming and going. But he made no effort to discover what was going on. He was up at daylight. He stepped across the sleeping men and went out to the corral. There, just as McLowery had promised, was the Contention horse. Frank McLowery came out of the house. He looked furtively behind him.

"I'll catch him for you," he said. Then, when they were out of earshot of the house: "Listen, you'll be all right so long as you're here at the house. But not a mile farther! I had trouble talkin' the man who had the horse into puttin' him in the corral. He's not goin' to take this lyin' down. Him and his bunch aim to stick you up on the way to town and take the horse back. That'll leave me in the clear, he thinks. So, watch yourself on the way home! And remember I told you."

"Thanks," Breakenridge told him.

They went back into the house and had breakfast. Curly Bill's dark eyes glinted a shade maliciously, as he watched Breakenridge.

"Hope you have a nice ride back to town," he said, and some more of the men laughed.

Breakenridge only nodded calmly. He had naturally an unreadable face. And now, as throughout the meal Curly Bill made oblique remarks which much amused the rustlers, he replied in apparent innocence to the outlaw's double-edged talk. When he got up to go to the corral, the whole bunch trailed out to stand interestedly and watch him saddle the hired pony. They yelled enthusias-

tic goodbyes. Breakenridge waved to them. The pony
was unwilling to face the road. Breakenridge, leading the
fine Contention horse, had trouble in spurring the pony
out on the homeward trail. But at last he got some distance between himself and the house. He looked back—
and a bunch of riders, just leaving the corral, were going
fast toward the pass between the Dragoons and the Mule
Mountains.

Breakenridge considered. The rustlers would be heading for Antelope Springs. That would be the place to
stop him, because his passage there would be through a
narrow, rocky cañon. He rode on and came from the Mc-
Lowery ranch-trail into the lumber road that led from
the Chiricahua Mountains to Tombstone. A lumber
wagon stood on the road, just ready to move. Breakenridge made his plan quickly. He rode in behind the
wagon, to get out of sight of the horsemen behind him.
Quickly, then, he shifted the saddle from the balky
pony to the Contention horse.

"Bring this pony in behind the wagon for me, will
you?" he asked the driver. Then he jumped the big horse
out from behind the wagon and went racing across country. The cowboys, who had been looking for him, let out
a chorus of Apache whoops. They followed him, quirting and spurring, and firing wildly. Breakenridge knew
the folly of attempting to shoot from the saddle of a
racing horse. He pulled in and lifted his carbine. He
pumped lead uncomfortably close to them until they
fell back. It was a hopeless race anyway, unless one of
their slugs, by sheer luck, found a target in the Contention horse's rider, for there was no animal among the
pursuers which could touch that horse. Breakenridge got
safely into Tombstone.

It was regarded as another Breakenridge trick. John
Ringo and Billy Clanton, coming upon Breakenridge
sometime later, shook their heads.

"You'll try one of those tricks once too often,"
Ringo told Breakenridge, only half-humorously. "You'd
better be careful. Next time you might get caught."

BREAKENRIDGE was not given much opportunity to consider possible reprisals from the rustlers. The feud between the Earps and the Clanton-McLowery faction was daily growing more serious. Both sides were breathing threats. The bases of the trouble were several, dating back to the attempt of Wyatt Earp's to recover Government mules from the McLowery place, but intensified by other, later events, like the chase after the highwaymen who killed stage driver Bud Philpot. That hold-up occurred in March, 1881.

Bud Philpot was driving and Bob Paul was riding shotgun at the time of this hold-up. Paul opened fire with his shotgun and hit one of the road agents. Their return-fire killed Philpot. The stage was carrying $80,000 in bullion and Bob Paul saved that treasure when he whipped up the stage and, under heavy fire from the highwaymen got clear. But a wild bullet from a highwayman, as the stage rocked away, killed a man named Roerig.

In a controversy which has persisted for half a century, it is pleasant to record one point of agreement between the Earp faction and the sheriff's office of John Behan: Bill Leonard, Jim Crane, Harry Head and Luther King were suspected both by Behan and by the Earps.

But the controversy will rage forever, over the hidden connection of the two factions with the robbery. Leonard, Crane, Head and King were members of the rustler element attached to the Clantons. When the posses of the deputy U.S. marshal—Earp, and the sheriff—Behan, took the trail, it was claimed by the Earps that the sheriff had only one motive in accompanying the Earp party—to be sure that the robbers would not be come up with. Luther King was arrested, but made his escape in Tombstone. Regarding that escape there are the customary two stories. Leonard, Crane and Head got into Mexico and when the two factions returned to Tombstone insinuations began.

The Behans, and a good many others in Tombstone, claimed that Doc Holliday—who was a tinhorn gambler

and what one would today call a homicidal maniac—
had been a member of the highwaymen and had actually
fired the shot killing Bud Philpot. And the truth of the
matter is that Holliday and Bill Leonard were close
friends, and that Holliday *was* mysteriously absent from
Tombstone at the time of the robbery. He had an excuse
for his absence, but could not offer any unquestionable
evidence in support of his alibi. The Earps, on the other
hand, maintained that Behan and Breakenridge (and
virtually everyone else connected with the sheriff's
office) were in league with the bandits—and with the
other criminal elements.

I have no means of knowing whether or not Doc
Holliday actually engaged in the robbery. Breakenridge
confessed that he had never discovered any evidence to
clear or convict Holliday. But there is nothing in the
dentist-tinhorn's record to lead me to believe that he was
incapable of such participation. On the other hand, there
is nothing in the record of Wyatt Earp to make me believe that he had any knowledge of Holliday's intent to
engage in the robbery. (Regardless of what he might
have discovered after the event.) And that a man of
Breakenridge's character—as it was made plain to
Arizona during some sixty years of residence there—
would have been willing to side even with Behan in a
shady trick—I do not, cannot, believe!

The Behan side maintained that Luther King's escape
from the custody of the sheriff was part of a plan staged
by friends of Doc Holliday, who wanted to get a witness
against the gambler out of the way. The Earp side, on
the other hand, maintained that the Behan men let King
go because of friendliness felt toward him and all other
outlaws.

However, gossip had been pretty well hushed when
Doc Holliday fell out with his mistress, "Big-nosed"
Kate. She was a notorious character and the story I have
heard, accounting for Holliday's infatuation for her,
does not bear printing. She got on a wild drunk and
swore to a statement charging Holliday with participa-

tion in that stage-robbery and murder. Johnny Behan arrested Holliday, charging him with the murder of Bud Philpot and Roerig. Wyatt Earp came forward with $5,000 bail and Holliday was released. Now, according to the Earp side of the business, Virgil Earp as city marshal locked up the woman to let her sleep off her jag. According to the Behan side—and Breakenridge has made the assertion calmly—she was fined for drunkenness in the sum of $12.50 as a slight punishment for making the charge against Holliday. The factions were very bitter in their accusations against each other.

IT SEEMS to me that both sides were willing, even anxious, to believe the worst about each other.

Tombstone's temperature rose to fever-heat, what with this feud between the Earps and Johnny Behan and the threats passing between the Earps and the Clanton-McLowery faction with which Wyatt Earp claimed the whole sheriff's office had "thrown in." Trouble was expected. Trouble came!

October 25, 1881, Ike Clanton and Tom McLowery drove into Tombstone and put their rig in a corral. Ike went to the Eagle Brewery to get a meal. Doc Holliday saw him go in and followed. He told Ike that he was tired of hearing of Ike's talk against the Earp side. He cursed him furiously.

"I ought to kill you right now!" he said.

Ike Clanton was no fighting man. Nobody believed that he was. His father, his brother Billy, were different. But Ike was merely a rustler and a talker. He was afraid of the cold-blooded little killer, Holliday, and when Morgan Earp came in and joined Holliday in threatening him, Ike got out as quickly as he could. Virgil Earp—city marshal—stood on the sidewalk outside the Eagle's door. He also told Ike that he ought to be killed.

Ike got away from them. He was unarmed and he was badly scared. He proceeded to drown his fright. By the time he reached the corral where he intended to sleep, he was so drunk that he could hardly walk. When he waked next morning it was to find his brother, Billy, and Frank McLowery, in town. Ike put on his gun. He told the others of the trouble with Holliday and Virgil and Morgan Earp.

He went out on the street, wandering aimlessly, it would seem. Virgil and Morgan Earp came up behind him. They "pistol-whipped" him, took his gun from him and marched him to the justice's office where he was fined for carrying arms in town.

Wyatt Earp and Doc Holliday came in.

Ike claimed—and it seemed plausible, considering the character of Holliday and the Earps—that the four men threatened him. At last, a gun was shoved toward him. He was told to take it, to "start something." He kept his hand away from that gun. Not without reason, he was confident that the moment he reached for the weapon, he would be shot down.

I say, not without reason, for it seems certain that the Earps had decided that the time had come for the clean-up of the Clantons and the McLowerys. This, of course, is not in accordance with the statements of the pro-Earp faction. But it seems to me apparent beyond doubt, from the evidence that appeared in the case and from the standpoint of mere common sense. The Earps were gunfighters; they were killers; their record in Kansas and in Arizona is proof of this. They felt that the Clantons and McLowerys would kill them, given opportunity. It was only human that they should have tried to assure themselves that they, and not their enemies, got the first shot.

And, so far, one's sympathy must be with the Earps. Certainly, they had the right to defend their lives against armed men. Nor can I get worked up about their abuse of Ike Clanton. Ike was a cowardly little mouthfighter. There is no record of his ever having gone up against a man on equal terms. But, once the Earps had made up their minds—as I believe they did make up their minds —to settle with their enemies, they seem also to have made up their minds that it didn't matter how they got the Clantons and McLowerys. The important thing was to get them.

So, Wyatt Earp left the justice's office and went up the street where he met Tom McLowery. By the testimony of at least one witness Tom McLowery had both hands in his pockets when Wyatt pushed his left hand into McLowery's face. According to this same witness, Wyatt then asked McLowery if he were armed. McLowery replied that he was not and backed into the street. Wyatt jerked his six-shooter and followed, beating McLowery over the head with the barrel. McLowery fell down, got up, was knocked down again and then, staggering and bleeding, was led away by a bystander.

BEHAN'S testimony, in the trial that followed "the battle of the O.K. Corral" was that he came out of a barber shop where the barber had been discussing the probability of a fight between the Earps and the cowboys. Behan said he saw a crowd at the corner of Fourth and Allen streets. Virgil Earp was standing close by holding a shotgun, and Behan—by his testimony—asked what the trouble was. And Virgil replied that "a lot of sons of bitches" were in town looking for a fight. Behan suggested disarming the men and Virgil refused. He said that he *wanted* them to fight and made no reply to Behan's statement that as a peace officer, the chief of police of Tombstone, it was his duty to prevent trouble. Behan saw Morgan Earp and Doc Holliday standing in the middle of the street where the crowd was gathered. Behan went on down Fourth Street and found Frank McLowery holding a horse. McLowery refused to give up his gun but he went with Behan to where Ike Clanton, Will Claybourn and Tom McLowery were standing.

Behan stated that he told all the cowboys that they must give up their arms. Frank McLowery again refused. Ike Clanton stated that he had no gun. And Behan's search found none. Tom McLowery also was unarmed. Claybourn claimed that he was not with the Clantons and McLowerys but was leaving town. The Earps and

Doc Holliday now came toward the group. Behan left the McLowerys and the Clantons and went ahead to meet the Earps. He tried to stop them but they merely pushed by and went on toward the McLowerys and the Clantons. Wyatt addressed the cowboys:

"You sons of bitches! You've been looking for a fight and now you can have it!"

Then, according to the testimony of Behan and other witnesses, someone of the Earp party shouted to the Clantons and McLowerys to throw up their hands and as the men—at least some of the men—put their hands in air the shooting started. Only Billy Clanton and Frank McLowery were armed. Doc Holliday fired his shotgun into Tom McLowery and killed him instantly. Morgan Earp shot Billy Clanton. Wyatt Earp shot Frank McLowery in the stomach and McLowery, staggering into the street, attempted to pull his pistol. According to Claybourn, not a shot had been fired by the Clantons and McLowerys when Tom McLowery fell dead and Frank and Billy Clanton had been fatally wounded. They did their shooting afterward.

There was a hearing before Justice Wells Spicer. The Earps produced their witnesses; Ike Clanton and Behan and others testified against the Earps. For the Earps, witnesses claimed that the cowboys had made many threats, that the Clantons and McLowerys had none of them put up their hands; that they started shooting at least as soon as the Earp faction. Breakenridge's mature opinion was the Clantons and McLowerys were not expecting a fight. It is a fact their rifles were on their saddles, that the McLowerys and Billy Clanton were apparently leaving town, and that, if they had been expecting trouble, they could have wiped out the whole Earp party with rifle-fire before Wyatt led his fighters into pistol range. No, it looks to me as I have said—the Earps had decided to settle the Clantons and McLowerys once and for all and, having made up their minds, they cared very little how the wiping out was accomplished. Some apologists for, or champions of, the Earps make

the point that the Clantons and McLowerys were un-
desirable citizens, that the Earps were the "Right
Side," so it didn't matter how the Earps killed them.
This point of view regards it as better for the community that they be killed. And, of course, the Behan
faction takes the ground that the famous "battle at the
O.K. Corral" was cold-blooded murder.

The pure truth will never be known. The killings at
the O.K. Corral will be forever justifiable homicides or
outright murder, depending upon the sympathies of the
historian. Justice Spicer, who was regarded as an Earp
sympathizer, listened to the conflicting testimony and
decided that the Earps had been justified in hunting up
the McLowerys and Clantons and killing them. He went
further—he stated that the nature of the dead men's
wounds proved them to have been shooting at the Earps.

Pro-Earp recorders of Tombstone events maintain
(chiefly on the grounds of Wyatt Earp's own statements) that Johnny Behan tried to lure the Earps into a
trap by telling them that the other side had been disarmed; that Behan was virtually the instigator of the
affair; that, in short, whatever Behan or Breakenridge or
any other anti-Earp man did was deplorable. The chief
error I find in this attitude is that Earp men adopt the
"whole hog" theory as their method—and the difficulty
with this all-or-nothing viewpoint is its essential fallacy
where human beings are concerned; its claim that only
black and white exist—and never a touch of gray. It is a
juvenile and hero-worshipping point of view. Particularly in this case, it has an inherent weakness—its
acceptance necessitates the belief that, in Tombstone,
the All-Heroes confronted the All-Villains. And instantly
the theory is exploded.

The provable fact is that the Earp crowd of efficient
gunfighters wiped out their not-so-efficient enemies and
that one man, at least, was shot down while unarmed.
For Ike Clanton escaped, dodging into Fly's photograph
gallery.

BREAKENRIDGE had no part in this affair. His regular duties kept him riding in and out of Tombstone. He looked for no trouble but—as was to be proved very soon—he side-stepped none when it came at him. Certainly, he expected more gunplay as aftermath of the slaughter at the O.K. Corral. For everyone expected reprisals, blows against the Earps.

Apparently, Wyatt Earp expected more trouble, even, than he had had before. His brothers, with Holliday and others of the faction, began to keep together; from five to eight of them always in a group and always heavily-armed.

But John Ringo was not impressed by their numbers. The story persists to this day, despite frantic pro-Earp recorders' denials, of his proposal to Doc Holliday and others of the Earp crowd that he and any or all of them "shoot out" the feud between the Earps and the rustlers —for Ringo, like Curly Bill, never made any bones about his cow-stealing.

But John Ringo was one gunfighter none of the Earps wanted any part of. The belligerent little Holliday *might* have swapped shots with him, but Wyatt Earp led his party inside Hatch's Saloon and left Ringo walking up and down the street, hands on the guns in his overcoat pockets, very much "on the prod."

"Who—" I was asking Breakenridge one day "— was the outstanding expert, both mechanically and temperamentally, among all the gunfighters you have encountered?"

"John Ringo!" Breakenridge replied without hesitation.

"Better than Wyatt Earp? Better than yourself, say?"

"Ringo would have made me look like an amateur," Breakenridge answered. "As for Wyatt Earp, certainly I had no reason to like the man, but I wouldn't deny that he must have been an expert with the six-shooter. And, if Earp had been given the job of gathering in Ringo, I think that he would have gone out and tried to bring

Ringo in. So would I. But probably it's just as well that I never had to go up against Ringo in a gunplay and my own opinion is that Earp felt the same way."

Word went around town that John Ringo was fighting drunk and making a play at the Earps. Behan sent Breakenridge who had always had more influence than any other with the outlaw—to bring him in. Breakenridge found Ringo pacing up and down in front of Hatch's place, his guns in the side pockets of his long coat.

"Johnny Behan wants to talk to you," Breakenridge told Ringo. "What are you trying to do, anyway?"

"I'm trying to stop this feud," Ringo said—and turned to look scornfully at the door of Hatch's place. "But that gang in there hasn't got nerve enough to come out here and settle it with me. They don't want to try any shooting to my face. What *they* want is a chance to put a shot into my back."

But he went to the sheriff's office with Breakenridge. And there Behan told him that he would have to take off his guns.

"And then go down the street and have one of those glory hunters pop me?" Ringo protested.

"Well you can't go around in Tombstone with guns on!" Behan said shortly and went out of the office.

"Well, that's a hell of a note!" Ringo said to Breakenridge.

"Behan is boss," Breakenridge told him. "I'll have to take your guns, John. I'll have to take them and—" he looked steadily at Ringo "—put them in this drawer."

When he went out of the office, Breakenridge remembered, the twin Colts were in that drawer. But when he returned they were oddly missing. And so was Ringo.

December 28, 1881, Virgil Earp—now exonerated by Justice Spicer of the Clanton-McLowery deaths—was serving again as city marshal. Walking the streets near midnight, he was fired upon by assassins and seriously wounded. The reprisals expected by everyone had begun.

The final complications of the Earp regime in Tombstone were increased when, February 10, 1882, Ike Clanton went before a justice of the peace at Contention and swore out a warrant charging the Earps with the murder of his brother Billy and the two McLowerys. The warrant was given John Behan to serve. Heavily armed, the Earps, naturally resisted arrest at the hands of one they conceived to be their bitter enemy. On March 17, Morgan Earp was playing billiards in Hatch's saloon when through the glass panel of the back door shots came, fatally wounding him, killing a bystander, and barely missing Wyatt. The O.K. Corral battle was having for echoes the roar of cowardly assassins' guns. The report of the coroner's jury charged Frank Stillwell, Pete Spence, two halfbreeds "and others unknown," with the crime.

Wyatt Earp resolved, then and there, to deal personally with the killers. James Earp had gone to California with Morgan's body. Virgil Earp was in no shape for gunplay. Wyatt started Virgil for California to get him out of the way. But, hearing that Frank Stillwell and others of the anti-Earp side were gathered in Tucson, he got together his federal posse—all gunfighters, including Doc Holliday and the horse-thief Sherman McMasters, who had once been charged with stage-robbery, and led them to Contention as escort to Virgil. He and Doc Holliday continued with Virgil and were guarding him on the train when it pulled into Tucson. According to the reports of that day, Ike Clanton and Frank Stillwell were at the station. Ike saw the Earp party and warned Stillwell that he had better get out. Ike then hurried off, for he wanted no gunplay with Wyatt or Doc Holliday. In the railroad yards there, Wyatt got off the train and found Frank Stillwell—who, without doubt, had come down to get a shot at some of the Earps. Wyatt killed Stillwell—the first blow struck, in avenging Morgan Earp's assassination.

There are—as usual!—two versions of the Stillwell connection with Morgan's death. Breakenridge points out (and he was no champion whatever of Stillwell, in fact, had once charged him with robbery) that from Tombstone to Tucson is seventy-five miles. Morgan Earp was murdered about eleven at night in Tombstone and Frank Stillwell was seen in Tucson the next morning. He *could* have made it, but only by hard riding. He seems entitled to this one point in possible defence. The Earps always claimed confessions wrung from members of the party of assassins made Frank Stillwell the leading spirit in Morgan's murder—and this may be true. Again, there is nothing but Wyatt Earp's word on which one can base an opinion and Wyatt, one must always remember, was a prejudiced witness.

After Wyatt Earp's return to Tombstone, Johnny Behan received telegraphic request from Sheriff Bob Paul of Pima County, requesting his arrest for killing Stillwell. But the telegraph operator, a man named Howard, was friendly to the Earps. He showed Wyatt the telegram before taking it to Behan. At Wyatt's request Howard held up the message long enough to permit the Earps to prepare for leaving town. They saddled their horses and brought them up in front of the hotel at which they stayed. Behan, by then, had the telegram from Paul. He saw the horses of the Earp party. He told Breakenridge and Dave Nagle to get their shotguns.

"I've got to arrest the Earps," he said. "Maybe they won't start a fight in the face of shotguns."

Behan and Nagle hurried away, but they had gone hardly a block, Breakenridge told me, when Wyatt's party came out of the hotel.

The Earp party now numbered six or seven. Beside Wyatt there was Doc Holliday, Sherman McMasters, Texas Jack Vermillion, and others. Behan, unarmed, as usual, stepped up before them as they came out.

"I want to see you a minute, Wyatt," he said.

"I've seen you once too often," Wyatt replied grimly.

And he and his party immediately swung into the saddles and rode out of town.

Wyatt had no intention of being checked while going about the wiping out of every man whom he suspected of connection with his brother's death. He took his posse out to the wood camp of Pete Spence, where he expected to find the two halfbreeds charged by the coroner's jury with participation in the murder. He found only one, a man called "Indian Charlie." He shot Charlie after, he states, getting from the halfbreed a full confession covering the details of the murder and giving the names of all those participating.

From the wood camp the party went on to Mescal Spring in the Mustangs. Again, there are two—and divergent—stories of what occurred there. According to the Earp statement, they rode up to the spring and found Curly Bill Brocius with nine or ten other rustlers, and Wyatt killed Curly Bill. Some of the men camped at the spring tell the other story, which runs to the effect that Curly Bill was at the time in Mexico and that only four cowboys were at the spring when the Earps rode up. One of the cowboys said that Wyatt Earp—who did the only firing—made a perfect target, for he was wearing a white shirt. This man, Arnold, said he drew a fine bead on Wyatt and hit him but that Wyatt's famed "steel vest" saved him. So, the Earps always claimed that they killed Curly Bill—whom they suspected of complicity in Morgan's death and the wounding of Virgil, and others, reliable citizens of Arizona have never believed that the Earps killed *anybody* at Mescal Springs, least of all Curly Bill. Among these was Breakenridge.

In Tombstone, Behan was assembling a posse. There is no questioning Behan's determination to pick men to follow the Earps who had reason to dislike them. He was afraid that Earp sympathizers would hamper his attempt to arrest them and he expected a fight. Breakenridge quarreled with Behan. Behan had told him to stay in town and turn over his rifle and outfit to John Ringo. Later, he told Breakenridge to get another outfit and come with the posse. Breakenridge refused to accompany the posse unless he could use his own arms.

AFTER THE departure of the sheriff and his posse, word came to Tombstone of the murder of a man named Peel by two masked robbers, in the Tombstone Mine office, at Charleston. Two hard cases named Zwing Hunt and Billy Grounds were shrewdly suspected of being the burglars with the nervous trigger fingers. Hunt and Grounds went to the Chandler Ranch, nine miles from Tombstone. There was a caretaker at the place, but the owner of the ranch was in Tombstone. Hunt and Grounds claimed that the man owed them seventy-five dollars. They sent a note to him in town by the caretaker, asking him to send out the money. They said they wanted to leave the country. But he came to the sheriff's office to tell that they were at his place. At a conference in the office it was decided to capture them on the authority of two old grand larceny warrants which had been hanging fire because of their absence in Mexico. Breakenridge was handed the warrants. He expected to go out as usual, alone, but was over-ruled.

"If they shot Peel, they're not going to surrender. You'll have to take a posse," Breakenridge was told.

Still he objected, feeling that he could do better by himself, but three men finally accompanied him—a jail-guard named Allen and two miners, Gillespie and Jack Young.

They reached the ranch just before daylight, tied their horses a little way from the house and worked up close. Breakenridge placed Young and Gillespie at the back door, behind a wood pile.

"You stay there quiet until daylight. Those cowboys will come out to see where their horses are and all you'll have to do is cover them. Allen and I will cover the front door. If they come out that way we'll do the same thing."

But Gillespie was going to run for sheriff. He saw a chance to make a reputation. Instead of waiting behind the woodpile for the cowboys to appear he marched up to the door and banged on it. A voice from within challenged him.

"It's the sheriff," he said.

Hunt and Grounds were standing by the door. They simply jerked it open, shot Gillespie dead and wounded his companion, Young, in the thigh. Neither man had a chance to fire a shot.

As Breakenridge stiffened with sound of the shots, the front door was swung open almost in his face and a teamster who had been stopping at Chandler's overnight ran out, yelling that he had nothing to do with Hunt and Grounds. One of the outlaws fired then through the open front door and the bullet struck Allen, Breakenridge's companion, in the neck, putting him out of the fight. Breakenridge caught hold of Allen's collar and dragged him off to the side where he could drop him over the bank of an arroyo, out of fire.

Having got Allen into the shallow ditch Breakenridge looked again at the front door. He saw movement there and jumped behind a tree as a shot came. The slug struck the tree-trunk that sheltered him. Breakenridge's shotgun roared and he heard the heavy thud of a body falling inside the house. Allen, now returned to consciousness, pushed his rifle over the edge of the arroyo. And from the back of the house Breakenridge heard Hunt yelling for Billy Grounds.

It was not yet daylight and they could see Hunt only as a vague shape. Both men fired at him, Allen using his rifle, Breakenridge shooting his pistol. They saw Hunt stagger and turn back. The teamster was now yelling that he was shot, too. Allen guarded against possible attack while Breakenridge ran across to the teamster and helped him to a house away from that in which the outlaws had slept. The fight had not taken two minutes. Coming back to Allen, Breakenridge told him that Hunt was certainly wounded and that he would go up the creek to look for him.

"You watch the house," Breakenridge said. "Grounds may have a shot left in him."

Daylight came. They could see Billy Grounds' feet in the door. Breakenridge went cautiously up the creek.

He had gone perhaps a hundred yards when the grass rustled ahead of him. He covered the spot with his gun. "Throw up your hands!" he yelled.

Zwing Hunt's hands came up above the grass and he answered:

"Don't shoot! You got me anyway!"

The posse returned to Tombstone with Gillespie dead in one wagon, Hunt and Grounds, badly wounded, in another, and Young and Allen in an ambulance sent out from Tombstone. Breakenridge was the only un-wounded member of the party. Breakenridge saw Grounds dying that night in the hospital—victim of Gillespie's grandstanding. Zwing Hunt recovered and finally escaped from the hospital with the help of a brother. He was killed by Indians in what was then called Rustler Cañon but today is known as Hunt's Cañon. His body was buried by soldiers from Camp Price and was later dug up by a posse for identification.

COCHISE COUNTY was now getting more peaceful. The removal of the Earps from Tombstone and the kill-ing or the emigration of many men prominent among the rustlers—including Curly Bill, whether killed or merely moved to greener pastures—had relieved the tension of the last two years. John Ringo was still around Galey-ville and Charleston, drinking more heavily than usual, but his time was short.

Coming back from a trip to Sulphur Springs Valley, shortly after Behan led his posse back from the unsuc-cessful attempt to capture the Earps, Breakenridge met Ringo, very drunk, heading for Galeyville. Breakenridge tried to persuade Ringo to go on with him to the Goodrich Ranch, but the latter, drunk and stubborn, went on his way. Probably, Breakenridge was last to see Ringo alive. He was found across the creek from the house of a family named Smith, near the mouth of Morse Cañon. His pistol with one exploded shell was beside him and there was a bullet hole in his head. "Buckskin Frank" Leslie, a well-known character in Tombstone, claimed that he had killed Ringo, but the claim was not regarded seriously.

In the November election of 1882 a Republican named Ward was elected sheriff. Deputy Sheriff Dave Nagle went in as city marshal. Breakenridge served with Sheriff Ward as deputy during that spring and summer of 1883. Then the mines closed down and Tombstone dropped within six weeks from a town of 6,500 people to less than 2,000. The gamblers left, the saloons closed. The day of Tombstone's glory was ended.

For a while Breakenridge ranched, but in the spring of 1884 he sold out and went surveying. In 1886 he was again behind a star, this time as deputy of U. S. Marshal Mead. Then a general election in Maricopa County made him surveyor of that county, but he retained his position as deputy U. S. marshal. He took Apache murderers to the Federal prison at Columbus, Ohio, trailed stage-robbers—and sometimes shot it out with the gentlemen, with one fatality that I know of—including the gang which robbed U. S. Paymaster Major Wham of $20,000. He arrested two men in connection with this famous robbery and saw them acquitted by a friendly jury.

Eventually, Breakenridge went into the service of the Southern Pacific Railway and for years, as special agent, led posses across the desert and into the mountains, chasing express and train robbers as in the days when he was "Tombstone's deputy." In 1925, while hunting up witnesses in the famous Lotta Crabtree will case, which had an old Tombstone angle, he re-encountered Wyatt Earp. They were both old men, Breakenridge a couple of years Earp's senior. Time had dulled somewhat the ancient hostility between them. So they could meet amicably and without rancor discuss the old days and recall the deeds of men long dead—Doc Holliday and Buckskin Frank Leslie, Curly Bill and John Ringo—even Johnny Behan.

Breakenridge, retired from S. P. service, had leisure to hunt up surviving oldtimers. He wrote a simple story of his life (I have drawn upon it liberally, as I have also drawn upon his talk and his letters to me). He planned another book, in collaboration with me. And then—January 27, 1931, he wrote me:

"I was taken sick the evening of December 28th . . . had to be operated on at once for appendicitis . . . yesterday they let me return home. They claim a very successful job . . ."

Four days later he was dead, in his eighty-fifth year, a modest, forthright soul, whose sense of humor was gentle, if keen, whose memory was like a filing cabinet, whose opinions were reasoned and tempered with kindliness. I wrote an obituary then:

"Billy Breakenridge is gone from us. Gone over the last hill that, maybe, is but the first hill. Gone to the Valhalla where staunch friends, unrelenting foes, red and brown and white, have waited years to hear his footfall. Slipped quietly out on that trail where the pony tracks point all one way . . . Billy Breakenridge has laid down his pen as he laid down his six-shooter some years before. But the shadow he cast has fallen into the long, tumultuous panorama of silhouettes that is Arizonan, western, history. It is not likely to become faded."

CHAPTER V · *Sure-Thing Killer*

BILLY THE KID

LINCOLN, ancient county-seat of Lincoln County, New Mexico, scene of "battle, murder and sudden death" in the famous Lincoln County War, today lies drowsing, a "finished" town, in the sheltering circle of the Capitán Mountains.

The twin rows of old 'dobe buildings that wall in the silent, dusty main street seem to hunch themselves, like old men who sit dreaming in the golden sunlight—like Florencio Chavez, who sits there upon his doorstep, tall and straight, staring fixedly upstreet past the McSween store and bank, to the old Murphy, Riley & Dolan store building that was, in the time of Billy the Kid, courthouse and jail.

And as his wise, ancient eyes turn backward, inward, the tomb-still street fills with men in overalls and blue jeans, men who wear the wide-rimmed Stetsons and high-heeled boots of the day and place and who carry long Colts sagging at their sides. Olive-skinned girls stand in the doorways of the dwelling houses; ponies stand hipshot, drowsing at the hitch racks before saloon and store. The men move up and down at their awkward horseman's gait, watching one another with steady, sun-narrowed eyes, or pausing for a moment to talk in caressing undertones to one of the smiling girls. For Florencio Chavez is looking backward nearly fifty years.

He sees—as he makes you see—Lincoln as it was in the days of John Chisum, the Harold boys, Jesse Evans, Tunstall, McSween, Major Murphy, Pat Garrett, and all the others who figured large in the Lincoln County War. . . . And this is the story:

John Chisum was king of the Pecos and all the Seven Rivers country. But the small cowmen nibbled at his flanks and up in Lincoln and the valley of the Bonito, the firm of Murphy, Riley & Dolan staked the squatters and the little cowmen, and kinged it in their role of merchant-banker-politician. A man had to be either a Murphy partizan or a Chisum sympathizer. The neutral mostly died young.

Alexander A. McSween, bringing his young and pretty wife with him to Lincoln *plazita*, was not only the country-side's lawyer but, with J. H. Tunstall, a young English capitalist, he owned a banking and mercantile establishment down the street from Murphy & Company's larger store. This made them commercial competitors of Murphy and, so, made them enemies of Murphy and, equally, made them pro-Chisum because they were anti-Murphy!

To McSween came a Mrs. Scholland, sister of Colonel Emil Fritz, Sutler Murphy's one-time friend and partner at the military post of Fort Stanton. Mrs. Scholland desired a divorce from her husband, a clerk at Fort Stanton. Now, McSween had known Emil Fritz, who had established the Fritz ranch below Lincoln, before the Colonel had taken his money and returned to Germany. Fritz still owed McSween for legal services.

Came the news of Emil Fritz's death in Germany and Mrs. Scholland asked McSween to collect for her—in accordance with her brother's will—ten thousand dollars insurance now due on her brother's life. But Major Murphy had both Emil Fritz's will and the insurance policy. The latter was security for a loan of nearly a thousand dollars, made to Emil Fritz by the firm of Spiegelberg.

Major Murphy refused to turn over to his enemy, McSween, any papers of the Fritz estate. Through legal process, the lawyer finally recovered the policy, but not the will. And he went east, on Mrs. Scholland's account, to collect the face of the policy. At least half of the amount belonged to him, for he had paid off the

Spiegelberg loan and advanced his own expenses for the eastern trip. But Murphy—who also owed McSween money—demanded of the lawyer the full amount of the policy on some yet unknown ground.

NOW, MURPHY went to the law. He levied on all the goods in the McSween-Tunstall store. Not content with this, he also levied on the horse-ranch which McSween's partner, Tunstall, the young Englishman, had established on his private account down on the Rio Feliz. Enters, now, Billy the Kid. . . .

"They say that Billito worked for John Chisum," Florencio Chavez tells you. "That is not so. I knew the Kid from the time that he first came to Lincoln with Jesse Evans, Frank Baker, Billy Morton, and Jim McDaniels. It was McDaniels, I always heard, who named Billy 'the Kid.' I know that he was often with John Chisum, but he was only riding around the country with him.

"The only times Billy the Kid worked was when he helped Frank Coe a little, on Coe's Ruidoso ranch, the winter the Kid hunted grizzlies over there, and when he took a job on the Rio Feliz, on the horse-ranch of the *Inglés*, Tunstall. I know these things, for Billito was my friend, and he told me of many matters which I hear now in twisted form.

"Was Billito a better snot with the Winchester than with the Colt? Just the same! Just the same! I have seen him and Jesse Evans—in the days before he fell out with Evans and others of his old friends—shooting with two Colts at a hat thrown into the air. They were both wonderful shots, Billito and Jesse. *Es verdad!* It is true.

"Billito was my *compadre.* I liked him. My house was his house. He lived with me whenever he felt like it. He was a good boy, I say—except when he was angry. Then —well, he was a devil!"

BILLY—*alias* "THE KID" . . . If I have put upon his record in the very beginning of my writing the valuation I believe correct, the designation that seems to me to place him accurately, I can still concede that there was something about this smiling little outlaw which sets him apart from others of the border breed—some quality that lends glamor to his rascalities, makes of him a character with the perennial appeal of *Robin Hood*.

Perhaps it was personality. . . . If Florencio Chavez had the words, I am sure that he would say so. For it is "Billito's" personality that Florencio and Frank Coe and the others recalled, not his actual deeds. Whatever it was—or is—that makes The Kid a legendary figure, is very real.

Perhaps it should not seem strange that man-made cañons in a great city were the birthplace of the Southwest's most noted killer, one who was to know deeper, more rugged cañons, a freer, wilder breed than the litter of sneaking, out-of-doorway thugs spawned by any metropolis. Still, there is always a suggestion of oddity to the fact that "Billy the Kid" came into the world in a New York slum.

William H. Bonney, they named him that twenty-third of November, 1859, when as a tow-haired, blue-eyed infant he arrived in the tenement home of his Irish parents. In viewing such as he, one longs for the good old days of the nursery-tales, when some token was given over the cradle of the fate, good or bad, that was to be the baby's. Here lay the youngster who would king it among as deadly an array of killers as this continent has ever known. Yet there was no sign!

In 1862, Bonney's family consisted of his wife and two sons. Billy was the elder. He decided to move down to Coffeyville—then on the very edge of the Indian Nations. Apparently, this stroke of pioneering exhausted him. He died shortly after arrival and Mrs. Bonney took her small sons to Colorado. There she met and married one Antrim and went with him to Santa Fé. Then they moved to the booming camp of Silver City, New Mexico about 1868.

Mrs. Antrim was "a fine looking woman" according to the guests of her boarding house. And she had a warm,

Irish heart that refused no call of the luckless ones around
her. Billy always spoke of her with tenderness—as he
spoke of his step-father with hatred. He said that
Antrim's cruelty kept him out of the house as much as
possible.

Silver City was like other frontier towns, filled with
hard cases, many of whom Billy met at the table in his
mother's house. He took on the color of his environment, as boys tend to do. He learned a great deal around
the saloons and other joints of the town; learned a very
great deal, indeed. He learned the fullest intricacies of
profanity; learned, first to play cards, then to deal them
in the fashion that entirely discounts luck as a factor;
learned the use of Colt and Winchester.

Ash Upson, pioneer New Mexico newspaperman, a
boarder at the Antrims', liked Billy. But, he commented,
the boy's furious temper was one of his outstanding
characteristics. When Billy was in a rage, nobody could
control him.

There have been many others of violent, almost un-
controllable, temper, in the West, who have mastered
themselves. But—and this, it seems to me, more nearly
explains Billy Bonney than any other factor—on the
frontier where life was a constant battle for existence,
killing was looked upon as a rather natural incident to a
quarrel. That viewpoint became a part of life, persisted
in the generation that followed Billy's. Force, or fear,
only, could halt the killing-rush.

Coming along some thirty years after Billy Bonney,
brought up in a Texas that was becoming "civilized," I
can recall incident after incident among the boys I
knew, sons of cowmen and the like. In particular, I recall riding with another, slightly older, boy after
strayed stock, and encountering two "toughs" from a
little German settlement. We argued and eventually the
four of us were rolling on the prairie. My companion
settled his enemy with a rock. Then he came to me,
where I sat triumphantly on my "man" and tried to push
an open "push-button" knife into my hand.

"Kill him!" he said excitedly. "Kill him!"

Arrival of the boys' father relieved me of necessity for making a decision. But that is not the point—that frontier point-of-view, that instinctive feeling that the proper settlement of an enemy was the enemy's death at one's hand, persisted, if not so strong among us as it must have been with the boys of Silver City. Not Billy Bonney, alone, moved automatically to snatch up the nearest weapon in time of fury. I am very sure of that!

He doubtless witnessed shootings and knife-killings, as he lived in Silver City between the ages of nine and twelve—between '68 and '71. The efficient man lived— he must have observed that. And so in his own fights— which were many—he was usually the winner because he was the more efficient battler.

He was about twelve when a friend of his, one Moulton, was attacked in a saloon by some "shoulder-strikers." Young Billy decided to help Moulton. He opened his pocket knife and jumped upon the back of a blacksmith who was rushing Moulton with a heavy chair. There was more motive to the boy's attack than friendship—this blacksmith had once insulted his mother and Moulton had whipped him at the time. Billy clung to the man's neck, stabbing him with his knife. The man fell dead.

Billy had to run for it. He went alone, though there was in Silver City at the time an older boy who had been his close friend for a year or more—Jesse Evans, who was to be connected almost to the end with the Kid's blazing career.

The many and varied legends which attempt to fill in the next half-dozen years of Billy Bonney's life at least have one common attribute—they are colorful. But little is actually known of the wandering years. He went to Arizona and picked up a nameless companion. They killed three Chiricahua Apaches in the mountains near Fort Bowie, took the "friendly" Indians' ponies and pelts and sold them to some emigrants.

They came back to Bowie in style! They were riding
good horses. They were well-dressed and well-armed.
They had money in their pockets to finance Billy's
monte-dealing. And he was particularly expert at
monte. . . . So the pair lived high around San Simon,
Bowie, San Carlos, Tucson.

Fort Bowie was the scene of another killing. A
drunken soldier-blacksmith quarreled with the young
monte-dealer, struck him and knocked him down. Billy
said briefly, some years afterward: "Then I come up
a-shooting."

ARIZONA was now too hot for him. He "hightailed"
for Mexico and again legend tells of countless adventures
of which Billy is the hero. But the truth seems to be that
he would do anything but work. If he could win from
the Mexicans at monte, that was good. If he couldn't
win, he could take their money at the point of a gun.
But—he would take their money! and nothing in the
known character of the youngster can lead one to believe
that he would hesitate to kill when that was convenient.
He had nothing of *Macbeth* in him. *Banquo's* ghost would
never wake him!

Tradition has it that he killed a Mexican gambler and
with one Segura moved to Chihuahua City, got into
trouble there and came fast back across the *frontera*.
Picture him, then—about five feet seven, lean, hard, cat-
quick of movement, his lank hair light brown, his eyes
blue but so flecked with brown that they seemed hazel,
long-chinned face seeming always to wear a grin because
of the prominent incisors pushing between his lips.
"Bucktoothed," the old-timers called him.

And about him was a careless gayety that those hard
men he met found very likable, outcropping of the
"personality" which set him apart from other gunmen,
makes him different, today, from Hardin and Longley.

Along the Rio Grande somewhere, Billy fell in with
his friend of Silver City days—Jesse Evans. This was in
'76 and until the latter part of the year the two young

desperadoes rode here and there, making their living in the fashion most convenient at any given time. West Texas, northern and eastern Mexico, New Mexico, came to know the pair well—and unfavorably. Joining forces with some cowboys of Evans' acquaintance—Billy Morton, Frank Baker, Jim McDaniels—they rustled stock, gambled, enjoyed themselves generally around Mesilla.

Then the *compadres* parted. They had been the best of friends. They did not look into the future—could not look forward to the day when the grinning "Kid" would sit in his saddle staring down at Morton and Baker, their killer in cold blood or hot, dependent upon the version one accepts.

BILLY—"THE KID," they were calling him nowadays. He told Jesse Evans and the others that he would see them on the Pecos, where they were headed from Mesilla. But word came to him, the old men say, that his friend Segura the Mexican gambler was in jail at San Elizario. Segura bribed a Mexican boy to carry word to his *amigo* and when the Kid got the word he was on the west side of the Rio Grande, five or six miles north of Mesilla. He listened to the messenger, grinned and nodded:

"Six o'clock, now," he said, looking at the evening sun. "By midnight I will be starting back from San Elizario with Segura."

"But it is eighty-one miles," the boy said doubtfully. "You will ride that distance in six hours? *No es posible!*"

But the Kid rode his gray horse some eighteen miles along the river-road to the tiny *plaza* of Chamberino. Here he sent the gray into the muddy Rio Grande and they battled the tawny flood to the other bank. Then the gray came racing toward the Texas line. Twenty-three miles to the Cottonwoods, from Mesilla; and on to Hart's Mill; past it into El Paso. He stopped here long enough to have a drink at Ben Dowell's and to let the little gray horse eat a few crackers.

It was after ten and he had still twenty-five miles to cover. Sometime around midnight, he was holding up the jailor at San Elizario, letting Segura out and helping him up behind the saddle. They crossed the Rio Grande into Mexico, stayed overnight at a friend's house, then recrossed the river.

Messages were waiting for the Kid when he got back to Mesilla. Jesse Evans was on the Rio Pecos near Seven Rivers. He wanted the Kid to come on, but warned him against the usual road through the Huecos and Guadalupes. But the Kid found a youngster named O'Keefe who would take the short trail with him and chance a meeting with the Apaches who were raiding.

In Las Cruces the Kid and O'Keefe bought Mexican mustangs for the trip. In El Paso they picked up a mule and provisions. They started out to cross two hundred miles of "Indian country" and on the second night, camped in the Guadalupes, cut an Apache trail. They had a fight with the Indians, lost their horses, were separated and only after much hardship did the Kid make the cow-camps along the Pecos. O'Keefe also got safely into Las Cruces and there found the Kid, who had come back to get his favorite gray horse.

For a while, in the Lincoln country, the Kid rode with his friends, Evans and Morton and the others. But he was restless. He was here and there, around Chisum's Bosque Bonito headquarters ranch, over on the Ruidoso with Frank Coe, then on the Rio Feliz with Tunstall, McSween's English partner.

Dick Brewer was Tunstall's foreman on the horse-ranch Tunstall had started. He and the Kid hit it off very well and for Tunstall himself the Kid developed a real affection.

"He was the only man that ever treated me fair about wages," he said once, long afterward.

He knew well enough that Murphy and McSween were enemies, but if he realized that riding on the Feliz was enlisting him on the weaker side, it probably worried him not at all. For by the time (February, 1878)

Murphy decided to include Tunstall's Rio Feliz ranch in his levy on McSween's property, the Kid was a conceded warrior of ability.

SHERIFF WILLIAM BRADY was called by his enemies "the Murphy Sheriff" and history seems to show that in every way he acted as a "yes-man" for the Murphy side. On February 12, 1878, in accordance with his boss's orders, he sent Billy Matthews with a small posse to Tunstall's place to attach the stock there. Dick Brewer, Tunstall's foreman, told Matthews that these were Tunstall's cattle and horses. Nothing of McSween's was there.

"But if you come pack later, with just one man," he told Matthews, "I'll let you look the place over for McSween stuff."

Tunstall was in Lincoln and there the word came to him that Matthews had been instructed by the enemy to raise a big, "fighting" posse to go back to the Rio Feliz and seize the stock. On February 16, he went back to the ranch, arriving there the next day. He refused to let Brewer fight to protect the stock. He preferred to take the matter to the courts. But he wanted to save eight or nine particularly fine horses, so early on the 18th the riders rounded up these horses and started for the county seat.

There was Tunstall on a fine mare. There was Dick Brewer, John Middleton, one Widenmann and the Kid. They were hardly off the place when Matthews arrived with his posse. Matthews' actions speak for themselves, tell the real purpose of this visit. He had a free hand to make his seizure. It was a civil process, requiring nothing of Tunstall. But he divided his force and sent Murphy's foreman, Billy Morton, with Jesse Evans and other hard cases, enemies of Tunstall, to overtake the young Englishman.

The day dragged on. The sun was low when Morton's heavily-armed riders came up with the little party that pushed the horses on toward Lincoln. Brewer and

Hardin were treated, "McDonald" might have a different meaning in Texas, today.

But he was never again to clash with Authority. He became a storekeeper, married Rhoda Carter, seemed to be traveling the road to prosperity as a merchant. He owned stores at Brown's Bluff on the Sabine, near Longview; at Mineola. It was in Mineola that he made a friendship which was to have a marked effect upon his later life. James S. Hogg, in turn district attorney, editor and governor of Texas. Bill McDonald and Jim Hogg were good friends; they were political and personal enemies; then they were friends again. They lived in a frontier community of fiercely individualistic viewpoint and they were fighters both. Opinionated, neither was apt to yield to the other's views. Which explains their falling out. Innate fairness, recognition by each of the other's worth. explains resumption of their friendship.

At Mineola, McDonald served as a deputy sheriff and quickly made a reputation for utter fearlessness, for outstanding gun-skill—and for discretion. This is not a usual combination. It meant, in Bill McDonald's case, that he was lightning fast "on the draw" but slow to shoot. Once he had the drop on a hard case, he simply marched him off to jail. At Mineola he had what amounted to a post-graduate course in peace officering—though he never thought of it in that way. Bad men came to town, listing to port or starboard with weapon-weight. They let out ferocious howls in Mineola streets or saloons—and a lanky young man with icy blue eyes appeared. He always "showed the best hand made on the draw." The bad men went to jail. Railroad gangs came to town to "take it apart." Prominent among the peace officers objecting to Mineola's dismantling would be that same blue-eyed young man—and Mineola remained intact, if the wrecking crew did not.

It was great training! Then McDonald sold out his store in '83, to buy stocker-cattle and strike out for open range. He was a cowman for a while; then he owned a lumber yard in Wichita Falls; and finally went back to ranching—this time in Hardeman County.

Excitement came always to Bill McDonald as steel comes to lodestone. He seemed during all his life to be magnetized for trouble. So it was, now, as quietly he trailed his herd toward the new home. There was a rough patch of country in this neighborhood known as the Cedar Brakes. It was the hangout of a tough bunch of whom the most notorious characters were the Brooken brothers—Bill and Bood. The Brooken Gang stole some stock from Bill McDonald as he trailed toward the ranch. He could not stop then to hunt the thieves, but he made a mental note—and it is of record that those mental notes of Bill McDonald's were rarely lost and never forgotten!

Margaret was the county seat of Hardeman. When he was established on the ranch, with his house built and some fences up Bill McDonald went over to the county seat and volunteered his services to Sheriff Alley. When he had received his deputy's commission, he looked to the hang of his six-shooter and started forth to learn the county. He was interested to know what supposedly respectable citizens were actually hand-in-glove with the Brookens and other outlaws. Presently, he was making arrests.

This was rather a novelty to the hard cases of the county at that time. They were very much annoyed when their friends were taken to town and jailed on grave charges. So they did the natural thing. They began to send threatening messages to Deputy Bill Mc-Donald; and to lie in wait for him to make those threats good. But then, as always, Bill McDonald seemed to bear a charmed life.

Partly, I think, his seeming immunity to lead was caused by his serene self-confidence. It never occurred to McDonald to take a backward step. He was a firm believer in the ancient adage that "the best defense is attack." So, when a dangerous moment arrived, McDonald moved so rapidly toward the other man that mentally,

Middleton were off to the side, looking for a flock of
wild turkeys they had heard. But with the sound of
hoofbeats on the road behind them, every man of the
Tunstall riders turned in the saddle to stare tensely.
There was a Murphy man in the lead—Billy Morton.
There were the four "Seven Rivers" cattle-thieves whom
Tunstall had forced Brady to arrest a little time before for
raiding his ranch: Jesse Evans, Tom Hill, George Davis,
and Jesse's brother. There were others, all enemies, all
whooping down upon them. Middleton screamed a
warning to Tunstall, who seemed not to realize his
danger. The others rammed in the hooks and sent their
horses jumping for shelter. Tunstall was left alone in the
road.

There are varying accounts of what happened. But
generally it is believed that Morton halted Tunstall,
disarmed him, then the bunch shot him down. Jesse
Evans or Tom Hill fired the first shot into the helpless
man. Morton is said to have shot Tunstall through the
head with the Colt taken from the prisoner, then to have
killed his fine mare. The indictments brought for this
murder name Jesse Evans, Frank Rivers, George Davis
and a Mexican named Segorio.

THAT NIGHT, Billy the Kid, possibly smarting under
the memory of his unvalorous flight before the posse,
made up a list of the men with Morton. He told it
around Lincoln that he would kill every man of them.
Or so the old-timers say.

At any rate, there began the last and deadliest chapter in the history of the Lincoln County War. And so
frequently, so prominently, does the Kid's name appear,
that "Kid" and "Lincoln" can hardly be mentioned now
except together.

McSween had Tunstall's foreman, Dick Brewer,
made a "special constable" and Brewer organized a
posse. He led a dozen men toward the Peñasco country.
On the little Rio Peñasco, a few miles from Pecos, they
found Billy Morton and Frank Baker. Ancient friendship

had been destroyed in the Kid's mind, for these two. He eyed them sullenly when they surrendered and rode in the middle of Brewer's warriors back to Roswell.

On the return trip to Lincoln the posse went by Agua Negra and there was a flurry of shooting. The Kid is credited with killing both the prisoners, March 7, 1878. Whether he shot them as they attempted escape, or killed them in cold blood, the conflicting accounts will never settle.

There was more work for Brewer's fighting men. Over in the Mescalero Apache Reservation, at Blazer's Mill, "Buckshot" Roberts was reported to be working. And Roberts had been one of Morton's posse.

He carried a load of buckshot in the right shoulder, this grim little ex-soldier. He could not lift a rifle above hiplevel. But that injury which might have turned an ordinary man's life into the paths of peace did not work so with Buckshot Roberts! It could not keep him from being a fighting man. All alone he faced Brewer, the Kid, George and Frank Coe, Charlie Bowdre, Dock Middleton, a couple of gunmen named Scroggins and Stevens, besides others not so well known. Frank Coe tried to persuade the crippled little ex-soldier, ex-Ranger, to surrender. Roberts refused. And around the corner of the house came the Brewer men shooting, so an eye-witness says.

ROBERTS OPENED fire with his rifle, shooting from the hip. He shot Jack Middleton. He shot a finger off George Coe. He jammed rifle-muzzle into the midriff of the Kid and only a misfire beat Pat Garrett out of the job he did three years later. Charley Bowdre shot him through the body and "Buckshot" staggered back into the house. He dropped his Winchester and snatched up a buffalo gun. Through the window he killed Dick Brewer. Then the Kid, now leader of the gang, gathered his outfit together—and they rode away from there. They wanted no more of that game little rooster, "Buckshot" Roberts!

"The Kid is said to have killed Sheriff Brady and George Hindman"—again it is Florencio Chavez reminiscing—"but I don't know. Brady had other enemies."

However, McSween himself furiously upbraided the Kid for this killing, by the testimony of Mrs. McSween. We are safe in believing that the Kid, Charley Bowdre, and others of his gang, hid behind McSween's corral wall. When Brady and three deputies—George Hindman, Billy Mathews and "Dad" Peppin—came along the street on April 1, 1878, the men behind the wall opened fire and killed Brady and Hindman, and went untouched themselves.

Now the McSween side "elected" John Copeland sheriff. Not to be bested, the Murphy side had Peppin appointed sheriff by Governor Axtell, who had always sympathized with Murphy.

Near the first of July, 1878, the Kid had to hole up at McSween's house in the face of superior forces commanded by Sheriff Peppin. With him were Harvey Morris, "Big Foot Tom" O'Phalliard, Jim French, Skurlock, Florencio Chavez and other Mexicans. And, of course, McSween. Charley Bowdre, with Hendry Brown and George Coe, held the store building next door. Downstreet, in the Montana and Patron houses, were some forty Mexicans of the McSween side.

Florencio Chavez remarks that it was considerable of a war that Lincoln saw during the next three days. Peppin had fully sixty men, three of whom were posted on the mountainside above the McSween place, firing buffalo guns down at the houses. The besieged fired through the windows and through loopholes. The first day passed tensely. The second day was marked by the killing of Charley Crawford up on the mountain by a nine-hundred-yard shot from Fernando Herrera in the Montana house.

Colonel Dudley, commanding Fort Stanton, came on the scene with a detachment of negro troops gatling-gun equipped. Dudley, like Governor Axtell, was pretty obviously on the Murphy side. He ordered the Mexicans of the McSween faction out of the Montana and Patron houses—clear out of town, in fact. He ordered McSween to have his men put down his arms, but made no provision for protecting the McSween-ites from Peppin's men. His offered protection was limited to Mrs. McSween and she refused it.

The end was in sight. . . . There were left in Lincoln to back McSween only the men in his house and store. The Peppin forces had closed in on these fortresses. Now, they set fire to the house.

"McSween," says Florencio Chavez indignantly, "was not a fighting man, but a brave man he certainly was. He would not touch arms. Even his knife was a tiny thing that he used for sharpening pencils. During the fight, he was not like one afraid of being hurt or being killed, but he moved about as one without hope."

The roof of McSween's house fell in. Darkness came. The men in the house looked at each other, looked at the Kid, who was generalissimo of their side. They knew that Peppin's men waited for the inevitable break from the 'dobe walls. But there was nothing else to do.

Mrs. McSween was gone. The Kid gave his orders. Harvey Morris was first to plunge through the back door which the Kid flung open. Francisco Semora was at his heels. Vicente Romero was third out—and third to die under the hail of lead that came from the Peppin men behind a wall not forty feet away.

"You, next!" the Kid told McSween and the lawyer walked out, Bible in hand.

Along the walltop orange flames stabbed the darkness. With the ragged roar of the volley, McSween fell across the other dead men. Beckwith, from Seven Rivers, "claimed him."

"Big Foot Tom" O'Phalliard, happy-go-lucky Texas cowboy, newest member of the Kid's bunch, leaped out. But he saw his friend, Harvey Morris, lying there. Tradition credits him with as brave an act as frontier legends chronicle. He dropped to his knees beside Morris. He lifted him up. Behind O'Phalliard Charley Bowdre yelled that Morris was dead; no use to stop. And O'Phalliard had discovered as much. But he did not hastily drop the body of his friend and run for his life. Gently, he let Morris down again, before he came to his feet and dashed for the shelter and safety of the dark. And the old men tell me that firing from the enemy was halted, while Tom O'Phalliard knelt there.

Of the others, Salazar, the fighting Mexican, was badly hurt. He shammed death and eventually got away. The others were not struck by Peppin lead. Only the Kid was left and it was he that the Murphy men most wanted. He leaped out with six-shooter flaming. He killed Bob Beckwith, who had killed McSween. He wounded a couple of others. But he won clear.

THE KID and his gang now "hung out" near Fort Stanton. They stole cattle and horses all over that section. They met no opposition and on August 5, 1878, they rounded up a bunch of ponies within sight of the Agency at Mescalero. The bookkeeper, Joe Bernstein, rode out and yelled at them to "let those horses alone."

There are two versions of the "period" to the Bernstein yell. Pat Garrett, the authorities generally, maintained that the Kid lifted his Winchester very calmly and shot Bernstein dead.

"Takes a bullet to teach some people to keep their noses out of other men's business," he is said to have remarked.

But you could have heard in that country until lately that a young Mexican named Sanchez, a would-be "bad man," was riding with the Kid's gang on that raid, and that it was he, not his leader, who shot Bernstein.

The Kid rode off to Fort Sumner, where he was to headquarter, dance and drink and gamble away the money got from rustling, until his death. O'Phalliard was with him, and Wayt, John Middleton and Hendry Brown. Bowdre and Skurlock stayed in Lincoln County for the time being.

September first, the Kid and his followers went back to Lincoln to help Bowdre and Skurlock move to Fort Sumner. September tenth found the Kid raiding Charley Fritz near Lincoln. He and Bowdre, Wayt, Middleton and Brown drove twenty horses toward Sumner and went on up the Pecos, stealing more as they headed for Puerta de Luna. Bowdre sold out his "interest" in the stolen stock and went back to his Mexican wife at Fort Sumner. The others pushed on toward the Texas Panhandle.

Early in the Fall, little Tascosa on the Canadian heard that Billy the Kid and a tough gang was camped near the LX. They held a conference, those grim cowmen of the Canadian. The first time the Kid rode into town, they sent for him. They informed him they knew all about him, knew of the reward offered for his arrest.

"But," they told him, "we are not interested in what happened over in New Mexico. We are interested, though, in what happens over here! So long as you don't throw the long rope over Panhandle stock, you're all right in Tascosa."

The Kid assured them that he and his men wanted only to be let alone. He promised to leave Canadian River stock alone. He said that he had a bunch of fine saddle horses for sale or trade.

The Kid's men got very friendly with the cowboys and the ranchers of that country. They drank at Mc-Masters' store with hard-faced riders of the Panhandle outfits. They danced at the *bailes* and gambled like any other bunch of cowboys-come-to-town.

Among the residents of Tascosa at this time was a young doctor, named Henry F. Hoyt. He was a noted athlete and very popular in the tiny cow-town. He and Billy the Kid became good friends and Hoyt had ample opportunity to observe the Kid. Too, he had a different point of view. . . . *He* studied the Kid, not as one cowboy might look at another, but as an Eastern man of orthodox training would weigh him. I think it is significant that Hoyt liked the Kid, found him a likable youngster, but very much the leader who would not be questioned or disobeyed by anyone in his gang.

Hoyt tells of one incident that illustrates the Kid's domination of those hard-cases who rode with him. John Middleton was a hard-case, but when he was boasting and quarreling in a saloon one day, very obviously "on the prod," the Kid walked in. One glance at Middleton and he had sized the situation:

"John Middleton, you damn' idiot, you go back to camp," he said to the hard case.

And Middleton—an older man—went back to camp as ordered!

This incident also proved what all the old-timers have said of the Kid:

He had a good brain. He knew that, more or less, the fate of himself and the men with him depended upon favorable public opinion here. If they made nuisances of themselves, the cowmen of the Canadian would not tolerate them. That meant closing of a market for cattle and horses that they might bring across from New Mexico—at the very least. It might well mean a good deal more! For no matter how hard Billy the Kid and Middleton and the others might be, plenty of men riding the Canadian were as hard, as efficient, as any the West could show! The Kid's reputation meant nothing at all to them.

Hoyt and the Kid became very friendly, as I have said. In fact, Hoyt gave the Kid a pretty braided-hair watch chain and that chain shows in the picture of the Kid made at Fort Sumner in '78 or '79.

The Kid appreciated the gift as he seems to have appreciated Hoyt's friendship. When the doctor was leaving Tascosa in late October, 1878, the Kid came riding in from camp. He presented Hoyt with his favorite race horse. At the Kid's own suggestion, to protect Hoyt if ever his ownership was questioned, the Kid went to the counter of the Howard and McMasters' store and wrote out a bill of sale. He signed it and had it witnessed by the two storekeepers.

Doctor Hoyt was interested to learn, many years later, that this was a typical bit of "Billy the Kid generosity"—for that race horse was the property of Sheriff Brady, whom the Kid's gang had murdered in Lincoln!

In Tascosa, Middleton, Brown and Wayt left the Kid. He and O'Phalliard went back to Fort Sumner. There, he got new recruits for the band which was to gravely annoy the cowmen of New Mexico and the Panhandle. Dave Rudabaugh was one of them.

PRESIDENT HAYES had replaced Axtell, the Murphy-partizan, with General Lew Wallace, author of *Ben Hur*. The new governor of the territory held conferences with prominents of both factions of the Lincoln County War. But he had little luck at clearing up the complicated task which confronted him.

On November 13, 1878, the Governor issued a proclamation, granting amnesty to all the men who had fought in the Lincoln County War, provided they would go peaceably home and lay down their weapons. Apparently, this did not apply to the Kid precisely as it applied to others of the warriors. At any rate the Kid seems to have ignored it for the time being.

In December he was "home" again—back in Fort Sumner. And in that same month, with Tom O'Phalliard siding him he rode down to Lincoln and was there arrested by Sheriff George Kimbrell who held warrants for him. He was put into jail, but soon got out and returned to Sumner. The gang continued its raids on the various ranches of the country.

February of 1879 saw the Kid and Jesse Evans shaking hands in Lincoln Plaza. Evans was then working for James Dolan as a cowboy and had come to town with his employer and one William Campbell, driving a herd of cattle intended for Thomas B. Catron. After some harsh words, Jesse and the Kid decided to call off their enmity. The party went over to a saloon and had drinks.

Coming out, they met Mrs. McSween's lawyer, a man named Chapman from Las Vegas. Campbell, pretty drunk, ordered the lawyer to dance on the sidewalk. Chapman refused and Campbell shot him dead.

Never again was the Kid to see Jesse Evans and, somehow, it seems a pity. . . . For these two were at the time probably—as Florencio Chavez has indicated—the two outstanding gun experts of the neighborhood. Jesse always claimed that the Kid *might* beat him at rifle shooting, but he said that he "didn't take off his hat to anybody in the world, when it came to handling a six-shooter" and certainly he and the Kid never seemed over-anxious to try out their skill upon each other.

The next month—March—some of Governor Wallace's messages seem to have got to the Kid. He came from Fort Sumner over to the little *plazita* of San Patricio and he and the Governor exchanged letters. By this time Wallace knew that there could be no real peace and quiet in New Mexico, so long as the Kid was free to raid up and down, stealing horses and cattle. Killings must come out of these rustling expeditions, and one killing inevitably leads to another. Wallace was very anxious to have the Kid surrender, stand trial, then—if convicted—Wallace promised to pardon him.

The Kid was as suspicious as any lobo. But, at last, Wallace prevailed upon the young outlaw to talk to him. And that brings us rather naturally to certain "biographers." . . .

FOUR OR FIVE years ago, a literary stranger came wandering through the Lincoln country, hunting material for a book on Billy the Kid. He was not among us long, but after he went away he produced a very detailed and thrilling and factual (and most readable!) "biography." The only draw-back we who live here find, about this saga, is its inaccuracy in most details. Dramatic writing does not relieve a historian of all necessity for facts.

Very vividly, this writer describes the Kid's visit to Governor Wallace in Lincoln. He tells how the Governor sat with General Hatch and Juan Patron and a group of Army officers, on a Lincoln porch; how they saw a lone horseman riding slowly toward them through Lincoln's main street; and how Patron remarked:

"That's the Kid!"

He goes on, then, to tell how the Kid looked grimly at the enemy-men before the Murphy store, keeping one hand upon his six-shooter, the other upon a cocked Winchester that cuddled across his lap. Vivid, too, is his description of the Governor's paternal interest in the young outlaw. He "recounts" most emotionally Wallace's appeal to the Kid to take off his guns and settle down, offering absolute amnesty to the Kid, and how the Kid replied—"as Rob Roy might have done"—that this was his native country and he would neither leave it nor unbuckle his gun-belts.

But—alas! for all this vivid writing. There still exist letters that passed between Governor Wallace and the Kid and Wallace's own account of his interview with the Kid.

In reality, there was no cool, grim running of the gauntlet of the Murphy men, in bright daylight. Wallace wanted no publicity as the Kid came in to tell him the truth about Lawyer Chapman's killing in Lincoln street, by the Dolan man—Campbell. So he wrote to the Kid:

"Come to the house of old Squire Wilson at nine o'clock next Monday night, alone. Not his office, but his residence. Follow along the foot of the mountain south of the town. Come in on that side and knock at the east door. . . .

"The object of the meeting at Squire Wilson's is to arrange the matter in a way to make your life safe. To do that the most secrecy is to be used. *So come alone.* Don't tell anybody—not a living soul—where you are coming or the object. . . ."

And the Kid answered that he would come and described in detail the way in which he was to be captured!

Eventually, he came in and in the room at Squire Wilson's house he met only Governor Wallace and the Squire. They arranged there, that night, how Sheriff Kimbrell was to arrest him. Evidently, the Kid trusted Wallace to pardon him if he were convicted in the courts.

It is a matter of record that he was arrested March 21, 1879 and that, at the April term of the court, he was in custody. He plead "not guilty" to the murder of Sheriff Brady and Deputy Hindman. Then, that same month, he walked calmly out of the Lincoln jail. Either he did not like confinement, or he had decided that his trust was better placed in his own six-shooter than in the promises of a politician like Governor Wallace. But, that same month, he was at Fort Sumner, testifying in the court of inquiry that was investigating Colonel Dudley's actions during the burning of the McSween house.

And then the gang went raiding up and down. The Kid had a special hatred, now, for John Chisum. In October he ran off more than a hundred head of Chisum's cattle and the gang rebranded these and turned them out on the range to let the new marks heal. Later, they rounded up the stock and sold them to Colorado buyers at Alamogordo.

1880 was to be a busy year for the Kid. Incidentally, it was a busy year for another man residing at Fort Sumner who was a fairly friendly acquaintance of the Kid. This second man was an ex-buffalo hunter, ex-cowboy, just then partner of Beaver Smith in a store-saloon. His name was Pat Garrett and he was nine years older than the Kid.

Joe Grant helped to make 1880 interesting for the Kid from the very beginning. Perhaps that was not his real name, but it was the "go-by" he gave when he came riding into Fort Sumner in January. He said that he came from Texas and he posed as a hard case. There seems small reason to doubt that there were some notches on his six-shooter. Grant made it a point to cultivate the Kid and his bunch from the moment of his arrival in Sumner.

One day in Hargrove's saloon in Sumner Grant got pretty thoroughly drunk. The Kid, with Barney Mason and James Chisum, came into the saloon. Grant was flourishing a pistol taken from a man there. The Kid got hold of it. . . . Presently, Grant went behind the bar. He began knocking glassware around with his pistol. Apparently, he was merely using his six-shooter as a handy club. But the Kid seems not to have been fooled by the pretense. There stood Grant, gun in hand, while everyone else in the place must go through the motion of the draw to get into action if need arose.

Grant pretended to mistake James Chisum. He said that he was "going to kill the old son of a bitch." The Kid interfered. He told Grant that this was James Chisum, not John. But Grant jerked up his pistol, snarling at the Kid. He let the hammer drop. But in the moment of handling it, the Kid had revolved the cylinder deftly. Now, the firing pin struck upon an empty chamber. The Kid whipped out his own gun and shot Grant through the head.

This exhibition proved more than the Kid's "triggernometry": It revealed his brain-workings. That Grant intended to kill him—and thereby make a reputation for himself—could not have been a mystery to the Kid, for when Grant was in his cups he let fall various remarks which revealed plainly the reason for his coming to Fort Sumner in the beginning. And he was out-guessed, out-maneuvered, and he died. . . .

Back and forth, and up and down, the Kid and his men rode like so many raiding Arabs. They ran off Indian horses from the Mescalero Reservation; they lifted Panhandle cattle up around Los Portales; they swept little ranches clean of stock. Then they took cattle, horses—like so many honest dealers—into Tularosa, Alamogordo, White Oaks, and sold them there.

The cold New Mexican Spring became the hot New Mexican Summer; Summer became Fall; and at last November came. The month was to be memorable in the annals of the Kid for two separate occurrences:

About the middle of the month the Kid, with O'Phalliard, Tom Pickett and Buck Edwards, stole eight fine horses and traded four of them to Rancher Jim Greathouse. Two, they turned out, and two they rode. Toward the end of November they were near the edge of White Oaks, attempting to run off some horses of J. B. Bell.

Deputy Sheriff William Hudgens organized a posse and set out on the trail of the gang. He trailed the Kid's party to Coyote Springs and there opened fire on the outlaws. After a quick exchange of shots, the Kid's bunch ran. The casualties were two horses killed, one being that which the Kid was riding.

Though the Kid took it on the run from Coyote Springs, he was not disposed to let this unusual, almost insulting, attack on him pass quietly. He came into White Oaks the very next day riding quite boldly. It was November 23, the Kid's twentieth birthday. He saw an enemy, one Jim Redmond, standing in front of Deputy Will Hudgens' saloon. He took a shot at Redmond but missed. As he rode fast out of town, he ran into Jimmy Carlyle and J. B. Bell, who had been in Hudgens' posse at Coyote Springs. The Kid shot at the two possemen and they returned his fire with enthusiasm. But neither side scored a hit.

The other "November event" of importance to the Kid—more important, as it turned out than even this "rebellion" of the citizens—was the election of Pat Garrett as sheriff of Lincoln County.

Garrett had moved into Roswell from Fort Sumner. Captain Lea, Chisum and other leading men of the country had decided that 1880-conditions were intolerable. They were tired of the Kid bulldozing peace officers, raiding with a free hand up and down the territory. For that matter, the Panhandle cowmen over at Tascosa had also reached the conclusion that something had to be done about the cow-thieves who came raiding from New Mexico. They had sent a stock detective named Stewart over into the Territory, to locate and identify the thieves, with a view of taking the law into their own hands.

Garrett had just begun to look around the country and make his plans for policing it, in November. So it was that Hudgens had been permitted to strike the first real blow at the Kid. It fell to Constable Longworth to make the second attack upon the Kid's apparent immunity. November 26th, Longworth raised a posse and went out to the Greathouse ranch, forty miles from White Oaks on the Las Vegas road. The posse arrived early in the cold morning of the 27th. Longworth had a good posse behind him. William Hudgens and his brother John had come, with James Watts, John Mosby, James Brent, J. P. Langston, Ed Bonnell, W. G. Dorsey, J. B. Bell, J. P. Eaker, Charles Kelly and Jimmy Carlyle.

With the first gray light of the November day, the posse saw a cook known to them come out of the house. Eaker and Brent captured him. The prisoner told them that the Kid, Billy Wilson and Dave Rudabaugh were in the house. Hudgens then scribbled a note and sent it by the cook into the house. It was addressed to the Kid and ordered him to surrender. The cook then came back accompanied by Greathouse and the two men bore the Kid's reply, which was to the effect that the only way that posse could take him would be dead.

Billy Wilson was in the house with the Kid and Hudgens, knowing that Wilson was charged with nothing more serious than counterfeiting, called to him to come out. He promised Wilson that if, after talking the matter over, he did not wish to surrender, he could go safely back inside. But the Kid and Dave Rudabaugh —both of whom were wanted for capital crimes—persuaded Wilson against surrendering. Wilson called to the posse-men that if Jimmy Carlyle would come in for a talk, he might surrender. He promised that Carlyle would be permitted to return as soon as the talk was over.

Carlyle insisted against the advice of the other men on going in to talk to Wilson. He laid down his weapons and went inside. When he got in he found the Kid's

party pretty well under the influence of the whisky
Greathouse had provided for their entertainment.

He was not permitted to talk to Wilson about surrendering. Instead, the Kid threatened to kill him. Time
wore on and the men outside waited impatiently for
Carlyle's return. The young blacksmith was the close
friend of most of them and they did not trust the Kid's
good faith. At last they sent a message into the house by
the cook: If Carlyle were not out within ten minutes,
Greathouse—the gang's friend—would be instantly
killed. The Kid sent back an answer:

"Carlyle is safe enough. But we won't let him go,
just yet. If we hear a shot from outside, we will know
that you have killed Greathouse and we will pay you
back by killing Carlyle."

Carlyle knew the contents of this answer. So, when a
shot was accidentally fired outside by a posseman,
doubtless Carlyle believed that Greathouse had been
killed, and that in a moment the Kid, Rudabaugh and
the others would kill him. He made a dash for a window,
crashed through and fell dead as the gang poured lead
into his back.

HALF-HEARTED and amateurish attempts to rid the
territory of the Kid and his gang were about over now.
That long-legged, slow-spoken, implacable and fearless
buffalo hunter, Pat Garrett, was in fact and in name
the sheriff of Lincoln County. He had been making his
plans for the speedy capture, or killing, of the Kid.
Carlyle's murder was poor diplomacy. "Jimmy" had
made many friends and now even those who had been
the Kid's apologists hardened against him.

Too, the feud between the Murphy faction and Mc-
Sween had burned out. Murphy was dead; McSween was
dead. The Kid was no longer leader of a fighting faction
in what might be called a "war." He was a plain cowthief, a killer as dangerous as a wolf. Garrett got help
that would never have been proffered him six months,
even three months, before.

The Kid, with Rudabaugh, and Wilson, took advantage of the posse's temporary withdrawal to get away from Greathouse's. Another posse came up and burned the house when they found the outlaws had gone. The Kid's party made Anton Chico afoot. Greathouse supplied them with horses, there, and they rode out, south, to Las Cañaditas. Here Tom O'Phalliard, Charley Bowdre and Tom Pickett joined them.

Garrett now really began to hound the Kid. The Panhandle cowmen had sent into the territory not only the stock detective, Stewart, but also a bunch of fighting Texas cowboys from the LX, the Frying Pan, the LS, the LIT and other outfits along the Canadian River. Garrett moved back and forth, with his brother-in-law, Barney Mason, trying to cut the Kid's trail. He recovered stock they had stolen, narrowly missed killing or capturing O'Phalliard in a running battle, and about the 15th of December he and Stewart came upon the Canadian River warriors, who were moving to recover Panhandle cattle stolen by the Kid at Los Portales.

Garrett and Stewart explained to the cowboys that they were to go down to Sumner and watch for the Kid. Lon Chambers, Lee Hall, Jim East, and three men known only by their nicknames of "Poker Tom," "the Animal," and "Tenderfoot Bob," were spared by Charley Siringo, the wagon-boss, to go with them. Garrett led his posse toward Fort Sumner. He had learned that the Kid had withdrawn from Sumner when he heard that Garrett and Mason were headed that way. Garrett did not believe that the Kid knew of his reinforcements under Stewart. He expected the outlaws to come back. The weather was bitter. Sumner was a comfortable, familiar place. It was, in a sense, the Kid's "home town."

Garrett's Panhandle cowboys had been friendly with the Kid up at Tascosa the Fall before. But that made no difference now. He had stolen their employers' cattle and all the drinks that they had had with him counted for nothing. He had gone one way on the trail, they had gone another. They took station in Fort Sumner as Garrett directed them, looked to the hang of their weapons.

Dark came. Garrett was watching the old hospital in which Charley Bowdre's Mexican wife occupied a room, for he figured that the party would come there first. Garrett's men played poker while they waited for the gang to come in. The night was very cold. Snow was falling, which made for better light outside. The room in which the posse watched was crowded, for Garrett had gathered in all the loose Mexicans he found wandering about town. None of these would spoil his plans if he could help it! None would carry word to the Kid that a posse waited for him. The poker game went on in a corner. It was almost eight o'clock. Lon Chambers came up to the door.

"Pat!" he called. "Somebody's coming!"

Garrett threw his hand down upon the blanket. He got up, Winchester in hand. The cowboys looked at him.

"Get your guns, boys," he said in his slow drawl. "Nobody but the men we want would be riding at this time of night."

One of the Mexicans followed Garrett out and the two joined Lon Chambers, who was standing guard at the side of the hospital. Barney Mason led Jim East and the others around the building, to cut off the gang if they should try to get into the plaza.

Through the snowflakes, their horses black silhouettes against the white ground, the little body of riders was plain. Garrett could even recognize "Big Foot Tom" O'Phalliard's tall form in the lead.

He and Chambers and the Mexican, standing under the porch roof, hugged the wall. Harness was hanging on pegs, there. It helped to shelter them from sight of the men approaching.

"That's him!" Garrett whispered to Chambers.

The riders came on. The head of O'Phalliard's horse poked under the roof of the porch. Garrett stepped forward then:

"*Halt!*" he ordered.

O'Phalliard's hand jerked toward his pistol, but before he could draw both Garrett and Chambers fired.

O'Phalliard's horse whirled and ran for a hundred yards or so, with the tall cowboy rocking in the saddle. Garrett shifted aim flashingly to fire at Pickett, next man of the gang. But his eyes were blinded by the retained vision of the flash of Chambers' shot. He missed and Pickett jerked his horse around and galloped "screaming as if he had been killed" toward the Kid and Bowdre and Billy Wilson. These halted with the first shot. Now, all of them raced away, followed by the fire of Jim East and the rest of Garrett's party. O'Phalliard's groans were heard, even in that uproar. He did not follow his friends. Instead, he turned his horse and rode back toward Garrett.

"Don't shoot, Garrett. I am killed," he groaned. He came closer and Garrett, suspecting a trick, barked at him: "Throw up your hands!"

O'Phalliard told him that he was dying; that he could not lift his hands. He begged Garrett to take him down from the saddle and let him die.

So they eased "Big Foot Tom" down from the saddle for the last time. They carried him into the old hospital. O'Phalliard knew that he was dying. He asked Barney Mason to have a letter written to his people in Texas, telling of his death.

Garrett eyed the groaning cowboy very grimly. He was disappointed. He had wanted the Kid and he had only bagged an unimportant subordinate. His mind ran over the problem, shifting details, speculating as to the Kid's probable next move. He hardly heard Barney Mason telling O'Phalliard to "take his medicine." Three-quarters of an hour later, O'Phalliard was dead. He might have been the nameless cowboy of the ballad and said, with truth—

> "Once in the saddle I used to go dancing
> Once in the saddle I used to go gay. . .
> Got shot in the breast and I'm dying today . . ."

The attack in Sumner was a heavy assault upon the Kid's pride and his confidence. He had strutted up and down Sumner, a "leading citizen." He had been the *beau* of the Mexican beauties of the town, honoring them by accepting their favors, fathering their children. He had swaggered it in the saloons, with none to face him. And now, Pat Garrett, whom he had laughed at, drunk with, had put on a star and come calmly into Sumner and sent him flying out!

Incidentally, but for a typical display of Kid-caution, Garrett would have had the Kid, not O'Phalliard, dying on the snow. The Kid told Garrett afterward that he "smelled a trap" in Sumner. And no trap would ever close on *him* if he could have what the moderns call a "fall guy"! He, not "Big Foot Tom," had been in the lead. But when they came to Sumner's edge, he got nervous, fell back:

"I wanted a chew of tobacco," he told Garrett—grinning. "I remembered that Wilson had some that was good and he was riding in the rear. So I went back—after that tobacco, of course."

From ranchers of the neighborhood, Garrett learned of the demoralized condition, the hangdog appearance, of the gang. He took his posse out to Brazil's ranch, to look for the Kid. But the house was vacant and they pushed on.

Presently, Garrett was sure that the Kid intended to hole up at the old stone house abandoned by Alejandro Perea, at Stinking Springs. And when they came quietly up to the deserted house, they knew that Garrett's "hunch" was good. Three horses were tied outside. Garrett knew that there were four men with the Kid. That meant that the Kid and one other had taken their horses inside the house.

Garrett told his party that he intended to kill the Kid on sight. The Kid had sent his one-time friend word that he would never surrender, that it was a business of "shoot on sight." Garrett did not mean to be last to pull trigger. And, too, if he killed the Kid, the others in the gang would doubtless surrender.

Gray light came slowly to the posse shivering outside that ruined stone cabin. Through the opening where once had hung a door, a man came. He was dressed exactly like the Kid. Garrett stared strainedly. In that chill half-light it looked like the Kid. The lank sheriff gave his men the signal by lifting gun to shoulder. Seven shots were fired. The echoes rang up and down with the sound of sheets of glass breaking. The man spun about and staggered back into the house. Billy Wilson lifted up his voice inside:

"Garrett! You killed Bowdre. He wants to come out."

"All right!" Garrett answered. "Let him *come* out—with his hands 'way up!"

As Bowdre started through the door, the Kid reached down, pulled Bowdre's cartridge belt around so that his pistol was in front. He pushed him outside:

"They've murdered you, Charlie," he said. "Kill some of the sons of bitches before you die!"

But Bowdre was too far gone to be looking for revenge, now. He reeled out with his hands lifted, came staggering toward Garrett.

"I wish—" Bowdre muttered. "I wish—"

But what it was he wished, he never said. He began to sway. Garrett caught him and eased him to the ground. He died almost immediately.

The light was growing stronger. The men outside watched the stone house. Then one of the ropes by which the horses were secured began to shake. Garrett lifted his rifle, aimed at that rope, then shook his head. He knew that he could not hit that thin, rippling target. Instead, he shot at the horse and dropped the animal dead across the door.

Then, he shot at the ropes holding the remaining two horses.

The old buffalo hunter, trained in a marksmanship that would shame the average target-shot today, made nothing of severing those two ropes with bullets. The

horses walked quietly off; came to the hands of the posse-
men. Garrett felt better. So he called to the Kid:

"Well, Kid, how you feeling in there?" the sheriff
asked, with grim humor.

"Pretty well," the Kid answered in like vein. "But
we haven't any wood, to make a breakfast fire with."

"Why, that's easy to fix," Garrett told him. "Come
on out and get some. You want to act sociable, Kid!"

"No," the Kid yelled back. "My business is too
confining, right now. I haven't got time to be running
around."

Garrett grinned at Jim East, lifted his voice again:

"Didn't you fellows forget part of your program
yesterday?" he inquired. "The way we heard it, your
bunch was to come in on us at Fort Sumner from a direction we wouldn't expect, then give us a square fight, and
after you had set us afoot, run us down the Pecos."

The rancher, Brazil, had told Garrett as much. This
remark—proving to the Kid that somebody he had
trusted had carried his boasting to the sheriff—seemed to
make him uneasy. He would not continue the banter, at
which he was normally quite adept.

Garrett and half his men went up to Wilcox's ranch,
three miles away, and ate breakfast. When Garrett's
party got back, Stewart took the rest of the posse over to
the ranch. Garrett had arranged with Wilcox to send
food and wood and horse feed over to the stone house. He
intended to stay there until he had captured or killed the
Kid's party. The day wore on quietly. In midafternoon,
the men inside drove out the two horses. The posse
captured them, as they had caught the other two. An
hour later, Wilcox's wagon came up with food and
wood. The posse built their fire and began to cook.

The odor of frying bacon, boiling coffee, had instant
effect upon the surrounded gang. Rudabaugh called to
Garrett:

"We want to surrender!"

"All right! You can all come out—with your hands
up," Garrett told him.

Rudabaugh came outside. He said the Kid and the others would surrender, if Garrett guaranteed protection from mob violence. Garrett made the guarantee. Rudabaugh went back inside and presently the Kid, Billy Wilson, Pickett and Rudabaugh walked out with their hands in air. The posse-men disarmed them, fed them, and took them back to Wilcox's.

A wagon went from the ranch to the stone house, brought in Bowdre's body and took it to Fort Sumner. He was buried beside Tom O'Phalliard.

By sundown, Garrett, with Stewart, Barney Mason, Jim East and Poker Tom, had the ironed prisoners on the road to Las Vegas.

The Kid was gay enough, on the trip back. He complimented Garrett on the shot which had killed the horse in the door of the cabin. But for that, he and at least one other would have ridden the two horses out of the house and off. But his racing mare would not cross the dead animal.

From Fort Sumner, Garrett took the prisoners to Gearhart's Ranch. There they stayed overnight, and made Puerta de Luna in early afternoon of December 25th. The storekeeper, Grzelachowski, gave them their Christmas dinner.

By afternoon of the next day, Garrett was taking his prisoners through a sullen crowd at Las Vegas, toward the jail. He was heading for Santa Fé, for U. S. warrants were out against all the prisoners but Pickett.

The temper of Las Vegas' people was ugly. Rudabaugh had killed the jailor here and it was feared that either the authorities would insist upon having him left for trial in San Miguel County, or that the Mexican population would try to lynch the prisoners. Garrett forestalled any official move by swearing out an affidavit to the effect that Rudabaugh was in transit under the aegis of a federal warrant.

This done, the grim sheriff felt his mind more or less at ease. No matter how threatening the mob might become, six-shooters and Winchesters would halt them.

Garrett had with him, as guards, Stewart the stock detective, Michael Cosgrove, the mail contractor, and Barney Mason. They boarded the train and when heavily armed Mexicans began to show signs of rushing the officers Garrett told his prisoners that it looked like a fight.

"If it comes off," he added grimly, "I'll give vou fellows back your guns and let you take a hand."

The Kid grinned:

"All right, Pat. All I want is a six-shooter."

But the Mexicans could not stiffen themselves to the point of facing those Anglos with their well known deadliness at fighting. They did delay the train's departure for forty-five minutes by covering the engineer with their guns. Finally, Mollay, a deputy U. S. marshal, crawled into the cab and jerked the throttle open.

In Santa Fé the prisoners were jailed and immediately began to attempt to escape. They had tunneled almost out of the jail when their work was discovered.

Rudabaugh drops out of the picture, now. Sent to the Vegas jail to stand trial for murder of the San Miguel County jailor, he was convicted, sentenced to death, but appealed and while awaiting action escaped and was never seen again in New Mexico.

The Kid was sent down to Mesilla—"Old Mesilla," we call it today, as we turn toward it from the highway between El Paso and Las Cruces and move toward the Rio Grande over a dirt road, to stop at last before the long, low 'dobe building in which Judge Bristol held court that March of 1881.

The last part of the Kid's journey was made by stage. Jim Gillett was going to Socorro with a prisoner and when his stage met the other it stopped while the drivers talked.

"I saw a pleasant looking young man on the back seat. I didn't pay a great deal of attention to him, for I was watching Enofre Baca pretty closely and, too, I couldn't see any official jewelry on this boy. Then our stage driver leaned to me and whispered that this nice looking young man was the notorious killer, Billy the Kid. . . ."

Judge Bristol assigned Judge Ira Leonard to defend the Kid. The first charge was that he had murdered Buckshot Roberts on the Mescalero Reservation, a Government area. Judge Leonard brought forward the information that, while Roberts *had* been killed within the confines of the Reservation, the spot upon which he had died was not Government property, but was the private holding of Doctor Blazer. He questioned the jurisdiction of the Federal Court and made a motion to quash the indictment. Judge Bristol agreed and the indictment was quashed April 6th, 1881. But, Bristol immediately ordered the Kid to stand trial for the murder of Sheriff Brady at Lincoln in April, 1878.

So, on the morning of April 8th, the guards came into court again, with the slender figure of the Kid between them, his leg-irons clanking, his slender, deadly hands held in front of him by the shining circlets of the handcuffs. Again, Judge Bristol must appoint counsel for him. He called upon John D. Ball and Judge A. J. Fountain (who was himself to be the victim of murderers a few years later).

The first day was occupied in the selection of the jury, but by evening of the second day, the all-Mexican jury had the case—and made short work of it. The Kid was found guilty.

They brought him back into court, April 13th, and judge Bristol sentenced him to be returned to Lincoln Jail and there between the hours of nine a.m. and three p.m. to be hanged.

The Kid rather expected Governor Wallace to pardon him and, in the days to come, when Wallace's silence was unbroken he became very bitter. With some justification, he felt that he, alone, was being executed, being made the demanded sacrifice for all the Lincoln County killings.

Again the Kid was taken to Lincoln. One of his guards was Robert Ollinger, who had been a close friend of that Bob Beckwith who had murdered McSween, and who had died under the Kid's lead that night in Lincoln. He hated the Kid. He drew ghoulish pictures of the Kid kicking at the end of a hangman's rope. He tried to provoke the prisoner into attempting escape so that he could shoot him down. And the Kid made no secret of his like-hatred for the long-haired and boastful Ollinger.

Lincoln County had just bought the old Murphy & Dolan store for use as a courthouse. Pat Garrett imprisoned the Kid on the second floor. All that he could do was to keep irons on the Kid's hands and feet and set guards over him. J. W. Bell was one guard, and Ollinger the other. Bell and the Kid got along well enough, but Ollinger continued hounding the prisoner.

On the evening of April 28th, the Kid and Bell sat alone in the room that was used for jail. Ollinger and the other prisoners were across the street at supper. The Kid looked at Bell.

"I want to go out in the yard," he said.

The good natured Bell got up without objection. He and the prisoner went out into the hall and down the narrow stair to the yard. Coming back the Kid walked ahead. The chain connecting his shackles was long. He walked fast, entered the building and, momentarily out of sight of Bell, raced up the stairs, whirled at the landing, leaped up the last flight and hurled himself at the door of a small room used by Garrett as a sort of armory. That door was locked but the ram of the Kid's shoulder burst it open. He snatched up a loaded six-shooter and ran back to the stair head. Bell, still unalarmed, had just reached the landing. The Kid fired at him and missed, yet did not miss. His slug struck the wall twelve feet below almost at Bell's side, ricocheted and pierced the deputy sheriff's body. Bell spun about and half fell back down the stairs to the yard, staggered a few steps and fell dead.

The Kid rushed then into Garrett's office. There was Ollinger's fine double-barreled shotgun. That very day the Kid had seen him load it—eighteen buckshot in each barrel.

"The fellow that gets them loads will know it," Ollinger had said with a long meaning stare at the Kid.

"Be careful you ain't the fellow," the Kid had replied.

Now he snatched up the gun and ran to the east window. He was waiting for Ollinger.

Old Geiss, a sort of janitor, had seen Bell die. He ran out to meet Ollinger—who had heard the shot and was coming back across the street. He was at the gate leading into the yard.

"Bob, the Kid has just killed Bell!" Geiss yelled.

From above the Kid's voice came now, no less deadly for the laughing note in it.

"Hello!" the Kid called. And Ollinger's head jerked.

"Yes, and he has killed me, too!" he said.

The shotgun roared and Ollinger fell over dead. Those eighteen buckshot, which he had so carefully put into the barrel of his gun, were in his body and not the Kid's, as there is small doubt he hoped they would be.

Now the Kid went out to the gallery that overlooked the street. He could see Ollinger's body. He fired the other barrel into it, broke the shotgun over the gallery rail and flung the pieces at the corpse. He yelled at Geiss, ordering him to bring up a file, then to get out Billy Burt's horse and saddle it.

Geiss flung up the file and went for the deputy clerk's fast horse. He had trouble with the nervous animal. The Kid sat in a window and filed away at one shackle while the old man tried to get a saddle on Burt's horse.

He was up there an hour after he had killed Ollinger. He was like a maniac or a drunken man. He sang, he danced, he whistled, he yelled. At last, he was in the saddle, riding out of town. He had a Winchester and two revolvers.

Pat Garrett was over in White Oaks collecting taxes. He heard of the Kid's escape next day, by letter. He came back and proceeded quietly, methodically, to pick up the trail.

THE KID was here, there, everywhere, for the next couple of months. Cow-camps, sheep-camps, even the friendly 'dobe houses of Fort Sumner, saw him. Garrett had no trouble in *hearing* about the Kid's visits. But he could never quite catch up with him.

This is perhaps the most appealing part of the Kid's career. Partly from fear, or course, but also out of loyalty to him, men and women fed him, sheltered him, lied for him. Men and women, both—but especially women. . . .

He would not leave that neighborhood. He could have ridden out of the country, clean. He would not do it.

Garrett was now joined by another Canadian River stock detective, John W. Poe.

On the night of July 13, 1881, Garrett, with Poe and his deputy "Tip" McKinney, came riding up to the outskirts of Fort Sumner. Poe had scouted the town that day, learning nothing. But he had a strong feeling that the Kid was in the neighborhood. The very vehemence with which certain citizens said that he must be elsewhere had made Poe certain. Garrett decided to go quietly into town and talk with Pete Maxwell, the big stockman.

They left their horses at the edge of town, in the camp of one Jacobs, an old friend of Poe's. They went afoot, then, to the Maxwell house—one of the buildings of the fort's old "Officer's Row." Garrett left Poe and McKinney on the porch. He went inside very quietly, into Pete Maxwell's bedroom at the corner of the house.

It was nearly midnight now. Maxwell was in bed. Garrett crossed the room and sat down. He asked Maxwell in a low voice what he knew about the Kid.

"Well, Pat, confidentially," Maxwell said cautiously, "he has been here, of course. But where he is at this moment I—I cannot say."

Garrett trusted Maxwell, but he knew the effect of the Kid's personality upon these people of Fort Sumner. He had had too many opportunities to witness the effect of the Kid's mere presence in a neighborhood. At Lincoln, had any other than the Kid killed two officers, he would not have ridden out of town. A volley of shots would have swept him out of the saddle.

Garrett sat there thinking. And at that moment a figure appeared in the doorway of the bedroom. Garrett looked up quickly. He could see that the man wore no hat and he had come too soundlessly into that door, to be wearing boots. His silhouette showed something like a knife outlined in his left hand, something that certainly was a pistol in his right hand. He came quickly, softly, toward Maxwell's bed. Garrett leaned a little.

"Who's that, Pete?" he whispered.

Maxwell made no answer. Perhaps the condition of his nerves did not permit an answer. Garrett was at a disadvantage. Here he was in a friendly house. He had left two men of his on the porch and this man must have come past them. It *must* have seemed to him incredible that this could be the Kid. The more logical thought was that this was some member of Maxwell's household, come into the old man's room on an errand.

Before Garrett could do anything, the man was almost at his elbow, leaning towards the bed, whispering:

"Pete! Who are those men?"

Then he realized that someone sat beside Maxwell's bed. He backed quickly across the room, the pistol rising in his right hand.

"*Quien es? Quien es?*" he cried. Maxwell whispered gaspingly to Garrett:

"*That's him!*"

And Garrett threw himself to the side, for he expected a shot at any moment. He jerked out his own gun, levelled it, fired at the Kid.

He heard the thud of the body striking the floor, heard a rattling, gasping noise, then silence.

Poe and McKinney came crowding into the doorway. Maxwell was up, now, rushing for the door. He was not even free of the bed clothes. He shouldered past McKinney and Poe. The three officers made a light. The Kid sprawled motionless. . . .

AND SO BILLY the Kid died with a gun in his hand. For
once he had been the victim, not the beneficiary, of luck.
He, like Garrett, was at a disadvantage in Maxwell's
bedroom. He, like Garrett, must have believed that anyone sitting in that room was logically a friend of
Maxwell's. It was simply that "the breaks" were this
time with the other man, not with the Kid.

How many notches were on his tally, when he died?
Tradition credits him with twenty-one—a death for each
year of his hectic life.

> "There are twenty-one men I have put bullets through,
> And Sheriff Pat Garrett shall make twenty-two. . ."

But, in a good many years of study, I have found
tradition a gossipy, exaggerating jade. Statistics, all too
often, blow great holes in the legends. And so it is with
the Kid's record, when we demand *evidence* and reject
hearsay. I can credit him with no more than eight
notches, for killings unquestionably done by his own
hand—

> The tough at Silver City;
> The soldier-blacksmith at Fort Bowie;
> Billy Morton and Frank Baker;
> Bob Beckwith;
> Joe Grant, the "bad man"; and
> Bell and Ollinger.

True, he was indicted for other killings—for that of
Buckshot Roberts and Sheriff Brady. But Charley Bowdre had shot Roberts through the body—a fatal wound.
The Kid was merely one of the party firing upon the
officers from behind the wall, joining in the volley that
killed Brady and Hindman. Whose bullets actually
caused these deaths, nobody will ever know.

The Kid is accused of Joe Bernstein's murder—and
with equal vehemence old-timers claim that he did not
fire the shot. The Kid is said to have admitted this
killing—and said to have denied it.

Jimmy Carlyle possibly fell under the Kid's lead, as he
leaped from the window at Greathouse's ranch. But—"a
fusillade" from the men in the house killed him. There is

no more reason to believe the Kid was Carlyle's murderer than to believe that it was Rudabaugh or Wilson who committed that cowardly and treacherous murder.

Then, of course, there were the three Apaches murdered near Fort Bowie by the Kid and "Alias"—but even the fact that three Indians were murdered is a matter of pure conjecture, unprovable.

The Mexicans "slain" by the Kid in Sonora and Chihuahua are of the same legendary breed. So are the Apaches he and O'Keefe are supposed to have killed in the Guadalupes.

Analyzing the Kid's "triggernometry," another quality of it is noted:

His tally of killings is "pretty sorry" by contrast with that of almost any other noted gunman.

He killed Beckwith in fair fight—but no particular *gunskill* was shown. He let go a burst of shots at the men seen vaguely above a wall's top. A lucky slug caught Beckwith. Any pistolman knows that sort of lucky accident.

Brady, Carlyle, Bernstein (if he killed them!), Baker and Morton—these died in what the Old West called "bush-whackings" or "dry-gulchings." Shooting at unsuspecting or helpless targets is *not* man-to-man gunplay.

Which leaves the Kid only one episode, on which to build his reputation for triggernometry—the affair with the bad man at Fort Sumner. And he shows very little, here, to enhance his fame! He was fast on the draw, a good shot, the old-timers tell me. But—he preferred not to have a row with Joe Grant on a "who's quickest?" basis. He preferred to get hold of Grant's gun, twirl the cylinder, assure himself of the first shot.

I wish that he had gone straight up to Joe Grant, as John Ringo went up to the "ferocious Earps" in Tombstone, to say:

"Come on! Let's shoot this out!"

But he did not. Nor have I ever found any incident in his record to make me alter that opinion of him which I have been voicing for years—that he was tricky, deadly, but a "sure-thing" killer; that as a gunman he was vastly over-rated. Pat Garrett said judicially that he was brave, a good shot—but no better, as he was no braver, than many another of his day.

An old sheriff who knew the Kid (and knew Garrett) when neither was notorious, says:

"Billy was absolutely the dangerousest man ever hit New Mexico. There never was nobody so poison to monkey with. He was a fine fellow—if he liked you. Jolly and good company. If he liked you, he'd give you his last two-bits and go right out and steal another one from somebody. I remember one time he give Pat Garrett his horse and saddle and bedding and had to steal another outfit for himself. That was when Pat first come off the buffalo range and was going to be a cowboy for Maxwell.

"But, if Billy never liked you, he was out to get you and he didn't care how he done it. He was not bothered by any fine points of etiquette, when it come to killing you."

A lot of nonsense has been talked about Garrett "taking advantage of the Kid"—mostly talked by those who know nothing much about the business. I have little patience with this point of view. When Garrett recognized the Kid's voice, there in Pete Maxwell's bedroom, he knew that if the Kid recognized *him*, there would be a shot. Like a sensible man, he shot first.

THAT LITERARY WANDERER in our midst, of whom I have spoken before, has written a very dramatic account of the reaction of Fort Sumner to the Kid's death. He tells how sullen groups stood around, remarking furiously that *Pobrecito Billee* had been given no chance; that they should go kill Garrett and Poe and McKinney. And how, next morning (the avengers having apparently been able to restrain themselves) they hurled savage imprecations after Garrett and his companions as they rode out toward Roswell.

Perhaps it is good literary technique to cover absence of fact by "vivid writing" but this particular story falls very quickly flat before a brief official document—the report of the coroner's jury. Alas for vivid writing! It does not bear out our Literary Stranger's tale about the community's sentiment.

That jury, composed of Fort Sumner men, had to go out of that room with their verdict known, and continue to live right there in Sumner. And if that verdict did not mirror the opinion of at least a majority of Sumner people, life for those jurymen was going to be a rocky road. It is logical, then, to assume that the verdict would not too radically offend the community.

And that verdict ran to the effect that this was a justifiable homicide, committed by an officer in the execution of his legal duty. More! Gratuitously, that jury added:

"And (we) are united in opinion that the gratitude of all the community is due to said Garrett for his action and that he deserves to be compensated."

Occasionally, we hear it whispered down here that the "killing" was merely "a put-up job," that the Kid still lives in Mexico. I heard that tale only yesterday on an El Paso street. I cannot credit it. Too many who knew the Kid must have been fooled. Old Silva, who laid out the Kid's body for burial, laughed at it. So does Florencio Chavez, who liked the Kid, who fought with him.

"*No es verdad*," says Florencio. "It is not true. I am sure of that. These tales of his slipping away from Fort Sumner, they have come with recent years. My friend Billito, he is dead. He was in many ways a good boy. Not half so bad as many others of his time here, anyway; not half so black as some stories make him. I cannot help thinking softly of him."

CHAPTER VI · *Two-Gun Marshal*

DALLAS STOUDENMIRE

THE NEW, the American-style, El Paso was "born" in 1881. For in that year four railroads came shoving toward The Pass. With the news, men and women of all classes and conditions realized that this sleepy little 'dobe village on the wide, shallow Rio Grande was destined to become a place of wealth and importance. In '81, the town's record was pretty much the hectic history of every western "boom camp." For every day brought swarms of new settlers.

"Bankers and merchants, capitalists, real estate dealers, cattlemen, miners, railroad men, gamblers, saloon-keepers and sporting people of both sexes, flocked to the town," the old-timers say reminiscently of that day.

"El Paso Street, the town's only business thoroughfare, was like the midway at a world's fair," Captain "Jim" Gillett recalls.

"Uncle Ben" Dowell, the leading saloon-keeper, had presided over a city council in years past, but that gesture toward community government "hadn't *quite* got there," to give the cowboy verdict. Now, the dusty, half-forgotten, civic machinery was oiled up for another try at it. Of main importance here is the fact that the city council immediately appointed one George Campbell city marshal and gave him, for deputy, the outstanding drunkard of the community, Bill Johnson.

Campbell was from Young County in North Texas and had been a peace officer before. Nothing has ever been said that would imply doubt of his personal bravery, but he was gravely handicapped for impartial execution of a policeman's duties, by a close friendship with what was known as "the sporting crowd." He was particularly friendly with the Manning Brothers—Jim, Frank and Dr. G. F.

Like many another policeman in this condition, Campbell found it very difficult to police the town and make justified arrests without treading on the toes of his friends, or—which is always worse—of friends of his friends. The city council grew impatient at what they considered the waste of a perfectly good calaboose. They began to speak sharply to Campbell.

In his turn, Campbell had a complaint; He thought that the arduous duties of city marshal were worth a good deal more money than the council paid him. He demanded a raise in salary and the council took this as excellent excuse for dispensing with his services. Apparently, they moved on the theory that one man could do nothing just as efficiently as two, and at but half the expense.

So Bill Johnson was brought in and informed that he was city marshal *pro tem.;* that he would thereafter walk and act and drink as such. He seems to have received the elevation very modestly, not to say indifferently. Certainly, it made no difference in his conduct.

But Campbell's friends were annoyed by his deposition. He had been the sort of city marshal to completely suit them and anyone could see that Bill Johnson was not apt to hold the office very long. If he should be replaced by a stranger—well, it could easily prove highly inconvenient. So—"Get Campbell back his job!" was the cry.

The plan was to show the city fathers what a wicked town El Paso had come to be; how necessary it was that some strong hand grip the reins; how desirable that George Campbell be reinstated at the higher salary he had demanded. So they decided not only to shoot up El Paso but to shoot her up as she had never been shot up.

They chose their night and the word went around to the sporting crowd. And at the signal—pandemonium broke loose! The actual number of shots fired will never be known, but windows were smashed and doors splintered and property in general pretty thoroughly wrecked. Townspeople not in the confidence of the schemers, unsuspiciously moving about the streets, galloped madly for shelter.

The next day's sun rose upon a badly-skinned, thoroughly alarmed, community. Those responsible must have been thoroughly satisfied at sight of the results of their work. But they had overplayed their hand; they had done their job too thoroughly. Mayor Magoffin was resolved to have no more of such pistol-play. He sent a messenger down the Valley to that thriving village, Ysleta, where Captain George W. Baylor was encamped with "C" Company of the Texas Rangers.

Captain Baylor replied to the mayor's request for a police-detail by sending Corporal Jim Fitch and five men. Fresh from fighting Apaches, trailing murderers and horse-thieves, bucking bad men, the Rangers embarked upon the new duty as upon a vacation—and the work proved to be a mere formality. Texas is one place where a home-raised prophet is *with* honor—if he prophesy with the tongue of a Texas Ranger. So these bronzed and level-eyed young men merely walked about the streets looking thoughtfully at men and events, and the result was a great, an obvious, a downright conspicuous silence.

But Rangers can be used in such capacity for no more than an emergency. Mayor Magoffin and the council realized this. They looked about for a heavy-handed marshal who had "a front sight on his gun," but who had "thrown his spurs away."

So, toward the end of a week of Ranger-policing, the stage came in from New Mexico, bringing a blonde six-footer with chin like a great rough-hewn oak block, with a drooping yellow mustache and small deepset, steel-hard blue eyes. The word had gotten 'round and the town watched arrival of this big figure and his smaller companion very curiously.

"Dallas Stoudenmire; Confederate veteran; Texas Ranger. . . . " the whispers passed from those who knew to those who wished to know.

Stoudenmire presented himself to the city council. He had heard that they were looking for a city marshal. He was looking for a job as city marshal. It did seem to him that, in view of such a coincidence, some arrangement could be made. They questioned him, wanting no more such experiences as that with George Campbell. He gave his history very swiftly and that same day it appeared in the papers:

Born in Abafoil, Mason County, Alabama, he had served during the Civil War with the Fifty-Seventh Cavalry and Thirty-Third Alabama Regiment; wounded four times; surrendered with Joe E. Johnston at Greensboro, North Carolina; moved to Colorado County, Texas; served in Captain Waller's "B" Company of the Texas Rangers.

But, even more impressive than his record was the presence of the man himself. He was lion-like as his blue eyes turned slowly from one to another of the councilmen. They hired him and remarked that Bill Johnson had the keys to the calaboose. He nodded; said that he would see Johnson.

He found the marshal *pro tem.* in a saloon and informed him that he wanted the calaboose keys. He stood impassively beside Johnson, big head slightly on one side, squinting a trifle as the smoke of his cigar curled upward past his face. Johnson refused to hand over the keys. He mumbled something about not knowing of a new marshal coming in.

His complaints were swiftly checked. Stoudenmire stretched out a long arm and seized the luckless deputy. Thoroughly, however dispassionate his expression, he shook Johnson until that worthy's teeth rattled in his head. Then Stoudenmire took the keys from Johnson's pocket and strolled out, without troubling to see if his victim intended shooting at him.

Stoudenmire's brother-in-law, "Doc" Cummings, opened the Globe Restaurant, the finest place of its kind in the locality. Stoudenmire went about the business of learning the town. In one sense, the geographical, there was little to know; the town was very crowded, with hotel accommodations utterly inadequate. Almost every corner had its saloon and there were very many more sandwiched between. An important adjunct to almost every drinking place was a gambling hell.

The Mannings operated two places—a saloon on the present site of the Hotel Paso del Norte and the Coliseum "variety theatre," farther south on El Paso Street. Jack Doyle had another variety theatre, only smaller than the Coliseum. Men and women "made" the town by night. It was almost impossible for late comers to get within sight of the gaming tables where faro bank, roulette, monte, chuck-a-luck, stud poker and other games were reaping their harvests.

But the city marshal had to know his people. That was difficult for a newcomer like Stoudenmire. In any such new town as El Paso was in the '80s, society is mixed indeed; a gentleman in one of the learned professions might be the town's worst citizen, while a saloon-keeper enjoyed the confidence of the best element and was known as a first-rate man.

BUT STOUDENMIRE did not leave El Paso long in doubt, concerning his fitness for the place he had been given. It was a short time only until a detachment of the Rangers went up the Rio Grande to a point near Canutillo, to investigate the report that the bodies of two Mexican youths—apparently murdered—lay in the brush up there. They found the corpses and returned with them to El Paso. Preparations were made for an inquest in an empty adobe store building on El Paso Street, about where the Hotel Fisher now stands.

It was rumored about town that these two Mexicans lived on the other side of the Rio Grande; that they had followed the trail of some of their stray cattle over the river, into the thick tornillo brush, where they had been set upon and killed. Some suspicion began to attach to Johnnie Hale, who managed a small ranch owned by the brothers Manning of the Coliseum Theatre. The Rangers believed that Hale and a man named Len Peterson had committed the double-murder.

The inquest naturally attracted much attention in such a place as the El Paso of that day. The parents and friends of the Mexican youths were there; ex-marshal Campbell and ex-deputy Bill Johnson were spectators; Marshal Stoudenmire attended, as did the Rangers. Johnnie Hale had been summoned and he had many friends.

A former Ranger of Baylor's company, Gus Krempkau from San Antonio, now a deputy sheriff of a nearby county, was selected as interpreter. The inquest proceeded. It dragged along until noon, with Johnnie Hale becoming more and more displeased with the trend of the testimony and more ready to blame the interpreter for the trend. Recess was announced. Actors and audience, those in the building filed out to the street. The Rangers went toward their quarters, but around the place of inquest a sizable crowd lingered. For almost everyone there knew everyone else, which is first requisite to thorough enjoyment of an inquest or trial.

Krempkau, coming out upon the street, was immediately buttonholed by Johnnie Hale, who objected pointedly and profanely to the manner of Krempkau's interpretation of Mexican testimony. Krempkau quietly insisted upon the honesty and accuracy of his work. His quiet insistence fanned Hale's rage and suddenly the ranch manager's hand flashed to his Colt-butt; the weapon twinkled out and there was the, to El Paso, familiar sound of a pistol-shot. Krempkau fell dead, with a bullet hole through his head. Stoudenmire whirled at the sound. . . .

There stood Johnnie Hale, with his Colt vaguely menacing the air before him; with a wreath of blue smoke filtering up from the muzzle. Krempkau was on the ground, stone-dead. Stoudenmire went into action with a volcanic suddenness that, the town was to learn, was habitual to him in times of stress.

He came running toward Hale who, if he had no ulterior motives now, certainly lacked presence of mind enough to hurl away his weapon and indicate his surrender. Stoudenmire opened fire on him, his first shot missing Hale and killing an over-curious Mexican gaping at the scene. But his second shot sent Hale crashing down to join his own victim.

George Campbell now whippeɑ out ɧis Colt. He began to back across the street, gun-muzzle weaving back and forth. As he went, he said half-absently aloud: "This is not my fight."

But Stoudenmire was one to take appearances at face value. There was a man friendly to Johnnie Hale. He had drawn his weapon and its muzzle was covering, if not the marshal himself, at least the general vicinity of that officer. Stoudenmire turned a little more directly toward Campbell and fired his third shot. So in hardly more than five seconds, four men had been killed. Even for old El Paso, this was an event worth mentioning over the drinks for a day or two.

Some there were, both of the city council and the leading men of the town, who nodded their heads in quiet satisfaction—not because an occasion had risen in which Stoudenmire must kill two gunmen, but because their judgment of him had proved correct; he could and would handle the roughest men when that became necessary; and the sporting crowd had learned the fact.

But there was no lack of dissenting voices. In every town, there will be an element which, while admitting a certain necessity, will yet refuse to admit its corollary— the necessity for stern measures to meet the emergency. So it was here. It was admitted that the town had a deal of "bad men" and that drastic measures must be enforced if these were not to rule roughshod the quieter element.

But, when the emergency came and force, lawless force, was met with force, legal force, certain ones of the town growled about "a reign of terror" and began to call the marshal "Stoudenmire the butcher." They were sure that something different, gentler, should have, could have, been done in the circumstances. Just what, however, they did not trouble to specify.

Among these voices was prominent that of the professional politician, W. W. Mills, who admitted that he was "the county's Republican party." Mills at this time held a political appointment—that of deputy United States marshal. But he desired two things—to be city marshal of El Paso or, if that could not be, to accomplish Stoudenmire's removal.

In this, Mills had the vigorous support of the sporting crowd—the Mannings and their followers. Mills, of course, had no idea of personally doing away with Stoudenmire. But the Mannings, Jim and Frank, were said to be intensely bitter about the killing of their friend, Campbell. None can prove their connection with the schemes by which Stoudenmire's assassination was attempted, but certainly they talked loudest.

As for Mills, what he said always depended on how he felt. And he was always the shrewd politician. In his memoirs (one of the three most egotistical books in the world), he remarks quietly that he found a way to let the council rid itself of Stoudenmire: He appeared before mayor and council with a telegram from the United States marshal of New Mexico, stating that Stoudenmire had accepted appointment as his deputy. This, Mills remarked, was equivalent to Stoudenmire's handing in his resignation.

The council then declared the office of city marshal vacant and Alderman Hague immediately nominated Mills. But, put to a vote, Mills found to his chagrin, that the council was not so desirous of being rid of Stoudenmire as he had believed—and as afterward he claimed it to be. For when the vote stood four and four, Mayor Magoffin quickly cast the deciding vote in favor of Stoudenmire, who had been nominated to succeed himself.

Now appears upon the stage (again) a man of the type often found upon the frontier—where of all places in the world he has least chance. It was that immortal of Owen Wister's, *The Virginian*, who remarked most truthfully that in the western country a man must do *well* the thing he tries; must deal cards *well;* must steal *well;* must be really quick with a gun if claiming such quickness. This, of course, applied to the old west, rather than to the country that now frames Harvey eating houses and curio shops. Weaklings have it easier out here, nowadays.

But in the '80s, efficiency was demanded and it was in the '80s that Bill Johnson dwelt in El Paso. The town's chief drunkard was Johnson and, in addition to that, or because of that, almost a simpleton—a moron we could term him, in terms of today.

Bill Johnson was the tool chosen finally by those leaders of the sporting crowd who had determined upon Stoudenmire's death. They plied the fool with free liquor until the world moved around him in a haze, with little of form and less still of proportion.

Stoudenmire, they told Johnson, had frightfully affronted him. Supersede him as marshal, he might have done; but he had no right to cuff him and shake him as if he were a cur dog. They dwelt on this insult. They impressed upon the drunken Johnson that he was now a pariah in the eyes of the community. They, of course, understood him; but in the eyes of the town at large nothing would wipe out that insult save Stoudenmire's blood.

Johnson nodded boozily. He agreed to kill Stoudenmire. But not openly; his prompters doubtless did not even suggest that. Anyone could see clearly the length of Johnson's chance in a shooting-scrape, against the burly and gun-wise marshal. They planned for Johnson the insulted one's revenge:

Today, as then, San Antonio Street lies east and west, running into El Paso Street—as the upright of a T joins the top-bar. In the '80s, the "run" of the town was San Antonio Street west from Neal Nuland's Acme Saloon at the present Mesa Avenue to El Paso Street, thence south for hardly more than three blocks—a sort of L-shaped midway. At the time of Johnson's decision to assassinate Stoudenmire, there was a pile of brick on the edge of San Antonio Street, at its juncture with El Paso.

Behind this heap of brick, one night, the plotters posted Johnson. They had armed him with a double-barreled shotgun. Stoudenmire, they knew, would soon be coming from the Acme Saloon on his round of the town. So, as a final precaution, just in case Johnson's shotgun should not work perfectly, a number of the sporting crowd ambushed themselves behind the thick adobe pillars that supported the "gallery" over the far, the west, sidewalk of El Paso Street. Thus they were opposite the mouth of San Antonio.

True to routine, Stoudenmire came like a bull straight toward the ambuscade. At twenty-five feet, Johnson, standing unsteadily erect, fired both barrels of his shotgun. He must have been amazingly drunk, for he achieved the astonishing feat of missing his target.

Stoudenmire never wore revolver-holsters. He had been presented with two fine silver-plated Colts, caliber .45, by Beneky and Pierce, pioneer hardware men. These he carried in leather-lined hip pockets. He maintained always that he could draw more quickly from his pockets than from holsters. Now, as Johnson's buckshot whined over his head, he proved at least that he could draw flashingly and shoot most accurately under fire. For Bill Johnson crashed down upon the bricks literally riddled with bullets.

Now, the discreet gentry on the west side of El Paso Street opened up from behind their pillars. Their aim was hardly better than their tool's. One bullet struck Stoudenmire in the foot, but failed to incapacitate him for a furious bullrush, straight across the street and into the rain of bullets. None of those doughty plotters cared to stay and face him! When they had scurried away, he went down El Paso Street and turned into a store, where a doctor dressed his wound.

A sort of venomous apathy settled over the sporting crowd, after this fiasco. Stoudenmire seemed to have a charmed life and the story of his putting to flight all the ambushed gladiators lost nothing in the telling. As for the marshal, he believed, with or without grounds, that Jim and Frank Manning were responsible for Bill Johnson's attack. So he watched them always.

He had a real deputy now—the veteran Ranger sergeant James B. Gillett. And in the very capable hands of "Jim" Gillett, Stoudenmire left the town in February of 1882, when he went back to East Texas to be married. Two days after his departure, Gillett was confined to his bed with a light attack of varioloid and Stoudenmire's brother-in-law, "Doc" Cummings, took it upon himself to represent the marshal's office.

In those days a man's trousers-pockets were vertical, top-opening affairs, which made very serviceable pistol-holsters. Cummings rammed a pair of .45s into his pockets and left the Globe Restaurant. First he went to Bill Coffin's Old Boss Saloon, standing on the corner of Overland and El Paso Streets and so almost across from the Mannings' Coliseum Theatre.

He had a drink—and another and some more. Then he announced that he was going over to the Coliseum and clean out the damned Mannings. It was quite possible that he might have achieved this purpose if he had let his .45s speak for him. But, lingering to drink in the Old Boss and go into detail concerning his plans, he afforded opportunity for word of his plan to cross the street ahead of him. (Argument still rages hotly between oldtimers, as to whether he lasted nine or ten seconds, upon entering the Coliseum.)

Jim Manning assumed the responsibility for the killing, but it was generally understood that a bartender of the Mannings did the actual shooting. Either way—whether Jim Manning or an employee killed "Doc" Cummings—it seems to have been a thoroughly justifiable action. The trouble was that Stoudenmire's opinion of it had to be given consideration! He was honestly fond of his brother-in-law and, naturally, he would consider this a score against him by the other side.

Jim Gillett considered all of this and when Stoudenmire came in with his bride, Gillett waited for him at the station. He told Stoudenmire the circumstances surrounding Cummings' death. Stoudenmire raved furiously; nor did he make any attempt to conceal his feelings:

"If the Mannings are hunting a fight, they can certainly have it!" he said.

THEREAFTER, relations between Stoudenmire and the sporting crowd grew very strained—as strained as the nerves of the townspeople who watched, expectant of a pitched battle on one of the two crowded streets of El Paso. All the elements were here for such a conflict as the Earps and Clantons staged in Tombstone.

So cool heads among the townsmen made a plan. A committee visited Stoudenmire; visited the three Manning brothers. Both sides to the feud were begged to patch up their differences. It was pointed out to them that under existent conditions, an explosion was bound to come; that such a fight would probably result in the death of innocent bystanders. Willingly, or unwillingly, the two factions finally agreed to a truce. An agreement was written and published on April 16, 1882. It is a rather remarkable document, which runs:

"We, the undersigned parties, having this day mutually settled all difficulties and unfriendly feelings existing between us, hereby agree that we will meet and pass each other on peaceable terms and that bygones shall be bygones, and that we will never allude in the future to any past animosities that have existed between us."

It seems an agreement fair enough, signed by Dallas Stoudenmire, Jim, Frank and G. F. Manning. The only trouble with such a paper is that it does not sufficiently indicate the real feelings of those who signed it. Certainly, if the "innocent bystanders" or those apt to become such in the event of a battle, now drew freer breath,

Stoudenmire and the Manning clan remained mutually suspicious.

Stoudenmire's emotions were not usually visible. But his friends noted that he was drinking more than usual; more than he could easily carry, in fact. In his cups he was quarrelsome and overbearing, even with his closest acquaintances, his best friends. This quickly brought a request from the city council for his resignation. He stalked into the council room to fling down the desired paper before them and glare about with fierce blue eyes: "You haven't treated me fairly," he growled at them; "and I can straddle the bunch of you."

And oldtimers who were there drawl reminiscently that he looked as if he would have welcomed an invitation to perform this somewhat obscure feat of "straddling." But the moment passed without violence.

Jim Gillett was natural successor to Stoudenmire and it may be interpolated here that in only one particular—utter fearlessness—did he resemble his predecessor.

Naturally, he was curious concerning Stoudenmire's feeling toward him. Would his former chief resent his elevation, particularly since Stoudenmire's resignation had been involuntary? Gillett admired Stoudenmire's good traits and had no desire to become embroiled with him. But Stoudenmire walked across to wish him luck. He reminded Gillett that a man-sized job confronted him.

It would have been natural in one of Stoudenmire's nature to exhibit resentment here. A belligerent character has been kingpin of a wild town; strongest of the strong; then suddenly is reduced to the status of private citizen. Peevishness at the deposition would be rule, rather than exception. But fortunately, at this juncture, Stoudenmire obtained appointment as deputy United States marshal for the western district of Texas, headquarters of this deputy-ship being El Paso. Apparently, this salved his sense of injury at loss of the other job.

Soon after this, Stoudenmire's official duties took him to Deming, New Mexico. Upon his return, he reached El Paso between midnight and dawn of September 18, 1882.

He wanted a drink and entered the Mannings' saloon. No credible report has ever been given of his actions there, or of what was said and done within the saloon.

But when Jim Gillett came on duty, very early that morning, the first important sight to greet his eyes was that of Dallas Stoudenmire's huge, frockcoated figure, reeling down the middle of El Paso Street. Very obviously he had been engaged in a drinking bout and that, with Stoudenmire, meant the probability, rather than the mere possibility, of trouble to come. So Gillett hurried to get alongside. He addressed Stoudenmire diplomatically.

As tactfully as possible, he suggested that Stoudenmire would be wiser to go home and get some sleep.

"I'll be glad to go with you," finished Gillett.

Stoudenmire flared up instantly:

"I don't need your company! I don't need anybody's company! You let me alone and I'll go home. Otherwise, I won't go at all."

Gillett saw that one imprudent word at this juncture would bring on a difficulty that might have very serious results. Stoudenmire's mood was too ugly to permit of reasoning with him. Gillett's thought here, as in the past, was to handle Stoudenmire in a common-sense manner. He had arrested Stoudenmire a short time before, in the Acme Saloon, where Stoudenmire and one of his former deputies were engaged in a shooting-scrape. Stoudenmire had shown no animosity for being "corraled" at the point of Gillett's double-barreled shotgun.

"I didn't wish to kill Stoudenmire, even if I could," Gillett says of that occasion. "At the same time, I didn't want to be killed by him."

So, wisely, he decided to take Stoudenmire at his word. He turned and left him. The big man, seeing that he was not to be forced to do anything, went straight home and to bed.

When Jim and Frank Manning came to their saloon and were told by the bartender that Stoudenmire had been in there "looking for them" they flared up. They said that Stoudenmire had broken his agreement. Jim Manning armed himself and went straight to the Acme Saloon, proclaiming that he was going to find Dallas Stoudenmire and "shoot it out with him." But Stoudenmire at this moment was peacefully asleep at home.

The Acme was owned by Neal Nuland, Cliff Brooks and Walt Jones. All were from Colorado County and all knew and liked Stoudenmire. It was in the Acme that Stoudenmire spent a great deal of his time, so, when at about three o'clock that afternoon he came downtown, he naturally drifted to the Acme.

His friends reproached him for hunting the Mannings in their own saloon and he exhibited surprise at the charge:

"Why, I wasn't hunting the Mannings, at all!" he protested. "I came into town 'way after midnight and I wanted a drink. That saloon was the first one I found open. I'll go down there and explain to them."

Walt Jones, of the Acme's owners, had been a deputy marshal under Stoudenmire and he is recalled as a very brave and dependable man. He announced that he would accompany Stoudenmire to visit the Mannings and they went out together.

At the Manning saloon, when they entered, they found Jim Manning at the bar and Dr. G. F. Manning playing a game of billiards. Stoudenmire went up to Jim and said that someone had evidently been spreading some lies. He asked for Frank Manning, saying that he wanted to explain things to all of them, together.

"Frank's in the gambling room," said Jim Manning. "I'll go get him."

As Jim went out, Dr. Manning dropped his billiard cue and came up to Stoudenmire. He was a small man, the doctor, and appeared even smaller against the great bulk of the ex-marshal. But he was a man of cold nerve and he looked grimly up into Stoudenmire's face, now:

"Dallas," he charged, "you haven't stuck to your agreement!"

"Whoever says I haven't tells a damned lie!" cried Stoudenmire.

Instantly, both men went for their guns. Walt Jones
risked his life to jump between them, but the effort was
useless. He was hurled back and Dr. Manning beat
Stoudenmire to the draw. He was using a double-action
.44 and before Stoudenmire, fuddled by drink, could
bring his guns into firing position, the little doctor had
fired a bullet straight at Stoudenmire's right breast. The
ball struck a large pocketbook and a packet of letters in
the coat pocket, else Stoudenmire would have died without firing a shot.

Again Dr. Manning fired. This second bullet wounded
Stoudenmire in the left arm and breast near the shoulder.
By this time Stoudenmire had got one of his Colts to
bear on Manning. He shot him through the right arm
above the elbow, knocking the doctor's weapon from
his hand with the jar of the bullet. Instantly, Dr.
Manning leaped for Stoudenmire, throwing both arms
around Stoudenmire's so that he could not raise his
hands to fire again.

Stoudenmire wrestled desperately to free his arms of
that embrace. The locked figures reeled around the barroom in a very waltz of death. They staggered to the
door and through it upon the sidewalk. Still, the little
doctor—terrier against mastiff—pinioned Stoudenmire's
arms; it was certain death if he were shaken off.

Marshal Gillett and one Joe Deaver, of Captain Baylor's Rangers, were standing in the door of Kerskie's
bookstore, talking. Gillett had no idea that Stoudenmire had reappeared upon the streets, until there came
the rattle of shots from the saloon. Then appeared men
running from the scene, anxious to get out of range of
the bullets. Gillett and Deaver whirled toward the
sound of the firing, but were nearly knocked down several times by those leaving the vicinity.

Stoudenmire and Manning, locked together, were
now visible upon the sidewalk and when Gillett and his
companion were within twenty-five or thirty feet of
the pair, Jim Manning jumped out of the gambling room
with a Colt's .45 in his hand. He opened fire on Stouden-

mire. He had but the big man's head for target and his
first shot, missing, splintered a barber's pole beyond
them. His second bullet caught Stoudenmire in the left
temple and killed him instantly.

He collapsed, dragging down Dr. Manning with him.
The doctor snatched up one of Stoudenmire's Colts and
began hammering his adversary over the head. Jim
Manning was pulling his brother away when Gillett and
Deaver came up, so swiftly had all taken place.

Gillett immediately placed the brothers under arrest
and Jim Manning nodded assent. Dr. Manning was now
unconscious from loss of blood and shock.

"All right, Marshal," said Jim Manning. "But please
help me to carry my brother inside. I think he's killed."

Deaver, Jim Manning and Gillett now picked up the
doctor, who was bloody from head to foot almost. Then
Deputy Sheriff Gonzales of the county came rushing up
to claim the prisoners. He said that the killing constituted a state offense. Gillett agreed with this and
turned over the Mannings to Gonzales' custody. He then
recovered Stoudenmire's twin silver-plated Colts from
where they had dropped and had the body removed from
the sidewalk.

Jim Manning was tried and acquitted for the killing.
As a matter of fact, he was hardly in danger of any sort
of conviction. The Mannings and Stoudenmire had
made so many threats and counter-threats that El Paso
had expected nothing else but an armed collision and the
citizens were relieved that no outsider had been killed or
injured during the battle. It was a day of personal settlement of differences; if a man passed the word along that
he intended to kill you, you were more apt to look to the
hang of your own gun than to have him put under bond
to keep the peace.

W. W. (familiarly known as "Billy") Bridgers, one-
time district and county attorney and a witness to the
Stoudenmire-Manning windup, remarks that there was
no fundamental ground for a conviction against Jim
Manning. He points out that Jim Manning, even had

there been no relationship between him and the doctor, was perfectly justified as a citizen in interfering to prevent a murder being done. Seeing that Dr. Manning was unarmed and striving to protect himself against the armed Stoudenmire, Jim Manning was within his fundamental rights as a citizen in preventing Stoudenmire from killing the doctor—even to the point of killing Stoudenmire to stop him.

But whatever the law of it may have been, this smoke-wreathed personal combat in the Manning saloon and outside of it marked the end of Dallas Stoudenmire, the two-gun marshal. A rather sorry ending but, perhaps, the only one possible if one reflects upon the metal of the man and his enemies. And in this day and time it is well to remember of Stoudenmire that, as city marshal, he was given a hard, thankless task and performed it very thoroughly, by the standards of his own day—the only standards with which he was properly concerned.

CHAPTER VII · *Behind the Star*

"JIM" GILLETT

UPON THAT twisting, wooded stream West Texas knows (and often curses bitterly) as the North Llano, a half-dozen tents shining dull-white in the brush showed where E Company, Frontier Battalion, Texas Rangers, were camped. It was the middle of January, almost—and a cold January, that year of 1878. The weather, though, was not cold enough to chill Lieutenant N. O. Reynolds' anger. Not all the frost of Kimble County could cool the inner fires of "Mage" Reynolds' six-foot frame.

"By Gad, seh!" he told First Sergeant Nevill of E Company. "How in the world four crack Rangers could let that dam' Dick Dublin jump right on top of 'em and then ride away, is more than I can see! The worst old 'brier-breaker' in Kimble County, Dick Dublin. And you let him get away!"

He tugged at his drooping blond mustache as he raw-hided the big sergeant. E Company was a picked outfit. When Reynolds had been promoted from sergeant to lieutenant, the September before, he had been given a free hand to choose his company from all the other companies' ranks. He had already been detailed to the hardest job in the State of Texas—the cleanup of those frontier counties of Kimble and Menard, where Indians still raided the ranches in the "light of the moon" and desperadoes of every stripe had congregated, feeling safe in the dense thickets of pecan, cedar, mesquite, live oak.

Dell Dublin, Dick's brother, and like him a murderer, had been captured only a few days before Nevill's failure to stop Dick, but Dick defied the Rangers. In particular, he breathed forth fire and destruction at three men of

Reynolds'—the Banister brothers and Corporal Jim
Gillett, all of whom he had known as cowboys.

"Send me Corporal Gillett," Reynolds snapped finally
and Nevill, glad to get away from his famous commander's
tongue, moved off quickly to hunt the young non-com'.

Presently, up to Reynolds' tent came a quick-moving,
muscular youngster, just past his majority, a dark-eyed,
dark-haired cowboy, five-nine or so, the son of a one-
time adjutant general of the State of Texas.

Reynolds looked grimly at him. He knew Jim Gillett
very well, for they had been privates together. The nine
years' difference in their ages had made only for a sort of
brotherly feeling between them. But, most important
just now, Reynolds knew that prior to his enlistment in
the Rangers thirty months before, Gillett had punched
cows in both Menard and Kimble Counties.

"Jim," Reynolds said slowly, "it's a scout after
Dick Dublin again. That man seems to be a regular
Jonah to this company. With him living only ten miles
from here, I've been awfully disappointed at not being
able to capture him. It's a reflection on all Company E.
There's one thing sure, though! If I can't capture him,
I'll make life miserable for him! I'll keep a scout in the
field after him constantly. You take John and Will
Banister, Tom Gillespie, Dave Ligon and Ben Carter.
Five days' scout."

"He's sent word to the Banisters and me that he aims
to use his quirt on us, like as if we were dogs," Gillett
nodded. "I know Dick and Ace Lankford both, mighty
well. In '73, when I was punching cows for Joe Franks,
the two of them hung around our outfit. Always armed
and cat-eyed—afraid of arrest. I've heard Dick say,
many's the time, that he'd never surrender. Well . . .
any instructions about route?"

"No, no! I rely too much on your judgment to hamper
you with orders. After you're once out of sight of camp,
you know these mountains and these trails 'way better
than I do. Just go and do your best. If you come up to
him, don't let him get away, that's all!"

The seven-man "scout" was in the saddle at day-break. A couple of little bronco-mules trotted after the horsemen, packing the camp-gear. John and Will Banister, who had punched cows with Jim Gillett, pushed up alongside him. They wanted to know what the particular reason for the scout might be. When Gillett answered with the two words, "Dick Dublin!" Will pushed back his hat and whistled long. And grinned.

Gillett led the party toward the Potter Ranch on Pack Saddle Creek. Old Man Potter and his two grown sons were ancient friends and allies of all the Dublin clan. Gillett hoped to find Dick hanging around the place. So, with the skill of much experience, the Rangers quietly "rounded up the ranch." They came quietly and swiftly, closing in from four sides on the one-room cabin. It was empty.

The next possibility was an old stock-pen far beyond any settlements, on the extreme headwaters of the South Llano. The cowmen of the vicinity used it to corral wild cattle. But this, too, was a blank today. They could find no trace of Dick Dublin in two days' scouting. The scouts turned back. On the evening of the fourth day, Gillett timed their arrival at Potter's for dark. Sundown came. They were within a mile of the cabin.

Gillett grunted an order. They swung down from the horses and each man unsaddled. John Banister and Dave Ligon remained with the animals. Gillett, with Will Banister, Tom Gillespie and Ben Carter, moved cautiously toward the house.

They heard a horse coming and squatted in the bed of a creek. They saw the horseman passing, a blob of shadow in the brush. They followed him. At last they were within fifty yards of the cabin, before which a fire blazed. A small wagon stood near the single door of the cabin. To one of its wheels a saddled horse was tied. On the Rangers' right, twenty-five yards away, Old Man Potter and one of his sons were unloading hogs from a second wagon.

"All right!" Gillett whispered tensely. "We'll streak it across and throw down on them before they know we're here. What we want is a talk with that fellow who just rode up. But we've got to make time crossing the open!"

They were hardly over the creek-bank when Old Man Potter dropped a squealing hog and spun toward them. "Hightail, Dick! Here's them dam' Rangers!"

Around the wagon jumped Dick Dublin. He was a big man, dark, with more of the look of a prizefighter than a cowman. There was no time to untie that horse. He raced for the brush, head down.

Gillett yelled at him to halt, then snapped out a Winchester slug for period. Dublin merely ran the faster. Gillett, the smaller, lighter man, ran after him. He saw Dublin sprinting up a little ravine. Again he yelled to the murderer. Dublin's hand went under his coat this time. Gillett, with a bead on the fugitive, squeezed the little .44's trigger. With the whiplike crack of it, Dublin crashed down upon his face. He lay still.

The others pounded up. Gillett was bending over Dublin, puzzling the odd course of his bullet, which had struck Dublin over the right hipbone and come out near the left collarbone. Ben Carter shook his head dolefully.

"A seven-hundred dollar shot," he mourned. "That reward was for his arrest and conviction."

With Dick Dublin's death, there remained in Kimble County only one other outstanding criminal. For E Company had swept those tangled fastnesses as with a broom. Outlaws who escaped capture decided to "buy a trunk." But on the Junction-Mason road, ten miles from Ranger camp, was the ranch of Starke Reynolds, horse-thief, wanted for assault to murder. And he was a slippery customer! Every scout in the field made it a point to round up his ranch when in the neighborhood.

In February of '78, Reynolds started for Austin with Gillett and four Rangers—including that Dick Ware who was to kill Sam Bass at Round Rock the following July—escorting a four-mule wagon in which rode five shackled

prisoners. They rode past Starke Reynolds' ranch and
Lieutenant Reynolds glowered at the silent place:

"Reckon there's no use rounding it up again. We've
done it so many times without finding anybody home.
But I certainly hate to have a spare set of shackles in the
wagon he could use, without having Starke use 'em!"

They went on. A quarter-mile. A half-mile. Then all
gaped ahead to where, four hundred yards down the
road, a small man sat a brown pony with a sack of flour
across the saddle before him. He saw the Rangers and
recognized them, as they recognized him. He spun the
brown pony on a dime and dumped the flour. Low over
the horn, he rammed in the steel and was gone for the
Llano bottoms, three miles away.

Lieutenant Reynolds was no slower. Nor were the
Rangers behind him. But the lieutenant's horse was a
racing animal. He had the lead and he kept it, in as fast
a race as the Rangers ever ran. That brown pony of Starke
Reynolds stretched the big race horse to a limber. A mile
was covered and a mile-and-a-half. Reynolds was yelling
at Reynolds:

"Surrender! You this-and-that! Surrender!"

Shooting from the saddle at that terrific pace was not
likely to result in a hit. But Reynolds thought that it
might scare the fugitive. He emptied his six-shooter and
his carbine, but Starke Reynolds saw the Llano bottoms
dark and thick ahead of him, over the scrubby live oak
and mesquite of the grade down which he rode.

Gillett rode up beside Reynolds. Carter, Ware and
Ligon were dropping out of the race, their horses all but
done.

"Can I go after him?" Gillett yelled at Reynolds.

The lieutenant turned a brush-scratched, bloody and
furious face upon the corporal.

"Yes! Stop him or kill him!"

Gillett shifted bridle-reins from right to left hand.
He snatched the little carbine from the saddle-scabbard
and drove in the hooks. His horse shot past Reynolds'
and in three hundred yards he and Starke Reynolds were

alone. Starke rode now with chin on shoulder. Gillett
was coming up on him. Without warning, Starke
whirled his pony to a stop, jumped off and leveled his
gun over the saddle.

"Damn you! Stop or I'll kill you!" he yelled.

Choice was taken from Gillett's hand. His horse was
running downhill and for twenty-five yards there was
nothing to do but let him go. Gillett pulled in at last
and jumped down, to take shelter behind the animal.
But Starke broke for a thicket, afoot. As he came from
behind the horse, Gillett fired instantly. The bullet
whined in Starke's ear. He jumped back behind his horse.
Once more he peered over the saddle. Gillett drew a long
breath and steadied himself for a shot. Before he could
pull trigger, Dave Ligon burst from the brush and
covered Starke. He flung down his gun.

' I wish that horse of yours had busted his leg!" he
told Gillett bitterly. "I wish he'd busted off all four of
his legs—right off at the shoulder! Hadn't been for you,
I would be gone in them Llano bottoms, by now!"

"The last old brier-breaker!" Reynolds grinned,
when they shackled Starke Reynolds in the wagon.
"Let's go!"

IN JUNE of '75, when that adventurous young cowboy,
James Buchanan Gillett, enlisted in the Texas Rangers,
the chief interest of the famous Frontier Battalion was
Indian-fighting.

By '78, the marauding Comanches, Kiowas, Lipans
and Apaches had been pushed well back. The Rangers
became a mounted police force, enthusiastically and
energetically putting the fear of *el buen dios* into outlaws of all varieties.

With mere word of their coming, hard cases went
quietly out and got their own or other men's horses and
"bust' down the timber" getting away. Yell "Rangers!"
into the middle of a group of men in a cow-camp, a
frontier saloon, a railroad construction camp of the
'70s and '80s, and *someone's* head was sure to jerk. There

was that history-less cook of the T. P. grading-crew
near Monahans. . . .

He looked up, one morning, to see horsemen coming.
All heavily-armed, splendidly-mounted, riding with the
peculiar saddle-swagger of the Texan who has put on his
hat, tied his saddle-rope to the horn and made up his
mind for the day. This cook stared. Then he moved. The
census of the camp was just the same as short one cook.
Late that evening, the Rangers rode on off. Quite some
time later, the camp again had a cook. He came shivering
out of a water-barrel.

"What yuh shakin' so about like a dog a-swallerin'
peach seeds?" the foreman asked curiously. "That on-
expected non-Saturday bath, or them-the' Rangers,
huh?"

The cook made noises through chattering teeth. At
last they took on the semblance of words:

"I do' know," he meditated. "Do' know which."

They were entering upon that period of service which
made the mere statement "ex-Ranger" about all the
entry a man need make, in the "references" column of an
application for peace-officer's job. The Frontier Battalion
with its varied duties, its demand for the Ultimate in
bravery, ability to meet frontier problems, was a very
College for Sheriffs and Marshals.

Jim Gillett was on the way to graduation. But he
had no thought of this as, early in '79, he received the
incredible news of Lieutenant "Mage" Reynolds' resignation from the service. He felt as if the bottom had
dropped out of everything. The finest commander of the
day was gone. Sergeant Gillett sat down, presently, to
take stock. He had had four years of varied service. He
had fought Indians with D. W. Roberts, perhaps the
most famous of the Indian-fighting Ranger-captains. He
had stood guard over John Wesley Hardin, Texas' most
noted gunfighter. He had ridden hellbent into Round
Rock with Reynolds in time to see Sam Bass die "and
Jackson in the bushes, a-tryin' to git away."

Mage Reynolds' resignation almost broke Gillett's heart. But he was rated one of the most efficient, cool-headed noncom's in the service, headed straight for a commission. He looked around him and chose to enter Captain Baylor's C Company as sergeant. For he had seen a great deal of the frontier, with Captain Neal Cold-well and Major Jones, the Battalion's commander. C Company was headed for El Paso and the chance of Apache-fighting.

In '79, seven hundred and fifty dangerous miles separated San Antonio and El Paso. The Indians still raided up almost within hearing of El Pasoans. Attacks on stages and wagons were the order, not the exception, in that wide, still wild, region. But Baylor's party pulled into Ysleta, the little hamlet twelve miles down-river from El Paso, after forty-two uneventful days. C Company made camp.

Baylor's assignment was not precisely a picnic. The limits of his territory were conspicuous by their absence. Here was a land of mountain and desert, with the ancient, bloody-banked Rio Grande lying in the dull-green of the *bosque* like a looping silver ribbon upon a green table-top.

Along the river, a day's march for Spanish soldiery apart, lay the villages of the sparse population—mixture of Spanish and Indian, speaking Spanish almost exclusively, looking to Mexico, not to the United States, as the mother-land. Outlaws brown and white abounded. The villagers were friendly; it was almost impossible to find them in the tangled greenery of willow, tornillo, catclaw and cottonwood. And if hard-pressed, there was always the other side of the Rio Grande where Mexican authorities would turn no hand to help Texas officers.

C Company had hardly stopped for breath, there in Ysleta, when fifteen Apaches raided a Mexican hay-cutters' camp near Fabens, some dozen miles downriver from Ysleta. The Mexicans howled and dived into the grass. They reported at Ysleta, one by one, each calling himself the sole survivor. Baylor, Indian-fighter by choice and training, took up the Apache trail.

They crossed into Mexico and with volunteers from that side, holed up the Apaches in that gloomy passage of the Sierra Bentanos called Cañon del Moranos. Rangers and Mexicans charged the Indian position.

Gillett found himself in the lead. A six-foot Apache, tastefully decorated with red and blue paint, lifted himself up and whanged away at Gillett. He missed. Gillett whirled quite unnecessarily to suggest to his men that they take cover. Not one was in need of that suggestion. The buck took another shot at Gillett. Tore off his Stetson-brim. Gillett was a better shot. He bored that Apache clean through the spine and the buck departed from the Cañon del Moranos on the Trail of Permanent Sleep.

During the day the battle raged noisily but harmlessly—except for one more Apache killed by the Mexicans and the death of Sergeant Swilling's white saddle-horse. Swilling cursed mournfully. He was thinking of the long, long walk home, over sand, in high-heeled boots. The Rangers gave him rough sympathy:

"Ah, cheer up, Sarge!" they said. "Mebbe, come evenin', you won't be *needin'* a horse."

There was no possibility of dislodging the Apaches from that wilderness of boulders, except by a murderous series of single-handed combats. The Mexican volunteers had an Apache to show the folks at home. The Rangers were not strong enough to do the job alone. They re-crossed into Texas.

But when that first-class fighting man, Victorio of the Apaches, deserted the Mescalero Reservation to raid in Mexico, C Company crossed the river again. When they came up within striking-distance, General Terrazas of the Mexican force refused to share credit with Texas Rangers. He demanded that Baylor go back. So Gillett missed the mop-up there by two days. Terrazas simply swamped Victorio.

He was Baylor's right-hand man, now—Sergeant Jim Gillett. Twenty-five, and he had crowded into those years more experiences than many a gray-beard could show for a life-span three times as long. He held the highest non-commissioned rank. But his pay was only $50 a month and a commission might not come his way for a good while. He watched his chances for both rewards and notoriety that might keep memory of him green among the Brass Collars at Austin.

In April, '81, his chance came for both. Reward-money and a blazing fame that made him News all over Texas. It came about over a small matter of so-dull a subject as geography. Perhaps, if he had been able to foresee the furore he would cause in official Mexico City, Austin, Washington, he would have held his hand— and his horse. Perhaps. . . .

It began in Socorro, New Mexico. The brothers Baca, Abran and Enofre, murdered A. M. Conklin, editor of the *Sun*, on the church-steps as he came outside with his wife on his arm. Then they fled Socorro. They had an uncle in Ysleta who was a county judge of El Paso County. The Rangers of Baylor's Company C knew this. They watched the Baca house. It was a long wait, but Gillett had the patience of the Indians whose ways he knew so well. He pounced down on Judge Baca's place and captured Abran. Judge Baca offered him a thousand dollars to let the murderer go. But Gillett preferred the reward at Socorro. He delivered Abran and collected his $500.

But Enofre had vanished. And Enofre was simply a walking draft for $500. Gillett, doing virtually all of the criminal catching for A Company (which was C Company re-designated), brooded over the business. Then he learned that a young Mexican answering to Enofre Baca's description was clerking in a general store across the Rio Grande in Mexico, in the village of Zaragosa opposite Ysleta. Gillett thought that one over.

There was no possibility of persuading Mexican authorities to surrender this murderer. Even today, a Mexican who commits murder in Texas and makes the wet bank of the Rio Grande may serve on the Juarez

police-force under his own name. He is in danger of
arrest only if seen kissing his wife in a public place. The
Mexicans are a very moral race.

"If Enofre Baca is to be tried in Socorro," Gillett
told Private George Lloyd, "I simply can't see that it
will be arranged in any way but whistling for him to
come back to Texas."

"I'll go with you and help you whistle," Lloyd
offered. "Two can whistle louder than one."

In such fashion did Gillett, having come to a blank
wall, proceed to jump the wall. He and Lloyd crossed
the river, made a detour and came into Zaragosa from
the Mexican side. They rode up to the store and Gillett
swung down. Lloyd sat his horse and held Gillett's
reins. Gillett went clink-clumping across the hard-
packed delta earth that made the store's gallery-floor.
Inside, a red-faced young Mexican with dark-red hair
was measuring calico for an old woman. There was no
mistaking the man. It was Enofre Baca.

Gillett stepped briskly up to the counter. Enofre
looked at him. Six-shootered American riders were
quite common on that side of the Rio Grande. The possibility that two Rangers would dare to come into a
thriving Mexican village, where virtually every inhabitant owned a gun, to attempt taking out from under
the muzzles of those guns a Mexican was just too far-
fetched to occur to any Mexican. For that matter, George
Lloyd had really owned no expectation of getting out of
the hornets' nest alive.

Gillett grabbed Baca's collar and whipped out his
pistol. He grunted at Enofre.

"Where I go?" Enofre gasped.

"Paso del Norte—and step lively!" Gillett answered.

The old woman promptly screamed and fainted. Two
other customers fled from the store. In a twinkling,
Zaragosans were alarmed by these witnesses' yells. The
church bell began frantically to clang as if the Apache
nation were sweeping down on the hamlet. With Colt-
muzzle at Enofre's temple, Gillett was hustling the

prisoner outside. So far, the whistling had been most effective. There only remained the small matter of breaking through the aroused Mexicans.

Up behind Lloyd Gillett forced Enofre. The church-bell clanged madly. The population was snatching up arms. Men were running for corraled or staked-out horses. Gillett and Lloyd rammed in the hooks. Out of the village they went on the dead-run. Four miles to the river! Four miles of deep sand!

The Mexicans were on their heels at the two-mile mark, firing wildly. Lloyd's horse began to fail. In the face of heavy, but wild, fire, Gillett pulled in and motioned for Lloyd to do the same. They jumped down, pulled Enofre off and hustled him up behind Gillett's saddle.

This made their race faster and easier. But the lead they had had coming out of Zaragosa was cut down by the minute's halt. George Lloyd looked behind, shook his head. Not fearfully; resignedly. Still, he could see no reason to change his original notion. It had been fool-hardy to try this. He saw no chance of making Texas safely.

But they plowed on through the sand. Somehow, they made yard after yard without being hit. The Mexicans' fire was low for fear of hitting Enofre. But the horses were untouched. There was the Rio Grande! a hundred yards wide. The Mexicans yelled savagely. Almost incredulously, Gillett saw the edge of the bank at his horse's forefeet. Down into the water he slid. Gillett roweled him. The Mexicans were on the bank, now. He expected to feel a bullet as they splashed across the shallow water. But with a grunt, his horse reared up and scrambled up the Texas bank. Gillett waved his hat.

There was kick-back a-plenty! Baylor gasped at sight of Enofre. He said that Gillett's raid was the most insane he had ever known. He combed the sergeant up and down. Mexico City protested furiously to Washington. Secretary Blaine wrote hotly to the governor of Texas. The adjutant general wrote Baylor. And Baylor

wrote his reply, dwelling on the impossibility of securing anything but lip-coöperation from Mexican authorities in recovering escaped criminals. Official clamor began to die down. But not local sound and fury.

Word went around Ysleta that a good man could
make some money, working for Judge José Baca. All
that was required on the job was a thorough job of
bushwhacking. If a man would lie in wait for that devil
of a Ranger-sergeant who had taken Judge José's nephew
back to Socorro for hanging, and give that *sarjento
diablo* a bullet through the heart, it would be worth
mucho dinero. Baylor spoke to the judge about it. And
that business fell quickly flat.

But up the river in El Paso, where the railroads had
come to turn the sleepy village into one of the fastest,
toughest, twenty-four hour towns in Texas, a couple of
men might stand at the bar of Neal Nuland's Acme
Saloon on San Antonio Street and yarn a little over the
red-eye. If the talk turned—as usual—to hairbreadth
'scapes, "that Ranger kidnapin' the Mex' murderer out
o' Zaragosa" was sure to be brought in by the local man,
to cap the "foreigner's" tallest yarn. And the local man
might add:

"You know what a Ranger sergeant's worth in
Zaragosa? Laid down? $1500—if the brand's Gillett!"

This was one of Jim Gillett's last jobs in the Rangers.
In El Paso, in the wagon-yard that stood where the old
red Federal building now is, Gillett and a detail came
within one pound of coffee of capturing the notorious
Curly Bill Brocius of Tombstone fame. Gillett had trailed
Curly Bill's party of four across the Franklin Mountains.
The men had stolen a bunch of work-mules near Tombstone and headed for El Paso. But when Gillett and his
detachment burst into the wagon-yard with Winchesters
leveled, they found only the Baker boys and Billy
Morgan. Curly Bill had gone out for coffee. Gillett
figured that Curly had come back in time to witness the
capture of his men and had slid back to disappear.

The Santa Fé railroad wanted a good captain of guards to ride money-trains. They picked out the Ranger sergeant who had whistled Enofre Baca back across the river in his own particular style of whistling. Gillett remained here a few months, until train-robberies were discouraged. Then he became assistant city marshal of El Paso, a deputy of the famous Dallas Stoudenmire, whose character and career I have described in another chapter. With Stoudenmire's resignation, Gillett became marshal.

His career as marshal I have always considered to be one of the most remarkable in western history. El Paso may not have been the *toughest* town in the west, in '81-'82 and immediately thereafter. *But it was tough as they got!* It was wide-open and the marshal had such men as Mysterious Dave Mather, Billy Thompson (brother of Ben the famous gunman), Colorado Charley Utter, and other gun-toters of the same caliber, to control. With the aid of two .45s swiveled on a bracketed holsterless belt, and a pair of sawed-off shotguns, Jim Gillett never took a backward step from anybody and never killed man.

Usually, when a row started in some saloon, it was quite enough for the belligerents to see the middle-sized figure of the city marshal pop through the door with a sawed-off shotgun in his hands; to hear his unvarying command:

"Gentlemen! Stop that, now! Stop it—or I'll have to *cut you in two!*"

He retired from his position in El Paso to go ranching with his old Ranger-comrade, C. L. Nevill. He became sheriff of Presidio County (as I have shown in writing of Bass Outlaw—the Little Wolf), serving also as deputy United States marshal. Today, there is no better-known figure in Texas than ex-Ranger Sergeant Jim Gillett, owner of the big Barrel Springs Ranch on Valentine Flat, bank-director, author, student of history, traveler—and frontiersman. . . .

For a frontiersman he has remained through it all!

A Gallery of Gunfighters

Bill Longley

John Wesley Hardin

Ben Thompson when Marshal of Austin

William Milton Breakenridge

John Ringo's Grave

"Billy the Kid"

"Billy the Kid's" Mother—From an Old Tintype

Sheriff Pat Garrett

Dallas Stoudenmire While El Paso's Two-Gun Marshal

James B. Gillett as a Ranger Sergeant

Long-Haired Jim Courtright when Marshal of Fort Worth

Company "D"—Texas Rangers. Captain John R. Hughes at Right in Front Row

Bass Outlaw

"Wild Bill" Hickok at Deadwood

*Sam Bass (center), Jim Murphy (right)—A Disputed Picture,
Presumed to Have Been Taken at San Antonio*

"A Brave Man Lies in Death Here—" Sam Bass's Grave at Round Rock, Texas

Sheriff John Slaughter of Cochise

Captain "Bill" McDonald, Texas Rangers

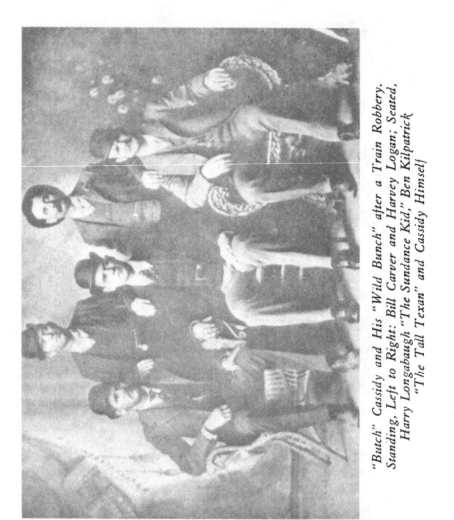

"Butch" Cassidy and His "Wild Bunch" after a Train Robbery.
Standing, Left to Right: Bill Carver and Harvey Logan; Seated,
Harry Longabaugh "The Sundance Kid," Ben Kilpatrick
"The Tall Texan" and Cassidy Himself

Tom Horn

General Lee Christmas

Photo by Eugene Cunningham—Guatemala City--March, 1920

CHAPTER VIII · *"The Hammer Thumb"*

LONG-HAIRED JIM COURTRIGHT

Publicity, in the old days, had almost as much to do with the forging of reputations as it has today. Old-timers like Captain Jim Gillett insist that many of the great gunmen are barely known, today. They claim that they knew many a gun-sharp the equal of Wild Bill Hickok, Ben Thompson, Bat Masterson, John Wesley Hardin, Clay Allison and all the others whose names have come down to us as synonyms for flashing, deadly weapon-work.

These men, they say, merely missed out on the publicity. For instance, let us have a look at "Long-Haired Jim" Courtright:

Captain Gillett points to Courtright, the veteran scout and marshal, as one of the wizards of the Colt who gets left out in the darkness, when the spotlight of publicity is being turned on the gunmen. Since the Captain was the contemporary of Hardin, Thompson, Courtright, Allison and Stoudenmire, et al., his opinion is highly interesting.

He saw Wes' Hardin demonstrate his skill with the sixes while that famous killer was held prisoner in Ranger camp. He watched Courtright, when the ex-marshal of Fort Worth was in El Paso, during Gillett's time as marshal there. He maintains that it would have been hard to know how to lay your bet, had a contest at gunplay been staged, between Courtright and *any* of the other noted gun-fighters of his day.

Of Courtright's earliest history, little is known except that he was born in Iowa around 1848, that he served as a trooper under John A. Logan during the Civil War and came to Texas as a young man. Between

Logan and Courtright a warm friendship sprang up which was to have results in later years.

Jim Courtright was tall above the average of men. His shoulder length hair and his deep-set eyes alike were black. His skin was naturally dark and, tanned as he was by years in the open, he needed only the Indian's high cheekbones, to pass as a red man.

Of the meaning of the word fear, he seemed utterly ignorant. This faculty, together with an amazing skill at handling weapons, plus a wide and intimate knowledge of the frontier, made him splendid potential material for an Army scout. Through the influence of General Logan, he was employed in this capacity and served with the Army over much of northwest Texas, Arizona and New Mexico. If Logan's word secured Courtright the detail as scout, his own outstanding ability was responsible for his retention of it. This ability seems to have been universally conceded.

While Captain Gillett was serving as city marshal of El Paso, Courtright came to town. Gillett says that the scout's popularity among Army men was manifested by the eagerness with which ex-soldiers living in El Paso sought out Courtright. He could not appear on the streets without having a group of frontiersmen or ex-soldiers crowding about him, leading him off to yarn about their time of service together. Someone was forever coming up to shake hands with him.

After Courtright quit the Army, he obtained appointment as chief of police in Fort Worth, Texas. Fort Worth, during the '70s and '80s, was a two-fisted man's town, second—if second at all—only to the El Paso of the same period. Men settled their disputes without recourse to the police. The six-shooter was worn openly and handily. The saloons were the clubhouses of the citizens and the natural belligerence of the frontier, increased by liberal quantities of stinging whiskey, led to many and bitter disagreements.

It was no place for a weak-kneed officer of the law The city marshal was supposed to keep order in whatever

fashion best served that purpose. Jim Courtright found
many opportunities to display both his grim fearlessness
and his uncanny speed and accuracy at weapon-play.

Politics was his weakness. He was not like Jim
Gillett, who concerned himself solely with the job of
policing his town and let the factions and the parties do
the electioneering. Courtright's Army life, perhaps,
made him a natural partizan. He had to be on one side
of the fence or the other. It was this tendency of his that
got him lined up with one faction in local politics. It was
the fact that he made a mistake in picking his side and so
chose the weaker one, which resulted in the loss of his
place as chief of police—or city marshal, as they called
the job in those two-fisted and turbulent days.

Now, down in El Paso, Colonel A. J. Fountain of
Mesilla, New Mexico, had come into town on an errand
which was to be of interest to the long-haired and fearless Courtright, though he knew nothing of it at the
time.

Colonel Fountain was a man of many interests. He
had been prominent in El Paso politics during the time
of the Mills brothers, Anson and W. W. He was now a
big figure in New Mexican politics and interested, also,
in the new mining camp of Lake Valley, above Rincon
in New Mexico.

He came to El Paso to talk to Captain Jim Gillett.
He said that this Lake Valley was a wild community, a
rip-roaring, twenty-four-hour-a-day place comparable
to the Kansas cow-towns just then models for all wild
communities. What it needed was a marshal of the Wild
Bill Hickok or Wyatt Earp or Bat Masterson type; a man
of cold nerve, good judgment, likable personality and—
prestidigital skill with a pair of long-barreled Colts or a
sawed-off shotgun.

"You come up and take the job," said Fountain to
Gillett. "I'll pay you just double what you are drawing
here. I know what you've done for El Paso and to my
mind you're the logical candidate for our place."

"Declined with thanks!" smiled Gillett, shaking his head. "No, Colonel, I'm getting tired of forever looking down the muzzle of somebody's six-shooter. In the Rangers and on this job, I've had a tin-cupful of bullets shot at me and I'm thinking of going into the cow-business. I'm ready to resign here, but I'm going to be a rancher, not the new marshal of Lake Valley."

Fountain was disappointed. But he knew that Gillett meant what he said. So he asked the marshal whom he could recommend for the place. Gillett recalled what he had heard from one source and another of Courtright's experience in North Texas:

"I know just the man for you!" he told Fountain. "Jim Courtright, the old Army scout. He's a man who can't be bluffed. And, when he has to be, he's a gun-fighter from the forks of Hard Water Creek. As good as anybody I ever heard of—and I'm not barring John Wesley Hardin or Ben Thompson or anybody else. He's been marshal up at Fort Worth but lost his job through politics. If he'll come to Lake Valley, I guarantee that it won't be long after his arrival that you'll see your hard cases hightailing for a healthfuler climate."

"Wire him," said Fountain promptly. "Offer him the place in my name. If he's the man you think he is, he'll be our best bet—since you won't come."

So Courtright came to El Paso for the second time, in reply to Gillett's telegram. Gillett gave him the highlights of the proposition and took him to see Fountain. The politician was much impressed by this tall, picturesque figure with the long black hair and the steady, Indian-dark eyes, who handled his Colts as a sleight of hand performer juggles glass balls on the stage.

They came quickly to agreement and departed for Lake Valley together. Here, Fountain introduced Courtright around the camp and the new marshal settled himself in the job. Two ore-thieves had been making life miserable for the mine-owners. They had the bad judgment to engage in battle with Courtright and paid for the slip with their lives. Thereafter Courtright went

quietly about his duties, with such grim efficiency that—
even as Gillett had prophesied—the "bad men" were
smitten with the fear of sudden death. They "hightailed" for places where no Jim Courtright was riding
herd on civic affairs. Lake Valley became downright
peaceful—for a mining camp of that day and place.

But the camp was like many another. The mines
played out and the population drifted to other, newer
camps. Regretfully, Fountain and his associates withdrew and Courtright's job was played out.

Now, General Logan entered the picture again. He
sent for Courtright and told his old scout that he had a
job for him. The General owned a cow-ranch in the
American Valley of New Mexico, a sizable and a valuable property. But at this time the profits were not coming into the pockets of the owner, which was the reason
for Logan's thought of Jim Courtright. The range was
being cluttered up with squatters and the herds were
suffering from rustlers.

So General Logan offered Courtright the position of
foreman. Just at this minute, he felt he needed the services of a bold man well-used to weapon-play, more
than those of an experienced cowman, who might not
measure up to the necessary height required to cope with
"hoe-man" and rustler. Courtright accepted and entered
into his new duties with all the determination which
marked him in any job.

THERE ARE conflicting stories as to the rights and
wrongs of the case of Logan vs. the Squatters. Everywhere in the West, the "nester" problem has been a
tangled one. The big ranchers, with much money in-
vested in their herds, occupying free range by virtue of
preëmption, felt that the "hoe-man" might have the
law on his side, but certainly did not have justice.

The nester claimed that he was perfectly within the
law when he settled on a choice section of watered land.
It was public land, this. But the cowman, seeing the
water upon which his cattle depended fenced in by some-

one who had waited for him, the cowman, to make the country safe, was very naturally provoked. He had to fight or get out. Since he had been in the country a long while, it was no more than human for him to think of fighting, rather than of accepting ruin merely because a vague and faraway lawmaker sided with the squatter.

At any rate, Courtright was working for a cowman. He had been given the task of freeing the Logan range of squatters. Being the man he was, he tried to earn his wages. He served notice on the squatters and moved to see that his notices were heeded.

There were two Frenchmen who had squatted on a nice bit of the Logan range. One day Courtright rode down with a companion, a very well known Panhandle gunman, a killer of very nervous trigger fingers, named Jim McIntire, to move the squatters.

The rights and wrongs of this particular case are, like the rights and wrongs of the whole business, lost in the mists of the years. But there was an argument with these Frenchmen which ended with the swift, deadly rattle of the Colts. Even discounting the expert quality of McIntire's gunplay, it is plain that these squatters bucked almost certain death, when they tried to match weapon-work with Courtright and any companion.

There was plenty of squatter-sympathy in the country. So the killing roused wide-spread and bitter feeling. So universal was it that Courtright and McIntire felt it wise to leave that region. Nor was it so simple as merely "rattling their hocks" out of the American Valley, New Mexico, then stopping out of range of enemy bullets. Warrants were sworn out; they were charged with murder.

McIntire began to think of South America. Courtright, it seems, was not yet convinced that he had to leave the country. Whether they came to Fort Worth together, to part there, is not clear. But Courtright came back and found that McIntire's sarcastic remarks about the "civilized" condition of Texas were well-founded. Legal papers were beginning to pass and repass over

Texas, New Mexico and Arizona. Telegraph wires were spanning the miles in this year of 1884. With the dawning of The Modern Era, the shooting of one man by another was becoming a public affair.

Courtright found that the mere riding fast out of New Mexico was no longer sufficient to sever a man's connection with the Territory. A thousand miles of distance did not now safeguard him. For a New Mexican agent was in Austin, getting warrants for Jim Courtright "and two companions." McIntire, of course, was one of these. But who that other may have been is a matter unknown to any of the oldtimers known to me.

A New Mexican officer, Richmond by name, arrived in Fort Worth. He had the warrants issued by the governor of Texas in response to a formal requisition made by the governor of New Mexico. But he chose not to proceed directly with the arrest of Courtright. Lieutenant Grimes and Corporal Hayes, of the Texas Rangers, were to assist him in making the arrest—when he requested their assistance.

Adjutant General W. H. King speaks caustically of the "mystery with which this agent saw fit to surround his movements in this matter." If one talks to an oldtimer who saw it all, the mysterious and meaningless actions of Richmond begin to seem an attempt to throw Courtright offguard.

The arrest was finally made on Saturday, October 18, 1884. When news of it spread over the city, there ensued the most intense excitement. There were—so General King remarks—"a long train of antecedent circumstances and rumors revolving about Courtright and his alleged crime," which "caused an outburst of real or assumed indignation among his friends when it was known that he was in arrest."

Jim Courtright was the sort of man who was either liked whole-heartedly or disliked with the same degree of feeling. In Fort Worth he had—as the adjutant general learned—many friends who would take risks in his behalf. The bulk of the town—even those who had no personal acquaintance with him—were in this matter sympathetic toward him.

Fort Worth has always been closely connected with the cowman. And the word was going around that Courtright was being railroaded to a necktie party. It was said and firmly believed that he, acting as agent for a cowman, defended his employer's property against a couple of Greasers of the worst character and killed them (more power to his .45s!). That the warrant for his arrest had been sworn out by friends of these Greasers, to get Courtright back in their hands, helpless. It was a dirty, underhand deal that would end in his lynching.

The actions of the New Mexico Sherlock lent color to the story. So when Courtright was taken to the union depot to await the arrival of the westbound T & P train, "an open, lawless and dangerous attempt at his rescue was made by a large crowd," so General King informed the governor. He continues:

"This attempt failed, partly through the coolness of the two Rangers who had Courtright in charge, and partly through the efforts of Judge Hood of the District Court, Sheriff Maddox and others, who assisted in keeping the mob from any overt act of violence, and succeeded in having the prisoner conveyed to the county jail."

Word of this mob's attempt to rescue Courtright reached Austin on Monday, October 20th. The governor ordered his adjutant general to take the first train to Fort Worth, to aid the civil authorities in preserving order and securing the execution of the law. But before General King reached Fort Worth he was notified by telegram of Courtright's escape the night before—Sunday night. He could only go on and investigate.

Richmond, the New Mexican officer, was afterward charged with both misconduct and folly. The charges seem mild, indeed, when it is known that he insisted on taking Courtright out of jail, on Sunday, to get his meals from an eating house. He ignored the protests of Sheriff Maddox and Lieutenant Grimes of the Rangers. In spite of the very obvious sentiment of the city, on Sunday morning he took Courtright down to a restaurant on Main Street—and picked the restaurant or was persuaded to go into the restaurant which was the known resort of many of Courtright's closest friends.

At noon he repeated the performance. At sundown he headed the little procession of four, back to the same place. But this time the meal was not to be eaten without interruption. The place was crowded with friends of Courtright. The favorite table of Richmond was known. The crowd pushed in to say good-bye to Courtright. The Rangers scowled, for this whole business of being under Richmond's orders and so made party to foolish risks was galling.

The crowd surged in as Courtright suddenly stood erect, a tall and very deadly figure, with a long-barreled Colt in each hand.

"I won't be going to New Mexico with you!" he informed the amazed Richmond.

The Rangers and Richmond were surrounded by armed men. They had not the ghost of a show for resistance. Courtright backed to the door. His horse was hitched outside. He sprang into the saddle when he had jerked loose the hitch-rope. Back to the furious Rangers and the amazed Richmond came his triumphant wolf-howl and the hollow, faraway cracking of his pistol as he did "the roll," beloved of the cowboy leaving town.

General King reached town on Monday night. On Tuesday morning he began his inquiry into the whole affair and absolved Lieutenant Grimes and Corporal Hayes of all blame. They had been told to act under Richmond's orders in all things.

Captain Schmitt of Company C, Texas Rangers, came in from Wichita Falls with Jim McIntire. General King feared some such demonstration in the McIntire case as had been staged in that of Courtright, but during a habeas corpus hearing the town remained uninterested. When the District Court ruled against McIntire, his counsel appealed. McIntire was held in custody of the Rangers until the Appellate Court sustained the decision of the District Court. He was then turned over to New Mexican authorities and escaped, to head for South America where Courtright, too, had gone.

Courtright remained for a good while in South America. Then, knowing well his West, he came quietly back to New Mexico and surrendered. The result was what he had anticipated:

The witnesses were scattered. A jury was empaneled from men who were strangers to both Courtright and the two Frenchmen; men ignorant of the case itself. And, it must be remembered that, anywhere in the West of the '80s, public sentiment dictated both charges and convictions; if there were sentiment enough against him to bring about indictment, there was sentiment enough to secure his conviction, almost regardless of evidence. Witness the bitter controversy that has raged for nearly thirty years, over the conviction of Tom Horn!

Jim Courtright was honorably acquitted. Eventually, he drifted back to Fort Worth. He did various things. Staring up at his faded sign on the wall of an old building near the Tarrant County court house, as a boy, I have heard that he traded horses, that he was a saloon "bouncer"; that he served as a deputy sheriff during the big railroad strike of '86. During this strike, some strikers were killed by the deputies and there was a good deal of hard feeling all around. But nothing to signify, to a man of Courtright's uncanny skill with weapons. He went his way quite unworried.

The oldtimers who knew him well used to marvel in my hearing over his skill. They said that his hands, snapping to the butts of the .45s in their cut-down holsters, were like racing snakes streaking into holes. He was a deadly shot with either hand—which was not so usual with gunmen who "pulled" as flashingly as he. Frequently, the man who was 'extra-quick on the draw" figured to make up, by the number of shots he fired, for any lack of accuracy in aim. But not Long-Haired Jim Courtright! And danger, tension, seemed only to increase his coolness, his dexterity.

THAT SIGN of which I spoke, on the old brick building near the court house, was the "card" of the T. I. C. Commercial Detective Agency, which he opened. With its inauguration, Jim Courtright became a gentleman extremely unpopular with the gambling fraternity. Not many would talk openly against a gun-fighter of his more than marked ability. But the T. I. C. Agency began a career of "shaking-down" in the manner which is, doubtless, old as several of our hills; on which Chicago's underworld has put a few modern improvements. It was a "racket."

For gambling was going on in Fort Worth, in violation of certain ordinances made, provided and comfortably ignored. To the gamblers came Courtright and his aides, "racketeering." The gamblers paid certain amounts regularly, in return for shut mouths on the part of the T. I. C. A sorry business and one which was just as certain to end in Colt Thunder, Colt Lightning, as are the smelly rackets of today. Jim Courtright had slipped down a long, long way, from the place he had once occupied in men's esteem.

His racket brought him in contact with Luke Short—and sparks began to fly, very quickly.

Short's name sticks out like a rubricated word in some old manuscript, on the records of Leadville, Colorado; Dodge City, Kansas; Tombstone, Arizona. Like Courtright, he was a product of the frontier, for his parents had moved from Arkansas down to Tarrant County in the early '6os.

Luke Short was never one to earn his bread by the sweat of his brow. Perhaps he had done enough work as a boy, in Cattle Land. He was a small man—around five-six in height, who never weighed a hundred fifty pounds.

He was expert—as were most Texas boys of his time and section—in all the craft of the cowboy. A dead shot and a game, cool and deadly opponent in the ancient game of killing. He went "up the trail" with a herd. But, unlike so many of the cowboys fulfilling their ambition in this manner, who returned to gather more

cattle and build names that survive to this day, Short
was on the trail of Easy Money. The cow-business was a
hard one. An oldtime cowboy learned "to do his sleeping during the winter" for he often worked twenty
hours a day. Hard, perilous work, too.

Luke Short wandered to Nebraska and with a partner
began bootlegging whiskey to the Sioux. When the
Army broke up this business, Luke drifted to Denver,
thence to Leadville, which was a hell-roaring community in those days. There were so many gunmen that about
the only way to be conspicuous, in that line, was to
wear no gun at all! In Leadville, Luke Short had a row
with a Bad Man and when the argument quickly
reached the "leather-slapping" stage, Luke out-slapped
him—a habit Texas men seem to have had in dealing
with mere outsiders; non-Texans.

He drifted about the cattle-towns of Kansas—Dodge
City and Caldwell and the others—as a gambler and
saloon-man. He followed his friends, the Earps, to Tombstone. There he killed the well-known gambler, Charley
Storms. He went back to Dodge and, in '83, fell out with
the city ring. The mayor and the sheriff were jealous of
such successful rivals in the saloon-keeping and gambling
way as Luke Short had always been. They ran him out
of Dodge.

He came back, though—with backers of such stature
as Bat Masterson, Wyatt Earp and the brand of desperate
warriors these gentlemen always enlisted in their vendettas. The mayor and the sheriff capitulated abjectly
and completely and in haste.

This, then, was the smooth-faced, soft-voiced, im-
maculately-clad little man who ran the White Elephant
Saloon; the gambler to whom Jim Courtright came with
his demand for protection-money. Short considered the
demand—perhaps thinking of that little business in
Dodge City, in '83. Then, in his soft voice, he invited
Courtright to take the short walk necessary to a jump
into the Trinity River, somewhat north of the White
Elephant.

Courtright might have believed that the dapper little man had water on the brain. For no matter how often he or his agents mentioned protection money to Short, there was always this reference to the river. And, except in time of flood, when she goes on a "high lonesome," the Trinity is neither a majestic nor a beautiful stream. Jim Courtright must have begun to feel that the frequency of Short's comments upon it would have been out of all proportion to a stream the size of the Mississippi.

Fort Worth realized that trouble between two such as Luke Short and Jim Courtright was inevitable. Nothing short of a miracle could prevent their feud ending in the smoke. Neither had ever been known to take a backward step. Sizing up the two men, the canny bettor put his stack of blues on the long-haired ex-marshal.

"Oh, yes," the oldtimers say, even yet, "Short was right quick with the plow-handles. But Jim Courtright—hell! he was a ring-tail' whizzer with red-striped wheels!"

Short remained quietly inflexible. He would pay Courtright's T. I. C. Agency precisely the whole of nothing. Courtright, in such a town and such a time, had to make good his demand. It was make Short knuckle under or leave, not only Fort Worth; Tarrant County; Texas; but the country. For that tale would spread and there was never a sick wolf who lasted long. Being Jim Courtright, he was not apt to "buy a trunk."

He got pretty drunk one night and remarked that there was a combination over at the White Elephant which was bucking him. But, he hinted grimly, it was going to be settled soon. The next evening—February 8, 1887—at about 7:30, an excited citizen dashed up to a young policeman and wanted to borrow a gun. He said that there was going to be trouble between Courtright and Short.

Courtright came looking for the stubborn little gambler and found him at around 8 o'clock. A mutual acquaintance brought Short outside of the White Elephant and the little man stood looking at Courtright, keeping his thumbs hooked in the armholes of his vest. The talk became somewhat heated. Short dropped his hands, as if to smooth his vest. It was no time for movements even remotely suspicious. In such times as this, many a man in Texas has committed suicide by reaching abruptly for his handkerchief!

"Don't you pull a gun on me!" Courtright snapped at him.

"Why, I'm not trying to pull a gun!" cried Short, in a pained tone. "I haven't got a gun there, see!"

He began pawing at his vest and all the time his hands got lower, closer to his belt, closer to the pistol on his hip. Jim Courtright was not one to be taken in by any such maneuvering. He "went for his gun," the right-hand gun. Short's hand flashed back to his hip. He had the edge, through the pretense of showing his unarmed condition. His hand was already close to gun-butt when Courtright started his draw.

Short's gun snapped out flashingly, as did Courtright's. And Short fired so wildly that he would have missed Jim Courtright, with that first shot, by two feet —but for the upward jerk of Courtright's hand. That first wild bullet tore into the hammer thumb of Courtright's hand; smashed it at the moment it was pulling back the big hammer of the single-action .45 Colt! As lucky a shot as the Old West ever heard of. It would be described for many a year around the cowboy's campfires, from the Rio Grande to Calgary.

Jim Courtright wasted no time, then, in reaching for his left-hand gun. Instead, he tried to throw the pistol from right hand to left hand, in what is called "the border shift." But that split-second of time required for the maneuver had given Short opportunity to correct his aim and drive three bullets into Courtright. Down went the long-haired gunman, dying, with no spectator gaping more amazedly at this reversal of the town's expectations than Short himself. A barber who had been shaving a man in the shop nearby, told me about it the other day. And he shook his white head again, after forty-odd years; the old amazement came fresh to voice and face:

"The man in the chair heard the shots, the same as I did. He lifted up, with the lather on his face, you know. He said:

" 'What's that?'

"I said: 'Jim Courtright's killed Luke Short! It was bound to happen!' Then I ran out and—it was Luke that had killed Jim!''

So Jim Courtright died, victim of perhaps the oddest bit of gunplay on record. Luke Short lived, by virtue of that freak hit scored by a wild bullet. Lived nearly seven years longer, to die peacefully in bed in Kansas, in September, 1893, aged thirty-nine.

As one remembers Jim Courtright, it is only fair to remember both sides of him. He was neither all good nor all bad—who is!—and if he died as what would be called today a "racketeer," before that he had lived as a good soldier, a valued scout and a fearless peace officer. Though he died the victim of a fluke shot, still he was one of the Great Gunmen of all time. A better gunman than the man who killed him!

CHAPTER IX · *Bayard of the Chaparral*

RANGER CAPTAIN JOHN R. HUGHES

"THE TEXAS RANGER can ride harder, fight longer, live rougher, and make less talk about it, than anything else that walks on two feet!" wrote a veracious chronicler many years ago—and the words should be graved upon a monument.

Texas Rangers! They had their beginning back in the '30s. For the Ranger force was born of the travail of Texas the Republic. Since then, its name has gone around the English-speaking world, as that of an organization without like or equal. The Rangers have given us names which must be interwoven with the history written and unwritten of Texas; of the frontier.

If, today, we were to set up a tablet and grave upon it twenty names of Ranger officers in whose very shadows the frontier crept forward, onward, the list must include such names as Jack Hayes, L. H. McNelly, D. W. Roberts, N. O. Reynolds, George W. Baylor—and John R. Hughes, ex-commander of Company D, Frontier Battalion, Texas Rangers.

His place among the famous Ranger captains is assured for several reasons. For one thing, he was longest a captain, if not longest a Ranger. Enlisting August 10, 1887, he resigned January 31, 1915, having held the rank of captain since 1893.

But this is the least of his qualifications for placement among the tall ones of the Ranger officers. His twenty-eight years of arduous, dangerous and varied service bridge the years between the oldtime force and that of today. Himself, he was ever the "horseback Ranger;" always the leader, rather than the commander, of his men. When D Company was given a difficult, dangerous assignment, Captain Hughes would never be found in a swivel-chair. On horseback, he was *taking* his men on the trail.

The stories they tell of him! They say that during his long service, he knew every loop and curve of the ancient blood-soaked Rio Grande, from El Paso to the mouth. No hidden retreat of outlaw or fugitive in the green and tangled *bosques*, or among the savage mountain fastnesses of this grim, wild, border-region but was photographed on his steeltrap memory.

As for the hundreds of "bad men" who struck right and left at lonely ranch and cowtown bank and treasure-bearing express car—the adjutant general's office, down at Austin, published annually what was officially termed a "Fugitive List." (Among the Rangers it was often called "Bible Two"—and read as Bible "One" never was!) It contained the list of "wanted" criminals sent in by sheriffs of Texas counties. Religiously, the Rangers pored over criminals' names and descriptions and habits. But Captain Hughes did more—he memorized the list of border-criminals. So, he could come to the scene of a crime and, very often, say with certainty that a certain man, or band of men, had committed a particular crime.

He made a study of the art of crook-catching. So, knowing criminals in general and those of his own territory in particular, he generally outguessed them. So successful was he that the newspapers had a stock-phrase: "Captain Hughes is reported on the trail of these men. If so, we expect word shortly of their capture."

Captain Hughes has probably been in more battles than any living Ranger. But like that Typical Ranger of whom the old reporter wrote, he makes "less talk about it!" One must go to the old reports of the adjutant general, to learn that he had any fights at all! I believe that it was a sort of hobby with him, never to lose a battle and never to let a prisoner escape!

From the very beginning, his experiences were of that sort from which a fictionist could—and would—make thrilling stories. Born in Cambridge, Illinois, he came to

the Indian Territory a husky youngster in his 'teens. He
lived with the Indians. He worked with Indian traders.
He was companion of such famous scouts as Jack Stilwell, who had been in the great Beecher Island fight
with Major Forsyth. He stood in a post sutler's store and
heard Stilwell give the news of the Custer massacre.

Working as cowboy for those contractors who were
furnishing cattle for the Indians, he became an expert in
all the branches of this trade. In 1877, when his employers lost their beef-contract, he accompanied a herd
up the trail from Fort Sill. In 1878, he went with Cross-P
cattle from Austin, Texas, to Ellis, Kansas, working for
Major Drumm. That same year he started his own horse-
ranch in Central Texas. It was before barbed-wire and
every day's work was a "rodeo." He captured wild and
half-wild horses on the range; he traded one broken
horse for a whole band of free-ranging wild ones—then
worked perhaps six months to capture his new possessions.

So for nine years. He might have ended his days a
horse-rancher, without even thinking of becoming a
peace officer. But a hard-case bunch of horse-thieves
came raiding his way. They ran off seventy good horses
and sixteen of these were Hughes' property. He was
much annoyed. So he made a deal with his neighbors—
if they would look after his ranch, he would follow the
stolen animals and the thieves. It is safe to venture
that, had those six "long-roping" gentlemen known
Hughes personally, they would have cut his sixteen
animals out of the herd and saved themselves future grief.

That was '84. West Texas and New Mexico alike
were unfenced wilderness. Scattered ranches; a few tiny
farms; a population of one person to many and many a
square mile—that about described it. Hughes' troubles
were many, as on May 1st he started out. But once he
cut the robbers' trail, he stuck to it like a bloodhound.
The days dragged by, became weeks; the weeks mar-
shaled themselves into months. Still he was riding,
getting fresh mounts, making inquiries; riding, riding,

riding. Across the wide, rolling plains of West Texas; up into that No Man's Land that was the Panhandle; south again on the twisting trail—and into New Mexico.

There, at last, he caught up with his men, who were in camp. Six against one. But he attacked them. You cannot get from him any thrilling picture of this fight. He says nothing of the Colt Thunder that rolled; of hot lead singing and whining in two directions. Briefly, matter-of-factly, he remarks that he "took the two surviving robbers to the nearest town and delivered them to the authorities."

He came jogging back from his—lacking fifteen days —year-long journey. He had traveled 1200 miles. But he had the horses! He found that he could no longer live peaceably in that section. The robbers' friends "had his name in the pot." One such rode up to his place when Hughes was absent, but found a Ranger there. He and the Ranger exchanged some six-shooter compliments. Then that "avenger" lit a shuck out of the Hughes bailiwick. Later Hughes and this Ranger cornered the fellow and when he refused to surrender, he was killed.

But this by no means ended the attempts on Hughes' life. As he remarks humorously, it seemed that, if he were forced to neglect his ranching to fight outlaws, it would be only sensible to have official status and draw pay for the work. So he enlisted in the Rangers at Georgetown, August 10, 1887, expecting to serve six or eight months. He rode horseback 700 miles to join his company at Camp Wood. When his command moved to Rio Grande City, that winter, he was plunged into all the danger and the excitement of Ranger service in the wild border-region.

Hughes it was who arrested the notorious Catarina Garza—chief figure of what was grandiloquently called 'the Garza War." Garza had a loud, self-published record as a dangerous man. But that failed completely to impress Hughes. He simply walked up to Garza and arrested him and—that was that.

In 1889 Hughes worked as guard for the Fronteriza Mining Company for awhile, but after six months came back to the Rangers; became corporal. At Shafter, the mining company was losing high-grade ore to thieves. Pinkerton men and local county officers, even another detachment of Rangers, had failed to locate the thieves, much less capture them. Hughes was detailed here and by clever detective-work and employment of an ex-Ranger as sleuth, four ore-thieves were surprised one night.

One Mexican stood guard over the thieves' horses. When Hughes ordered the other robbers to surrender, all four opened fire. The horse-guard threw lead for a time but seemingly became discouraged with his lack of success. He hightailed and was not followed, Hughes and his men being busy with the others. The battle raged for an hour. When the smoke blew away the Rangers had killed three Mexicans, who fell with guns in their hands.

They were buried on a hill, in a place chosen by Hughes. He put the white crosses where they would gleam, at night, between the two branches of the ore-thieves' trail into Mexico. It was an object-lesson which these people could understand. It stopped the thefts.

Hughes was definitely a Ranger, now. He had found himself possessed of all the qualifications, physical and mental, for this ever-thrilling, ever-interesting life. Bass Outlaw resigned (under a little pressure!) as sergeant of Company D. Captain Frank Jones appointed Corporal Hughes in his place.

He was already well-known as one of the most daring and efficient Rangers in the Frontier Battalion. His exploits were colorful. They made wonderful "copy." Newspaper men gave him such complimentary titles as "A Bayard of the Chaparral." A big, dark-haired, dark-eyed, still-faced man, expert shot with either belt-gun or Winchester, when he sat mounted he was the very picture of *The Ranger*.

In June, 1893, Captain Jones went down below San Elizario hunting cattle-thieves who were supposed to live around Tres Jacales—"Three Shacks." He had with him five men. Failing to discover the thieves, he was returning along a trail that twisted, now into Mexico, again back into Texas. His detachment ran into the thieves.

These immediately dashed for the brush and finally holed up at a tiny village. The Rangers were fired upon from the place by a large number of Mexicans. Jones was badly wounded, after wounding one of the fugitives. He kept on fighting from the ground until he died. More Mexicans were swarming up, minute by minute. The Rangers were driven back. Captain Jones' body was recovered next day through the mayor of Juarez, Mexico. Four Mexicans were arrested on that side of the river and lodged in Juarez jail.

CAPTAIN JONES had been idolized by his company. Nobody doubted that, if the Mexican authorities failed to execute the murderers, their names would be written large on a special fugitive list of D Company. Nor that close attention was being paid to the activities of the Juarez courts.

Meanwhile, on July 4, 1893, Governor Hogg had appointed Sergeant Hughes to command of the company. This promotion was praised by the state press, for, as has been said, Hughes was becoming very well-known indeed.

The Mexicans responsible for Captain Jones' murder were released from Juarez jail. Now enters the tale one of those famous clouds of mystery. To discover what happened, one consults yellowed clippings, by which it is learned that one of those Mexicans has been found dead near the scene of Captain Jones' murder—broken heart, doubtless. . . . That another has been found dead —must have been apoplexy. . . . That still a third has been found mysteriously hanging to a tree. *That* sounds like suicide! But—at any rate—the released murderers died. All of them!

A "horseback Ranger's" life being what it was, it would take the book he refuses to write, to give more than the high-lights of Captain Hughes' service. His weeks had seven full days, four times a month. An old adjutant general's report lies on my desk. Above the seven-notched barrel of Bill Boggs' old .45, which holds it open, I find a biennial report. It is a tabulation of the activities of the Ranger companies. By its evidence, little Company D, Captain John R. Hughes, commanding, "rambled right smart" during the two years covered by the table. Members of Company D rode horseback 26,000 miles; they accomplished 139 "scouts"!

The life of a Ranger captain in those days was no career for a home-loving, ease-hunting man! There were entirely too many odds and ends of nobody's business which always became Ranger business. Horse-thieves to hunt, up in the wild and desolate Guadalupe Mountains. Cattle-smugglers of the swarthy breed who ambushed Captain Jones, to lure into fancied security, then land upon in some gray dawning with a grim, bullet-pointed charge out of the Rio Grande's sinister green *bosques*. Murderers who overawed a whole community, to be located and taken dead or alive. Brand-blotters and butchers of other men's cattle to build cases against and put the shackles on. Or a prize-fight to stop!

In '96, certain gentlemen decided to stage the Fitz-simmons-Maher embroglio in El Paso. But these parties to the decision had not taken into account the fact that Charley Culberson was governor of Texas. Nor that, of all the many, many things Culberson could not endure, prize-fighting was least endurable. For the reformers were against the spectacle of two men hitting each other with fists. As usual, they made a great deal more noise than the quiet, respectable citizens who wanted to see Fitz and Maher shoving the chamois.

Prize-fighting was evidently considered by Culberson as worse than murder or any of the forms of robbery. For, whereas the appeals of county attorneys and sheriffs, for Rangers to handle situations involving felonies, were often refused with the remark that "no Rangers are available," mere threat of this fight brought four companies of Rangers to El Paso, away from the districts where their services were needed for police purposes.

Captain Hughes' company was among those present. And a pleasant time was had by all! For to the sporting element local to El Paso in that day, was now added a constantly augmented swarm of outsiders. The uncertainty, the delays, attendant upon staging the fight, gave it the widest possible publicity. In addition to the Ranger captains, Adjutant General W. H. Mabry came down. Now, I don't *know* that he shared the hope of many Rangers that the fight would be held somewhere barely out of their jurisdiction, but within easy eyeshot. But it is of record that he came to El Paso.

Old John Selman, the famous gunman, was El Paso's city marshal at the moment. On one night, his arrests numbered twenty-six burglars! There were riots and near-riots. One evening, a deputy sheriff and a gambler fell out over a card-game. They adjourned to the street very courteously, to avoid damage to the bar-fixtures and bystanders. A special Ranger threatened them with arrest and this cramping of a gentleman's style so provoked the gambler that he opened up on the Ranger instead of on the deputy sheriff. While a number of shots rattled out of the pistols, nobody was hurt. The two principals of the original row were arrested by Sergeant "John L." Sullivan.

Some three or four hundred men collected in the street outside the saloon in which the prisoners were held. All were armed; the vast majority were hard characters whose great delight was to find—or stage— such a scene of excitement. For they had a most profitable way of spotting the jewelry in a saloon crowd, then shooting out the lights and snatching the valuables—to the accompaniment of murderous assault if necessary.

It was a moment of relief to the Rangers when the fight was moved away from El Paso. Not even in the old days when the railroads first came, had so many toughs been seen assembled.

The Big Bend country was an outlaws' paradise. In its savage fastnesses lurked two-gunned outlaws, Mexican and white. Peace officers usually gave the Bend a wide berth. So it was no more than natural that, to Captain Hughes, the Bend seemed due for a cleanup. He rode down after a particularly desperate and misguided Mexican. Merely because he had cut stick for the Bend and now lived a hundred miles from the railroad, this foolish *bandido* felt himself secure from the attentions of all authorities.

At a little Mexican store on the river-bank, Hughes saw his man among a bunch of Mexicans. He rode up and "threw down" on the wanted man. After the capture, the other Mexicans ducked behind clumps of brush and opened fire. Without losing the magic of the drop, Hughes replied so earnestly to the attackers' fire that those who had not already become permanent residents decided to emigrate rather than to settle. That night he took his prisoner on a skilfully executed detour, thus evading the waiting Mexicans. He landed his prisoner in jail, up on the railroad.

It was in the Marfa-Alpine country, in '96, that Hughes had what he recalls as one of his "most interesting little battles." To him at Ysleta came word that some men were camped in the Glass Mountains, stealing fine saddle and race horses and apparently getting ready to rob a train. He loaded some men and horses in the mail car of a passenger train and was soon on the trail of these prospective Long Riders. He had a warrant issued by Judge Van Sickle of Alpine.

Hughes had in his party Rangers Ed Bryant (later to become well-known as chief deputy of Sheriff Seth Orndorff in El Paso) and Thalis T. Cook, with Deputy Sheriff Jim Pool of Marfa, a rancher named Jim Stroud and a cowboy named Combs who had lost a fine horse to these fellows.

In the meanwhile, the horse-thieves had been de-predating in Brewster County. They raided a house and a report came into Alpine, to the sheriff'a office.

Captain Jim Gillett had just turned over the shrieval honors and dignities to a successor who, at the time the runner came in, was off tax-collecting. A young office-deputy, a relative of the new sheriff, came to ex-Sheriff Gillett with word that some tough cases had robbed "the Frenchman's" house. He asked if Gillett would go out.

"It's no business of mine," Gillett told the boy. "But if the sheriff is away, I'll get a citizens' posse to-gether and we'll round up the place. But if the robbers aren't there, or close by, we can't leave our business to chase them all over the country."

The posse went out and performed that classic maneuver of the old Rangers called "rounding up the ranch." But the robbers were gone, leaving a trail that headed for the Glass Mountains, miles away. The citizens spent the night foodless and blanketless and with dawn they started back for town. On the way, they met Captain Hughes' party. Jim Stroud had no "long gun" and borrowed a fine specially-made .45-90 from Gillett.

Captain Hughes' party, well-equipped for a cam-paign, went on. They found the thieves' old camp and studied it carefully. No signs of coffee-making or bread-baking were there, so they decided that the bandits must be pretty sick of a straight beef diet. The trail from the camp pointed generally toward Fort Stockton and showed a number of horses being driven.

Hughes thought that one of the ranches in the neighborhood—the Star or McCutcheon's—would be raided by the men they were following, to get flour and coffee. So he headed for the Star. There the trail petered out. But the terrain in that region is too rough to permit of crossing the hills except by the passes. So Hughes divided his party and sent them scouting the passes in an attempt to cut the trail.

Thalis Cook, Jim Stroud and Beau McCutcheon made up the lucky squad. They came suddenly upon the robbers, who opened so hot a fire on them that they ducked back behind a hill. The robbers came after them a little way, shooting. Cook had taken from Stroud the .45-90 Gillett had loaned him. He opened up on the robbers and drove them back. Then he settled down to keep in touch with them. Stroud and McCutcheon, who had no rifles, went racing back for Hughes.

When Hughes came up, he found Cook and the bandits comfortably exchanging personalities. One of the robbers would rise up and beckon imperatively to the Ranger: "Come on and fight, you This-and-That!" Cook would shake his head and beckon just as enthusiastically to the robber. "Bring your fight over and put it in the pot!"

He described the robbers' position on a mountain-point and gave his idea of the best plan of attack.

Combs had been expressing himself very bitterly about the loss of his fine horse to these thieves. So Hughes and Cook drafted him to join them in a charge on the robbers. The rest of the party went down to head off the men, in case they made a break for the plains. There was hot firing on both sides as the two Rangers and Combs moved forward. Combs put a hand to his ear. It came away wet with blood.

"They shot me!" he yelled.

"Why, that's fine!" Thalis Cook assured him over-shoulder, as he lined his sights on the robbers. "You see, there's nothing like being cool, in a squabble like this. Now, that blood-letting will cool you off, so you can do some real fighting and—"

One of the bandits showed himself an inch too much, trying to get a shot at them. Thalis Cook's finger tightened on the trigger. The man pitched down, dead. Cook was one of the finest rifle-shots in the Frontier Battalion.

Captain Hughes moved off, looking for a place where he could crossfire upon the two survivors. One of these was now afflicted with a burning desire to remove from the locality. The three robbers had tied their horses before the battle began. A chance-shot of the posse cut the hitch-rope of this emigrant's horse. So he had only to jump on and slam steel to the animal. The men below him hesitated to fire, for he looked rather like Captain Hughes. So he got a long start—got clear away for the time being.

"Come on out of that!" Thalis Cook yelled at the remaining bandit. "You're goin' to get yourself cut off pocket-high, if you don't. Grab your ears! Come on out!"

"All right! Calf rope!" the robber called in reply. "You have killed my brother."

He stood up. Hughes, who had returned to Cook's side, moved in with Cook to make the young fellow a prisoner. He was not "grabbing his ears," but he had no weapons in sight, where he stood near the body of his brother. Abruptly, his lax attitude vanished. His hand whipped around behind him and came out with the pistol he had rammed in the back of his waist-band. He fired, but Hughes and Cook were pumping lead at him before he let go the big hammer of the hidden pistol. He crashed down dead, almost across his brother's body.

These were the Friar brothers, Jube and Arthur. Hard case cowboys, like Sam Bass; like the Daltons; like Butch Cassidy and all the tribe, whom the old song describes so neatly:

> First took to drinking
> Then to card playing;
> Got shot in the breast
> And I'm dying today. . .

When they had carried the bodies down to where they could be sent into Alpine, they found that the warrant for the arrest of these horse-thieves and house-robbers was saturated with blood. It was returned to Judge van Sickle, with this lurid verification of the indorsement scrawled upon it.

The man who fled from the fight was not long at liberty. He was arrested and all his protestations that he knew nothing of the Friar boys failed to keep him out of the penitentiary. He was for years bitter against Captain Hughes. A man for whom he rode the range says that a bunch of his cowboys, including this ex-convict, were once on a cow-hunt in the Big Bend. Sitting by the camp-fire, the old fellow announced his intention of killing Hughes on sight.

"Why—" a cowboy lifted a little, where he was hunkered with a cup of coffee, to shade his eyes and stare at an approaching horseman "—you're the *luckiest* fella! Which if I had yo' luck, I would play the lottery for a livin'. Yonder comes Cap'n Hughes now! I'd know him in a thousand. . . ."

It proved to be the brother of the outfit's owner. He got off of his horse and sat down by the fire to eat. A hoarse, whispering voice sounded, out in the grease-wood and mesquite, minutes later, calling for the cow-boy who had announced "Hughes."

"Is it—Is it—you know who? 'T ain't? 'T ain't! Well, by Dad! It shore is mightily lucky for him it ain't!"

THIS "INTERESTING little battle" was nothing at all, compared to a holding-of-the-fort which Hughes had to do in early 1904. A fight with *bandidos* who slam lead at you and at whom you slam lead is a clean and simple business of killing or capturing the targets or dying, yourself, from lead-poisoning. But mixing into a brawl where lawyers are using writs and mouth-filling techni-cal terms for ammunition is—quite the reverse.

Captain Hughes and most of D Company were sta-tioned at the little town of Alice in Jim Wells County, when in faraway New York City the ball started rolling. A famous criminal lawyer—criminal in both practice and practices—named Abe Hummel, had let his foot slip. District Attorney Jerome had long been ambitious to see Hummel in stripes and when he stumbled upon a little matter of subornation of perjury, he saw his opportunity. The chief witness was a railroad conductor, Charles F. Dodge. He it was who had done the perjury at Hummel's instigation. Hummel learned of Jerome's plans and—Dodge vanished. A detective in Jerome's employ traced Dodge and an agent of Hummel's to New Orleans, thence to Houston, Texas. These two were bound for Mexico by way of Eagle Pass. Houston officers took Dodge from the Sunset Limited. He vowed that he would never return to New York. Hummel had boasted that a million dollars would be spent, if necessary, to prevent Dodge's appearance against him.

Texas now saw the beginning of its most tangled— and possibly its most sordid—legal battle. Jerome hired local attorneys to represent him against the native lawyers who were acting with members of Hummel's firm, sent down to introduce high-pressure legal jigglings of the New York brand. Writs and appeals and injunctions and—a layman knows what! were flying.

All of which prefaced the arrival in Alice of a red-faced pleasant little man who looked like one of the drummers who made the town. He hunted up Hughes and his blue eyes twinkled at sight of the big, dark-haired, dark-eyed and still-faced captain of Texas Rangers. He introduced himself after that inspection. He was the detective Jerome had sent down to find Dodge and secure the runaway witness' arrest. He explained the case, thus-far:

"Dodge is aboard a sea-going tug with one Kaffen-burgh, who is Hummel's nephew and a member of the firm. They have a fellow named Bracken with them— he's been with Dodge ever since the conductor skipped. They think they're going to get that tug-captain to take 'em to Tampico. But he has orders from his employers to bring 'em to Point Isabel and land 'em there."

"What do you want me to do?" Hughes asked in his quiet, precise voice.

"Well, you're the head of the Rangers in this district. You're not subject to wire-pulling. And here's a man for whom Governor Lanham has issued an extradition warrant, honoring a requisition of the governor of New York. Our man, a detective sergeant of the New York City force, was going to start for New York with Dodge when he was served with an injunction forbidding him or the chief of police to arrest Dodge under that warrant. Hummel's gang secured a new habeas corpus hearing for Dodge. It failed and Dodge was handed over to our detective sergeant.

"But an appeal was taken from that decision. Dodge got out on twenty thousand dollars cash bail. It would have been the same if bond had been set at a million! I went to Austin, to arrange for another extradition warrant. I left the sergeant to keep an eye on Dodge. He let him slip away. I knew that Dodge would jump bail and I wanted that new warrant so that I'd be ready for him.

"Now, the party's going to land at Point Isabel and come to Brownsville. That's first step toward a jump into Mexico. Will you have some of your men on hand, to meet the party when it comes ashore at Isabel? Not to arrest them. They're still within the jurisdiction of the Southern District of the Federal Court. Technically, Dodge hasn't jumped his bail. I want the Rangers to keep an eye on 'em and if Dodge starts to cross the line, arrest him."

The detective, having made his arrangements with Hughes, hurried by stage to Brownsville. Meanwhile, Dodge and his companions had landed under Ranger surveillance at Isabel. They hurried by train to Brownsville. A Ranger-Sergeant was with them, waiting for a move toward Mexico. But they went on to Alice, with the Ranger and the detective trailing. They intended to take a train at Alice for Mexico. They believed themselves free of the hounds, now.

But when they strolled into the smoking car of the National of Mexico, a big, dark-eyed, calm-faced man in citizens' clothing also came strolling in. He stood with hand at small, dark mustache, looking about. Dodge and his companions thought nothing of him until he informed them gently that he had to arrest Dodge, who was wickedly attempting to jump his bond. That remark set them slumping in their seats, gaping at Captain Hughes. They had been so sure that their trail, from Houston, had been covered!

The agents of Jerome had secured their second extradition warrant from Governor Lanham. The Governor telegraphed Captain Hughes* to take charge of the prisoner and deliver him to the New York officers for transportation back to that state.

But all was not so simple as the mere arrest of Dodge. The commander of D Company would have arrested whole regiments of Dodges without batting an eye. But now began the tortuous writhings of our marvelous legal system. Hummel and his Texas agents knew every wrinkle of this game and there was money to burn. No matter what the cost, Dodge must be kept out of a New York court!

So in Nueces County a new writ of habeas corpus was applied for. A Nueces County officer came galloping over to Alice to get Dodge. Captain Hughes listened attentively, then referred to his telegram from the Governor. He shook his head:

"I'm sorry," he said courteously. "But I don't find a thing in this telegram about turning the prisoner over to you. Sorry! Come over again, some time."

The next application for habeas corpus was brought in Bee County. A Bee County officer lit a shuck over to Alice. If he had met the Nueces County man on the road, it would have saved money for his county! Hughes referred again to his telegram. He asked what part of New York City Bee County might be in.

*W. U. TEL.

Austin, Texas, Feb. 15, 1904
Capt. Jno. R. Hughes, Alice, Texas.
Hold C. F. Dodge to await requisition from governor of New York.
                                        S. W. T. Lanham, Gov.

"For, you see, this telegram says I have to deliver him to a New York officer. . . ."

There was by this time about as much excitement in that section of Texas as the inhabitants could bear. A great deal of it was born of the high-powered legal lights and lightnings, for this was Law on a scale to which Texas had never become accustomed. But a good share of the furore was due to that famous telegram of Captain Hughes'.

The judge of the Federal Court at Houston now took a hand in the squabble over Dodge's custody. He ordered the United States marshal at Alice to take the prisoner. But Hughes had been paying no heed to the legal thundering around him. He had a perfectly plain order from the only authority he recognized. So, for the United States marshal's benefit, he once more got out the now immortal telegram. It was growing a trifle frayed of creases, but it was just as potent as on the day Hughes received it.

To the United States marshal he stated his simple code: He obeyed the Governor; and all the writs, the thises, the thats, which lawyers could think up, then twist and pull-haul about, made no difference whatever. The Texas Rangers had that prisoner and until the Governor rescinded his original order—well, Hughes would like to see somebody try taking the prisoner away from him!

At last, Dodge went to Houston, in what was termed the joint custody of Captain Hughes and the United States marshal. (I have always liked that word "joint" as used in this case!)

This was not the end of the Dodge case. But it was the finish of Hughes' connection with the most famous fugitive in Texas' history. Eventually, the conductor went back and testified. Jerome won his long fight to put Abe Hummel behind bars. Down in Alice, Texas, an imperturbable Ranger captain moved calmly about his business. He had done precisely that, in the face of the most gigantic network of legal and extra-legal efforts to take a Ranger's prisoner away. But then—he had been armed with all the authority any Ranger ever needed— an order from the Governor and a well-oiled six-shooter.

How many battles the Captain has fought; how many criminals he has captured; how many hard case gunmen it has been necessary for him to kill—these things nobody knows but himself, or is likely to know! There was one fight up in the Indian Territory of which he will talk—a little. A bullet so wounded his right arm that he had to learn shooting all over! He learned so well that those who met him during his twenty-eight years in the Texas Rangers rarely guessed that he had not been *born* left-handed.

Today he lives in El Paso—in the Ford—and most particularly he lives in the Present. He is not one to day-dream much of the Past. There was a time when he had good reason to believe that silver would never show in his dark hair. But he is with us today, erect as ever he was; as keen-eyed. It seems likely that for many a year to come he will be a familiar and honored figure on the streets of El Paso and Ysleta. When he does lay down the hand he has played so well, his chosen epitaph will be that of the old cowman—

> When my old soul seeks range and rest,
>   Beyond the last divide,
> Just plant me in some stretch of West
>   That's sunny, lone an' wide.
> Let cattle rub my tombstone down;
>   An' coyotes mourn their kin;
> Let hawses paw an' tromp the moun,'
>   But don't you fence it in!

BASS OUTLAW

THEY SAY that he had but one qualification of the true Texas Ranger, this insignificant-seeming little man: He could pull a Colt so rapidly that eye could hardly follow hand and, once out, the bullet from that Colt bored its target with deadly accuracy.. At short range, he killed the "fool quail" of West Texas with a .45 and filled the Ranger camp-kettle.

But, if he were as brave as other Rangers, when on a "scout," he was of a quarrelsome disposition that kept him embroiled with the men of his company; or with the citizens he was detailed to coöperate with or to protect.

He was a native of Georgia and enlisted in E Company of the Rangers in '85. Two years later, he joined D Company. He was appointed corporal in April, 1890 and advanced to sergeant when Sergeant Fusselman died with boots on, in the Franklin Mountains near El Paso, killed by Mexican horse-thieves.

Considered in the light of Bass Outlaw's reputation as a gunman, his picture offers a puzzle to the physiognomist. His pale blue-gray eyes, his receding chin, seem indexes to an insignificance that certainly was not the keynote of this suspicious little wolf's character!

Perhaps his uncanny dexterity with the six-shooter gave him a confidence, a boldness, not innate. Perhaps the respect in which his gunmanship was held by the average man pulled up his chin, pushed out his chest. It has happened before.

The manner in which he left the highest rank—sergeant—ever to be attained by him in the Rangers, must have soured him:

Captain Frank Jones commanded D Company at the time. Bass Outlaw was senior non-commissioned officer. So, when Captain Jones left the Rangers' camp at Alpine, to come to El Paso on business, Outlaw was acting commanding officer.

He left the camp and rode into Alpine, to begin the drinking that Captain Jones (or any other Ranger captain) would not permit. He came to the Buckhorn Saloon and there found an old Ranger out of N. O. Reynolds' famous company, Abe Anglin, now out of the service. Anglin and Outlaw got into a card-game. As the night wore on, Outlaw lost steadily. Drank steadily, too.

Near midnight, the checks and money on the table were all on Anglin's side. Bass Outlaw was virtually "clean."

When Anglin reached out to draw his winnings to him, Outlaw reached for money and checks with his left hand. His right dropped to the butt of his pistol. Anglin, in shirtsleeves, unarmed, was in no position to argue with Outlaw. But, nevertheless, he did argue with him. Outlaw snarled that he had been robbed. Anglin, the old Ranger of the Indian-fighting days, was not one to be intimidated. The quarrel waxed hotter. The bartender of the Buckhorn sent a hurry call for Sheriff Jim Gillett, whose home was not more than a hundred yards from the saloon.

So, the men watching the argument, saw the sheriff come through the door, a wide-shouldered, square-faced, dark-haired man. Outlaw and Anglin still argued heatedly. Sheriff Gillett hurried back to them. He caught Outlaw by the shoulder with left hand, leaving his right free for gunplay if that were necessary. He worked him toward the back-door and into the yard.

Some of the men at the bar followed them outside. For here was Bass Outlaw, not alone in his opinion that he was a ring-tailed whizzer with a six-shooter. Here was Sheriff Gillett, with a record six years long as a Ranger, supplemented by his record as captain of guards for the Santa Fé and as city marshal of that wide-open, hell-roaring border town, El Paso. No pistoleer, but a highly efficient officer who could handle his Colt just as flashingly as the bad men, when necessary. No wonder they followed, those men from the bar. Here were the potentialities which, so many times, had made for flashing, smoky gunplay in Cattle Land.

In the yard, Gillett upbraided the sullen Bass Outlaw for starting a row in the saloon. He reminded him that he was commanding officer, during Captain Jones' absence, of the whole Ranger company.

"You ought to be ashamed of yourself!" the Sheriff told him, "Now, you get on your horse and go back to camp."

Outlaw was just drunk enough to be in ugly humor; just sober enough, possibly, not to want an argument with the Sheriff.

"All right, I'll go back to camp," he agreed. "But we'll all go back and have a drink, before I go."

He led the way back into the Buckhorn. Gillett—who never drank—stood watching, to see that Outlaw kept his promise to go back to camp. Outlaw lined up the saloon's patrons at the bar. He rammed a hand into his pocket and brought out silver. A quarter-dollar dropped to the floor and automatically, Bass Outlaw moved as if to recover it. But he only began the move! His head jerked to the Sheriff, who stood watching him grimly.

There are those who watched who say that they could not see how both of these men could live until morning. Outlaw was always dangerous and when half-drunk, more dangerous than usual. He had boasted, time and time again, that no man could cross him and live. As for Gillett—the man who could for two years police Old El Paso, neither killing a man nor taking a step backward from such as Dallas Stoudenmire, the brothers Manning, "Old John" Selman, Ben Thompson's hard case brother, Billy, "Mysterious Dave" Mather, he was not a man to try to outface, when he stood behind the Law!

Bass Outlaw kicked the quarter.

"I don't want that money!" he remarked and looked at Gillett again.

His meaning was plain to everyone. He was a suspicious little wolf! He distrusted everybody. Now, he distrusted the Sheriff. If he bent—so his thought ran—would Gillett take advantage of that to kill him? Gillett understood. The silent accusation both hurt and angered him. He picked up the coin and tossed it contemptuously on the bar.

When Captain Jones returned to Alpine, he heard the tale from a prominent citizen—not from Gillett nor Outlaw. He called Outlaw on the carpet. The reputation of the little sergeant meant nothing at all to Jones.

"I told you not long ago that the next time you drank on duty you'd be finished!" he said flatly. "Now, sit down at that table and write out your resignation from the Ranger Service."

There was a battle of eyes for a brief moment. But Captain Jones looked the little "bad man" down. Sullenly, Outlaw did as he was ordered. He received a voucher for the pay due him. When he went out, he was furious. Not at Jones, who had kicked him out of the service. His grudge was against Sheriff Gillett. Quite erroneously he insisted that Gillett, for fear of him, had reported his misconduct to Captain Jones. There is little reason for believing that Bass really held that opinion. Certainly, his encounters with the Sheriff had not been such as to give him an impression that Gillett was worried about his gunplay.

But he took his voucher, muttering threats. He went down the street. There was in Alpine at that time a general store owned by an ex-Ranger who is now one of the most prominent of Texas cowmen—Joe D. Jackson. For some reason, the cranky Bass liked Jackson. At this moment, he owed him money.

JACKSON REMEMBERS vividly how the little man came snarling into the store, to fling down his voucher with an oath.

"Cash it for me!" he told Jackson. "Take out what I owe you. That's the last payday."

"I—heard that you were going to quit," Jackson remarked cautiously. He knew the whole story—just as he knew how Jones had heard of it.

"Quit!" cried Bass Outlaw furiously. "Jones kicked me out. The old devil! He looked me in the eye and made me give him my resignation. I quit because I don't want any trouble with him. But I'll tell you something: Gillett won't grin long about this! I'm going to kill him for telling Jones."

"You listen to me, now, Bass," Jackson said earnestly. "Gillett didn't tell Jones a thing. Get this killing idea out of your head."

"The hell he never! You're saying that because you're a friend of Gillett's. He was the one that ran to Jones and he's the one I'm going to settle with."

"He did no such thing!" Jackson insisted. But he says that he had little hope of making Bass believe the truth—and he couldn't very well tell the little wolf who *had* gone to Jones, for that man would have stood no more chance than a child, if set to slapping leather with Bass. But if he could not prevent a shooting-scrape, at least he might give Gillett some warning.

"He did no such thing!" he repeated, thinking furiously. "Here! I'll go to Gillett and ask him point-blank if he talked to Jones about you. You know him. If he says he didn't, you'll have to take his word for it, won't you?"

"He won't say he never told Jones—because he did. But if he denies it—"

Jackson waited for no more. He went hurriedly out and hunted up the Sheriff. Gillett made a contemptuous, wordless sound.

"Where is he, now? He's just trying to run a bluff. And it won't *sort o'* get there. Sweet thing if a sheriff has to be bluffed in his own county-seat, by the like cf Outlaw!"

They found Outlaw. Very flatly, Gillett told him that he had no need to go tattling to Jones or anyone else.

"You're just like anybody else, in Brewster County," he said grimly to the sullen Bass. "You won't have any trouble so long as you don't make it. But if you do start trouble, I'll know how to handle it."

"All right," Bass muttered, staring at his boots. "If you say you never, that settles it. But," he added viciously, "I'd like to find the man that did tattle!"

Alpine breathed more easily with this understanding. Bass doubtless saved his own life by admitting error. But with two such pistoleers involved, battle might also have ended Jim Gillett's long and useful career. They might well have killed each other.

After this, Bass hung around town, broke, at loose ends. While he slouched from one saloon to another, with the toes of his boots getting thinner and dustier, he remembered something. He sat brooding over the memory. Finally, he came to the Sheriff and addressed him as if there had never been any trouble between them.

"Cap'n," he said friendly enough, "I'm going out of town for a little trip. I need a saddle-gun to carry. I sold mine when I got hard up and I wonder if you'd loan me that .44 carbine of yours. I'll take good care of it."

So Gillett loaned him his chiefest treasure—that 1873 model Winchester number 13401 which had been, at the time he purchased it, the world's last word in saddle-guns. He had killed Dick Dublin the murderer with that carbine; had dropped a big Apache buck in the Sierra Ventana with it. But he let Bass Outlaw take it, and the last shot ever fired from this Winchester dropped a deer for Outlaw.

Outlaw thought that nobody guessed what took him on mysterious rides out of Alpine, to return and sit brooding over his whiskey-glass, his angular, rather sullen, face more forbidding than usual. But Gillett grinned to himself. He knew the bee that buzzed in Outlaw's shabby Stetson—knew more of it than Outlaw himself. . . .

In September of '91, a G. H. and S. A. passenger train came to an unscheduled stop on the Horseshoe Curve east of Sanderson, Texas. It was around three of the morning and six grim, deft gentlemen of the Updrawn Bandanna ilk boarded the train. They looted the express car, chatted with "the boys"—as they termed the train crew —broke into the news butcher's box and helped themselves to candy and fruit and finally departed, taking a small amount of silver money out of the through-safe.

"So long, boys!" they yelled back cheerfully to the trainmen. "We'll see you-all in San'tone and celebrate."

Captain Jones and a squad of Rangers, which included Bass Outlaw, cut the robbers' trail and followed it southwest from the G. H. tracks toward the Rio Grande. That is a rough, rough country and trailing— even for the famous Joe Sitters—was slow work. At last Sitters shrugged and pulled philosophically at his big mustache. Jones looked at him expectantly. He was best trailer in the Rangers, Joe Sitters.

"Scattered and gone," Sitters gave his verdict.

Gillett, as sheriff, was working on the case, also. He believed that he knew the robbers' identity. He went with Captain Jones on several subsequent scouts after the men but without success. He chanced not to be on the scout when Jones located the robbers in camp on the Rio Grande, a hundred miles south of Marathon.

The robbers caught sight of the Rangers. They set fire to their camp and rode off hell-for-leather. Nobody had ever come upon any of the silver money from the express car and its amount had been swelling in the usual fashion of word-of-mouth reports. All over that great scope of greasewood flats and arroyo-gashed foothills, the word was that the gang had taken around $50,000 out of the express-car and, crowded by Jones' Rangers and Gillett's sallies here and there, had buried the loot in a cane brake close to the camp from which Jones had run them. Money sacks containing sugar and coffee, found at that place, seemed to verify a part of these rumors.

Jones kept after them, with the help of Sitters' trailing. He finally cut a hot trail between the River Pecos and the town of Ozona. The Rangers "took after" them and there was a breathless chase. The leader jumped in his saddle with the rap of a slug that sent dust puffing from his coat. Better than the Rangers, he knew how badly hurt he was; how impossible it would be to outride those seldom-outridden gentlemen, the Texas Rangers behind him.

He whirled his horse aside and gave it the steel. Into a thicket he sent the animal plunging. Up came the Rangers, interested in a riderless horse trotting away from that brush. There was the roar of a pistol. But when they charged the thicket, they found only the man's body, with a hastily-scribbled will beside him. He was a man of pride, that boss-robber. He was not going to be arrested and have his family dragged into a long court-session. The three others of his party were captured.

As two cowboys met in the mesquite and greasewood, in the days afterward, they would stop their horses and with leg crooked comfortably around the saddle horn, build a Durham cigaret and look toward the Rio Grande, showing across the flats as a dark line, where it ran through the *bosque*.

"They ain't never found that money, yet. . . ." they would say to each other. "Hell, ain't it! Fifty-sixty thousand, buried down there, for somebody to find. Express-company says only a little bit was in that safe. But they wouldn't want the truth to get out.

"Reckon not," they would finish it, wisely. "Bad for business. Well . . . I'd sure like to dig it up. . . ."

And as they turned away on the business of cow-hunting, two bronzed faces would "hang on the shoulder," staring as if hypnotized, away toward that cane-brake where wealth untold was buried—according to the story.

At crossroads stores and blacksmith shops, in ranch-houses over the Big Bend and the Davis Mountains country, at the bars—oh, most particularly at the bars!

—of saloons in El Paso, Sonora, Fort Stockton, Alpine, Menard, the tale was told and retold until it became part of the buried treasure legend of the Southwest.

And this it was which pulled Bass Outlaw from Alpine for those long, mysterious trips horseback. He would come back again, beard-stubbled and dust-coated, to loaf awhile. Then thought of that buried silver in which he believed so implicitly would torment him into the saddle again. Hole after hole he dug in the cane-brake, sweating all day, lying by his fire of nights with the scream of the cougars and the faraway, mournful howl of coyotes, drifting to him. In all his life, the little wolf never showed so much of persistence and industry. But at last he gave it up and looked for a job.

DICK WARE put him on as deputy United States marshal. Ware was that famous ex-Ranger of E Company, who killed the notorious train-robber Sam Bass at Round Rock. He was a splendid peace officer and partial to ex-Rangers as deputies. In addition to this appointment, Bass Outlaw also became a special Ranger, attached to D Company, after the death of Captain Jones and the succession of Sergeant John R. Hughes to the captaincy.

On April 4, 1894, Dick Ware came to El Paso to attend court. He brought Bass Outlaw with him and also another deputy-marshal, Bufe Cline. Bass was in bad humor, this day. There had been a great deal of work to the building up of certain cases which Ware was to present at this term of court and it had fallen to Bufe Cline to do the long and tedious job. Consequently, when the cases were worked up and time came to serve subpoenas and other papers, Ware turned these papers over to Cline. It was the usual procedure. The man who had done the preliminary work was entitled to the fees paid for serving the papers.

But Bass Outlaw conceived that he had a grievance against Dick Ware because he had been given none of the fee-bearing summonses in the cases. Ware's explanations in no way soothed the little gunman. He flung out of Ware's presence like a sulky child. Ware paid no attention to him. He was not the sort of man to be worried by the peevishness of Bass Outlaw or any other man, no matter what his record might be as a gunfighter.

On the street, later, Bass met an acquaintance and unburdened himself of his grievances. This man, Frank Collinson, with another named Ernest Bridges, saw that Outlaw was "on the prod." He was snarling about Dick Ware's favoritism to Bufe Cline. He seemed on the verge of going into court to shoot it out with Ware. Collinson and Bridges tried to talk him out of his ugly mood. They suggested that he go to his room and that reminded Bass of his favorite girl, down at Tillie Howard's joint on Utah Street.

He said that he was going down to the sporting district and they had to go with him. Bridges objected and Outlaw looked at him with hand on his gun. He said that Bridges was going to go down to Tillie Howard's whether he wanted to or didn't want to. And that was that!

At the door of the Bank Saloon Collinson and Bridges saw Old John Selman, the famous gunman who the next year was to shoot John Wesley Hardin in the back of the head. They were much relieved to see the constable. Outlaw and Bridges set out for Utah Street and Selman trailed with Collinson, to see that Outlaw's savage humor resulted in no damage to the reluctant young Bridges.

When they got to Tillie Howard's Bass asked the Madam for his favorite of what the old newspapers used to call "the fair Cyprians." She, it seemed, was busy with a client and Tillie refused to permit Bass to interrupt. He went snarling around the house, leaving the others in the parlor. He went out into the back yard. A pistol-shot sounded.

"I reckon Bass must've dropped his pistol," Constable Selman remarked. But he got up and moved toward the back door.

Tillie Howard knew Bass and his ways when drinking. She came running as the three men moved toward
the rear of the house. She was not monkeying with Bass.
She had her police whistle out and she was blowing it.
Selman got into the back yard just as Ranger Private
Joe McKidrict and Constable Chavez jumped the fence
to investigate the pistol-shot and the blasts of the police
whistle.

McKidrict had come up from Ysleta, D Company's
station, to attend court. He was in the neighborhood of
Utah Street only by chance. He knew Bass Outlaw as a
special Ranger attached to his own, Captain Hughes'
company, also as a deputy of Dick Ware. It may be that
he knew Outlaw's propensity for getting a cargo of
drinks aboard and then starting out to "shoot things up."
For the tale of Bass' enforced resignation had traveled
widely.

At any rate, he faced Outlaw without alarm. When
he saw that Outlaw was half-drunk and had obviously
been shooting off his pistol aimlessly, he counseled the
little gunman to go sleep off his jag and not disturb the
peace again. Outlaw was in no humor for orders or sug-
gestions. He jerked up his pistol with a furious oath:
"You want something, do you?" he snarled.

The gun roared there and McKidrict fell with a bullet
through the head. With thin face contorted, Bass fired
another bullet into the boy's body.

Nobody there knew how much farther his homicidal
rage would take him. All of the little group were aghast
at this senseless murder of the unsuspecting McKidrict.
Old John Selman, veteran of many such scenes, was first
to whip out of his near-stupor. He went for his gun and
Outlaw, catching from the corner of an eye the movement, turned a little and fired at Selman mechanically.

Had he waited a split-second, he might have kept a
notch off of George Scarborough's gun, just two years
and one day later. But his bullet only bored through
Selman's right leg; his second bullet—he must have

been firing as fast as he could jerk back the hammer and release it—also striking the old constable in that leg.

Selman got his gun out and shot Outlaw through the body, the slug going just above the heart. Outlaw ran to the fence and jumped over it into the alley. He had got a block away when Ranger McMahan, also from Hughes' D Company, encountered and arrested him.

McMahan saw that Outlaw was seriously, if not fatally, wounded. He helped him to the backroom of Barnum's Saloon at Utah and Overland Streets. This was a sporting-joint and on one of the beds in the rear section of Barnum's, they let Bass drop. He looked around at the gathering crowd. The curtain was sliding down on the last act of the little killer's life and he seemed to understand it. He lifted himself dramatically upon an elbow:

"Go gather my friends around me," he gasped, "for I know that I must die!"

It sounds for all the world like a couplet from one of those old ballads the cowboys love to sing. But, quite apart from the testimony of oldtimers who were there, there is no reason to doubt that Bass made precisely that melodramatic cry. They were so often a sentimental lot, those old killers! A man with gun-butts so notched that they looked like a bear-cub's teething-ring, when he came to face death by noosed rope or singing lead, might cry out touchingly for his pet canary or his old gray-haired mother.

That first shot of braggadocio, fired in Tillie Howard's backyard, had jerked McKidrict's head around a little after five in the evening. By nine o'clock, Bass Outlaw lay dead on the mattress of some nameless courtesan in Barnum's back-room.

As a gunfighter, he was an oddity, in a way. He was the type observers were always expecting to see kill someone. He told Captain Hughes many times of killing a man in Georgia and taking it on the run for Texas. He once suggested to Hughes that they go out after some wanted men and collect a reward easily.

"We'll let drive at 'em, then yell 'hands up!' " he suggested. When Hughes begged to be excused, that brilliant plan failed to end in murder.

Sometime later, with Hughes and others, Rangers and county officers, he fought a battle with the Odle brothers at Bullhead, in Nueces Cañon. The Odles were killed, but nobody could say who had actually owned the deadly lead.

So, skilled though he was in the mechanics of gun-slinging, he vanishes from the picture anything but a hero, with two notches on his pistol. He vanishes, too, with the sinister distinction only too often marking his type of Gunman—he had killed a man worth a thousand like himself.

The casket of young McKidrict lay in state at Company D's station, Ysleta, twelve miles down the Rio Grande from El Paso. It was banked with flowers by the children of that little village, whose special friend Mc-Kidrict had been.

As for Bass, there is record of nothing but the most routine ceremony at his funeral. To one of so sentimental a dying-cry, this difference in treatment of murderer and victim would doubtless have been a blow, had he known of it.

But at any rate—

So died Bass Outlaw, the little wolf, boots on!

CHAPTER XI · *"The Magnificent—"*

WILD BILL HICKOK

"HE CAME out of Ben Thompson's Bull's Head Saloon.
He wore a low-crowned, wide black hat and a frock
coat. His hair was yellow and it hung down to his
shoulders. When I came along the street he was standing
there with his back to the wall and his thumbs hooked
in his red sash. He stood there and rolled his head
from side to side looking at everything and everybody
from under his eyebrows—just like a mad old bull. I
decided then and there that I didn't want any part of
him."

It is Brown Paschal, a famous oldtime Texas cowboy,
recalling the day that he came into Abilene with a trail
herd and caught his first glimpse of the marshal of
the town who was a topic of conversation among cowboys from the K. P. steel in Kansas down to the "brushy
country" where Texas cowboys gathered "mossy horn"
steers hardly wilder than the men chousing them from
the thickets.

"A mad old bull. . . ." The phrasing seems to me
particularly happy. For by the time James Butler Hickok
—ex-Free State warrior, ex-stage driver, ex-Army scout
—came to the hell-roaring Kansas trail town, to replace
Marshal Tom Smith and police the wild cowboys, the
crooked gamblers and prostitutes who preyed upon them
he *was* very much like a bull—the biggest and fiercest and
proudest of the herd.

Wild Bill Hickok. . . . He lived thirty-nine years on
the frontier. Thirty-nine hard and fast and crowded and
—*vivid* years. He left a name behind him, one of the
greatest reputations of the frontier. He has become a
figure gigantic and omnipotent as one of the mythical

creatures of the Norse sagas—credited with Homeric battles and incredible slaughters. The actual Hickok has been all too often lost in the haze of myth and legend. And this is bad, it seems to me. For Hickok really did amazing things, deeds worthy of recounting and the fact that he, after all, was no more than a man (if an unusual man), heightens the drama. For one expects the near-incredible from a superman and it does not so impress one as would a lesser feat done by—John Smith.

So, if nothing else is achieved in this brief study of Hickok, perhaps he will emerge as a living, breathing human being, an historical figure in whom an adult can believe!

LaSalle County, Illinois, was Hickok's birthplace, May 27, 1837, the date. He lived the usual life of a farm boy, working, riding, hunting, until 1855, when he went to Kansas—then in the throes of her struggle with the Border Ruffians. Very early, Hickok became accustomed to violence, for he was bodyguard of General Lane, of Free State fame. He served too, as constable of Monticello Township, Johnson County; he "took up a claim" and ranched a while. In 1858, according to the story he told Mrs. Custer, he was set upon by a gang in Leavenworth and killed five of them—his first killings, if this were not merely a bit of romancing.

Sometime in '59, Hickok went out as a wagon driver on the Santa Fé Trail. He became an employee of the stage company, driving stages to Santa Fé, sometimes taking charge of a way-station. He was badly mauled by a grizzly, in late 1860, and in the spring of '61 was brought from Santa Fé to Kansas City by his employers. He recovered from his wounds and was sent to Jefferson County, Nebraska, to the Rock Creek Station of Russell, Majors and Waddell, who operated the Overland Stage Line, the Pony Express, and a huge freighting business. David McCanles, a North Carolinian some nine years Hickok's senior, was owner of the Rock Creek property and agent and superintendent for the stage company, to which he rented the place. McCanles put Hickok to work as a stable hand—and apparently did not fancy him. He looked at Hickok's curving nose and short chin. "Duck Bill," he nicknamed the new hostler. By report—which I think should not be taken too seriously, since it seems part of the justification built by Hickok apologists in the traditional manner—McCanles bore down pretty heavily on the new hand.

He is said to have handled Hickok roughly, wrestling him around before spectators, pretending that it was no more than horseplay. By the same reports, Hickok bitterly resented McCanles' treatment of him, but could not match the station agent because of his weakened condition.

Some two months after Hickok's arrival, McCanles made arrangements with the stage company to buy the station, payment to be made in monthly installments. He then turned over the agency to a man named Wellman and himself occupied, thereafter, the relation to the company of a hay-contractor—and, of course, a creditor in the amount due on the property.

TROUBLE came in July of 1861. It seems to me that it had two roots. McCanles had a buxom mistress living in a cabin across the creek from the "East Ranch House" which was the stage station. Hickok saw her and must have made overtures. For McCanles warned Hickok to stay on his own side of the creek if he wanted to live. That, I believe, was one reason for the belligerent McCanles' attitude toward the stage company employes. The other grew out of the company's failure to make payments promptly as the agreement had provided.

McCanles did not receive the June installment on the purchase price. He hounded Wellman for his money and Wellman finally went down to the company's division office at Jacksonville on the Missouri, to try to get the money. While he was gone (one must keep in mind that Hickok's apologists are presenting this testimony) McCanles made himself highly objectionable to the common-law Mrs. Wellman, with threats of ejection of the company from his property.

When Wellman returned bearing, not money, but excuses, McCanles was furious. In most of the accounts of this Rock Creek incident, McCanles is made out a criminal, Wellman and Hickok a couple of plaster saints. More important to our examination, McCanles' attitude is translated into terms of downright unreasonableness. By inference, one gathers, he had no right to object to the delinquency of the stage company. Everything he did (according to the general run of commentators) was wrong, if not actually criminal. Hickok and Wellman were entirely in the right.

I confess that I cannot accept this view. Without going as far in the other direction as Hickok's apologists have gone toward whitewashing him, it seems to me that McCanles was a rough, two-fisted sort of person, possessed of a great deal of natural acumen in business matters, not at all the sort to be put upon by a man or a corporation. He had sold property to the stage company and stipulated certain terms. The company defaulted. Legally and morally, McCanles had the right to demand fulfillment of the agreement's terms or return to him of his property. And both were refused him.

The biological urges of Hickok, as he looked across the creek at McCanles' comely property, have only collateral effect in that, as McCanles observed the glances, he was roused to keener irritation.

Wellman returned from Jacksonville on July 11th. McCanles, sleeping on the unsatisfactory answer that night, rose on the morning of the 12th determined upon a showdown. Many years later Sarah Shull was discovered by Frank Wilstach, who was engaged in writing a book about Hickok. She is reported by Wilstach to have said that McCanles rose, that morning of July 12th, and said that he was going down to "clean up" the men at the stage station. Wilstach asked her if the money owed McCanles had anything to do with the resolution. She answered "no." But she offered no substitute reason. She

leaves us to believe that McCanles had no reason for
"cleaning up" the stage station. We must believe that,
as in the case of the immortal chorus girl explaining her
marriage, "it was a Wednesday and—seemed the thing
to do!"

William Elsey Connelley, late secretary of the Kansas
Historical Society and biographer of Quantrell and
Hickok, makes what seems to me an error in reasoning,
in connection with this testimony of Sarah Shull. He
says that "McCanles was well armed, although it has
been denied that either he or his men were armed." This
is a statement that does not bear examination. No
authentic testimony has ever been given on the subject.
Connelley is letting his opinions slip into his record and
giving them the weight of evidence. He explains his
positive assertion that McCanles was well armed when
he visited the stage station by the vague assertion that,
since McCanles told the Shull woman that he was going
to "clean up" the men at the station, he *must* have been
armed!

This is of a piece with the "evidence" offered by most
of the hero-worshipping Wild Billians.

But there is no doubt that, on the morning of July
12th, McCanles went to the stage station and discussed
with Wellman the matter of the delinquent payment.
And that, receiving no satisfactory reply from the agent,
he returned that afternoon with his cousin, James
Woods, his son Monroe, a boy of twelve, and a McCanles'
employe named Gordon.

Connelley and other biographers make much of the
fact that McCanles went to the station to create violence. But, even by the testimony of the pro-Hickok
faction, McCanles actually made formal demands upon
Wellman for return of the property. As for his intent to
commit murder—which is the implication one gets from
the Hickok side—I may be pardoned for emulating that
faction, and drawing conclusions from facts as I see them,
in saying that, if McCanles intended to start a shooting
affair at the station, it seems odd that he should permit

his young son to accompany him into the very forefront of the trouble.

Be that as it may, McCanles and his companions went to the "East Ranch House" and, upon arrival, Mc-Canles left Woods and Gordon at the stable and with his son Monroe went to the house.

This "evidence" is all very confusing to me, because the statements intended to make McCanles appear the unwarranted aggressor in the affair are so double-edged, when one examines them closely. Summing it up—

By the testimony of the pro-Hickok faction, Mc-Canles leaves Sarah Shull's, accompanied by two well-armed men. He states that he is going down to "clean up" the men at the stage station. But he lets his small boy trail along into what will obviously be a line of fire. And, when he arrives at the stage station, he doesn't ride up with these two members of his party and proceed to wipe out the men in the house. Instead, he leaves Woods and Gordon at the stable. All he says to them is that, if they hear or see a "serious disturbance" at the house, they are to come to his aid. Is this merely confidence on the part of the villain McCanles? And, how are Woods and Gordon to know whether the "serious disturbance" they hear is caused by McCanles getting hurt, or by Mc-Canles carrying out his stated plan of "cleaning up" the men in the house? And, what sounds are they to expect? Shots? And, if shots, how are they to distinguish between the shots which tell of McCanles killing Wellman and Hickok, and shots that may be flying the other way?

It seems to me that the Hickok people are making a very common error, in presentation of their evidence. They make it *too* good. The result is that it seems overdone and makes the examiner suspicious. Every bit of "evidence" presented can be logically turned to indicate that McCanles came (armed or unarmed, *I* cannot say, and neither can anyone else at this date, with absolute conviction) to make formal demand of Wellman, the representative of the stage company, for return of his property being held by the company, contrary to agreement. To me, all the evidence appears to support this theory.

When McCanles and Monroe got to the East Ranch House, Wellman appeared. McCanles made formal demand of him for return of the property. Wellman replied that, as mere agent, he had no authority to turn over the station. Then, as McCanles became more threatening, Wellman went back inside the house. Mrs. Wellman appeared and became abusive. McCanles told her that his business was with men, not women. She went back inside.

Hickok now appeared in the door. McCanles asked him what *he* had to do with the business. He added that if Hickok wanted to mix in it, he had only to step out and be accommodated. If not, McCanles wanted Wellman. Now, according even to the anti-McCanles side, the belligerent North Carolinian had only a feeling of irritated contempt for Hickok. And those who seem to believe that McCanles should have been made nervous by the "terrible Wild Bill" Hickok should remember that, at this time, Hickok amounted to precisely nothing in McCanles' opinion. It is doubtful if Hickok had ever killed a man up to this time. (The story of the five men killed in Kansas, with which he regaled the romantic and impressionable Mrs. Custer in later years, has no foundation whatsoever in any actual records that I know.)

No—McCanles looked upon Hickok as a very ordinary young man who had been pushed into an unimportant place here at Rock Creek by the company. So he looked at Hickok and Hickok looked at him. Let us discount the romantic account of Hickok's steady, almost magnetic, eye that has almost the quality of the fabled basilisk's. All we can know is that Hickok looked out of the door at McCanles, who had been his boss; that McCanles, demanding that Wellman come out, added that if he did not he would come in after him. Hickok stepped back into the house.

Young Monroe McCanles waited outside while his father left the south door of the house and went to the west door. When he stepped inside he faced Hickok and Wellman. There was a calico curtain across a part of the room, strung on a lariat. Hickok kept edging toward this curtain. McCanles watched him.

By testimony of the stage company's side, McCanles was nervous. He asked for a drink of water, now, and Hickok came to the bucket and dipped up a gourdful, handed it to McCanles and once more moved toward the curtain. McCanles ordered Hickok to halt. Hickok did not obey, but continued toward the curtain. He stepped behind it, where McCanles could not see him.

McCanles told Hickok to come out from behind the curtain or he would pull him out. Hickok is said to have answered:

"There'll be one ———— ———— less, if you try it."

Considering the claim that McCanles was "well armed" and there on murder-bent, it seems odd to me that he did not shoot Hickok then, before he could get behind the curtain; odd, too, that Hickok should have so calmly disregarded the order of an armed and desperate man.

By the testimony of those attempting to clear Wellman and Hickok, later, it was admitted that immediately a shot was fired from the shelter of the curtain and that McCanles staggered backward into the yard with a bullet through his heart.

When Woods and Gordon, down at the stable, heard the shot and saw McCanles fall to the ground, attempt to move and die, they ran toward the house. They separated, Woods heading for the west door, Gordon going to the south door. Woods was just entering when Hickok—standing concealed behind the door—shot him twice with his pistol. Woods was fatally wounded. He ran back out, to the north side of the house, and fell in a bunch of weeds. Gordon, appearing at the south door as Hickok shot Woods, turned to run. Hickok fired at him again and mortally wounded him, but Gordon did

not fall. (Strange actions, for *three armed* men: Not a shot
fired by any of them, even into air!) He ran toward the
stable, toward his horse. Hickok shot him once more
and followed him at the run. But Gordon, despite his
wounds, outdistanced Hickok, who emptied his pistols
without scoring another hit.

There are two stories concerning the murder of James
Woods, who sprawled in the weeds at the end of the
house. One charges "a woman"—that would be either
Mrs. Wellman or Sarah Kelsey, step-daughter of a stock-
tender named Baker—with chopping the dying Woods
to death with a grubbing-hoe, and attempting to murder
young Monroe McCanles, who bent over his father's
body. The second (and later) version makes Wellman
Wood's murderer.

From the other house, across Rock Creek, two men
came running. These were a pony express rider and a
stage driver. And a man named Hughes, who had pretended to be a friend of both McCanles and Wellman,
came up from where he had been hunting in the creek
bottom. Hickok called Sarah Kelsey's stepfather, the
stock-tender Baker, from the stable. He accused Baker of
being a member of the McCanles faction. He was about
to shoot him when Sarah Kelsey threw her arms around
Hickok and prevented the killing.

Now, a bloodhound belonging to the McCanles side
was put upon the trail of the luckless Gordon. The dog
led Hickok and his party straight to the dying man.
When he was found, Hickok or some other of the party
shot him dead.

Hickok, Wellman, and the pony express rider Brink
were arrested and charged with murder. In the unsettled
condition of the neighborhood it was impossible to expect anything like a regular trial. Actually, the three
defendants were never taken beyond a preliminary hearing before a justice of the peace. To quote Connelley:
"no motive for the *crime** was shown." So Hickok and
his companions had to shelter, first, under the technical-

*Italics mine.—E. C.

ity that they were "defending government property"—
the wagons and stages used in transporting U. S. mail
—and secondly claim self defense.

It is hard to see how even a backwoods justice could,
by any strain of the imagination, call the chopping to
death of Woods in the weed patch "self defense," or
view the cold-blooded murder of Gordon by Hickok's
party as "self defense," whatever might have been said
about the killing of McCanles by Hickok from behind
the curtain. But, small matters like that seem to have
worried the defense not at all—any more than they have
worried Hickok's whitewashers for the last seventy
years. Doubtless, in maintaining that this was anything
but an heroic deed on the part of the Galahad-like
Hickok, I am once more in error.

I have the feeling that Hickok rather squirmed, in
after years, at memory of that affair in the Rock Creek
station. Otherwise, I think, he would not have found it
necessary to remodel the story for the benefit of the
romantic and impressionable wife of General Custer,
and others whom he met in later years. This revised
version has been current these many years, now. It recounts how Hickok heroically defended the stage company property against the "ferocious McCanles gang of
horse thieves and killers" and in a hand-to-hand struggle worthy of a Fenimore Cooper hero, laid about him
with knife and pistol until from fifteen to fifty ruffians
sprawled lifeless about him and he himself was merely a
walking collection of wounds.

But truth sometimes outs. And when I view the real
record of Rock Creek, I can find nothing of which
Hickok could be proud. It seems to me that, at Rock
Creek, for one reason or another, and without real
justification, Hickok was guilty of murders for which almost any fair jury would have given him, at the least, a
long penitentiary sentence.

THE QUESTION has often been asked, when and where
—and why—did Hickok get the sobriquet "Wild Bill."

The most commonly accepted story (it came from Hickok himself, however) is that, some time in August, 1861, Hickok served as wagon master for the Union forces out of Ft. Leavenworth, and lost his supply train to a bunch of guerrillas. They chased Hickok into Independence (and I think we need give no attention to this story as repeated by Connelley, that he fired upon the pursuers and "killed some of them" because, manifestly, he had no way of telling whether he killed anyone or not). In Independence he went into a saloon owned by a friend of his and found a bunch of roughs in a brawl. With a pistol in each hand, he drove the gang outside. Later, passing through the public square of Independence, he was cheered by some of the townspeople who had suffered from these roughs. One woman shouted (according to the legend):

"Good for you, Wild Bill!''

Hickok's time of service as scout during the Civil War has accounted for a myriad of amazing yarns. Story after story tells of his activities, alone or in company with other scouts, when he dashed through large bodies of Confederates, laid them low in swathes, but escaped himself without a scratch. Many, if not most, of these tales bear upon their faces the question mark with which any student of history must mark them. There is—just for instance—the matter of percentage, in the business of fighting. This has been crystallized into a proverb concerning the pitcher going once too often to the well. No matter how incredibly efficient a man might be with his weapons, no matter how amazingly mounted he might be, there would come a time when, chased once too often by the enemy, a shot would bring him down. But this never happened to Hickok—according to the fables recounted by word of mouth and between the covers of books, even today.

But, actually, Hickok seems to have been attached to various Federal units operating in Southwest Missouri, Northwest Arkansas, and the Indian Territory. That he was a valuable man there is no reason to doubt. That he served bravely in dangerous territory is equally certain. But that he was a demigod one may be privileged to doubt! He risked his life daily. Sometimes hourly. He became adept in all the art and craft of scouting, and his fellows in that dangerous business acclaimed him as a master of the work. He must have been unusually valuable to his commanders, for he was constantly in demand. But to credit him with the feats described in the childish tales one finds in most "biographies" is merely to make the adult question everything told about him—including the things he really did.

IN JULY, 1865, Hickok was in Springfield, Missouri. And here in Springfield, he engaged in what was (so far as I know) his first "man to man" encounter, in which he and another armed man "shot it out." Springfield, at this time, had more than its fair quota of belligerent heavily armed men. Prominent was an Arkansas man named Dave Tutt.

Over in Yellville, Arkansas, the home of Tutt, Wild Bill had pursued his (apparently) usual course and looked with much favor upon a pretty sister of Dave's. To say the least, Hickok and the girl had been *very* good friends. But her brother Dave and Hickok were friendly enough for a while. But there appeared in Springfield a girl whom Wild Bill had known very well three years before, having met her while upon a scouting trip. This was Susanna Moore.

She joined Bill at Springfield, but the relationship seems to have been broken off quickly and Susanna became the intimate of Dave Tutt. The result was bad feeling between Tutt and Hickok. They needed only an excuse for a fight. Apparently, Tutt was not one to be impressed by Hickok's record as a scout and gunman. On July 21, the two men clashed on the square after a quarrel during a gambling game. Tutt fired first at Hickok and the latter (walking with his pistol drawn) rested gunhand upon left arm to steady it and shot Tutt through the heart. The range was about seventy-five yards. This would seem to place Hickok as a cool and a deadly marksman. There was no question here, incidentally, of the "quick draw" for which Hickok has become so famous in tradition: He saw Tutt coming across the square. He expected trouble. He drew his dragoon Colt and challenged Tutt, ordering him not to cross the square. When Tutt fired and missed, Hickok very deliberately fired his shot.

There seems no question but that the killing of Tutt was perfectly justified and that Hickok had attempted to avoid trouble with the brother of his one-time *inamorata*.

In February, 1866, Hickok was appointed a deputy marshal, to operate against deserters and horse thieves around Fort Riley, Kansas. By the records he was an efficient officer, arresting many men, recovering much stock, occasionally battling the criminals.

When General Hancock was ordered to war against the Indians, in 1867, Hickok—he was known everywhere as "Wild Bill" now—was attached to the command at Fort Riley as a scout. In this service he risked his life on every trip made into the Indian country in search of information for his commanding officer. And, as courier, carrying messages between the officers at various stations, he had more than one fight with the Indians. He continued in the Government service, officially a deputy marshal, but serving also as scout, courier, or guide for troops, during 1868. And it is on this section of his career that so many of the wildly incredible Hickok stories are based.

Sometimes, it seems that every oldtimer who was within a thousand miles of the Plains forts recalls Wild Bill ("vividly!") and, to bolster up his own splendid history, feels it necessary to add another bit of gilt to Hickok's record. This is bad, for there is no need to exaggerate the danger Hickok faced, the daring he exhibited. The records show that he was one of the most valued men on the Plains. And that none but a man exceedingly brave, cool, and efficient, could have survived in that work is axiomatic. The fables merely cloud the record, tend to cast doubt upon his real exploits.

Coming to 1869, we leave behind the Indian fighting days, the war-time period of Hickok's life. Not that the Indians were settled—far from it! But in this part of the plains country the red man was no longer to raid; the settler was coming in, frontier towns were springing up and—most picturesque, if not most important—the vast herds of Texas longhorns were crawling up the Chisholm Trail to stock northern ranges, to give beef to Eastern states. And the cattle trade was to be important to Hickok, was to furnish him with a new job that was a rather natural development of his peculiar training. Hickok the Scout was gone. "Wild Bill" the Marshal stood in his place.

HAYS (or Hays City), Kansas was typical of the frontier towns along the western course of emigration. A trail connected Hays with a greater thoroughfare, The Old Santa Fé Trail.

Hays offered the traveler rough comfort and rude dissipation—a plenitude of saloons and gambling joints and bawdy houses. Here cowboy and freighter and soldier drank and bucked the tiger and "got roostered," in the expressive old Western term. And when they fell out, the crash could be heard a long way. They were hard men and they fought to kill. A hard man was needed to keep them even moderately in order. And so Hickok came to Hays.

In mid-August, 1869, he was elected sheriff of the county. In his policing of Hays, Wild Bill did not depend entirely upon the two pistols he always wore. He patrolled with a sawed-off shotgun across his arm and also carried a bowie knife. He was very successful in law-enforcement in this "hurrah" town. He insisted upon saloon keeper and gambler and red light character observing certain fundamental rules of decency. He enforced his edicts with an iron hand.

There are stories about several Hickok killings at Hays, but the best known (and the most definitely authenticated) concerns the death of one Strawhan, a typical frontier desperado. There was not much of detail to the killing. Strawhan and Hickok had trouble in Ellsworth. Both returned to Hays. Coming into a saloon one night, Hickok saw Strawhan, but made no sign. Strawhan, doubtless thinking himself unobserved, pulled a pistol. But before he could fire the watchful Hickok had drawn and killed him.

The story of that lightning draw and its deadly ending went forth. "Wild Bill" Hickok was showing the same efficiency as a peace officer that he had demonstrated while a scout. All over Kansas and Missouri his fame was spreading. He was a very different person from that gangling hostler who had committed murder—rather than homicide—at Rock Creek stage station. He had a reputation and he began to act the part.

Not in any swaggering fashion! He seems never to have strutted, or talked bombastically. Men who disliked him have said that in his manner he was quiet, courteous. Strangers who expected to meet a strutting bully were always surprised. But—he liked the limelight. He was a personage and he knew it.

One thing one must understand about Hickok, if one is to credit him with neither too much nor too little: Like all of his kind, *he was a killer*. All his training had made him ready to kill. It is the penalty of a gunfighting reputation that the owner must be ready to defend his title. And the inevitable corollary is watchfulness—intense suspicion. Hickok developed this habitual alertness, this readiness to shoot fast and accurately at the first move another man made.

A gunfighter's reputation is much like a snowball. It increases tremendously as it travels. This was true in Hickok's case—particularly true! Whether or not he encouraged the telling of amazing stories of his feats of arms, of his innumerable killings, those stories *were* told. Go anywhere on the Plains of that day, clear over into

Missouri, and you heard of Wild Bill Hickok, who had killed Indians by the hundreds, Confederate soldiers by the score, and was credited with dozens of desperate hand-to-hand encounters with the ruffians of various wild towns. Too, even the Rock Creek affair had by now become something creditable; become an homeric battle, waged against terrific odds, in the interests of the right.

So, when Wild Bill first assumed the work of policing Hays City, his reputation reacted for him and against the man encountered. Facing the terrible "Wild Bill," the average rough was inclined to be nervous. And in any gun battle split-seconds may be of terrific import.

After he had policed Hays for a time, policed it efficiently and killed two or three men, even the fables recounted about him were difficult to deny. Not that the wild, essentially masculine men—who were a good deal like so many bulldogs walking up and down and glaring at each other—accepted Hickok's rule unquestioningly. On the contrary!

There was General Custer's brother, an officer in the Seventh Cavalry. He felt that his position in the Army rendered him immune to authority other than that of the military, but when he rode drunkenly up and down the streets shooting up the town, Hickok took him quietly into custody. The incident rankled with Custer. He got some rough characters—tradition is hazy as to the number, it may have been two, or three, or four—to help him kill the marshal who had so humiliated him. Custer and his helpers found Hickok in a saloon. One of the soldiers lunged at Hickok, while another caught him from behind. Hickok got an arm free, pulled a pistol, poked it over his shoulder and killed the soldier behind him. His second shot got the soldier in front of him and killed him also. Now, men of the town jumped up and forced their way between Hickok and Custer and the other soldiers and drove them out of town.

After this incident Hickok was persuaded to leave the city to avoid more trouble with the Seventh Cavalry.

AND SO we come to Abilene . . . Joseph McCoy had made Abilene. There were a few log huts on the site when he decided that the vast herds of Texas longhorns could come up to Kansas and there meet railroad steel and be put aboard stock trains bound for a market. McCoy had both vision and courage. He bought the entire town-site for five dollars an acre. He built a hotel, the famous "Drovers' Cottage" which appears in every story of the trail herds. As early as 1867, Abilene was a wild and woolly frontier town, a typical boom town in which stores and saloons and brothels sprang up overnight. T. C. Henry was elected mayor and Tom Smith, famous peace officer of Kit Carson, Colorado, became the first marshal.

Tom Smith was the antithesis of Hickok. A big, two-fisted man, he saw little use for weapons. ("Any officer can bring in a dead man!" he told Billy Breakenridge.) When the trail herds came up to Abilene, accompanied by wild Texas cowboys, Smith watched over the saloons and dance halls and red light dives. When trouble developed between the cowboys and the townspeople, Smith would jump down from his big white horse, run into a saloon and take the cowboys by surprise and hammer them unconscious.

The Texans, at that time, were not fist fighters. As a matter of fact, a Texan rather *disdained* so ineffective a method of dealing with an enemy. He was used to men red and white and brown who had to be killed to be settled. He fought with weapons—and Tom Smith lived *because* of that fact. Lived for a time. Eventually, he was murdered by a coward's bullet. Joseph McCoy became mayor of Abilene and he, looking about for a successor to Smith, thought of Hickok, whose record at Hays he knew.

November 2, 1870, Smith died; 1871 was to be Abilene's Great Year. A marshal was urgently needed. A marshal of a particular type. Right here history is divided between those who feel that the employment of Hickok was a mistake and those who maintain with Mc-

Coy that none other could have done anything at all with Abilene the booming.

Abilene, in early 1871, was an island in the middle of a sea of Texas cattle. Herd after herd came up—was bedded down, waiting to be sold, waiting its turn to move up to the stock yards. Up and down zigzagging Texas Street moved the cowboys, those just arrived long haired and wearing shabby clothing; those who had been paid off, barbered and newly outfitted. Texas Street at night was a miniature Broadway, ablaze with lights. Saloons, in particular, were myriad. The Alamo was the finest and the most famous. But Ben Thompson and Phil Coe owned the popular Bull's Head, and there were the Longhorn and many others, inviting the cowboys in.

Hickok did not come to Abilene as marshal. He was already there, headquartering at the Alamo and gambling for a living, when McCoy, conscious of the necessity for a marshal, and mindful of the effect of a reputation, thought of the tall gambler down at the Alamo.

Abilene people were already very conscious of Hickok's presence. As he sat at a table in the Alamo Saloon, the citizenry and the transients crowded about to look at the famous Wild Bill, whose blazing record as an Army scout had been so lately augmented by the deeds credited to him in Ellsworth and Hays City.

And he was a figure to stand out in any company! The six feet of him were perfectly proportioned. He was wide-shouldered, lean of waist, with hands and feet as small and shapely as a woman's. He affected a black frock coat and the finest, whitest linen shirts. His boots were made of kid, or the thinnest, finest calf, and he paid as much as fifty dollars the pair. Add to the natural handsomeness of aquiline face golden-brown hair parted in the middle and hanging over his shoulders, and eyes that seemed, now blue, now gray, and the picture was one to remember.

McCoy was more impressed by Hickok's reputation as a killer, than by his looks. He observed how men swung wide of Wild Bill, how his mere presence quieted

rowdy gatherings. He went to the town trustees and persuaded them to indorse his choice of Hickok for city marshal. So, April 15, 1871, Wild Bill became marshal of
Abilene at a salary of $150 the month and half the fines
paid into the city court. (Tom Smith had drawn $250 a
month, with the same ''cut.'')

Abilene now saw a different policy of law-enforcement. No more of the Tom Smith method! No more cowboys knocked unconscious and carried on the marshal's
shoulder to the lockup. No more steady patrolling of
saloon and dive.

A less apparent, but more sinister, atmosphere was in
Abilene. This was inevitable. Wild Bill was no fist-
fighter! Like the cowboys, he used deadly weapons in
his battles. He did not want trouble. One may believe
that he did not *expect* trouble. And—if I may judge from
the testimony of old cowmen who knew Abilene and
Hickok—he moved on the theory that everybody should
realize that Abilene had a ''shooting marshal,'' and
that the man who raised a row might very well die
because of it.

He did little patrolling. He continued to headquarter
in the Alamo, to gamble and fraternize with the ''sports''
who made their money from (not to be uncharitable and
say ''preyed upon'') the Texas cowboys. The Texans said
that he sided with the dive-keepers who robbed them.
Many Abilene people regretted Tom Smith and disap-
proved the trustees' choice of a marshal who was as
much a creature of the ''vice dens'' as the ''wild men'' he
was supposed to control.

I hasten to say that these are not my opinions, but
contemporary views even more strongly stated by those
who held them very sincerely. I pass no judgment upon
Hickok because—in effect—he seems to have preferred a
poker game to a prayer meeting. Unpopular as the belief
is in certain circles, I hold it the inalienable right of
every man to walk the path he chooses—so long as he
tramples no other's toes; to drink whisky instead of
sarsaparilla—or refuse to drink either; to—in short—go

to hell if he so elects, without being arrested. Every single man, that is. Married men have no rights.

But—the point that must be considered by every biographer of Hickok is the divergence of opinion concerning his eight months in Abilene. And it must be remembered that not only the Texas men accused him of standing in with the harpies, Abilene taxpayers also objected to his associates, his habits, his system of policing.

Such hundred-per-centers as William E. Connelley *pooh-pooh* the accusations of Ben Thompson, maintain that Hickok's career in Abilene was irreproachable. They call Thompson a mere gambler and saloon-keeper.

But when we find a number of Hickok's employers (for the Abilene taxpayer *was* his employer) remarking that the gunlaw was not enforced, save in the most desultory, spotty fashion; that Hickok permitted drunken cowboys to stop citizens and make them buy drinks; that he rarely interfered save in the more serious brawls; that he consorted with the women of the cribs— why, then, I think, we must consider the fact that both the Texans and the Abilene folk made the same charges!

Hickok never went carelessly about town, as Tom Smith had always done. "Cat-eyed!" an old-timer once summed up Hickok for me. "He *slid* into a room, keeping his back to the wall, watching the whole crowd like a hawk. He looked like a man who lived in expectation of getting killed."

He had plenty of feminine company in Abilene, as always, everywhere. There was Susanna Moore, from Springfield. She seems to have borne Wild Bill no grudge, for killing Dave Tutt. She came to Abilene and shared a cottage with him. And there were various beauties of the bordellos. And, there was Mrs. Lake, who brought a theatrical company to the trail herd town and "fell with a crash, clean through to the basement" when she met Hickok.

IT WAS a woman—if one takes the Texans' version— who caused the enmity between Hickok and Phil Coe, an

Austin (Texas) gambler who—while no gunman in any sense of the word—*was* a fighter and, moreover, a big man, and handsome, a figure as impressive as Hickok himself.

It seems quite possible that some light and lovely lady of the "Hell Hole of Women" may have brought these two bulls of the human herd to battle. But there was for undercurrent the hostility of the Ben Thompson-Phil Coe faction (the Texas men) for Hickok.

Thompson was spokesman for this side. He charged Hickok with getting a share of the spoils stripped from the cowboys by crooked gambling and over-charges on drinks. He claimed to have stepped between the town-harpies and the Texans and, thereby, to have incurred Hickok's enmity. Be that as it may—and it is a point bitterly-disputed to this day—Hickok never "made a play" at the gunman Thompson. Nor did Thompson *hunt* a chance to "shoot it out" with Hickok. I have an idea that these two champions of pistoleering were neither of them too sure of the result of such an encounter.

But Phil Coe was a different case. Far from being a gunman like his partner, Thompson, he rarely carried a gun. This was a known characteristic. It would have been strange if, in a place like Abilene, where a man's gun-ability was a general topic of conversation, Wild Bill had not known that Coe was a fist-fighter. Very strange.

Thompson was not in Abilene in October, 1871, when the trouble between Hickok and Coe came to an explosion. He had gone to Kansas City some time in July to meet his wife. On a drive, his buggy had overturned. Mrs. Thompson's arm was so badly broken that amputation was necessary. Thompson's leg was broken. So, in early October, the formidable Thompson was on the road to Texas.

In Abilene, Coe and a bunch of cowboys were celebrating. The Texas men had sold out and were ready for the trip home. They went up and down the streets, and when they met a poorly-dressed man, they descended on him, stripped him naked and crowded him into the nearest store, there to outfit him from head to foot. They stopped townsmen and forced them to buy drinks for the crowd. It was all very rough, very noisy and—by cowboy-standards—very harmless. Certainly, it does not seem the proper setting for a planned murder.

Hickok received complaints about the spree. He went out and warned the cowboys to be quieter. Then he bought the drinks and went back to the Alamo. The celebration continued. Coe's party came to the Alamo and in the street a pistol-shot sounded. Hickok jumped to the door—by one account—with a Colt in each hand. Coe, from the sidewalk's edge called that he had shot at a dog. But (according to this pro-Hickok version, we must remember) he lifted his pistol and Hickok fired at him. Coe's shot went wild, Hickok's found its target.

The Texas version, given by men in Coe's party, has Coe replacing his gun after his first shot and turning to face an empty-handed Hickok, who reproved Coe mildly for shooting inside town-limits. The incident was ended, when Coe turned away and Hickok suddenly whipped a pair of derringers from coat pockets and shot the big Texan, then jumped back inside the saloon.

I find nothing in Hickok's record to make this incredible. It parallels the killings at Rock Creek. It was a very human thing to do—if not admirable. And there was no danger attached to the course—as marshal of Abilene, opposed to one of the Texans whom the Abilene people so distrusted and disliked, town sympathy would be with him.

Coe then pulled his pistol and fired at Hickok, but only lodged his lead in the door around the marshal. Mike Williams, a special policeman and close personal friend of Hickok, came running up. Wild Bill, hearing only the pound of the footsteps behind him, whirled and fired without thought—proof, again, of the "cat-eyed" state in which he lived. Mike Williams dropped dead.

Coe lived for two or three days; then a friend, Bud Cotton, took his body back to Texas. En route, he met the crippled Ben Thompson and they went on together with the body.

Hickok continued as marshal until November 13, 1871. When he left Abilene it was to wander awhile and wind up in Buffalo Bill's show—then touring the East. The performances were pretty terrible, typical *Scout-of-the-Plains* "plays," in which the Hero rescued the Lovely Heroine from Marauding Redskins. Hickok was in no sense an actor and he did not like his part in the theatricals. He came back West, to drift for a time over Colorado and Wyoming. In Cheyenne, March 5, 1876, he married Mrs. Lake, the lady who had "fallen" for him with the crash described by Abilene residents in 1871.

The Black Hills, then opening up to miners, attracted him. In Cheyenne, Hickok got together a party of some two hundred would-be miners. He guided them safely into the Black Hills, then returned to Cheyenne with his wages in his pockets. He met an old friend, "Colorado Charley" Utter, and they went to Deadwood as partners. They located claims and were proceeding with their developments when the rumor went around that Hickok was to be offered the post of marshal in this most lawless of lawless mining camps. The underworld element seems to have been very much worked up about the possibility of Hickok being hired to police Deadwood. And an incident or two of his time in the camp did not tend to lessen their fears: Hickok is said to have once walked into a saloon filled with gunfighters, "confessed" bad men.

"I understand that some of you two-by-four gladiators have been making remarks about me," he told the assembled crowd. "So I came by to tell you that if I hear any more talk about what you're going to do to Wild Bill Hickok, this camp is going to have the biggest bunch of cheap funerals ever seen in the West. Line up, all of you! I'll take charge of your artillery."

And he disarmed a half-dozen of them forthwith and walked out.

In Deadwood at this time, was a cross-eyed, broken-nosed man named Jack McCall, an ex-buffalo hunter, who spent most of his time in carousing around the toughest dives of the camp. By common repute McCall was the tool of Tim Brady and Johnny Varnes, leaders of the toughs in Deadwood, the anti-Hickok element. Brady and Varnes kept McCall drunk and primed him to kill Hickok, telling him of the reputation he would make, assuring him of immunity for the murder.

About mid-afternoon of Wednesday, August 2, 1876, Wild Bill was playing poker with some friends in a saloon. Incredibly, he sat with his back to an open door. He did not do this unconsciously. He had complained to the other players that it was contrary to his habit. They laughed at him and refused to let him change his seat.

Jack McCall came into the saloon. He passed the poker game and no one paid any attention to him. That was the sort of figure he was in camp—a bum of no importance. He moved a little closer to the game, to Hickok's rear. Surely, Hickok was not himself that day! He was looking down at his hand when McCall's Colt roared and Hickok slumped forward to the table, the faint smile still upon his face, still holding his cards. He slid from the stool to the floor. McCall swung his pistol around to cover the other men in the barroom. He backed out of the place to the hitch-rack, where he had a pony. But, when he tried to swing up, the saddle turned—slipping under the pony's belly. He fell, scrambled up, ran along the street.

That famous character, "Calamity Jane," a close friend of Hickok's, pursued the murderer. She found him in a nearby butcher-shop, dragged him out and back.

One might think—if one's mind tended toward the ominous—that August second was fated to be Hickok's last day. The back to the door, the carelessness in ignoring a man behind him, but—odder still—the fact that, of the six loads in McCall's pistol, only that cartridge which had at the first click killed Hickok would explode!

"Aces and eights" is "the dead man's hand" throughout the West. And the superstition dates back to that hot August afternoon in Deadwood, when the famous gunman's stiffening fingers revealed his two pair—aces and eights.

McCall narrowly escaped lynching. Then a frontier court was formed at a miners' mass meeting. The brutal and cringing McCall was put on trial. He was about twenty-five and an eye-witness reported that in the bloated face was not a redeeming feature.

McCall's defense was that Wild Bill had killed his brother some time before. Apparently, the jury was selected by the men who arranged for Hickok's assassination. At any rate, the vote stood, eleven for acquittal, one for conviction, the final verdict being "Not Guilty." McCall left Deadwood, but he got drunk and fell to boasting in Custer City about the murder. He laughed at the story he had told, about avenging an imaginary brother's death. He had under-estimated the indignation of decent men. These moved quickly and, in the early days of October, 1876, McCall was arrested by a deputy United States marshal. Brought to Yankton, South Dakota, he was put on trial for murder in a regular court. Within a day he was convicted and sentenced to death. On March 1, 1877, he was hanged.

Hickok was buried at Deadwood by Colorado Charley Utter and other friends, August 3, 1876. In 1892, over his grave in the cemetery a life-size statue was erected. Today, that statue is defaced in many places by the chipping of curio hunters. But, if the statue vanished entirely, Wild Bill would not be forgotten. His name would remain famous in the West. And, if famous for a great many things that actually he never did, still there remain authenticated incidents galore, enough to set his name high on the list of great scouts and super-gunmen.

CHAPTER XII · *"He Was Born in Indiana"*

SAM BASS

As the faraway blast of the train whistle carried to them across the Nebraska prairie, six men crawled from under the platform at Big Spring station on the Union Pacific. They looked down the track. The locomotive's headlight shone like the one yellow eye of some huge animal rushing at them through September darkness.

Joel Collins looked at the engine, turned back to the five men grouped around him. They watched him tensely.

"We've gone over the job enough. All of you ought to know your places by now. But, just for luck, once again—I and Heffridge stick up the engineer and the fireman. We'll bring them out to you, Berry. Nixon will help you hold 'em. Bass and Davis to go through the express car. We'll help you, Sam," he added to the stocky, dark young man beside Jack Davis. "Everybody clear in his head?"

They nodded, then huddled under a tree until the train pulled in. Then—Collins on one side, Heffridge on the other—the engine crew was covered by six-shooters. Sam Bass nudged Davis:

"Come on, Jack!" He showed large white teeth in easy grin beneath dark mustache. "Let's go cash in our old white-handled six-shooters!"

Davis followed him at awkward trot up the side of the train. At the express car Sam Bass rapped with pistol muzzle on the door. The door slid back raspingly. The messenger put his head out. Sam Bass's pistol muzzle jumped forward:

"Throw up your props!" he commanded.

Beside him, moved Davis. He caught the threshold of the express car's door and scrambled up, jostling che

messenger aside. Sam Bass followed when Davis had
covered the messenger. They searched the man, removing
his pistol and taking what money was in his pockets.

"Well," Bass drawled, grinning at the messenger,
"let's open up that big box there, and see what Mr. Express Company has got for us hard-working cowboys."

"I can't open that safe," the messenger told them,
nervously. "Nobody can, this side of Omaha. That's a
through-safe. It's locked at San Francisco to be opened
at Omaha and not *till* we make Omaha—"

Footsteps grated on the loose gravel of the right-of-
way outside the car. Jack Davis stepped forward with
six-shooter coming up. He lunged out viciously and
rammed his pistol muzzle into the messenger's mouth.

"You're a God damn' liar!" he snarled. "You'll
open that box or it'll just be nearly hell for you! You—"

The messenger staggered back. His lips were beginning to bleed. Desperately he mumbled that he could not
open the safe.

"You can kill me—but I can't open it, I tell you! If I
could, don't you think I would? Look here!"

He turned aside; snatched up sheets of paper. They
showed the destination of the safe's contents but Davis
—uneducated cowboy—stared helplessly at them. He
looked at his companion. Sam Bass took the papers and,
like Davis, stared at them without understanding. He,
too, had barely more than ability to painfully scrawl his
own *Sam Bass* and make out a few figures.

"What's the trouble?" Joel Collins's authoritative
voice demanded, from the doorway.

"This feller won't open the safe," Jack Davis told
their leader. "He says he *can't* open it. But I bet you I can
find the way to talk him into it!"

He glared threateningly at the messenger as Collins
swung easily up into the car, to take the papers which
Sam Bass held out to him.

"The man's telling the truth," Collins shrugged.
"He can no more open that box than we can. Let him

alone." Then his eyes wandered to the bulk of the safe; he shook his head regretfully.

"Two hundred thousand dollars in it—but *we* can't touch it! Get going! What's here that we *can* use?"

Sam Bass stared at his leader. His dark eyes rolled to the safe. His lips were moving, forming four words over and over—*two hundred thousand dollars!* Suddenly, he glared around the car. There was an axe standing against the wall. He made two strides toward it, going awkwardly, but fast, in his high-heeled boots. When he snatched it up the messenger shrank back, but the stocky cowboy came blindly past him. His fury was directed at the squat, formidable shell which held, for kernel, a sum of money too vast for him to really comprehend. He swung up the axe, brought it down in a terrific swing against the safe door. The car rang with the clangor of metal smashing upon metal in blow after tremendous blow. He gave over the attack only when he was panting, dripping perspiration, too weary to lift the axe more.

Davis and Collins had been poking about the other end of the car. Collins lifted his voice as the stocky cowboy let the axe sag to the floor and mopped his face with a shirt sleeve:

"Here's a bunch of silver bricks. But they're too heavy for us to handle!"

BASS LOOKED about him. Something about the messenger's manner, some subdued triumph, caught his wandering gaze. He looked sinisterly at the man for an instant, then his roving eyes came back to the scarred, but intact, safe. Beside it, unnoticed before, were piled small wooden boxes, a half-dozen of them. Upon them were blobs of sealing wax. Sam Bass stepped closer to them, staring without comprehension at the stars imprinted upon the wax.

"What's in these-here?" he demanded of the messenger. The man shrugged:

"I don't know. Some kind of shipment going through."

"You don't know," Bass drawled. "Well, that's nearly hell! But those boxes ain't no safe! We can get into *them!*"

He picked one up; found it heavy. He slammed it against the floor. And, with sight of the yellow gold pieces rolling over the floor, he lifted his voice in a shrill cowboy yell that whirled Collins and Davis, brought them rushing to him; brought Heffridge's head and shoulders thrusting through the doorway.

Collins looked the boxes over and made a quick estimate:

"There's ten thousand dollars in each of those boxes —sixty thousand dollars. Boys, we've hit a damn' bonanza!" he said excitedly. "Sam, you and Davis go shake down the passengers. Hightail! The rest of us will get the boxes off."

Bass nodded and crossed to the door of the car. Davis followed. They dropped down to the right of way, ran along it to climb into the nearest passenger coach. A savage yell from Sam Bass sent the passengers crowding into their seats. The train was well-peopled but out of all the passengers coming from the Pacific Coast, out of all the train crew, there was none daring enough to attempt resistance in the face of these six cowboys. Bass and Davis went calmly through the cars, taking money and watches from the trembling passengers. When they were done they had some four hundred dollars in money and a good deal of jewelry.

"We got everything," Bass reported to Joel Collins, who nodded and turned to the engineer:

"You can hightail, now," he said.

They watched the train vanish, then picked up their boxes. It was nearly a half-mile to where their horses waited, securely hidden in a motte of trees. The boxes made heavy burdens, but none there was conscious of weariness! Ten thousand dollars apiece. . . . Joel Collins, as cattle-buyer, had owned that much, time and again.

But not the others. Sam Bass voiced the opinion of the whole crowd, when he lifted his drawling, humorous voice:

"Well, Joel, it looks like we hit our racket at last. Yes sir! This train robbing business, it beats sticking up Black Hills stages for six dollars apiece—and sometimes not even getting the six dollars—like that business last month when you and Heffridge killed the driver and *still* he run his team into Deadwood and we couldn't catch him. We have got enough to go back home and play Old Solid now. There'll be some eyes bug out in Denton, when I ride in and begin to chunk twenty dollar gold pieces around!"

"We won't split the money, yet," Collins decided. "Our play is to start the Old Solid racket right now. We'll bury the money down on the river. Then we'll drift into Ogallala and loaf around a day or two. If we start running, right off, they'll catch onto us. It would be nearly hell, to get heeled now!"

With the boxes before them on the saddles, they rode the three or four miles to the South Platte, and there dug a hole in the sandy bank. Then Joel Collins, one time trail driver, Texas cattle-buyer, led his gang back to Ogallala, whence they had moved down upon Big Spring for the robbery.

They were old hands at this stick-up business, now. In Texas, and around Deadwood after coming north, they had practised robbery with much boldness, if with little success. Joel Collins was older, and shrewder, than his followers. He had come up the trail with a herd bought on credit, with Bass and Davis for herders. Selling out in Kansas, he had embezzled the money due the Texas owners of the cattle and proceeded to "blow" it in the dens of Deadwood with a free hand.

But of the six of them, none was apt to give himself away by any amateurish nervousness. Collins felt safe in returning to Ogallala, where excitement would be most feverish. So, they circulated in the brothels, saloons and stores, watching, listening, discussing the robbery, but catching no suspicious glances turned their way. There was nothing remarkable about any of them. They looked like any of the wandering cowboys who used Ogallala.

They heard plenty of talk about the Union Pacific robbery, but the sheriffs and express and railway company detectives were not expecting that daring bandit sextette to show up right in Ogallala.

So, after a couple of days, shrewd Joel Collins felt safe. He led them back to the gold *cached* on the South Platte's sandy bank.

Back on the South Platte, they made camp and dug up the boxes of gold. They had brought with them from Ogallala sacks of striped ticking. Each man dumped the contents of a box into his sack. When this was done, Joel Collins looked around at them:

"We can't stick together any longer," he told them. "It won't be safe. We had better split up in couples and scatter out. I'm going back to Texas."

"Same here!" Sam Bass said—and grinned slowly. "Like I told you-all the the other day, I'm going to cut a dash in Denton County nobody will ever forget. I want to show old Dad Egan—he's the sheriff and I used to work for him—a few."

"Texas suits me," Heffridge said. "I'll pair up with you, Joel."

"Texas for me, too," Jack David remarked. "I'll side Sam." Berry and Nixon were for Missouri.

NOT ONE of the groups would ever see another. Booncompanions of the cow-trail, the saloon and the bordello, partners in many a stage robbery, they had caroused together, shared dangers as they had shared beds and bottles. But when they parted here, it was for all time. Three were marked for quick death. Two would disappear—vanish quite—into obscurity deeper than the grave, for most graves bear headstones. The sixth—

That was the stocky, dark cowboy with the slow, wide grin and the drawling, humorous speech—Sam Bass —who would gain something like immortality in a crude ballad that has held the cowboy's fancy these fifty years. And *he* had less than a year to live, as he rode southward beside Jack Davis that bright, cool September day. . .

But no hint of tragedy came to him as he and Davis jogged toward the Kansas settlements. At night when they made their camp, they hitched the horses with their lariats and to the end of the ropes fixed their sacks of gold pieces. Sprawled beside their fire Sam Bass, who had a gift of talk when the audience was sympathetic, told his companion of his early life.

He was born in Lawrence County, Indiana, July 21, 1851. At ten, Sam was taken into the home of an uncle, and when he was about seventeen he left Indiana and started for Texas, coming at last to Denton County.

Common labor had always been his lot—sawmill work, teaming and punching cows. A hard life and a poverty-stricken one. The "easy money" he had always hunted had never come his way—until now. But wealth had come his way at last, and it had worked a change in him in these few days since the train robbery, too! He could look back almost humorously upon his days of petty gambling, of racing quarter-horses around Denton, and at the Dallas Fair, when little Johnny Hudson had ridden Sam's famous "Denton Mare" and a hundred dollar bet won bulked like the hoard of the state treasury.

He was changed. The good-humored, "no-'count" teamster and cowboy who had trailed shrewd, unscrupulous Joe Collins around San Antonio, gathering cattle, "rolling" drunken Mexicans for a few dollars, was a full-fledged bandit, now. More! In his own mind he was a fledgling bandit-chieftain. He thought of Texas trains, Texas banks, that could easily be held up—by the daring leader of a loyal gang. He told Jack Davis his plans for the Texas business.

"Sam Bass's Gang. . . ."

He liked the imposing sound of it. But Davis was more concerned with the present. Besides, he was already rich—that hitch weight yonder, against which his horse tugged, was a fortune. Ten thousand dollars in bright, new gold pieces. . . . He hardly heard Sam Bass's rambling talk of Denton folk, whom he would stagger with sight of his wealth, and with daring deeds of mask and six-shooter. Jack Davis kept a roving gaze on the horizon, turned often in the saddle to look across the flat prairie that was marked by their trail.

And they had good reason for uneasiness, whether they knew it or not! The telegraph had carried warnings to sheriffs all around. The soldiers were riding with the peace officers. Nebraska and Kansas fairly buzzed with activity.

But these shabby riders jogged into a Kansas village and somehow escaped suspicion. They listened to the latest news about the great robbery. Then they traded their saddle horses—one for an ancient buggy, the other for a harness horse.

Perhaps it was here that they first heard of the fate of Joel Collins and Heffridge, killed at Buffalo Station, Kansas, on September 26.

Collins and Heffridge were unaware that the party had been trailed out of Ogallala by a man named Leach, a daring ex-employe of the express company. This man had seen the gold dug up and had overheard enough of their talk to learn their real names and where they were going.

So Collins and Heffridge rode boldly up to Buffalo Station, talked with Sheriff Bardsley of Ellis County and, when followed by soldiers, admitted their real names. But they tried to shoot it out and were killed by the troopers.

Bass and Davis, in the old buggy, drove quietly through Kansas. They came up to the camp of a squad of soldiers set to hunt for them. The officer stepped forward to question them. They listened quietly, their feet on the striped ticking sacks of gold in the buggy's bottom. Sam's white teeth showed beneath dark mustache in his easy, good-humored grin.

He and his partner knew nothing at all about express robbers—whether named Bass and Davis or Smith and Jones. They were two "flat-brokes"—farmers leaving Western Kansas for a better location where they could get jobs. As for two riders with a pack horse, they had seen so *many* roving cowboys—

He finished by asking permission to camp near the military! And he and Davis borrowed the troopers' frying pan and coffee pot. They cooked their meal with troopers idling about them. The next morning they promised the officer to keep watch for the much-wanted Bass and Davis. Then they drove on south.

THEY MADE an uneventful trip of it, the rest of the way through Kansas, down through the "Nations" and into Texas at Red River Crossing. Sam Bass—always a cheerful soul—grew happier as Denton came nearer. Jack Davis was more thoughtful—Denton was not his home town, anyway.

The days grew colder as the buggy creaked on. For October was gone. November had come before they made Denton. Because of Davis's insistence, Sam drove on down to Fort Worth. And here they parted. Sam was determined to cut his swath in Denton, where there would be a home-town audience for the gallant, desperate deeds he would do. Davis wanted to head for South America. Neither would alter his determination. So— Jack Davis vanishes from our record. He headed for New Orleans—and obscurity. Unless—

Two of us were riding north through Nicaragua in early 1920, following the cattle-trails that wound through scrubby brush near Lake Nicaragua. An old man rode up to our camp one day—a lean and alert old fellow, tanned to the rich red-brown of saddle-leather, who might have been eighty—or fifty.

He was very curious about us; concerned about our getting safely through to Guatemala. When I mentioned days on the Texas range, as explanation of our confidence, he warmed immediately.

"I haven't seen Texas since '77," he said thoughtfully. "I lit a shuck out of Fort Worth in early winter, that year. Changed my name—came down here—been here ever since."

He talked on. Hartman looked at me sidelong. I was thinking furiously—trying to fit that fall of '77 into outlaw history as I recalled it. But too many men were "buying trunks" about that time. Nor did this old exile say anything that served as a clue.

It was in Managua, later on, that I mentioned the old man to an oil-scout long in the Republics. He knew the man. Indifferently, he nodded:

"I've heard him talk about Texas and the old trail herd days. He went up the trail from San Antonio with a couple of hard cases and, I gather, they sold the cattle and stole the money. When they had blown it all in they started out as road agents and stuck up stage coaches and trains. He's well-fixed, now."

The oil-scout could supply no more than these tag-ends of the old man's reminiscences that he had pieced together. But, to me, they bore a surprising likeness to the history of Joel Collins, Sam Bass and the vanished Jack Davis. And the fact that my old expatriate did *not* claim to be the lost member of the gang, but only dropped enough hints to parallel Jack Davis's history, is to me more impressive than an unsupported claim could be. Perhaps I shared a meal with Jack Davis—perhaps not. My belief is that I did.

Sam returned to Cooke County, which adjoins Denton County on the north. He had a well-developed bump of caution and it seemed better to him to have a look around—through the eyes of friends—before showing himself boldly in Denton. He must have remembered how that Army lieutenant in Kansas had displayed full knowledge of the Collins Gang. And the deaths of Collins and Heffridge, so soon after the Big Spring robbery, must have pointed to what we should call today "inside information."

So, at Cove Hollow in Cooke County, Sam camped near the cow-camp of Bob Murphy. The Murphy family was well-known throughout this region. Sam Bass knew them all, but perhaps knew Jim Murphy most intimately.

Sam learned from his friends that, on October 12, the *Denton Monitor* had published an account of the Big Spring robbery, naming Joel Collins as leader. But as yet, Sam himself was not suspected (in Denton) as one of the gang. From his camp in the impenetrable thickets of Clear Creek Sam went after dark into Denton. The man he sought was Jim Murphy's cousin, Frank Jackson, a tall young cowboy dare-devil who was, just then, practising the tinner's trade in town.

To Jackson Sam told great stories of the wealth that was to be made as a train robber. For proof, he showed his pockets, crammed with twenty dollar pieces. He enlarged upon his ambitious plans. He painted a bright picture for this young ex-cowboy whose idea of bettering himself was working in a tinshop. It was a story hard to turn aside from, a future hard to resist. But Frank Jackson was not easily persuaded to leave the way of honesty. It was not until the third visit that Sam, forcing handfuls of gold pieces on Jackson, was able to persuade him to become member number one of the proposed gang. The second recruit was another Indianan, Henry Underwood, then living in Denton County. Underwood was a reckless young cowboy three years Sam's junior, but two years older than Frank Jackson.

Sam was talking largely around the county of the money he had made, racing horses and selling mines in the Black Hills. Not everybody took stock in these tales. Sam had not amounted to much around Denton and it was hard to believe that he had so greatly prospered. It began to be whispered that Sam's unfailing supplies of gold pieces came from some other "lead" than the claims he told of locating.

Sheriff Everhart of Grayson County was one who doubted. So was Deputy Sheriff Gerren of Denton County.

Everhart began to make some investigations and soon learned from the express company that Bass was one of the robbers wanted for the Big Spring job. The Sheriff also got the names of the others. And he came to believe that Henry Underwood was none other than Nixon of Collins' bunch.

Meanwhile, Sam had taken his two recruits to San Antonio for a spree on express company gold. Sheriff Everhart and Deputy Gerren followed. But they quarreled upon arrival in San Antonio and as a result Sam Bass and the others were not molested. But they did learn now that the sign was up against them. The telegraph had brought word of Berry's killing in Missouri by officers, of Nixon's disappearance. Sam Bass knew that large rewards were offered for his capture. So he led his two men back to the security of Cove Hollow.

On December 20, 1877 Bass, with Jackson and Underwood, committed the first robbery to be charged against the newly-organized "Sam Bass Gang." They held up the Fort Worth-Cleburne stage. The result of this robbery could not have made Sam enthusiastic. They took eleven dollars from the passengers!

Underwood went home to spend Christmas. Sheriff Everhart rode up to the house on Christmas Day and arrested him, insisting that Underwood was the wanted Nixon, despite the fact that any number of Denton citizens could have testified that Underwood was in Denton County at the time of the Big Spring hold-up. But Everhart collected a reward and Underwood was taken back to Nebraska as a train robber.

After Underwood's capture, in mid-February, 1878, Sam and Johnson stopped the Fort Worth-Weatherford stage at Mary's Creek. Then they picked a spot for holding up the Sherman-Gainesville stage, but on the ground Sam lost his nerve for some reason. They rode off without making the attempt.

Sheriff Egan was one man for whom Sam owned much respect. And he knew that Egan—like Everhart—was looking for him. So he rode very cautiously, keeping to the densely-wooded country, visiting Denton, Rosston, Fort Worth, after dark.

He and such companions as might be riding with him would come into the edge of a town, choose an outlying saloon for their drinking, fling down gold with a grand flourish and swagger out to the horses. Then they would rouse the neighborhood with wild cowboy yells and volleys of pistol shots.

Seaborn ("Sebe") Barnes now threw in with them. Sam also recruited one Tom Spottswood and the gang held up the H. and T. C. train at Allen Station in Collin County. Spottswood then went home and was instantly suspected—as Sam and the others seem not to have been. Sam rubbed his black head at the news:

"Well, that's nearly hell!" he said. "But no more than I expected: Any man that'll rob a train inside fifteen miles of home, and then go home and try to play Old Solid—well, he ought to be captured! But he's a good'n'. So, if they have him in jail at McKinney after we get a stake, we'll try to get him out. But the next man that goes home, after this, and gets caught, he can go to hell!"

THE WHITTLED gang consisted now of Sam Bass—"Old Honest Eph," the others called him in camp—Frank Jackson, or "Blocky," and Seaborn Barnes—"Nubbins Colt." They struck the H. and T. C. again, this time at Hutchins in Dallas County. The local authorities seem to have had no idea that these familiar men, who rode so carelessly and openly through the cross-timbers, seen by any who passed that way, could be the perpetrators, of the skilfully-executed robberies. But Sheriff Egan of Denton County was informed of Sam Bass's connection with the Big Spring robbery and he knew to a dollar the amount offered by the express company for the Union Pacific robbers.

In March, 1878, Henry Underwood reappeared. He had broken jail at Kearney, Nebraska and brought with him a desperado who used the alias of "Arkansaw

Johnson.'' Sam was highly-pleased. It began to look like a real gang. Apparently, the frenzied efforts now being made by various authorities to capture him for the Union Pacific robbery—and to take the unknown local train-robbers—worried him very little. He left Barnes, Jackson and Underwood in camp and with Arkansaw Johnson went over to Dallas County. Here he recruited a couple of unknowns and hid under the station-platform at Eagle Ford, a tiny station some six miles west of Dallas.

Shortly before midnight of April 6, 1878, the T. P. train came out from Dallas and was robbed, not a gun being fired in the whole business. But his two recruits left Sam afterward, nor have they yet been identified. Public excitement had risen. The Governor was called on to take action. The region began to swarm with detectives and State forces. June Peak of Dallas was commissioned captain of Rangers and ordered to recruit a special company. The very multiplicity of the plans and planners wrought a confusion which worked to Sam Bass's advantage, then and later.

It has been believed that Peak's commission was given him on the score of familiarity with the densely wooded region in which the robbers holed up. Too, he had an excellent record as a peace officer. But his company of untrained men were hardly Rangers—in the true sense of the term. Peak did as well as he could with them, but had such a veteran outfit as N. O. Reynolds's Company ''E'' been detailed to capture Bass, the result must have been very different. Reynolds had the name of being the Frontier Battalion's champion bad man-exterminator.

On April 15, 1878, Sam committed his last robbery—that of the T. P. train at Mesquite, just east of Dallas. The full tally of his ''regulars'' was there—Arkansaw Johnson, Underwood, Barnes, Jackson and, of course, Bass himself. In addition, he had Sam Pipes, Albert Herndon, William Collins, William Scott and five unknowns. Certainly, an imposing gang for one stick-up!

Since this is the last recorded holdup, it may be interesting to consider here a tabulation made of the results of Sam's various robberies:

December 20, 1877—Fort Worth-Cleburne stage, robbed by
Bass, Jackson and Underwood; total secured..........$ 11.00
Received by each of three $3.33.

February 15, 1878—Fort Worth-Weatherford Stage, robbed
by Bass and Jackson; total secured (with two watches)   70.00
Received by each of pair $35.00

February 23, 1878—H. and T. C. train, Allen Station,
robbed by Bass, Jackson, Barnes and Tom Spottswood;
total secured.................................   1280.00
Received by each of four $320.00

March 1878—H. and T. C. Train, Hutchins Station, robbed
by Bass, Jackson and Barnes; total secured...........   400.00
Received by each of three $133.33

April 6, 1878—T. P. train, Eagle Ford; robbed by Bass,
Arkansaw Johnson and two unknowns; total secured...   50.00
(some registered mail was taken; little value apparently)
Received by each of four $12.50

April 15, 1878—T. P. train, Mesquite; robbed by Bass,
Underwood, Barnes, Jackson, Pipes, Herndon, Collins,
Scott and Johnson, with five unknowns; total secured...   150.00
Received by each $10.71

"Grand" total of Bass's Robberies..................$1961.00

Bass seems to always have taken an equal share, so on this basis he received for his seven months of "labor," between the first robbery on December 20, 1877, and the end of his career on July 21, 1878, the munificent sum of $514.87! His followers made even less than this amount, for few of them were present in every robbery.

After Sam's death, the inevitable ballad (purporting to be a narrative "poem") was written. John Denton of Gainesville gets credit for the song. It is a piece typical of the muddled and hero-worshipping ballad-monger in general. One verse "relates" the tally of Sam's gang—

Sam had four companions, four bold and daring lads;
They were Richardson, Jackson, Joe Collins and Old Dad;
Four more bold and daring cowboys the Rangers never knew;
They whipped the Texas Rangers and ran the boys in blue.

Taking the last assertion first, actually, Sam and his gang did their fighting with the Rangers ‘‘over the shoulder.’’ Their chief aim when Rangers were near was to ‘‘break down the timber’’—and to do that with all the speed attainable. The reference to the‘‘boys in blue’’ has always puzzled me. I was ‘‘raised’’ in that country and I never heard of any soldiers being drawn into the ‘‘War.’’ It may refer to policemen; there were plenty of these and some seem to have owned a well-developed ‘‘bump of caution.’’ More probably, it refers to nothing at all; is merely ‘‘chucked in’’ to make a rhyme.

As to Sam's ‘‘four bold and daring lads’’—Richardson is a stranger—both to me and to all my records; Jackson is the only member of the Bass gang mentioned; for Joel Collins and ‘‘Old Dad’’ Underwood (Nixon) were of the Collins gang—as was Sam.

> Sam had another companion, called Arkansaw for short,
> He was shot by a Texas Ranger by the name of Thomas Floyd;
> Oh, Tom's a big six-footer and thinks he's mighty fly,
> But I can tell you his racket—he's a deadbeat on the sly.

Sheriffs and their deputies; United States Marshals and *their* deputies; railroad and express company detectives; posses of citizens; June Peak's homespun Rangers —all swarmed in Sam's back-yard. The posses and officers' parties fired on one another; they harried the citizenry of Denton County.

‘‘Did you ever see Sam Bass; then you're an accomplice!’’ was the hysterical war cry of the peace officers. Indictments for‘‘harboring’’ were drawn by the sheaf.

Sam ranged back and fourth like a hunted wolf. I imagine that it is on this part of his career that the cowboys have based their feeling of sympathy for him. He and the gang continued to ride into Fort Worth or Dallas after dark, buy drinks all around from some saloon, then leave town at the gallop, yelling and shooting off their pistols. But they were caught on Salt Creek and in the exchange of shots Arkansaw Johnson *was* killed—by Ranger Sergeant Floyd, according to the

ballad and to June Peak's statement; by Deputy Sheriff
John Carroll of Denton County, or Deputy Sheriff John
Stoker of Tarrant County—according to *their* claims.

After this fight Henry Underwood fled and was never
seen again. (Sam said he was glad—"Henry couldn't
stand the racket.") Henry Collins also deserted, as did
Charley Carter who, like Collins, was a raw recruit in
this business and who found more lead than gold in
Sam's mining ventures.

Jim Murphy, the Denton cowman who had been
friendly with the gang (he was Frank Jackson's cousin)
was arrested, charged with active participation in the
robberies. Major John B. Jones, former chief of the
Texas Rangers and now Adjutant General of the State,
persuaded Murphy to make bond, jump it and return to
Bass, for the purpose of informing the officers of their
movements. For Bass was planning now to hunt greener
pastures and Major Jones wanted to capture him.
Murphy was a pliant tool. "John Denton" is both
veracious and detailed:

> Jim Murphy was arrested and then released on bail;
> He jumped his bond at Tyler, then took the train for Terrell;
> But Mayor (*Major*) Jones had posted Jim; that was all a stall.
> 'T was only a plan to capture Sam before the coming fall.

MURPHY WAS not received with warmth on his return
to the gang. Sam Bass had turned wolf. Remember that,
in all his robberies, his escapes and his unexpected encounters with posses and officers, he had never killed a
man. He had passed up opportunities. But now, he was
really on the dodge; really hunted. He was fearful,
suspicious, desperate. By Murphy's account, Sam and
Sebe Barnes stood over him with drawn pistols, assuring
him that his treachery was known and that they intended to kill him. Frank Jackson saved his cousin's life;
he told Sam that only after his death could come
Murphy's.

They decided to try for Mexico, planning to rob some
small bank enroute to get money for their future. So,

early in July, they left Denton County—forever. Murphy's story of their travels perfectly illuminates the
character of these now-reckless, now-fearful, cowboy-
robbers. For as they rode, they roped such horses as
pleased their expert eyes, leaving their own animals in
place. Sam, according to the Fugitive Lists furnished the
Rangers and peace officers, was not much of a talker—
"five feet seven inches high; black hair; dark-brown
eyes; brown mustache; large white teeth; shows them
when talking; has very little to say"—was the description. But on the road, as in camp, he talked with
humor; and the cowboy picturesqueness of word and
thought salted what he said:

"What do you reckon Old Mounts'll say, when we
lift his saddle horse? I would like to be hid around! The
old rascal will walk out in the morning and find his
horse and saddle gone and he'll say:

"'I just *know* that Sam Bass got 'em. I wish I had
never got that long range gun! He *said* he would make it
cost me ten dollars every time I shot it!'"

He speculated about the banks on the road ahead of
them:

"We'll just go down the country and cash these old
white pistols of ours for a good roll of greenbacks. Old
Banker, he wouldn't trust us if he could help himself.
But I think when I drop my old white pistol up to his
ear, he'll throw his old top to one side and wall his eyes
like a dying calf and say:

"'Here are the boys! they want a little money, of
course. The cussed old express company can't furnish
'em enough, so I guess we'll have to let 'em have some.
This must be Colonel Bass! I have heard a heap of talk
about him, but I never saw him before'."

Jim Murphy was still fearful; twice Frank had saved
his life. But he was scared; to cover his nervousness,
play boon-companion, he talked much in camp. He
mentioned the Dallas and Wichita railway. Sam snorted:

"Oh, the hell! Give us a rest! The Dallas and Which-
a-Way! Now, ain't *that* a bonanza! I would have pulled

it, but the time I come across it, the poor thing was bogged up in Elm Bottom and I'd as soon hit a woman as to tap it. Besides! If I *was* to rob it, I'd have to rob the poor sick thing on credit—and that's no good in this business!"

In Waco they looked over the banks, but Murphy persuaded them to make no efforts here—he had not been able to warn Major Jones, at Austin, and he wanted to pick a bank well ahead and have the Rangers—plenty of Rangers—lying in wait. At Waco Bass preached a whole sermon—if with no thought of doing it—on the subject of robbery. Flinging down a twenty dollar gold piece on a bar, he started dourly after it; half-turned to Jim Murphy:

"Jim, here goes the last piece of '77 Union Pacific money I had. It hasn't done me a damned bit of good."

They came to Belton and here Murphy found opportunity to scrawl a frenzied note to Major Jones: "We are on our way to Round Rock to rob the bank. For God's sake be there to prevent it!"

Major Jones immediately despatched Corporal Vern Wilson (who was to die in California trailing the bandits Sontag and Evans) to the camp of Lieutenant N. O. Reynolds, at San Saba. From dark to dawn young Wilson rode, killing his gray pony on the sixty-five miles to Lampasas. Here he caught the stage at daylight and reached Reynolds twenty-four hours after departure from Austin. Within thirty minutes, Reynolds and Wilson were in a light spring-hack (Reynolds had been ill and could not ride a horse; Wilson was exhausted), with Sergeant Nevill, Corporal Jim Gillett, and six other Rangers, on horseback. One halt was made next morning for breakfast—after sixty-five miles at trot, lope, trot. The remaining forty-five miles was made without check. (*These* were real Rangers!)

Meanwhile, Privates Dick Ware, George Harold and Chris Connor had gone to Round Rock from Austin. The following morning Major Jones and Maurice Moore, a deputy sheriff, arrived on the scene. Deputy Sheriff

Grimes of Williamson County was notified of the planned robbery and of Reynolds's coming. Jones suggested that Grimes watch for suspicious strangers, but warned him on no account to attempt an arrest without the Rangers. Bass was known to be desperate—and he and Jackson were experts with the Colts, if they had never put deadly skill into play.

Bass had planned to rob the bank on Saturday, July 20, 1878. Jim Murphy was nervous on Friday evening. When they left their camp outside of town to have a last look at the morrow's battleground, Murphy dropped behind on the pretense of getting horse-feed at a store. Bass, Barnes and Frank Jackson rode on, hitched their horses in an alley just back of Hightower's livery stable and walked up the alley to the corner. They entered Copprel's store, intent on buying tobacco.

Deputy Sheriff Grimes, heedless of Major Jones' strict instructions, looked after them. He turned back to Deputy Sheriff Maurice Moore, who stood beside him. He said he had seen a pistol on one of the strangers. It seems incredible that he should not have thought of Sam Bass, since he was looking for robbers. He said he would go in and see about the pistol. Moore stood at the door watching.

"I believe you have a pistol," said Grimes to Bass, walking toward him.

"*Yes!*" the three replied, as one man.

They whipped out their six-shooters. Bass was wearing his; Jackson and Barnes were each carrying saddle-bags with pistols inside. Two fired at Grimes; he died with six bullet-holes in him. The third opened fire on Moore, who was standing in the doorway. They rushed past him as he returned their fire. Dick Ware, the Ranger, heard the first shot fired and came running out of a barber shop. The trio opened fire on him. A bullet from Bass's pistol struck a post an inch from Ware's head. He killed Sebe Barnes and shot Bass through the body as the outlaws backed down the alley toward their horses. Ware's .45 slug cut two cartridges in Bass' belt and penetrated the right kidney.

LIEUTENANT REYNOLDS had ended his long ride but a few minutes before. He left his detachment on the edge of town and came riding in to find Major Jones. Frank Jackson, lank, twenty-two year-old six-footer, was by this time fighting Dick Ware, George Harold, Chris Connor, Major Jones and several quick-shooting citizens. If a train-robber can be a hero, Jackson was heroic, then. He returned the enemy-fire with his right hand and with his left helped the fatally wounded Bass into the saddle. Then he got on his own horse and he and Bass rode out together in a hail of lead. Lieutenant Reynolds had missed them by barely five minutes.

They got away from town in the darkness. Bass knew that he was dying. He would not listen to Frank Jackson's proposal to stay with him. So Frank rode reluctantly away and the next morning the Rangers—of whom only Captain Jim Gillett of Marfa survives— found Sam dying under an oak tree. The Rangers carried him into town and put him in an empty school house under guard. Major Jones vainly tried to get information from him concerning his associates, but Sam shook his black head stubbornly:

"I won't tell. It's against my profession to blow on my pals. If a man knows anything, he ought to die with it in him." Then, after a long pause: "I'm going to hell, anyhow . . . The world is bobbing around me. . ."

During the day he grew weaker. The Rangers stood three-hour guards over him—a man outside, a man inside, the barn-like school room. At noon Corporal Jim Gillett and Private Banister relieved the guard.

Banister took up his post at the door. Corporal Gillett sat with Winchester across his lap, near the outlaw's pallet. A yellow negro youth had been pressed into service as nurse to the dying man.

The afternoon wore on. Bass shifted on his pallet and said weakly:

"Water!"

"You ain't strong enough to drink," the negro told him.

"Get him some water!" Gillett ordered quickly.

The negro turned to the water bucket in a corner. But when he came back, Bass was dead. It was his twenty-seventh birthday, Sunday, July 21, 1878.

Sam met his fate at Round Rock, July the twenty-first;
They pierced poor Sam with rifle-balls and emptied out his purse.
Poor Sam he is a corpse and six foot under clay,
And Jackson's in the bushes, a-trying to get away.

Sam Bass was buried there in Round Rock, ten months after birth of his great ambition up at Big Springs. As a train-robber, he doesn't belong in the same category as the James Boys, the Youngers, the Daltons, the Jennings Brothers. But he had a cowboy dash and swing to him that has made him almost the favorite character of the range riders. Even today, one will not ride long through the cow country, without hearing some Knight of the Chaparejos lift up his voice to tell how—

Sam Bass was born in Indiana. It was his native home.
But at the age of seventeen young Sam began to roam.
He first come down to Texas, a cowboy for to be;
A kinder-hearted feller you seldom ever see.

As a gunman, he was efficient enough. It was simply that he was no killer by instinct. So we have no long and gory tally of six-shooter notches against his name. But he practiced diligently with the pistol. When Murphy began to run with the gang, Sam took him out on the prairie and had him shoot at marks. He warned Jim that it might be necessary to do some straight shooting—especially if "Dad" Egan the Denton sheriff came close after the gang!

And an old Indian harness-maker I used to know, a man who dated back to Quantrell's days, if not to Quantrell's band, once grew unwontedly talkative as we discussed gun-harness of various kinds and the trigger-nometry experts credited with designs of special nature.

Ben Thompson is generally given credit for designing the shoulder holster.

"Mebbe," the old Indian grunted doubtfully. "Me, I makum two shoulder holster for Sam Bass one time. He show me how."

He could have done a good many killings, this grinning "kind-hearted" cowboy. But during the battle at Salt Creek he was willing to lie quietly in cover and let officers pass almost within arm-length of him. He would not kill unless cornered. We know that he let Frank Jackson persuade him not to kill Jim Murphy—whom he knew very well he *should* kill. He passed up chances to do assassinations from behind walls in the Billy the Kid fashion. He tortured no prisoners in the James manner.

He "was cowboy," typical cowboy. And the cowboys of the years since his death have sensed that, have recognized an errant brother through his trail. He had all the careless improvidence, the open-handed generosity, the "ride-the-river" loyalty, the reckless daring and the gay swing of the cowboy breed. And so they have added *Sam Bass* to the repertory of Range Ballads.

Jim Murphy went back to Denton and for some months after closing of that fatal trap in Round Rock, Murphy led the life of a pariah. Even the peace officers who had used him in their schemes had no respect for him. He heard that Frank Jackson (still in hiding; still uncaught as I write) had passed the death sentence upon him. There are two versions of his death:

The Murphy family, it is said, was subject to scrofula or some similar disease, with attendant eye-trouble. Jim Murphy suffered from the disease. He was treated by Dr. Ed McMath, who officed at the Lipscomb drug store on Denton's courthouse square. One story has it that he drank a poisonous eye-wash in a moment of despondency. But Johnny Hudson, who had ridden Sam Bass's Denton Mare, recalls that Dr. McMath was accustomed to treat Jim's eyes with belladonna and administered it while Jim lay flat on his back.

While being treated, Hudson states, Jim raised himself suddenly and some of the belladonna ran into his mouth. In a short time he was very ill, suffering convulsions. All during the day he lay in the drug store. During lucid moments he sat up and demanded his pipe, or begged Dr. McMath to "do something for him."

Late that day he was seen to be dying and was removed to the family home on East McKinney Street and there, during the night, he died. Burial was made in the city cemetery of Denton. Hardly "unwept," if certainly "unhonored," for he left a wife and three or four children. And not "unsung!"

> And so he sold out Sam and Barnes and left their friends to mourn.
> Oh! what a scorching Jim will get, when Gabriel blows his horn!
> He may have got to Heaven—there's none of us can say—
> But if I'm right in my surmise, he's gone the other way!

And if you go to Old Round Rock cemetery, today, you will find a stone over a grave. A sister put it there, a mournful inscription:

SAM BASS
Born July 21, 1851—Died July 21, 1878
A Brave Man Reposes In Death Here.
Why Was He Not True?

CHAPTER XIII · *Sheriff of Cochise*
JOHN SLAUGHTER

COMING UP the trail from Devil's River, John Slaughter's herd crawled like a sluggish serpent, heading toward a market in New Mexico. Slaughter himself was the trail boss. He rode calmly, but alertly, a small, muscular man with short beard no blacker than his eyes, neatly dressed in wide Texas hat, flannel shirt, trousers tucked—not rammed hit-or miss—into the legs of expensive boots. Conveniently low on his thigh, his six-shooter sagged, to reinforce the Winchester that rode across the saddle before him.

Near Fort Sumner the herd was stopped. The outfit made camp. Slaughter said nothing of import to his riders beyond giving curt orders softened by his drawl. But then, he never talked much. They did not expect him to discuss the bad man he had run off from the herd, back on the trail. Indian-fighter, ex-Confederate soldier, ex-Texas Ranger, 33d Degree Cowman, John Slaughter made his decisions and his moves in a sort of remorseless silence.

This "Bad Man from Bitter Creek" had a rep'. Men said that up north he had downed a dozen men. Gallagher, he called himself when not roaring out the "Bitter Creek" name he preferred. Bad, he doubtless was. But when he tried to run a blazer on this grim little cowman, Slaughter had run him.

"None of these steers is yours," he said. "Hit the trail. Keep going."

But, though "Bitter Creek" had gone, Slaughter's riders expected him back, "on the prod". What their employer expected, none cared to ask.

He came back, this notorious killer who made his living by "cutting the herds" of timid drovers. And he was decidedly "on the prod". Nobody carries a shotgun to a friendly meeting and Gallagher's Greener was plain to be seen. He rode straight at John Slaughter—who was out in the open, away from the cattle. Slaughter's rifle came up, before "Bitter Creek" was in shotgun range. At the sound of the shot, Gallagher's horse jack-knifed, throwing his rider.

Gallagher rolled over. He dropped the shotgun, jerked a Colt. He moved toward the short, grim figure. And, in the expressive old Western phrase, "when he came, he came shooting!" But Slaughter, too, was shooting—and shooting straighter. . . He was shooting a rifle, too. He broke the bad man's arm. He sent three shots in succession through Gallagher's body. And he stood grimly by while Gallagher died.

Slaughter's cowboys looked one at another, then at the silent figure of their employer. They saw, now, that Slaughter had been expecting Gallagher, had chosen the ground and the weapons for the inevitable battle—and had quietly and efficiently fought it. Both his shooting and his generalship had been better than those of his opponent. Keep this unimportant killing in mind! It is a forecast of "John Slaughter's way."

He went calmly, inexorably, on his chosen course. What was his, he demanded, to the last dogified calf. He made no threats, he took no backward step. He drove his cattle over trails famous for the rustler-depredations along them. But—

John Chisum, so the story goes, became acquainted with John Slaughter. "No law west of the Pecos!" men said in the '70s. But what little there was usually operated in favor of Cow King Chisum. So, when Slaughter and his cowboys cut fifty-sixty head of steers out of Long-I herds, John Chisum objected. He had a bill of sale. Slaughter looked at the paper and nodded:

You ought've known something was wrong with 'em, when they were that cheap," he told Chisum sardonically. "They're mine and I'm taking 'em."

And take them he did, Chisum making no further objection.

Other outfits which had picked up strays from Slaughter's trail-herds were visited. If trouble threatened somehow Slaughter was ready for it, first man behind a horse, or out in the open where his rifle commanded the approach to his position.

Arizona called to Slaughter. It was virgin range for his cattle and the mines were drawing thousands of settlers to eat the beef he could raise. He knew the country, too—knew it well from trailing cattle. In his customary silence he made, first his decision, then his plan.

He left the Texas Panhandle in the spring of '79 and Slaughter cattle took the long trail toward Arizona. The long, slow-moving procession of horned beasts poured forward toward the Rio Grande far ahead. Texas was crossed, its wide, rolling plains. New Mexico's mountains loomed ahead, and the herd crawled across wide and shallow streams that, flooded suddenly by spring rains, became racing, dangerous rivers.

Slaughter married enroute. At Tularosa, pretty mountain town that lies below the Lincoln County of Billy the Kid fame, the grim cowman married Viola Howell. The herd came on, across the gypsum dunes of the White Sands, swimming the flooded, swollen Rio Grande that the Spanish called the Rio Bravo, and on across New Mexican plains to Arizonan mountains.

By late summer Slaughter had his ranch in the San Pedro Valley. He could sell every head of stock he had in the booming territory. His other herds came out from the Panhandle.

The little Texas-bred Confederate soldier and Texas Ranger, who had been born in Louisiana October 2, 1841, was an established figure in Arizona. He knew cattle as few men knew them. He had grown to manhood on the vast ranges of the Lone Star State, and had trailed his herds to Kansas during the post-Civil War boom.

He watched his opportunities and began to supply Arizona with Mexican beef.

Any man who took money into Mexico in the '80s virtually hung his life on the front sight of his pistol—and prayed that it would stick! Bandits swarmed in Chihuahua and Sonora. The Apaches left their reservations and moved back and forth at will, murdering and stealing stock.

But—John Slaughter's way was to make his decision with full knowledge of the odds against him and go his road. He made trip after trip into Mexico. He and Roberts, his foreman—another cowman of Slaughter's own stripe, "out of the old rock"—carried thousands of dollars on each journey, to pay for the Mexican steers.

On one buying trip they had $12,000. In a Sonoran village Slaughter's *vaqueros* heard that a gang of *bandidos* were planning to murder Slaughter and his men, to get the money. The Mexican cowboys had no such faith in their *amo* as the Texas riders had owned. It may be they knew less of him. They deserted and Slaughter, Roberts and a negro were left. Slaughter led his party out of the Sonoran village when dark had come. He chose good fighting ground and when the bandits came racing on the trail, they met lead from Slaughter's sheltered force. They broke under the deadly fire, ran back and—John Slaughter went calmly on with his cattle buying.

Expectation, doubtless, was father of the report carried by Slaughter's deserters across the line, that Slaughter had been killed by *los bandidos* and the cattle money stolen. When the new herd came back into Arizona, Slaughter was greeted as one from the dead.

He had little time to be amused. The small battle had been a mere incident in a life crowded with hard work, long rides, Apache-fighting. For his San Pedro ranch was in the Indian country. He saw much of the cavalry, more than he cared to see of the Apaches. Tom Horn and other scouts were often at his ranch; the Slaughter cowboys were always alert for Indian sign and a chance to get into a fight.

HE WAS established in Arizona. He had many friends, for all his taciturnity, his grimness. Men knew that he was one "to ride the river with" and they swore by him. But, also, and just as naturally, he made many bitter enemies. He hated a crook of any kind. Particularly he hated the rustler and the horse-thief.

Other cowmen hated them too. It was natural for men who had gathered their possessions in the face of terrific hardship and danger to resent a sticky looper's easy annexation of that hard-won property. But John Slaughter's intensity of nature made his hatred of a thief a deadlier emotion than worked in his neighbors. Marauding Apache or white or brown rustler—they were all alike to him: Creatures to be wiped out for the community good, nonconformists for whom there was no place.

Nor did he clutter his mind with technicalities. The issue as he saw it was quite simple: Was the man a criminal? That answered, he had no more to say. He declared a sort of martial law—his own. He constituted himself judge and executioner and proceeded without delay to settle the particular case. That same unemotional, remorseless efficiency against which Gallagher's blowhard attack had failed, only increased with the years. Arizona knew no deadlier man than this successful cowman, John Slaughter, facing an enemy.

It was not that he had Thompson's or Hardin's flair for flashy gunplay. By casual comparison with them Slaughter seems almost colorless. But actually he was in unspectacular fashion the very type of warrior who would probably have killed a swaggering Wes Hardin or Wyatt Earp and gone on about his business, had they infringed upon his rights.

So, without posing as a gunfighter, John Slaughter went his way buying and selling cattle, building up his ranch, killing Apaches when necessary, staring levelly and grimly into the faces of the Clantons—who were his troublesome neighbors—and the other rustlers and

criminals who "hung out" in Charleston and old
Tombstone.

The old-timers tell many a story of his adventures
with "bad men." There was the time when Slaughter
and his wife were driving out of Charleston. He had a
shotgun with him—and very near his hand—for there
were plenty of men in Charleston anxious to kill John
Slaughter, if the killing could be safely done.

He drove along, keeping his usual Indian-like watch
upon the wild country about them. He saw half a dozen
hard-riding horsemen heading toward a motte of
willows which loomed ahead on the trail. There was
no doubt in Slaughter's mind about the intention of
those men, no doubt about their identity. He recognized at least two of them—Cap Stilwell and Ed Lyle.
Mrs. Slaughter also saw the men. One look at her husband's rock-like face was enough to tell her that here
was danger. Slaughter pushed the lines into her hands,
picked up the shotgun.

"Now," he said "we'll go on. If those fellows open
up on us, you drive on out of danger. I'll fight from the
ground."

Mrs. Slaughter was a woman well-trained for emer-
gencies such as this. She "poured the leather" to the
team. The buggy bounced and jolted over the rutty
desert trail. The bushwackers came leaning low over the
saddle horns, quirting their mounts. But Mrs. Slaughter
was ahead when the willows were reached, and, once
the shelter was passed the killers gave over the attempt.
Perhaps they did not care to see John Slaughter over a
shotgun's deadly muzzle—out in the open.

They turned back toward Charleston. John Slaughter
and his wife went on.

But that was by no means the end of the incident,
John Slaughter being the man he was. He came into
Charleston a short while afterward. He encountered Ed
Lyle in a store and immediately, in typical Slaughter
fashion, he jumped the outlaw. Six-shooter in hand he
looked grimly at Lyle.

"I'm not going to kill you," he told the gunman. "Probably I ought to, but I'll give you this chance: This country isn't big enough any longer to hold the two of us. Twenty-four hours from now I'll be looking for you. I had better not find you."

Ed Lyle may have had his moment of indecision about obeying Slaughter's warning, but it could not have been protracted. When the twenty-four hours were gone—so was Ed Lyle! And he never came back.

Cap Stilwell was next to be met. When John Slaughter walked into a saloon and Stilwell saw him, there seems to have been no doubt in Stilwell's mind concerning Slaughter's errand. For he "slapped leather" instantly. But he was bucking a man who was just as fast on the draw as he needed to be. Slaughter's gun snapped out first. But he did not let the big hammer drop. He was not a man who did unnecessary killing, any more than he was a man who shrank from necessary gunplay. Stilwell's pistol hand sagged to his side. He waited, expecting to be killed. But Slaughter merely gave him the ultimatum which Lyle had obeyed and Stilwell followed Lyle's example. He, too, left the San Pedro country.

In a sense, this forbearance of Slaughter's is more impressive than blazing gunplay. It would have been far easier to kill Lyle and Stilwell than to take the chance of getting the drop on them. Showier, too! Many a gunman of the typical barroom variety would have built up his reputation, put more notches on his gun, by killings in such circumstances. But Slaughter— as everything I have said about him should make clear —was no "glory hunter." He wanted no reputation for killing. He was not that swaggering type which "cut its notches deep."

The quick obedience of Lyle and Stilwell—dangerous men both—is a good index to Slaughter's character as the San Pedro region understood it. They knew better than anyone else, what sort of efficiency Slaughter indicated by the calm contempt he showed them. It was such a contrast to their own method! *They* wanted a half-dozen to one. They wanted a safe ambush before facing this man. But Slaughter merely walked into town, produced his six-shooter. He drew fast, yes! But merely as a sort of incidental safeguard. He looked them in the eyes and told them to get out before he killed them—as he could have killed them at that moment.

Many another story is related today of narrow escapes of John Slaughter. "Curly Bill" Brocius—he who killed Marshal White in Tombstone with the road agents' spin—and other outlaws often trailed Slaughter as the cowman went on his cattle buying expeditions. They wanted that sack of money that Slaughter carried —but they wanted it only if they had a chance to get it on their own terms. Not one of them had the nerve to buck John Slaughter's gunplay alone. Nor did any half-dozen of them want to face Slaughter except they could stage a "dry gulching." It is not of record that any of these attempts succeeded. Sometimes, Slaughter's escapes seemed almost miraculous. But escape he did and his name grew in the imagination of Arizonans. He seemed to bear a charmed life.

As remarked before, the Clanton family were Slaughter's neighbors in the San Pedro. They were notorious stock thieves. But when they began to throw the long rope over Slaughter's cattle they suffered a quick check, of a sort they were not accustomed to. Slaughter took his fighting cowboys, rode over to the Clanton place and recovered his property. Not without a warning to the Clantons, of course. He expressed his opinion of the family quite freely.

The Clantons were not a quiet tribe. Ike Clanton, in particular, a very brave mouth fighter when drunk, made a great many threats against Slaughter. Then he cut across Slaughter's range one day and ran into the grim cowman. Slaughter ran him off. Ike considered this the last straw. He proceeded to get pretty well in liquor and explained to such part of Arizona as was within hearing what he would do when next he saw

Slaughter. Perhaps word of this came to Slaughter. Perhaps not. But—

Again, Slaughter and his wife were riding along the road to the ranch. In the moonlight Mrs. Slaughter saw a horseman whose course seemed to vaguely parallel the trail.

"That man," she said tensely to her husband, "has a gun in his hand."

"Why, so have I!" Slaughter replied almost humorously. He continued to watch Ike Clanton. And Clanton rode on.

COCHISE COUNTY, Arizona in general, saw the change that came with flooding of the mines at Tombstone. Easy money was gone. With it departed many of the camp followers of prosperity. Too, many of the strongest figures of the day and place packed up and moved on toward better camps.

Wyatt Earp and his pack of killers had vanished after the tragic fiasco of the O.K. Corral. "Curly Bill" Brocius was either dead or gone north—depending on which version of his vanishing one wished to accept. The days of outlawry on a great scale had passed and in the place of the almost Homeric killers and rustlers who had once celebrated in Charleston, Cochise County suffered a very plague of petty thieves.

John Slaughter went his quiet way very efficiently. He did whatever was necessary for the guarding of his property. But down in Tombstone men were talking things over and in the course of their conversation John Slaughter's name was often mentioned. They came to him, at last. They asked him to run for sheriff. Something, they said, had to be done. Conditions were intolerable, worse than in the wildest old days.

Slaughter listened to them—not that they told him anything particularly new or strange, for he was perhaps as well informed about general conditions as any man in Arizona. Nothing in his face told his feelings.

But at the end he nodded acceptance. He agreed that a clean-up was due. He felt that he could accomplish it.

He became sheriff in 1887 and, at distinct personal financial loss, moved down to Tombstone to take up the duties of his office.

In a sense, Slaughter was a unique personality. It was not that in appearance, in viewpoint, or in his actions, he differed from many other western peace officers. He was unique because he carried the hard, grim efficient frontier code to an extreme. He summed up all that all the other western sheriffs were—in one man. He embodied all their courage, their ability with weapons, their hatred for a thief, their contempt for the twisted ways of lawyers.

He had a direct sort of mind. His mental processes cut straight across all quibbles to the sensible, practical conclusion. When he saw around him men who were known criminals, men who openly violated all common laws protecting property and life, those men were not—if John Slaughter could prevent it—going into a court as persons even theoretically "innocent," to engage in games of legal hide-and-seek. Nor were they going to walk out adjudged innocent, when everybody knew that they were guilty, simply because of technicalities that their attorneys could bring into play.

One must understand the characteristics of this short, grim, silent—and *brainy*—man, if one is not to charge him with a ruthlessness of thought and action which must give an aspect to his personality entirely unfair to a great pioneer.

So much for his inner man. As for his externals—his impressiveness could not come from bulk. He lacked six inches of attaining the six feet of height owned by many men about him. He was very dark—hair and eyes and beard, with skin bronzed almost to Indian copper by his years out of doors. It was his eyes which impressed all those old-timers who knew him, which are recalled now whenever John Slaughter's name is mentioned.

They were very dark, very steady; they owned a penetration that was almost uncanny.

This was the man who settled down in the sheriff's office at Tombstone, with his own ideas concerning the scope and nature of a sheriff's duties. (Incidentally, one could wish that he, not the well-meaning, soft-natured Johnny Behan, had been Cochise's sheriff in the days of the swaggering Earps! History might well have been very different.)

John Slaughter began to move around Tombstone, about Cochise County, until his wide, white Stetson hat, his fancy stitched boots, his white-handled Colt, and the brown impassive face with cigar always in a mouth-corner, became very familiar, even to those who had not known him as Slaughter, the cow man.

He had his own methods of keeping the law a respected force. It was merely an extension, not a variant, of the method used in the case of Ed Lyle and Cap Stilwell. Ruthless? Certainly! But highly efficient—and certainly as fair as any average process of the courts: When he knew of a man who was "riding with a sticky loop," Slaughter rode up to that man's place and served an ultimatum: In effect, he said to the rustler: "Cochise County hasn't a bit of room for you. Settle up your affairs and get out!"

Not many were bold enough to argue the point. But if a man did inquire concerning the alternative, Slaughter would tap his Winchester, or perhaps state briefly: "If you're here past that deadline, I'll come looking for you. You'll stay here as a permanent resident."

It was not often he took the trail of a thief or other criminal with company. When word came into his office that a crime had been committed, Slaughter was wont to saddle up his horse, ram his Winchester into its saddle scabbard, look to the hang of that famous white-handled six-shooter, and start out. He would return after a time, bringing back a stolen horse or a few head of rustled cattle, and a horse or two with empty saddle. Rarely did he bring back the criminals. It was common rumor that he settled that criminal as soon as he found him.

In a sense it was very ruthless. But from time immemorial the penalty for major crimes, in the West, has been death. That is, wherever a frontier community tried its own cases by community rule rather than by book law. With the coming of courts, of politicians, "book law" with its mild penalties was put into effect in communities which, the day before, had dealt with that same caliber of crimes in a much more effective, if much severer, fashion.

Apparently, John Slaughter had little use for courts. But, neither had the other honest folk of the community! Slaughter was the sort of sheriff they appreciated. He saw eye-to-eye with them. So, they might talk among themselves about the peculiarities of John Slaughter's almost unfailing recovery of stolen property, and his equally unfailing failure to bring in a criminal. But private discussion was as far as the matter got.

He had a young deputy who was to achieve some notoriety in later days as a train robber, but who at the time of his employment by Slaughter was an honest and respected citizen. Burt Alvord was this deputy's name. Alvord was perfectly in sympathy with the sheriff's attitude toward criminals. Talking about old Cochise, just the other day, an old-timer suddenly slapped hand down upon his knee and burst out laughing:

"I was just thinking," he told me, "that in old John Slaughter's day, one of the funniest things we ever had to watch was the two ends of one of Slaughter's cases: I mean, where he saddled his horse and led Burt Alvord out after some horse-thief or rustler, and when him and Burt come back into town, leadin' a couple of stolen horses and maybe an extra horse or two with empty saddles. For it was one of old John's ideas that the proper time to tell a man to halt was after you had fixed him so's he couldn't do anything else *but* halt!"

And that was John Slaughter's way! He did no killing that he considered unnecessary. He put no notches

on that white handled six-shooter. He never spoke of
the men he had killed. He discouraged any consideration of himself as a gunman. But he shrank from no
necessary gunplay. For he knew very well that, for 95%
of habitual criminals, there is no cure this side of the
grave. From that premise, he reasoned in a manner not
accepted by some other criminologists, it is true. But
that his logic was good logic, one can hardly doubt.
Slaughter thought that the community at large did not
wish to be annoyed by the habitual criminal. Some
communities, of course, continued to send their habitual
criminals to prison, free them at the expiration of their
sentences, return them to prison after their next violation of the laws. But Slaughter—like many other
direct-minded and straight-thinking people—saw no
sense to this method.

Very typical was the case of a California-bred
Mexican named Soto. Soto was a leader among his own
race, a well-to-do man. John Slaughter had very strong
suspicions about the source of his prosperity. There was
a band of outlaws who engaged in cattle-rustling, and
horse-stealing, stage holdups and burglaries with, for
natural aftermaths, some murders now and then.

Presently, Slaughter and Burt Alvord were in posses-
sion of a case against Soto. It was a perfectly satisfactory
case—despite the fact that it could not have been taken
into any court with the faintest hope of securing a
verdict against this shrewd and daring Mexican. It was
a case quite satisfactory to the only tribunal concerned
at the moment—Slaughter, himself. He was sure that
Soto was the chief of this outlaw gang. The evidence
collected made him sure of this. He needed no more. A
particularly irritating double-murder of cow-buyers
roused Cochise's sheriff to action a little quicker than
he might otherwise have been.

He went to call upon Soto. But he was not going to
rush matters, so he brought back Soto as a prisoner
charged with this double killing. A jury promptly
acquitted the Mexican and Slaughter faced him unemo-

tionally as he stepped out of the courtroom a "free" man. Soto returned Slaughter's dark stare confidently. The sheriff had lost. He had won.

But if Soto thought that he dealt only with a Cochise County jury, he was badly mistaken! What the jury might do was no particular concern of Slaughter's. Perhaps he knew too much about juries in general! He minced no words. He told the Mexican that he was guilty of those murders and of other crimes. He told him to get out of the country. He set a time limit— some say ten days, some say a month. There is no possibility at this time of deciding just which period was that stipulated by the grim little sheriff. For the two persons who knew are no longer present to testify.

But, no matter what the time was, Soto at first blustered, saying that he would not be run out of Arizona, out of Cochise, by any man—not even this terrible sheriff. But, like Ed Lyle, and Cap Stilwell, and some others, somehow the day of the deadline found Soto gone.

He did not go far, merely to Sulphur Springs. Nor did he reform. A number of mysterious crimes were committed in his vicinity and John Slaughter's farseeing eye took note of the peculiar coincidence of Soto's presence and the commission of these crimes.

Did he kill Soto? John Slaughter was the only person who could have answered that question and there is no record that he ever mentioned that incident. He was always riding quietly out of Tombstone and as quietly returning. Perhaps it was on one of these rides that he decided to make a call on Soto. The actual evidence we have is meager. It runs about as follows:

John Slaughter was riding in and out of Tombstone at about the time Sulphur Springs Valley missed Soto . .

Nor was Soto's the only case at that time. It was—to quote a phrase that is almost an Arizona classic—"John Slaughter's way!"

Not always, of course, did the outlaws of Slaughter's section of Arizona receive quietly a warning to emigrate

—"buy a trunk," was the expressive western phrase. Nor were his encounters with the gentry standing on the Law's left hand always motivated by crimes commited in Slaughter's baliwick. There was the case of the train robbers from Sonora.

In May, 1888, a half-dozen train robbers stuck up the N. A. and M. train south of Nogales. They killed the locomotive fireman, the conductor and the express messenger. Then they plundered the train and rode fast for the border at Nogales. They had taken some $15,000.

Four of the gang were Mexicans. They made their way toward Tombstone, which brought them within Sheriff John Slaughter's ken. He knew that they were somewhere in the neighborhood of town, but his search for them was not at first successful. One of them— Slaughter and Burt Alvord knew—was named Robles. He had a brother, a woodcutter named Guadalupe Robles, living at Contention.

It was Slaughter's thought that, with the natural family attachment of the Mexican, Guadalupe Robles would hide and help his brother Manuel. So, Guadalupe was shadowed and presently the sheriff and Deputies Lucero and Alvord slipped up to the wood camp of Guadalupe in the Whetstone Mountains. When they came to the camp in the dawn they found only two of the four Mexicans they hunted. Guadalupe Robles was sleeping beside his brother and Deron, the other train robber.

Slaughter challenged the sleepers and they jumped up shooting. Slaughter killed Guadalupe Robles with one shot as the woodcutter cocked his pistol. Deron was wounded, as was Manuel Robles. But Manuel got away. Deron was taken and died of his wound.

Agustino Chacon, nicknamed "Peludo"—"the Hairy One"—because of the heavy beard he always wore, was more fortunate than other outlaws who crossed John Slaughter's path. Chacon was an unusual Mexican. He and his gang rode up and down committing robbery and murder, carousing and boasting. Slaughter was very anxious to catch this desperado, for Chacon was telling his people what would happen to the sheriff if ever he were so unfortunate as to be found by the terrible Peludo. But when finally Chacon slipped into Tombstone, and Slaughter and Alvord with double-barreled shotguns went down to a shack to take him, Chacon burst out the back door where Slaughter was waiting, was miraculously missed by the buckshot Slaughter sent at him, and vanished out of Cochise County. It was not until 1902 that he was finally hung for murder, the execution taking place in Solomonville that summer.

JOHN SLAUGHTER retired from the office of sheriff of Cochise County leaving a record matching the finest traditions of the Old West. Hard-handed, ruthless, some might call him, but it was a hard and savage country over which he was called to bring the law. As I have said before, he had no tolerance for the quibbles and technicalities of the lawyer. Nor did he willingly take the chances of having his own hard and dangerous work undone by the freeing of a man whom he had arrested, and whom he knew to be guilty of one of the frontier's major crimes.

He was always a practical person. He had no visionary, unworkable theories concerning crime and criminals. And Cochise County was a better place for the honest man and woman to live in at the expiration of his term as sheriff.

My friend, the late Billy Breakenridge, whose own story is set forth elsewhere in this book, once told me that Slaughter did not have so tough a crowd to contend with as had Johnny Behan. But, he hastened to add, it was plenty tough and John Slaughter did the necessary things to bring to book—his "book"—the cow thief, the highwayman, the murderer.

After his retirement from the sheriff's office, John Slaughter returned to his cattle-empire. He had created from the wilderness along the Mexican border the great San Bernadino Ranch, in the valley of the same name.

He made it a show place. He entertained the great and the small with even-handed hospitality. The years were not uneventful—there were a few Apache raids in the '90s, and the Mexican revolutions after Diaz's fall sent ripples northward to wash against Slaughter boundaries. But he was always master of his environment. Down to the time of his death—1922—he governed his hundred thousand acres of splendid range and was ranked one of the leading citizens of Arizona, the West.

I know of no monument erected to Cochise's sheriff—none of bronze or stone. But a monument to John Slaughter exists in the memories of Arizona—in the memories of all westerners—who hold him one of the real pioneers who fought and worked, to carve from savage wilderness a great state.

CHAPTER XIV · *"Rush One Ranger"*

CAPTAIN BILL McDONALD

"CAPTAIN BILL McDonald is still a famous name in Texas. In the East, probably McDonald was better-known than any other Texas Ranger. Partly, this was due to the fact that in his own person Bill McDonald spanned the forty years between the Smoky Seventies and the first decade of the 1900s. But, also, he was famous as the Westerner who was known and trusted by two Presidents of the United States—Roosevelt and Wilson.

He was a great peace officer! He was one of the really great Ranger Captains, worthy of mention with McNelly, Hall, Reynolds, Hughes. And yet for a while his feet were set upon the same trail that the outlaws Bill Longley and John Wesley Hardin traveled! It seems to me a mystery—as well as a blessing—that he was not, like those two twisted, bulldog personalities, forced into outlawry!

Given his two-fisted, chin-out nature, his utter fearlessness, his disregard of odds, and his amazing ability at gun slinging, if he had been thrust outside the law by the savage, stupid barbarities of the Bloody Shirt forces during Reconstruction, it seems to me that Longley and Hardin would not have surpassed Bill McDonald in reputation for grim gunplay.

Thirty years ago, it must be, since I first saw the man, in Dallas. Tall, angular, at once awkward-seeming and cat-quick on his feet, his lined face was weathered to the rich red-brown of saddle leather, and made notable by prominent nose and gray-blue eyes of a live, alert directness.

He rejected me for the Rangers that day, I recall. And my father laughed and reminded him that some boys not so *very* much older had made good Rangers. Then, as we went on around the courthouse, he told me what I have just written—that Bill McDonald was one of the great Rangers, the typical Ranger.

In later encounters with "Captain Bill," I heard him tell of outlaws and man-hunts and Rangers he had known. He was a born story-teller and some of those drawling accounts stick with me yet, like the clear picture of the man himself, who had every attribute to make him the hero he was of us Texas boys.

He was a Mississippian, born September 28, 1852, son of that Major Enoch McDonald of the Confederate Army who died at the head of his regiment, charging Corinth breastworks in October, '62. Bill McDonald had to act the man at ten. He had been raised in the woods and fields of the big plantation and he could ride and shoot and "cut a trail." He was the man of the house during the rest of the Civil War. Then, in 1866, the ruined family moved to Texas.

In Rusk County the McDonalds set to work to rebuild their fortunes. Young Bill worked with his uncle, grew to what the frontier considered manhood without showing any particular abilities to distinguish him from the other wild youngsters of the neighborhood. He worked on the farm, he went hunting, he "sparked" the girls, and he had a drink or two to be devilish.

Then, in '68, he got in trouble with the military authorities who ruled Texas under Reconstruction. In Rusk, as in other Texas counties, sight of a blue uniform on negroes was a constant affront to the people. Two negro murderers were lynched and the soldiers came down to lesson Rusk County people. Bill McDonald joined enthusiastically in efforts to resist them. And he was arrested. Through the defense made by Dave Culberson he was acquitted—and was more fortunate than two other youngsters of whom I have written, who came in rough contact with the Federals in that bitter time. If he had been treated as Longley and

at least—physically, very often—he threw his opponent off-balance. He had that great advantage that always accrues to the man who knows his own mind and moves fast and surely in executing his intentions. So, the hard cases got nowhere very rapidly in their attempts to scare off or kill Jim Alley's new deputy.

Hardeman County was beginning to fill up with settlers. The town of Quanah appeared like a mushroom. The coming of the railroad was responsible for the new settlement and it had the hard character of such towns the West over. The railroad construction gangs were attended by the usual procession of gamblers, red light women, parasites and killers of various calibers. McDonald was in the thickest of the troubles in Hardeman. And very soon his peculiar abilities as a peace officer were recognized by authorities both State and Federal. He became a Special Texas Ranger attached to McMurray's company. This appointment wiped out county lines for him, as a Ranger had authority in any part of the state. Also, he received commissions as deputy under two United States Marshals.

As Deputy United States Marshal of the Northern District of Texas and the Southern District of Kansas, he had authority over a vast jurisdiction—including the wild region then known as the Indian Territory, which in the '80s was a favored haunt of the West's toughest outlaws.

COW-THIEVES were a very scourge to the stockmen of the Panhandle when Bill McDonald pocketed his commission as Deputy United States Marshal and opened up his war on outlaws. Usually, he took the trail of outlaws alone. Into the wild fastnesses of that region called appropriately No Man's Land, he followed the tracks of stolen stock, surprised his quarry and popped into sight with six-shooter in his hand—then rode quietly back with his prisoners. His became the best-known name in all that region, so much so that many a hard case, hearing that Deputy Marshal Bill McDonald was on his trail, saved the authorities trouble by simply leaving the country. Occasionally, McDonald coöperated with the sheriffs of the various counties, but this, usually, was in cases where the sheriffs wished to go along, or where there were apt to be too many outlaws to herd, once they had been captured.

Full days were McDonald's, during the late '80s. For he was waging ceaseless war against killer and thief in No Man's Land and the Indian Territory. Load after load of prisoners came into Kingfisher, Guthrie, Wichita Falls, for trial or for delivery to outside officers. His prisoners were of all sorts—ranging from petty larceny thieves to killers. Apparently—which is to say, from everything that I ever heard McDonald say, or heard said of him—the lanky frontiersman made little distinction between the types representing the two extremes of outlawry.

When a bandit was to be taken, Bill McDonald went out after him, and if he caught up with him, yelled a demand for his surrender. That was all! Whether the man ahead was .22 caliber or—.45 caliber, to use the westernism, he made just as big a target for McDonald's gun. He was a gunfighter—a gunman—and I use the phrase in the same sense that one uses swordsman. He was lightning fast on the draw, an amazingly accurate shot—when he had decided that shooting was necessary.

Paradoxically, this efficiency of McDonald's worked to the advantage of the other man, as a heavyweight champion's boxing ability works to the advantage of a noisy weakling on the street. The records are full of killings by peace officers which were the direct result of nervousness. A sheriff or marshal half-afraid of a criminal's gunplay very often killed that criminal as safest expedient. But McDonald—like Jim Gillett, John Hughes, and some others I have noted in these chapters —owned both a dislike for killing and—self-confidence. Many times, he risked his life to disarm a man, and to bring in a live and dangerous prisoner, when it would have been the simplest, most justifiable, procedure to shoot quickly and bury his man. Which explains the comparatively meager tally of McDonald casualties, in a savage and lawless region.

During his service as Deputy United States Marshal, McDonald made the acquaintance of some notorious outlaws against whom he was to brush in later years. There was Bill Cook, a hard case who led a gang of thieves and killers more noted at one time than those overly-ambitious bank- and train-robbers, the Daltons.

IN JANUARY, 1891, Bill McDonald came back to Texas in no small way. Captain McMurray resigned as commander of B Company and McDonald applied to his old friend Governor Jim Hogg for the position. He received the appointment and took command of Company B, which then had its headquarters at Amarillo. There was plenty of work in the Panhandle of that day, for a Ranger captain. It was cow-country, a land of great ranches and enormous spaces.

Wanted men from other states, other parts of Texas, found haven here, safe from their pasts. It was easy to "make a living"—if at the expense of their neighbors. In some counties the outlaws became sufficiently numerous to say what men should be elected to the county offices, and put in their own kind. So, when complaint was made by honest citizens to the governor of intolerable conditions, and the Rangers were ordered to the scene, the commander of the State forces might find himself "coöperating" with a sheriff in league with the very men he was supposed to capture.

McDonald campaigned against the outlaws in precisely the same whirlwind fashion that had made him famous a little farther north. His company consisted of six or seven men, usually, two or three of these being non-commissioned officers. In person or by deputy, McDonald brought in cow-thieves and murderers and other criminals wherever they could be caught. Of course, various prominent hard cases began to make threats against McDonald.

One Matthews, in particular, came into Quanah for the avowed purpose of "settling" McDonald. With the sheriff of the county and with two other men he confronted McDonald on the street. McDonald watched Matthews closely and, when the bad man reached into an overcoat pocket for his pistol, McDonald whipped out his own Colt. The Hardeman sheriff stood slightly in front of Matthews and the gunman slid behind him. McDonald, sidestepping as Matthews fired, caught a bullet through coat-collar. McDonald's flashingly fired slugs went into Matthews, but were stopped by a plug of tobacco and a notebook.

The sheriff had no yearning to be a breastwork! He dropped to the ground as Matthews fired again. McDonald, surprised that he had not killed Matthews, shifted aim. A bullet struck McDonald high up on the left side as he leaned forward. That bullet went through the lung and along the Ranger's back. He staggered and Matthews jumped forward for another shot. McDonald leaned, to slap at the other's gun and succeeded in spoiling Matthews' aim. The bullet went through McDonald's hat rim as the Ranger fired his third shot and, this time, dropped Matthews.

Matthews' two companions now opened fire on McDonald. One shot him twice in the left arm. As he whirled upon them, cocking his pistol, a bullet struck him on the right side. His fingers numbed; he could not complete the act of cocking the .45 by hand. Grimly, he raised the pistol to his mouth and caught the hammer in his teeth. Those flaming blue eyes, staring over the Colt, unnerved these two. They whirled and ran!

Matthews sprawled dying in the street, but McDonald was hardly better. He staggered over to a post, put his back against it and slipped down it to sit on the ground. Quanah was sure that Matthews had "got his man." But McDonald had no such notion. He told his wife and his friends that he would get well and, though recovery was long and slow, get well he did. It was a typical McDonald gesture.

He lived. In fact, he was very much alive during the years following, as many a criminal would have testified on oath—and with an oath! All the daily routine of Ranger work was his, with such slightly unusual matters as trips to Mexico for runaway bank officials, and helping to prevent prize fights.

This last mentioned event was the famous Fitzsimmons-Maher "battle" originally scheduled to take place in El Paso in 1896. Charlie Culberson was governor at this time and—a very moral young man was Charlie. Particularly hateful to him was the idea of a brutal battle between two men in a ring. So, he convened the legislature in special session and had a law passed, forbidding prize fights within the State of Texas. This done, he convened in El Paso another "special session"—this time of Rangers. The whole affair is remembered by Texas as High Farce. Culberson withdrew from territories where they were urgently needed practically every company commander of the Frontier Battalion. The captains and their men mobilized in El Paso in the strength of a young army. He sent Adjutant General Mabry to assume charge of them. I have an idea that the group picture taken on the steps of the El Paso courthouse, during the preparations for the fight, shows the largest gathering of Ranger captains ever assembled. John Hughes (who could have stopped a dozen such fights single-handed!) Brooks, Rogers, McDonald, and General Mabry, all were here.

Eventually, Promoter Stuart decided that Culberson really would *not* permit the fight to be held in Texas. McDonald, like most of the other Rangers present, was not particularly in sympathy with Governor Culberson's anti-fight attitude, but it was a matter of obeying orders. When the Governor said that no prize fight could be held—no fight *would* be held. The "battle" was held in Mexico, across the Rio Grande from Langtry, Texas. The sports writers sat before the reeling porch of Judge Roy Bean's "Law-West-of-the-Pecos-and-Cold-Beer" establishment. They used the porch as desk, while writing the meager details of that fight which Fitzsimmons won almost with a single punch.

The absence from the Panhandle of Captain Mc-Donald and Sergeant W. John L. Sullivan (one of the outstanding Rangers of all time) was naturally capitalized by outlaws. One of the old Bill Cook gang, which McDonald had encountered a time or two in the Indian Territory, was named Lewis. He and a partner, Crawford, rode into Wichita Falls to hold up the City National Bank. Perhaps they were nervous. Certainly, they were loose on the trigger. The cashier was killed and a bookkeeper was wounded, before Lewis and Crawford scooped up some six hundred dollars and ran out. The robbers swung up on their horses and went fast out of town. But pursuit came quickly and a posse, firing on them, killed Lewis's horse. For a while the two men rode double, then they took a horse from a man coming into town. Later on they stole two fresh horses and got out into the country.

McDonald and his Rangers did not arrive in Wichita Falls until afternoon of the day of the robbery. They mounted immediately and took up the trail. It led them into the bottom of the Wichita River, into scrub timber and thick brush. Time after time the trail crossed the river and the questing Rangers must wade the icy water. Late that night the two bank robbers were rounded up in the brush. McDonald came upon them, sitting with rifles across their knees, waiting to kill their followers. It was a typical McDonald capture, which is to say, almost undramatic. McDonald merely rose up behind them and yelled. Lewis and Crawford put up their hands and by the time the other Rangers came up he had two prisoners and the stolen money.

Back in Wichita Falls, a mob formed quickly to lynch the prisoners. The town was roused by the murder of the bank cashier. McDonald had ridden out of town, looking for a rumored third robber, said to be hiding in the country. He rode back into town to find a mob milling around the jail door. He charged with his rifle and backed the mob away from the jail.

Local authorities now assumed charge of the prisoners. McDonald rather disgusted, left town. He was hardly out of sight when the mob surged down upon the jail, took out Lewis and Crawford, and strung them to telegraph poles.

IT WAS IN 1897 that McDonald and his company were ordered to San Saba, to put down a gang which was terrorizing that section. The gang leaders were exiling or killing citizens whom they didn't like, or who merely owned property coveted by the terrorists. It was a difficult assignment. Those who guessed at the gang's membership were afraid to tell what they knew or suspected. Everywhere he turned McDonald faced a stone wall of fear-caused silence. There was no way of estimating the strength of the gang. But McDonald was no mean detective. He moved quietly about the country, checking cases of mysterious murders, until he had collected enough information to form a background for the whole sinister drama—and had discovered, too, some of the characters of the cast.

Bill Ogle—who is still well and unfavorably recalled in the San Saba country—was a man of whom McDonald heard a great deal. Presently the Ranger was certain that Ogle was a leading spirit, if not the leading spirit, of the gang. Ogle was said to be a very dangerous man, but McDonald informed him that he had the evidence to connect Ogle with a murder committed some ten years before—the hanging of a man named Brown.

"And you're going to hang, just the same as Jim Brown hung!" McDonald informed Ogle.

Very much to the amazement of San Saba, the terrible Ogle did not whip out a six-shooter and kill the daring Ranger, then and there. Instead, he wilted like the cowardly murderer McDonald had informed him he was. Presently, he was trying to sneak out of the country.

But McDonald had anticipated this. His Rangers pounced upon Ogle and jailed him.

Now McDonald began to get information from those who had been afraid, theretofore, to open their mouths about any of the doings of the Ogle gang. He and his Rangers rode about the country, calling upon suspected terrorists, and displaying so much information about their deeds that some weaker members of the gang got out of the country, and those remaining hurried to explain their connection with Ogle.

Ogle was tried in Llano County and sentenced to life imprisonment. And the final result of McDonald's work was the complete wiping out of as choice a collection of night-riding assassins as Texas ever knew. A wipe-out, too, in the face of predictions that, at best, McDonald would learn nothing; that, at worst, he would die from a mysterious bullet.

There was never a let-up in the work of Company B —or any of the other companies of Rangers in the state— in the early years of 1900. Thumbing over the reports of the Adjutant General, reading between the lines of these terse statements, analyzing the tabulations of prisoners captured, miles ridden, one begins to understand what was required of a Ranger commander in those days not so log behind us. A typical extract from the Adjutant General's Report reads:

"Since January 1, 1899, the officers and men of the Frontier Battalion have been very actively engaged in running down the criminal element in the west, and in subduing lawlessness in other portions of the state. The Rangers have only been used in other portions of the state as direct request was made by the civil authorities of cities or counties needing them." And—"It is probably appropriate to mention some prominent features of the work of the Rangers during the past two years, *outside of the duties usually performed by them*, in the way of scouting the sparsely settled district of the west, and the work accomplished in recovering stolen cattle, arresting thieves, murderers, etc."

Then the Adjutant General continues:

"During the month of March, 1899, Captain Mc-Donald, with two men, was ordered to Columbus, Colorado County, for the purpose of preventing trouble there between the Townsend and Reece factions. Captain McDonald went alone, his men not being able to reach him in time, and his courage and cool behavior prevented a conflict between the two factions. The district judge and district attorney both informed him that it was impossible to handle the situation, but he told them that he would make the effort, and he gave the members of each faction a limited time in which to get rid of their weapons, stating that he would put those in jail who refused to comply. His order had the desired effect."

And from a letter from an Assistant Attorney General:

"At the request of the sheriff, county attorney, and other local authorities of that (Henderson) county, Captain McDonald and Private Old were sentthere to assist them and myself in the investigation of that horrible murder which was then enshrouded in a mystery that it seemed almost impossible to uncover. Before the Rangers reached us, the people in the neighborhood seemed afraid to talk. About the first thing that Captain McDonald did was to assure the people that he and his associates had come there to see that every murderer was arrested and convicted, and that he would see that all those who assisted him would be protected. They believed him and soon began to talk and feel that the law would be vindicated, and I am glad to see that it was. The work of the Rangers in this one case is worth more to the state, in my opinion, than your whole department will cost during youradministration."

In this case three of a lynching mob turned state's evidence and eight of them received life sentences through McDonald's efforts. B Company policed longshoremen's strikes, guarded courts, supervised elections, under McDonald's command, in addition to the business of catching thieves and murderers which one thinks of, usually, as the Ranger's work. But Rangering had become a more complicated profession in the early years of the twentieth century. More and more, Captains Hughes, Rogers, Brooks and McDonald were really State Police.

McDonald's name was known all over Texas, now, as a detective, so much so that a request from county authorities to governor or adjutant general for Rangers might include the sentence: "If Captain McDonald can be spared, we should like very much to have him."

So it was, in late 1903, when McDonald was ordered to Trinity County to investigate a murder. He caught his man but he realized that solving one murder mystery in this lawless region was never going to alter or improve conditions there. He was pretty sure that he, or some other Ranger, would be back in Trinity County and that soon. Which was a surmise soon to be justified! Quoting from his report covering the first half of 1904, we include the shooting of a bad negro and another visit to Trinity County:

"January, 1904: I, together with Private Delling, went to Corrigan and Livingston to look after some witnesses. I went after a bad negro for Sheriff Brooks. The negro was armed with a shotgun and considerable shooting occurred. After the negro ran out, he shot at me and I wounded him in the side. . . .

"February, 1904: . . . I was ordered to Groveton by Adjutant General Hulen for the purpose of investigating the murder of an old lady, Touchstone, who was murdered for her land and money and thrown out the door for the hogs to eat. After investigation, I found that her throat had been cut and that she had been killed outright . . . I arrested Ab Angle, who had run off, as principal, and five others as accomplices. These parties were indicted by the grand jury."

This curt report tells nothing of the painstaking detective work necessary in that criminal-ridden neighborhood, where arrests were made for "burglary and rape" and for murder of the most cowardly sort—and the prisoners were either turned loose by local officers or escaped in the courts. Yes, McDonald's life was a busy one, as well as a dangerous!

In 1905 he had a little pleasure by way of vacation—wolf hunting with the party of President Roosevelt. A warm friendship between the two forthright men was the result of this expedition. But the hunt was followed quickly by one of the most sickening tragedies in Texas criminal history—the murder in Jackson County of a Mrs. Conditt and her four young children. Headquartered at Alice, Texas, McDonald found the crime within his jurisdiction, and he began his investigation.

At the scene of the crime the Conditts' neighbors believed that a negro boy had committed the outrage. But McDonald had his own theory concerning the murders. He could not believe that one boy had done five murders in the circumstances that surrounded the multiple crime. Clear into 1906 he worked, talking to negroes, checking evidence, watching and listening. And there were bloody shirts and crimson handprints to be checked and identified. The final result was a triumph for Ranger sleuthing. Two negro men were hanged for the murders and another negro and four negresses were also indicted. McDonald's reputation was much increased. And in 1906 occurred another event which was to enhance the name of both McDonald and the Texas Rangers.

THE TWENTY-FIFTH INFANTRY, a negro regiment of the regular army, was stationed at Brownsville on the Rio Grande, in 1906. In August of that year, between ten and twenty of the black soldiers came to town armed and opened fire at random, raining bullets into houses and stores, with the result that a bartender named Natus was killed and several other citizens wounded, including the chief of police. Then the shooters disappeared.

The affair caused terrific excitement, not only in Brownsville, but—as I recall vividly—all over Texas. Negro soldiers have never been popular in the South and the Brownsville Affair seemed to prove the justice of Southern whites' antipathy for any black man in a

position of responsibility or authority. And when the
Army officers at Brownsville "could not learn" the
truth of the matter, Texas sentiment was near the boiling
point. For this wanton outrage committed by uniformed
men of the Army was only the climax of other incidents
which Brownsville had suffered at the hands of negro
troops. Bill McDonald was particularly angered for
Brownsville was in his bailiwick, and he could see no
energetic effort on the part of other authorities to investigate the affair, fix the blame, and begin proceedings
looking to the punishment of the guilty.

At last, he went to Brownsville and began to make
his own inquiries at the post. He found the Army
authorities anything but helpful. All the negroes, the
officers told the Ranger, had been present at roll call—
ergo, none could have been involved. Probably it was a
gang of Mexicans from across the Rio Grande. They
were satisfied with the soldiers' explanations. And so
their answers ran.

But McDonald knew negroes. Not for nothing had
he been brought up on Southern plantations and farms.
It was his intimate understanding of the negro mind
which had brought solution of the Conditt murder
mystery. So, at Brownsville, he listened with growing
irritation to vague talk from Army officers when he
wanted facts. At last, he demanded that the negroes be
brought in for his examination. And presently he was
tangling the soldiers, involving them in a mass of
contradictory statements. He matched what he learned
at the post with what his Rangers were learning in the
town and got something like a true picture of the affair.

Theodore Roosevelt had his eye on Brownsville.
And, dissatisfied with the results attained in Army
"investigations," the President mustered out the regiment. Later investigations made by the War Department through the work of private detectives bore out
the belief of Bill McDonald that the negro soldiers with
the help of their non-commissioned officers had been

guilty of the shooting, with its attendant casualties—
which might well have been much larger than they were.

Texans applauded President Roosevelt's action in dis-
banding the regiment. And the name of Bill McDonald
was heard everywhere in the state, for his insistence at
Brownsville, in the face of every difficulty that red tape
could rear, was well known. And—it was just what
Texans expected of a Ranger. Particularly of Captain
Bill McDonald!

THE BROWNSVILLE business almost marked the end
of McDonald's Ranger service. For, in January, 1907, he
was appointed State Revenue Agent of Texas by Governor Campbell and he literally put down the sword to
pick up a pen. And our concern with him is done,
though as a financial agent of the state he was no less
quietly efficient and forthright in his methods than in
the Rangering days. He was to visit Roosevelt in the
White House, serve as virtual bodyguard to Woodrow
Wilson for a time, die honored of every Texan who
knew him, personally or by repute. He was one of the
great Rangers, a typical frontiersman with little patienc
when the letter of the law, instead of its spirit, was in
voked, a man who—Texas likes to recall—

"would charge Hell with a bucket of water"!

CHAPTER XV · *Boss of the Wild Bunch*
BUTCH CASSIDY

Hᴇ ᴡᴀs perhaps most typical of "cowboys gone wrong," this stocky, tousled and goodhumored Utah leather pounder. As he broke bronc's along the Sevier, or "cow hunted" in the valleys and upon the great mesas and across the dreary deserts of southern Utah, there was nothing about him to distinguish him from the other hard working, hard living, punchers of the 1880 breed. George Leroy Parker was his name. He used it, then.

They say that as a buster he had few equals; that he owned a natural wit, a salty brand of humor, which made him favored on the spreads he worked for. When work was done; when cowboys hit town for primitive pleasures—to drink whiskey and dance with the pretty girls of Circleville, or Green River; to gamble at faro, monte, or stud poker; to shoot off their pistols and race their wild eyed horses down the streets—George Parker was a leader in the wild horse play.

That is about all we know of him, as he was in those early days. Men I know, who "were using around" western Utah, eastern Colorado, southern Wyoming, between 1888 and 1906, and who knew this cowboy as one of their own kind, tell me that he must have been born between 1865 and 1870. They make their guess by memory of him as he appeared when he drifted back to Dirty Devil Creek and the Robbers' Roost Mesa of Utah, in '96.

The face of the West was changing, by the middle '90s. Settlers were coming into the vast open reaches of the cattle states; land was going under fence and under ditch; towns were springing up; cowmen who had paid their hands a bonus for every calf they could steal and brand were now growing virtuous—for some of those hands were deciding that if a calf was worth five dollars to the boss, it was worth ten to themselves as nucleus of a herd. This naturally made their late bosses highly indignant! More important, still, the wild element was drifting from Texas' more settled sections, from the more "civilized" parts of other western states, into the savage wilderness that stretched from the Animas Valley of New Mexico to southern Wyoming.

They were hard men, used to taking chances; many were outlaws when they pushed into the wild region along the Colorado. They found no honest source of income and, quite naturally, they began to run off a few head of horses and cattle from big outfits, trail them north or south out of the home country and sell them for enough to finance their sprees in the cow towns.

Perhaps, in the beginning, seasoned horse thieves, rustlers, from other states were the principal depredators. But native cowboys were inspired by the example, or fell in with veterans on the range or in the little town, and were made thoughtful by talk of "easy money." So it was with George Parker. He began in fashion insignificant enough—but progressed!

He was already "a little on the rustle" when he crossed into Wyoming in '89. He knew the secret places of the Uncompaghre, of Castle Valley, of San Rafael Swell, of Robbers' Roost, of Brown's Park; knew the dim trails that connected fastness to fastness along the "high lines" that gave a view of the surrounding country across which law men must ride.

He and Al Hainer were partners in a little homestead, in Wyoming. They were about average, by the standards of citizenship of that day. They drank and gambled and rode the range from Lander roundabout, up to the Lost Cabin and Owl Creek country. Then they sold out and vanished—exactly as many others drifted in those days in that country. Nobody thought much of it; word might come in a month or a year that they were in Montana, or Idaho, or far south in Chihuahua or Sonora; alive or dead.

They showed up months later, in Lander. They had plenty of money and they told various stories of making it in Colorado. And they disappeared after whooping it up a while in Fremont County's "hurrah" cow capital.

Then, that spring of '94, a Fremont County deputy made a quiet trip. He was a good man; he had been selected to strike a blow at the horse thieves who had made life a nightmare for ranchers of that section; against whom the Stockgrowers' Association had taken steps both officially and unofficially.

He came back, this Calverly, with a bunch of stolen horses and with two prisoners well known to Lander. "Butch Cassidy" was the name George Parker had taken. Perhaps it was because his family down in the Sevier Valley of Utah were respectable folk—a sister was later assistant postmaster at Circleville. But Wyoming knew him as Cassidy; the Pinkertons were later to dig out his real antecedents.

Cassidy—to take up now the name by which he became notorious—had a gash in his head where Calverly's slug plowed through the scalp. He had a fractured jaw. For when Calverly and a fellow deputy had come upon their men in camp below Green River, Al Hainer had surrendered, but Cassidy had fought savagely before Calverly's pistol barrel had smashed his face.

Sentiment was mixed, there in Lander. As it was mixed in such cases all over the West, at that time! Cassidy was a friendly, a likable, soul. Lander had known him well, liked him well. And he had done little more than many others; stolen a few horses, that was all. But he was convicted and sentenced to two years in Laramie penitentiary. Hainer was acquitted.

Just a cowboy . . . who hadn't "kept his twine on the tree . . ." Circumstances had sent him to the penitentiary for a light sentence. A shift in the circumstances of his capture might have seen Cassidy dangling in some cottonwood motte at the end of a noosed lariat; might have ended with him lying beside his camp fire staring sightlessly upward.

But it is highly doubtful if he thought about that! His kind usually owned a dogged fatalism. They said to themselves—and to one another!—that when their time came, it would arrive beyond all escaping. A bullet would be marked—and it would surely brand them. That was the way they felt about it. They lived in accordance with the belief.

Along in January, 1896, Cassidy was pardoned by Governor Richards. His time was drawing to a close when he applied for the pardon. Whatever the Stockgrowers' Association knew, now, of Cassidy's former activities and associates, and however forebodingly they looked forward to his release, he had but a few months to serve and Wyoming gained little by keeping him behind bars until his last day was served.

He and the Governor had some talk. Quite a while later, down in the Robbers' Roost of San Juan County, Utah, Butch told some "long riders" about it. The Governor, he said, had offered to pardon him if he promised to reform.

"I told him," Cassidy said soberly enough, to the *buscaderos* there at the Roost, "that it was no use promising to go different. I was already in too deep. But I said I would promise not to worry Wyoming, if he'd pardon me out. He took me up."

The State of Idaho might very well have wished that the promise had been made to her chief executive! For Cassidy had told Governor Richards barest truth, when he said that he was not reforming.

There had been time to think—and time to plan—there in Laramie. And if Butch Cassidy had made a New Year's resolution, a couple of weeks before his successful plea to Richards, it must have been a resolve to aim at bigger things in outlawry!

After all, it was a very logical decision: There was really less work, and hardly more of danger, involved in robbing a bank or a train, than was connected with running off a thousand dollars' worth of horses. And the pay was ten, twenty, even a hundred times, greater! The

Daltons had proved that, over in an Oklahoma already grown too thickly settled for easy escape after a blow. And every good little *buscadero* knew that the Daltons' gory finish at Coffeyville had been due to a combination of three factors—foolish bravado in trying to rob more than one point, bungling technique during the robbery, and—hard luck!

No—with Bill Doolin, Anderson, Dynamite Pierce, Tulsa Jack, still loose and on the make, there was nothing about the Daltons' career to check an ambitious outlaw.

So, like many another, the man who came out of Laramie pen' was a long rider far more dangerous than the happy go lucky young rustler who had entered prison. Outwardly, though, he was the same overallsed and tousle-headed cowboy, with the quick grin and the good-humored blue eyes, when he left Laramie, drifted down to Green River, Wyoming, and began quietly to look up friends.

Take a look at the country, as Butch Cassidy could visualize it where he stood drinking quietly at a Green River bar, getting word of the outlaw fraternity from soft voiced, watchful eyed riders.

Something like ten years before, Granville Stuart, president of the Montana Stock Association, had opened a war upon the rustlers of the Yellowstone, the Missouri, the Musselshell. Fighting Montana cowboys had cleaned up the state; driving the sticky loopers into Idaho and Wyoming; decorating many a limb with the swinging corpse of a stubborner than usual horse thief.

From central Wyoming, then, south through Utah and Colorado, into Mexico and Arizona, the rustlers had spread. There were ranchers aplenty who profited by trading with rustlers, or who owned sympathy for them because they themselves were of lawless instinct; many more who were discreetly averse to complaining of the rustlers who were constantly riding past their places.

The long rider, then, was sure of finding food for himself and his horse, word of officers' presence, news of his fraternity, wherever he rode. And a stranger to any section of that country was foolhardy, who spoke to a casual acquaintance about the *buscaderos*. As some Pinkerton detectives were to learn!

Nonsense by the ton has been written by the blood and thunder fictionists of the Sunday supplements, about "The Wild Bunch," and "The Hole in the Wall Gang." Foolish imaginings about military organization and discipline, Masonic passwords and initiatory ritual, binding together into a closely welded army hundreds of outlaws from Jackson's Hole to far Cananea. With "General Butch Cassidy" in command, moving gang units like tacks on a map.

The truth of the business is that here was a vast scope of wild country, stretching from Wyoming to the Mexican line. To it gravitated naturally outlaws of many sorts, joining there with native products of the land. They joined themselves into gangs of convenient size and chose as their hangouts natural fortresses like Castle Rock in the Henry Mountains, and the Robbers' Roost.

Their connection, gang to gang, was of the loosest nature. An outlaw riding north or south was informed as to trails and gang fastnesses ahead; was sure of shelter and assistance from his kind. Stock stolen in one part of the country could be traded north or south or east or west for stock stolen elsewhere.

These were cowboys-turned-outlaw, for the most part. And still they owned qualities for which the cowboy has been famous always—loyalty to one another, good humor, recklessness, the ability to live hard and uncomplainingly where a stranger must have died or surrendered, and above all a rough bigness of nature.

They were not only feared by the general run of citizens; very often they were well liked. Cassidy was, for example. And there were few cold-eyed killers among them; fewer petty thieves; still fewer cowards.

In the aggregation of gangs, then, there were all sorts and conditions of men: Outstanding figures who

were known everywhere; subordinates by the dozen
whose names are today unknown; wild boys who might
join in a single job and never afterward do more than
passively sympathize with outlaws.

The tallest figures of the two principal gangs—"The
Wild Bunch" and "The Hole in the Wall Gang"—were
the brothers Logan, Harvey and Loney, and their
cousin Bob Lee, all of whom went under the alias of
"Curry" at one time or another; Harry Longabaugh,
known more usually as "The Sundance Kid" from his
hailing place; Flat-nosed George Curry; Camella Hanks;
and, somewhat later, two young Texans who had served
apprenticeship in "Black Jack" Ketchum's Arizona-
New Mexico gang—Will Carver and Ben Kilpatrick,
"The Tall Texan."

All of these were well known at the time when
Cassidy was merely an ex-convict from Laramie. Most of
them he knew. Without doubt, he had worked with
Harvey and Loney Logan before his arrest. So, as he
gathered up the lines broken during his time of imprisonment, he was neither friendless nor without objective.

Presently, with some of his own kind, he was riding
toward the eastern border of Idaho. He needed a stake;
so did the others siding him. And two of "the boys"
were awaiting trial in the Green River jail, for rustling.
They needed money for lawyers.

The gang came quietly into Montpelier, Idaho. They
walked into the bank. Accounts vary as to the amount
for which they "cashed in their six shooters"—as the
buscaderos used to phrase it. But it was plenty! For they
drifted back to Green River, left several thousands there
with lawyers for their friends' defense, then "cut their
suspenders" for Hanksville, down in Utah.

They made Robbers' Roost and amused themselves
with drinking and shooting at marks and playing poker
—with twenty dollar gold pieces for chips. When word
came from sympathizers—sometimes borne by a friendly
sheriff!--that the excitement was dying down, they
came out of the Roost to spree in the little Mormon

villages, sometimes staying in a town long enough to throw over the bar of a favored saloon keeper enough to pay for his establishment! Easy come—easy go! How does the old Long Rider ballad put it?

> "Long riding, she's an easy life!
> A life that's full of fun.
> The prairie is our lodging house,
> The moon, it is our sun.
>
> "Dancing, drinking, gambling, fighting,
> Are the pastimes of the gang.
> 'Enjoy yourself!' the password is,
> For tomorrow—you may hang!"

And so the Montpelier money went!

That was the beginning of Butch Cassidy's real career, a career which is picturable only in a sort of patchwork, made up of pieces gathered here and there from official records, from the word-of-mouth of men who knew him and liked him.

Because of the conditions of those days; because of the efficient speed with which the outlaws moved and struck; because of the secrecy with which they managed to clothe their activities; no such thing as a chronological record of Butch Cassidy's forays can ever be written. Even the Pinkertons, who were steadily on the trail of the men terrorizing the railroads, worked often for months to discover which known outlaws had done a particular job. Doubtless, Cassidy, Longabaugh, the Logans, and other outstanding leaders, got credit for jobs they knew nothing of. And doubtless, too, they struck blows never charged to them.

The "boys" would get together, at Castle Rock where the "Blue Mountain Gang" and the McCartys holed up; at Robbers' Roost; outside of Spanish Fork; over in the Brown's Park country of Colorado; get together almost anywhere! They would talk over various banks, trains, mining camps, and pick the one offering most money at the time. A sufficient number of men were selected and the job was done.

It might be a Cassidy job, or a robbery engineered by Logan or Camella Hanks. Detectives for railroads, express companies, banks, taking up the cold trail, nosed about to learn the names of the men concerned. Sometimes they managed to pose as men on the dodge and worm from outlaws the information they wanted. But there was rarely any assurance that what they were told was the truth. Charley Siringo, working for the Pinkertons in the interest of northern railroads, worked four years and covered 25,000 miles, and little if any of the data he collected could be used in a court. Chiefly, the detectives' labor was valuable in building up a vast fund of statistics concerning the outlaws; information which would help to smash an alibi, or identify a criminal, when he was picked up.

One of Cassidy's earlier robberies, and a typical Cassidy job in the efficiency, the cool daring, of its execution, was staged in the little mining town of Castlegate.

Cassidy and Bob Lee (sometimes known as Bob "Curry" and, like his cousins Harvey and Loney Logan, a cool and desperate man) rode up to the edge of the little town the night before payday at the mining company's office. They were merely two such shabby figures in old hats and faded coats and overalls and high heeled boots as any Utah town was used to seeing. They attracted no attention in Castlegate where they drank a little, gambled a little, and otherwise comported themselves like common riders. But the next day—

The paymaster and his guard got off the train with a money pouch. Miners crowded about, waiting for their pay. And Butch Cassidy, with Bob Lee siding him, rode quietly up the street, covered the two men as they swung from the saddles, and took the money from the paymaster. Many of the miners were armed—it was no more than a custom of the day and place. So were some of the citizens of Castlegate. But Cassidy and Lee rode out of town with lead singing their way, untouched. Cassidy and Lee had not fired a shot; the robbery had been executed with a cold precision that made for speed.

"Those fellows couldn't shoot!" Cassidy said afterward, grinning. "No use of us shooting back at them."

The pair had planned every step of both robbery and escape too thoroughly for a helter-skelter pursuit to worry them. They rode south into Castle Valley, across San Rafael Swell, and made the fastnesses of their hangout without seeing a posseman.

Cassidy was now an unquestioned leader of the outlaws—*among* the outlaws might be a better phrase, because of that looseness of organization of which I have spoken. He was one of those becoming prominent on the Pinkerton lists. Robbery after robbery was staged. Big cattle companies were all but ruined by the raids of the gangs operating out of the Hole in the Wall, Brown's Park, "The Rock," or "The Roost."

From Alma, against the Arizona line in New Mexico's Catron County, up to Jackson's Hole in the Tetons and the Hole in the Wall on Buffalo Creek, there was a constant movement of long riders. Word would come to the railroads or express companies that hard cases were in a certain neighborhood. Trains would carry guards heavily armed for a time; banks would be watched by county and city and special officers.

But the gangs would strike their blow—most usually in a place other than that expected by the corporations. They would run; scatter; vanish. Laboriously, the Pinkertons and allied detectives would take up the trail. Geography was with these raiders. A gang could strike in Wyoming, Utah and Colorado, all within a couple of days.

"We—I mean the boys, wasn't educated much," an old-timer told me not long ago. "But two things we— I mean the boys, was learn'd in: Professors couldn't have learned us—I mean the boys, anything about g'og'aphy and counting money!"

Routt County, Carbon County—others in Wyoming, Nevada, Utah and Colorado, heard the explosions that marked blowing of a money safe; heard the thudding of outlaw horses' hoofs; organized posses and "took out after" the flying raiders. Sometimes they caught up with the gang they hunted; and battle followed in which possemen or minor outlaws fell. But more often the long riders' knowledge of the country, their efficient plans, let them keep well ahead of the law. Sometimes they sent word back to sheriffs that they were lying in wait for the posses. In these cases wise sheriffs simply turned their horses around.

News of the Spanish American War's outbreak filtered into the fastnesses where the various gangs of the West were holing up. Old-timers tell me that nowhere did patriotism flame higher, indignation over the *Maine's* sinking wax hotter, than among these two fisted fighting men. The majority of them wanted to get into service and get over to Cuba. There was vague talk of organizing a separate outfit, all their own. And so it came about that three governors had cause to worry . . .

They were supposed to be gathering around Steamboat Springs, the tall ones of the *buscadero* clan. Wild rumors went the rounds of sheriffs and other officers. For the various gangs of outlaws were particularly active as '98 came in. And with word of massing of the long riders, it seemed certain that they intended a homeric blow at the corporations which were their chosen prey. Various meetings of officers were held. The governors of Utah, Colorado, Idaho and Wyoming conferred by wire.

But the impossibility of getting into the army was soon recognized by the outlaws; and the danger of putting themselves in uniform was also seen. Perhaps a few of the rank and file did slip into fighting units; one or two lesser lights of my acquaintance almost certainly saw service in Cuba. But the majority gave over the notion and "business as usual" was the order of the day.

The country had been well roused. Local authorities gathered posses and struck blows at various gangs in Wyoming, Utah, and Colorado. Some outlaws of more or less prominence were wiped out; some good officers and citizens died in the hills.

But the leading figures of the long riding fraternity continued to flourish; the Logans, Harry Longabaugh "The Sundance Kid," Butch Cassidy, Flat-nosed George Curry, Ben Kilpatrick, Will Carver and their like.

Logan led a gang with Flat-nosed George, to rob the Union Pacific at Wilcox, Wyoming, in a country where he had many allies to shelter him and inform him of official movements against him. Cassidy was credited with joint leadership of this stroke, but he always denied that he had broken his pledge to Governor Richards. And verification of this denial came to me a few years ago, from an old-timer who maintained that, at the time of the Wilcox holdup, Cassidy and some subordinates—of whom this old-timer was one—were leaving northern Mexico. Cassidy had been laying plans for a gigantic raid on Mexican *rancheros*. The old outlaw insisted that Cassidy could not have reached Wyoming in time to take part in the Wilcox affair.

Logan's bunch came very near to grief, after Wilcox. They found themselves hotly pursued by a fighting deputy and a posse of cowboys who were strictly "on the prod." The posse caught up with the *buscaderos* and opened fire, but were driven back. Gathered by the deputy once more, they charged again. They holed up the outlaws, chased them away from their mounts, and it was luck as well as hard fighting that let Logan's outfit escape before officers could make the distance from Casper to reinforce the cowboys. The deputy sheriff leader had been killed, but the waddies were still full of fight.

The aroused country was too hot for the outlaws. They separated, hearing that attack was planned on their northern fortress at the Hole in the Wall. Somewhere in the south, they met Cassidy. He got some of the unsigned currency taken in the robbery; went to Alma, New Mexico; opened a saloon under the name of "Jim Lowe." He was accepted as a quiet, likable business man, as in other places, at other times, he had been accepted as whatever he said he was.

Some others of the Wild Bunch, the Hole in the Wall outfit, were not doing so well. Pinkertons, swarming everywhere, posed as cowboys, prospectors, geologists, outlaws; they sent to the Denver office, where the famous detective McPartland presided, reports that contained the rumors and the hearsay that they wormed from outlaws big and little. The sum total of it was vast. Relayed over the country, acted upon by various officers, it made life highly interesting for a dodging long rider.

Loney Logan, alias "Loney Curry," Harvey's brother, was thus traced to the old home town of Dodson, Missouri. Pinkertons and local officers killed him as he resisted arrest. Elza Lay, alias "Bob Mc-Ginnis," had been an old Utah side kick of Cassidy. He drifted into New Mexico, fell in with Sam Ketchum, brother of the notorious outlaw "Black Jack" Tom Ketchum, and raided with Sam and other Arizona long riders, killed Sheriff Farr, was wounded and captured and when tried went to Santa Fé penitentiary for life.

Bob Lee, cousin of the Logans, sometimes called "Bob Curry," was captured by Pinkertons in Cripple Creek, returned to Wyoming and sentenced to ten years for complicity in the Wilcox robbery. Harvey Logan swore that he would strike the Union Pacific a blow in payment for Loney's death and Lee's capture. He took Ben Kilpatrick, "The Tall Texan," and another man, rode from a friendly cowman's place near Dixon, Wyoming, up to Tipton. There they stuck up the Union Pacific and rode back to the ranch from which they had started. They were concealed there until it was safe to ride on south. They reached Arizona; made that country too hot for them.

Meanwhile, "Jim Lowe" dispensed liquor in the wild little community of Alma, hail fellow with cowboy and miner and solid citizen. Word came to the Pinkerton office in Denver that Butch Cassidy was in the neighborhood of Alma. An assistant superintendent went there to investigate. He was an Easterner and much bewildered by this environment. He found no

officers in whom he might confide. For Alma was in a
section so lawless that the sheriff could not hire a deputy
to serve there.

The Pinkerton man confided, willynilly, in some of
the town's leading men. Jim Lowe listened with particular interest. And when some of the wild bunch of Alma
moved to string up the hated Law, it was Jim Lowe who
saved him. The Pinkerton man left Alma—hurriedly. So
did Jim Lowe! He sold out his saloon and went west toward the Arizona line, to find Logan and his gang, now on
the run from Arizona toward Wyoming. But the Pinkerton office in Denver regarded Jim Lowe as a gentleman,
if not precisely a scholar. It was useless for an operative
to write Denver and suggest that Jim Lowe and the
notorious Butch Cassidy were one and the same! That
assistant superintendent knew Lowe, who had saved
his life.

On the road toward a rendezvous with Logan,
Cassidy and his outlaw companion met another party,
also in search of "Kid Curry." This second band of
searchers chanced to be Sheriff Beeler. Cassidy and his
compañero were promptly captured—the second arrest in
Butch's racing career. But he was hard to capture and
twice as hard to hold. He escaped that night from the
posse's camp, riding a bareback horse. And when he
overtook Logan's gang, he mistook them for another
posse and dodged out of sight. Not until he stopped at
one of the secret postoffices of the long riders did he find
a message telling their identity.

He made Baggs, Wyoming, and was hidden there by
a friend. Beeler and the Arizona posse thought little of
state lines. They followed the "Kid Curry" trail clear to
Baggs. Like the Pinkerton man in Alma, they talked to
the wrong man. They told Cassidy's friend that they
were trailing Kid Curry, and he told Cassidy. That night
Cassidy rode quietly out of town, well armed, crossing a
bridge held by two Beeson men. They took him for a
rancher and spoke to him courteously as he rode past.

We come toward Trail's End. . . . Flat-nosed George Curry died with his boots on, down in the Mormon country, resisting arrest. Lesser lights were being nosed out by detectives working for express companies, railways, banks. Logan and a selected band, with Cassidy as fellow commander, stuck up the Great Northern train at Wagner, Montana, getting over a hundred thousand dollars in unsigned currency consigned to a Helena bank, and a great deal of other money and valuables from the express safe.

They exchanged shots with a sheriff who chanced to be on the train, mounted and rode south, closely pursued. They divided the loot, scattered and shook off the posse.

Cassidy, Logan and Longabaugh are credited with the robbery of a bank in Winnemucca, Nevada, in which over thirty thousand dollars was taken. They marched into the bank, held up the employes, dumped the loot into a sack and escaped. It was a typical Wild Bunch job. The posse following simply reached a place where the horses of the outlaws seemed to have taken wings. It was usually that way. These were frontiersmen, cowboys who knew all the tricks of the Indians with whom they had lived in Utah, Arizona and Colorado.

They had money galore—and in one sense this money was their downfall. For circulars had been flooding the country since the Wilcox robbery, warning bankers and storekeepers to watch for certain bills and notify officers if they appeared. Whenever one of the gang scissored off a few tens or twenties from a stolen sheet, and signed an imaginary bank official's name to it, the detective nearest that point of passing descended upon the spot.

But they were quite cheerful, happy go lucky, the five leading spirits of The Wild Bunch. They foregathered in Fort Worth—Butch Cassidy, Harry Longabaugh, Harvey Logan and the two Texans, Will Carver and Ben Kilpatrick.

They lived at the old Randall Apartments for a time. They bought "town clothes," loud suits and curly

rimmed derby hats and fancy vests. They indulged in
watch chains hardly thinner than plow tugs. They were
living the life of Riley. They thought about heading for
the Argentine, where so many cowboys had been going
lately. So they had a souvenir made, a group photograph showing them in all their sartorial glory. That
picture proved to be a bad investment.

A detective happened to see it at the photographer's.
He recognized Will Carver instantly, for Will had been a
prominent man in Arizona and Texas since the middle
'90s, along with Bronco Bill and the brothers Ketchum.
Other detectives supplied the identities of the other subjects. The trail was picked up. It led to San Antonio,
thence to Bandera and Kerrville.

Officers of West Texas were warned to look for a
group of the most dangerous outlaws in the country.
Logan was particularly deadly—a killer of the cold-
blooded, efficient sort. The number of notches on his six
shooter was large. Will Carver would kill upon occasion,
though his homicides seem to have been usually forced
upon him. In April, 1900, he had killed the famous officer
George Scarborough (who had killed John Selman in El
Paso), over in the San Simon Valley of Arizona. Longabaugh, too, would shoot. But Butch Cassidy had no
killing record, whatever.

After staying a while on the ranch of Ben Kilpatrick's people near Eden, Texas, the gang had to move
on. For one of them—Carver is generally charged with
the deed—killed an old fellow named Oliver Thornton
who, it was supposed, saw them and recognized them.

They camped on the outskirts of Sonora, Texas, and
Sheriff Briant was suspicious of them. When Will
Carver, one of the Kilpatrick boys and another man or
two entered town to buy horse feed, Briant hastily
gathered some men together and rushed the feed store.
He challenged the men and they opened fire. Will Carver
was killed instantly. The Kilpatrick boy was badly
wounded but survived. The outlaws in camp took it
on the run when the shots sounded.

Ben Kilpatrick annexed Carver's common law wife, Laura. They bundled up the stolen money and departed for St. Louis. They were not a pair to settle down quietly in enjoyment of so much cash. An old St. Louis detective sergeant says that reports came quickly of stolen bills passed in St. Louis. City detectives, wise in the ways of flush cowboys, combed the sporting district and located "The Tall Texan." By a ruse they captured Kilpatrick, then found Laura in a hotel, very fine in "cowgirl clothes." The pair were swiftly indicted.

Out in the gang's old haunts Harvey Logan heard of their arrest. He went back to Rawlins where he had *cached* some of his share of the Wagner money. Apparently, he was inspired by the cowboy's instinctive loyalty to friends. Charley Siringo was in Rawlins at the time. Logan saw him but Siringo never saw the little outlaw. He heard later that Logan had gone East to finance his friends' defense. But Fate had other cards to deal. . .

In Knoxville, Tennessee, Logan was arrested, indicted and given a long sentence. The Wild Bunch said that more of the buried Wagner money was dug up and sent East, to pay Logan's way out of jail. That was "Kid Curry's" last official appearance. The Wild Bunch as a major outlaw institution has vanished. Call the roll!

Bob Lee, lieutenant of Cassidy at Castlegate, of Logan at Wilcox—in Laramie for ten years. Elza Lay, as dangerous as any rider of the "high lines"—"doing the book" in Santa Fé. Flat-nosed George Curry—dead with boots on in Green River neighborhood. Will Carver, whimsical and deadly, cowboy troubadour brooding through the years over a faithless wife—dead in Sonora, Texas. Camella Hanks, veteran outlaw and boon companion of Cassidy and Logan—on the dodge, with death waiting in San Antonio. Ben Kilpatrick "The Tall Texan"—Atlanta penitentiary, fated to die under Express Messenger Trousdale's ice mallet near Sanderson, in 1912. Cassidy and Longabaugh and Logan —all were to make South America.

Logan's end is not recorded. Most credible report (to me) is that placing him on the Andean slope, beginning a climb that took him out of sight forever.

Cassidy and Longabaugh hung together, once they met in Buenos Aires. W.D. Connell was in "B. A." in 1906, with a chosen group of Texas cowboys come to rope and ride against the Argentinos. As a cowboy on the old WS outfit near Alma, Billy Connell had known Saloon Keeper "Jim Lowe." Cassidy renewed the acquaintance. When he and Longabaugh were leaving for Chile, Cassidy traded his white handled Colt .45, for Connell's longer barreled Colt. As I write this, that old .45 which Butch had carried on raids that marked the high water line of loot for cowboy-outlaws, lies before me. There are no notches on it. None could have been put on it, according to the record. Butch Cassidy was unique, in that for years he could dominate the hard cases among the Long Riders without having to kill, that in his many daring robberies he never killed.

He and Longabaugh were hardly of the type to become peaceful Chilean *rancheros*. Presently, they fell out with the authorities. A raid was made on their house. Longabaugh, they say, was killed while asleep. But Butch Cassidy from the shelter of a stone corral fought a deadly day-long battle against the charging *soldados*, until that long barreled Colt had from Billy Connell had but one live shell in its cylinder.

We may picture the square faced, blue eyed cowboy, there behind the stones of the corral wall. Sweat will be cutting the mask of dust and black powder grime. One shell left; one slug; and outside the soldiers gather for a final charge. One shot—and the soldiers pushing up cautiously suddenly rush forward. The *Yanqui* is dead with long Colt beneath him.

George Le Roy Parker, alias "Butch Cassidy," is a legend.

CHAPTER XVI · *"Railroaded?"*

TOM HORN

Iᶠ ʜᴇ ʜᴀᴅ been all good, or all bad, Tom Horn would not have offered us the complicated study that his case presents. He would not now live in the memories of the old-timers as martyr or murderer—as he does live in their memories, the rôle assigned to him depending upon the sympathies of the speaker.

But he was neither fiend nor plaster saint and, since his record has been created for modern readers almost wholly by small-calibred "feature writers," in newspapers, it is small wonder that nothing like a rounded picture of Tom Horn has yet been painted. Newspapers, almost without exception, deal with the raw, primary colors. Newspaper writing is usually hasty writing. In handling topics demanding research, the careful weighing of evidence, any newspaperman is handicapped by the necessity for making a deadline. Very rarely is his story marked by evidence of careful assembling of facts.

So—reams of sloppy copy have been written about Tom Horn. Almost every anniversary of his death is marked by a "story" rehashing a hundred other old newspaper stories. These are notable, usually, for the misspelled names and misquotation of facts they contain.

For thirty years, or since he made his last appearance upon the gallows at Cheyenne, in 1903, I have been hearing stories, reading opinions, concerning this Missouri farm boy who scouted in Apache campaigns, broke world's records for steer-roping, served in the Spanish-American War, terrorized cow-thieves in Colorado and Wyoming, and finally was hanged in Cheyenne, convicted of a cowardly—and stupid—murder.

Tom Horn's history is a complicated record. But, also, it must prove fascinating to any student of the Old

West, or any student of men. Horn is called by certain Army officers and their clique a mere common laborer, a monumental liar, a murderer and—whatever else occurs to them at the time of discussing him. By some Army officers who did not live to write letters to newspapers or publish time-misted and distorted memories, he was called a daring and reliable scout. By cowboys who knew him well, he was (and is) recalled as a good friend and one of the experts of their craft. By certain cowmen and their newspaperman friends, in Wyoming, Horn and his employers have been and are bitterly attacked, he for committing murders at which they hint, his employers for hiring him to do the murders.

All in all, this controversy which has raged since the January day of 1902 when Horn was arrested has produced much more of heat than of light. It has been remarkable for superficial thinking, for twisting of facts to make a point, and for very careless writing.

My own purpose, in considering Horn, is to attempt putting together the pieces of the puzzle which, assembled, will make something like a true picture of the man, bits of information found in widely separated places. Naturally, any such consideration of a figure so controversial must affront the partisan of either camp. Tom Horn's champions may complain that I credit him with too little. His enemies (the Retired Army Officer clique and certain interests in Wyoming) will froth furiously because I credit him with anything at all.

But the man interests me as other gunmen, good and bad, interest me. In writing of him, I have no ''missionary'' purpose, no partisan interest. The reader of my chapter will form his own opinion from such facts as I can marshal. It seems to me that, whether Tom Horn really murdered a fourteen year-old boy as climax to a long succession of assassinations, or whether he was railroaded by a bunch of political time-servers, such facts as are unquestionable make the best ammunition for both his defenders and his attackers.

My judgment of Tom Horn is formed by several years of study of all the material I could obtain, plus the opinions (favorable and unfavorable) of men who knew him and lawyers who did not—but considered the records of his trial.

Before one can sit as judge on Tom Horn the Gunman (good or bad), weighing the evidence for and against him, it is necessary to look briefly at his fifteen years in Arizona. For in Arizona Territory—the Arizona of *Wolfville Days*—Tom Horn became a frontiersman, a cowboy, an Indian fighter. In the Arizona of blue-shirted cavalry, raiding Apaches, wandering prospectors, gunfighting cowboys, Tom Horn received the education which made him the terror of rustlers in Wyoming.

TOM HORN says that he reached Arizona, a big country boy from Scotland, Missouri, in 1875. He was big for his age and generally taken for a man, though not fifteen. By his own account, he had come to Kansas from Missouri, worked for a little while at Newton, then pushed on into New Mexico where he became a stage driver, and late in '75 drove a company mule herd to Beaver Head Station near the Verde River.

Retired Army officers and their friends have written many pages to prove that no civilian ever did anything worth while in Arizona. Arizona history belongs to the Army, by the testimony of some of these. Those civilians employed by the Army seem to have been so unimportant of status, so trifling of character, by these accounts, that an unprejudiced observer rather wonders why they were let to cumber the ground around the posts. And then one encounters the testimony of an occasional officer lauding the deeds of those very scouts and interpreters who "classed as laborers" as one retired colonel recently wrote with high disdain.

But—whether or not Horn ever did anything in Arizona—there is no questioning the fascination the frontier held for him. He had always had "Indian ways,'' his mother complained. In his Missouri boyhood he had been by choice a hunter. Now, he looked out over the savage, sinister mountains that lifted ruggedly from yellow desert, where ''bronco'' Apache or horned sidewinder rattlesnake lurked behind rock or cactus. It was the heart of ''the Indian country,'' a land of spines, of terrific heat, of immense and inhospitable distances. He looked at Arizona and liked it.

THE HISTORY of the Apache campaigns is a record of which no white American has reason to be proud. The Apaches' country was wanted by the whites, as other Indians' country had been wanted in other days. The Apaches were herded onto reservations and the Army received the unpleasant chore of policing wild men who had been free to roam and fight at will.

Indian agents receiving appointment through political ''pull'' regarded their positions only as Government-given opportunities to graft. The Indians of any agency were utterly at the agent's mercy and—rarely had he any mercy.

When the Apaches' natural restlessness and belligerence were increased by injustice and oppression at the hands of these grafting agents, the result was trouble.

On the Army fell the burden of protecting settlers from the Indians who slipped away from the agencies on marauding expeditions. And the officers commanding the various detachments were of all sorts ranging from good to indifferent. The troops they commanded were good fighters when a fight was toward. But the Army itself recognized the need for civilian scouts and interpreters, when trailing Apaches across their native land. At any rate, around the posts were Americans, Mexicans, half-breeds serving in these capacities.

Horn was much around the Army. He became acquainted with Al Sieber, perhaps the outstanding scout of the Apache campaigns. Sieber was wise in the ways of the Apaches. Even Army officers, never noted for giving a civilian credit for anything more than two arms and two legs, have admitted (in writing) his abilities. Horn spoke Spanish fluently and spoke Apache at least well enough to associate with the Indians.

Sieber made countless scouting expeditions to look into the feeling of the Indians, to investigate the illegal making of liquor, to arrest criminal Apaches, to guide detachments of cavalry. Horn went with him.

"Often-times I needed the help of a man I could rely on, and I always placed Horn in charge," Sieber stated after Horn's death. "For it required a man of bravery, judgment and skill, and I ever found Tom true to the last letter of the law to any and every trust confided to his care. . .

"In making my side-scouts alone, I would always place Horn in charge of all Indian scouts left behind in camp. This required a man who was cool and had judgment to control and handle these scouts. On other side-trips, when I took a few pack animals, I ever made it a point to take Tom with me, as it very often required me to have a man that I could rely on in every way, as I often-times had to split my crowd after being out. I would always put Horn in charge of one set of scouts, tell him where and the time to meet me, and what to do; and I never had him fail to obey my orders to perfection. No matter what came up—rain or snow, clouds or sunshine—Tom was there to meet me. . ."

High praise—from that grim, taciturn old scout! Geronimo was always a trouble-maker. A sub-chief of the Chiricahuas, he aspired to supreme command. Regularly, he left the reservation with a band of the more warlike Apaches and went raiding into Mexico. He would be persuaded to come back and after a while would leave again, "to get the horses the Mexicans raise for me!" as he put it sardonically.

Horn was developing. At twenty-three, he was an outstanding frontiersman and a veteran campaigner. It was training that would make of him a Thieves' Nemesis in later days, a figure whose mere presence in a neighborhood scared rustlers into flight. He was as much an

Indian as any Apache and he had, in addition, the intelligence of the white man.

In the intervals of scouting, he found time to locate some mines in Aravapai Cañon and to learn the tricks of cowpunching on Arizona ranches.

In 1885, when Geronimo made his last and worst outbreak, Horn accompanied Captain Emmet Crawford into Mexico. In early 1886, Crawford's force—composed of scouts and pack-train only—with Lieutenant Maus as second-in-command, crossed the border. It was on this expedition that Crawford's force met a body of Mexican cavalry and was fired upon. Crawford was killed. By all accounts (including those of the Army) Horn conducted himself most heroically. With Lieutenant Maus he brought Crawford's body back into the United States.

Later, he was in Mexico with Captain Lawton, when Lieutenant Charles Gatewood went down with White Mountain Apaches to attempt a contact with Geronimo.

General Nelson A. Miles had relieved General Crook in Arizona and the War Department was demanding an end of the Geronimo raids. Miles had his plans for finally settling the Apache trouble, but these plans depended on getting Geronimo back into the custody of the Army—a difficult task, since Geronimo had taken refuge in the wild Mexican mountains and military expeditions, generally, found the Apache only when the Apache was quite ready to be found—in some very cleverly located ambush from which they could empty Army saddles.

This, incidentally, is no overdrawn statement. Even the Army officers of the day, such as Lieutenant Britton Davis, admit that the soldiers' pursuit of Apache was absolutely useless. And an old Apache scout now on the Mescalero Reservation above Tularosa told me, fifteen years ago:

"No white soldier carrying a cook stove could ever catch an Apache—unless the soldier had something the Apache wanted!"

This grim old Indian laughed at his memories of that campaign, when the heavily equipped troopers came lumbering after the Apaches. He said it was like a cow trying to climb a tree after a squirrel.

Enters, now, a highly controversial subject—the meeting of Gatewood with Geronimo. Lieutenant Gatewood was one of the very best of the Army's young officers—and none who knows the real story of the Apache campaigns (which exists only in part in Army records) could have any wish to detract from Gatewood's record.

With his two Apaches, Gatewood came up with and passed Lawton. He took Horn and the little party went into Geronimo's camp. Geronimo was persuaded to meet with General Miles in Skeleton Cañon. Did Gatewood accomplish this, alone? Did Horn twist Geronimo at Gatewood's request? Did they, together, accomplish the task set Gatewood by Miles? I don't know! Nor, I think, does anyone else.

Army authorities credit Gatewood with the accomplishment. Horn claimed that he, acting under Miles' orders, finally got Geronimo to Skeleton Cañon.

It seems impossible at this late day to sift all the evidence, and to determine exactly just what credit goes to this man, or that man. The Army claims that the military alone were responsible, deserve credit, for the arrangements resulting in Geronimo's final coming in. Horn states for himself that he, also, had his part in this business. The Army denies it. But the final result was that Geronimo was gathered up quickly by Miles, who had determined to make a clean sweep of all the Apaches, and who took into custody both the renegades who had been killing Americans and running into Mexico, and those "friendlies" who had never been renegades, but on the contrary had gone with the Army and fought Geronimo and the other hostile chiefs.

Miles made no distinction. He simply bundled up all the Apaches he could find, put them on a train and sent them to Florida.

NO, WE will never know just what part Horn played in this event of the Apache campaign. But this we do know by the testimony of others—that this blue-eyed, six-foot dare-devil was an outstanding figure on that savage frontier. He was as much an Apache as anyone of Geronimo's band. And he had intelligence of a high order, and a bravery that even the never-enthusiastic Army officers attest by letters.

These are points important, not so much historically, as psychologically. We need not bother about the particular activities of Tom Horn in Arizona. But we will never understand the man who remains one of the disputed figures of Western history, if we do not see what sort of person settled down in Arizona after this campaign.

In 1887 Horn, though interested in a mine, served as deputy under sheriffs such as Bucky O'Neil of Yavapai County. He saw the bitter fighting of what he called the Pleasant Valley war. This was a business of night riders, of lynchings, of ambushes, and of open killings. But, by all reports (including Al Sieber's), Horn stuck straight to the middle of the road. As a deputy sheriff he was a mediator. He leaned to neither faction in the "war."

He was a great cowboy, particularly noted for steer-roping. He was consistently a winner in this event. He travelled to the various rodeos, in Arizona and around about, contesting. When Gila County was organized Glenn Reynolds became sheriff and Horn took a star as Reynolds' deputy. The famous Apache Kid was arrested in the fall of '88 for murder. Horn was to be one of the guards to take the Apache Kid to the place of trial. He was also to serve as interpreter. But on July 4, '88, in Globe, he had made a record for roping and tying a steer. So, when the Territorial Fair at Phoenix was announced for the same date as that set for the Apache Kid's trial, Horn decided to defend his record at Phoenix, rather than to go with Reynolds as a guard.

He went to Phoenix and, while he was there, contesting, the Apache Kid was tried and convicted. As
Sheriff Reynolds and Deputy "Hunky Dory" Holmes
were taking the prisoners to the penitentiary at Yuma
to serve life sentences, Apache Kid and his five Indian
companions attacked the two officers and killed them.

Horn always blamed himself for their death. He
learned that the escape was a plan of the prisoners con-
cocted as they rode along. They talked over their plans
quite openly because neither Reynolds nor Holmes
understood the Apache tongue. Horn felt that if he had
been one of the guards, he would have known what the
Indians intended, or his presence would have kept them
from talking over their plans. The fact that he had won
the steer-roping contest against a very bitter rival was
an empty triumph.

In 1890 Horn finally got out of the mining business.
He and his associates sold their claims to some New
Yorkers for $8,000. He went to work for the Pinkerton
agency at Denver under James McPartland, the detective
famous for breaking up the Molly Maguire terrorists
in Pennsylvania. From 1890 to 1894, by Horn's own
statement, he was in the employ of the Pinkertons.

He never talked much about his experiences during
those four years. Old Charley Siringo, then a Pinkerton
man, has mentioned Horn a time or two in his own book
of reminiscences. I have the idea that Siringo was just
a little jealous of Horn. He (Siringo) was "the cowboy
detective" and he wanted no rivals. Nobody who knew
Siringo, either personally or through his writings, could
ever doubt that Siringo's bump of self-esteem constituted
quite a large section of his head. Without knowing
anything about the famous Nickell case, Siringo dis-
misses Horn as a common killer and says that he came
to an ignominious and a merited end. In fact, Siringo's
statements concerning Horn conflict with everything
that we know of Horn himself, and serve to illuminate
Siringo rather than Horn.

Apparently the life of a detective was too tame (and perhaps too dirty?) to suit Horn. When he had real criminals to track down, or when as in the Apache campaign, there were savage and dangerous Indians to trail, he liked it well enough. But sneaking and strike-breaking were Siringo's meat, not his.

HE AND Operative Doc Shores got in one bit of excitement during his service as a Pinkerton man. A train had been robbed on the Denver and Rio Grande railroad between Cotopaxi and Texas Creek. Horn and Shores took the trail, but so many amateur detectives were swarming over the ground that they were actually arresting one another!

But, when the sheriffs' posses had quit, Shores and Horn followed the trail of two men across the Sangre De Cristo Range, then back to the east side of the mountains and down through Huérfano Cañon and east of Trinidad. The two detectives followed into Clayton, New Mexico, across the Texas Panhandle and into the Indian Territory. At Washita, they caught one of the robbers named Burt Curtis. Shores went to Denver with him. Horn waited for "Peg-leg" Watson, the second man. When he rode up, Horn simply stepped out and said: "Someone has come!" Watson threw up his hands. Later, Horn captured a third man of this same train-robbing gang.

Horn himself gives the date of his resignation from the Pinkerton service as 1894. This would make him a Pinkerton man at the time of the farcical, if deadly, "Powder River Invasion" in 1892. Whether or not Horn was with the famous "regulators," seems impossible to determine. It is claimed that he was in the party which staged the comic opera war—and it is denied as vigorously. But there is no doubt that his sympathies were always with the cowman against the rustler. His chosen companions for years had been cowmen and honest cowboys, as his service had always been on the side of Authority.

And it seems certain that he worked as a stock detective in Brown's Park, Colorado and that, at the time he reached Wyoming (about '94) he was at once an expert cowboy and a deadly tracker-down of cattle thieves. There were cowmen in Wyoming at that time who had need of a fearless, straight-shooting, rider, to protect their herds against the onslaught of the thieves who made ranching a profitless occupation.

Until the outbreak of the Spanish-American War, Horn was a familiar figure on the cow ranges and in the contest arenas of various rodeos. But, with coming of the war, Horn could see in the newspapers the names of various cavalry officers whom he had known in Arizona. They were getting up in rank, now, filling positions of responsibility and influence in the War Department and in the field.

There was Dr. Leonard Wood, who was organizing the Rough Rider regiment with Theodore Roosevelt as his second-in-command. Horn had ridden with Wood in Arizona when he was an Army surgeon. There was Maus, now a ranking officer. There was Lawton.

Horn, nearing forty years of age, was yet anxious for service. Apparently, he had little difficulty in recalling himself to Maus. He was given work in the Army pack train. On service, he contracted fever and came back to Iron Mountain. His illness kept him from going to the Philippines with the Army. That he was highly regarded by some of his superior officers is attested by letters from Maus and others, in which occur such phrases as:

"I can say this of Horn; that he is one of the bravest men I ever saw. He was with me in Arizona, distinguished himself for gallantry and action with Mexican troops and Apache Indians . . . in the Sierra Madre Mountains. He is energetic, speaks Spanish fluently, and would be invaluable as a scout or packer or whatever you could give him. He was my chief of scouts and I have a high regard for him. . ."

". . . Mr. Horn's service, in the capacity of chief packer of all the pack trains in Cuba (eight in number) deserves the highest commendation and praise. He was indefatigable in all his hard work and exceptionally correct in his reports of what had been done. . .''

But the attack of fever made it impossible for Horn to go back into military service. He stayed at the Iron Mountain ranch of John Coble. Eventually, he rode the range again as cowboy and stock-detective.

Toward the end of the last century, Wyoming, like most other western states, was torn by the struggle raging between big cowmen and small, cowman and farmer, cowman and sheepman, cowman and cowthief. The war was fought on the open range, fought in the little town and the city, fought with bullets and with ballots. Both sides were frequently ruthless in their methods. Both sides numbered among their members strong and weak, brave and cowardly. And in official places sat honest and fearless men upholding the law, and dishonest, grasping individuals serving only the side that elected them. In many counties only one side could get fair treatment.

That was the stage. Tom Horn, a great cowboy, a fearless, efficient man—trained, remember, in the danger and the ruthlessness of Apache campaigns, was to play his part upon it—play what was to be his Last Act.

He worked at various times for individual cowmen and for groups of associated cowmen who hired him as their stock detective. As a representative of the cowmen, his duties were to guard against the stealing or butchering of his employers' stock, or the blotting of their brands. Naturally, he had to be constantly in touch with range conditions, had to watch suspicious characters.

It was a task always difficult and usually dangerous. Any motte of trees, any little ravine, was apt to hold a long-roping gentleman bearing a Winchester or Colt, thoroughly averse to being surprised by the like of Tom Horn. He would be rather more apt than not to express his resentment by a shot. Some of the old-timers remark that ''stock detective'' was just another term for ''thief killer.''

There is no questioning the general truth of this statement. Even today, on every range from Montana to the Rio Grande, in wild, deserted places one may stumble upon the bullet-pierced skull of rustler or detective. The stock-detective might be pardoned for shooting, rather than arresting, a man caught red-handed in the sovereign range crime.

There was the problem of trying to get a conviction—frequently in a hostile court—of the man arrested by a stock-detective. Millions of words of fiction have been written, describing the warfare between big and little cowmen and the political creatures of both. That fiction is often based on proved cases.

Tom Horn evolved a system: He made himself out so terrible, so omniscient—and omnipotent!—that the mere rumor that Tom Horn had been seen in a certain section brought cold sweat out upon men of guilty consciences. Frequently, a rustler would "buy a trunk"! Horn studiously cultivated his reputation for Indian skill at tracking, Indian ruthlessness.

It may be said that I am building up a strong presumptive case against Horn, by depicting the natural temptation to constitute himself judge, jury and executioner of cattle-thieves, and by recounting the reputation he had in Wyoming. But it is impossible to judge the man without considering all the factors in his case and when we come to the particular case of little Willie Nickell's murder, I think that the surrounding circumstances will be of value in judging that incident. There is no doubting the impulse that moved the owner of cattle and his employes—cowboys and detectives both—to do for themselves what the courts refused to do! Nor is there any question about Horn's calculated purpose to make himself the rustlers' bogeyman.

But, if Horn ever did any of the killings that were charged to him, he never left any actual evidence of his guilt. Usually, it was a matter of first wondering if he were in the neighborhood and if he had any possible motive. Presently, in the fashion of rumors everywhere,

it was shifting form—Tom Horn *was* in the vicinity of
a certain killing; Tom Horn had reason to kill the
victim; so, ergo! Tom Horn *had* killed the man.

ONE CASE I feel impelled to include because it was
described very vividly by my friend Bud Cowan, old
cowboy and intimate of Horn. In his "Range Rider"
autobiography, Bud tells of his friendship for Horn and
their association in the Iron Mountain country. Coming
to the spring of 1896, he says:
   "After the spring round-up, when we were gathering
horses for the beef round-up, Powell was killed up on
Horse Creek. I got in on that event by accident.
   "George Shanton and I were riding up Horse Creek,
about a mile below the Powell ranch, when we met
Tom Horn. He was riding like a wild Indian. We both
waved at him, but he never stopped.
   "We went on up to the ranch, and as we topped the
hill, just above the meadow, we saw a wagon with
part of a load of hay on it, and Mrs. Powell and her
little boy. We could hear them crying from where we
were. We ran up to the gate and went through and on
down to the meadow; when we got there Powell was
dead. George and I looked at each other and we both
understood why Tom Horn was in such a hurry when
we met him on down the road. . .
   "Nearly everyone around there knew in their hearts
that Tom Horn had killed Powell, but they couldn't
prove it in court. Billy Powell had been climbing up
in the rocks above the meadow a few days before his
father was killed, and he saw Tom Horn run to his horse
and get on him and ride away. Tom was arrested for
murder, but he proved in court that he was fifty miles
away from that locality at the time of the killing. As
for us, we pledged ourselves to secrecy about meeting
Tom on the road, because it wasn't healthy for anyone
to know too much in that country, and the least said was
quickest mended."

That is Bud Cowan's statement and he has amplified
it to me since then. He and Mrs. Powell believe that
Horn killed Powell. As for myself, I cannot judge. But
it was the sort of killing that if only for its clumsiness—
seems to me foreign to what I know of Horn.

And, in this case as in many others, more than Horn
had motive for killing. In most of the cases of mysterious
killings charged to Horn, it must be remembered that
other gun-carrying men were riding the ranges. It seems
logical to assume that if a rancher hired a man to kill
thieves and himself had the opportunity to kill one, he
would hardly hesitate. But Horn was a spectacular
character; his name was the natural peg on which to
hang an unsolved killing.

And yet, the records show, until 1901 no murder, no
killing, had ever been definitely and factually connected
with Horn. In that year he was riding the range in the
Iron Mountain country. This was a section of country
some fifty miles square, settled chiefly by small ranchers
but bordered by large outfits. And by report it was a
hotbed of rustlers, said to contain more hard cases to
the square foot than any other part of Wyoming!

Among the ranchers were two who had homesteaded
their places in the '80s—Jim Miller and Kels Nickell.
They were at outs. In February, 1901, Miller stabbed
Nickell during a quarrel, but failed to kill him. The
families hated each other; even the children fought.
Horn, riding constantly, seeing and hearing everything,
was frequently at both places.

Then, that summer of 1901, Nickell added new cause
to the many reasons his neighbors owned for disliking
him. He imported sheep into the country.

JULY 19, 1901, the neighborhood was thrown into a
turmoil by discovery of the body of Willie Nickell,
fourteen-year-old son of Kels Nickell, near a gate three-
quarters of a mile from the Nickell house. The boy had
been shot twice and it was judged that the killer had
come up to him, looked at him, then moved the body

from the gate to a point sixty feet away. The clothing
of the boy was saturated with blood and gravel was
stuck to it. Under the head, according to witnesses, was
a "small rock." Much was to be made of that "little
rock" later!

Living on the Miller place at this time, teaching
the Miller-Nickell school, was a girl from the East,
Glendolene Kimmell. She was very much attracted to
the big, good-looking Horn, who seemed to her to represent the Westerner, the Frontiersman, as she had heard
of the type. Horn had been a frequent caller at Miller's.
Miss Kimmell had heard many tales of Horn; had heard
him tell of his experiences in Apache-land, on the range,
in the arena. Next to the Cobles of the Iron Mountain
Ranch, Miss Kimmell was perhaps his stanchest friend.

At the time of Willie Nickell's murder, the neighborhood seems to have been in a state of turmoil unusually
violent even for that troubled region. Victor Miller, son
of Jim Miller, had long been quarreling with the dead
boy, according to the young schoolteacher. And
Nickell's sheep were much and violently discussed, like
the quarrels of Kels Nickell and Jim Miller.

When the inquest upon Willie Nickell was held—
July 22d—it was hinted around the neighborhood that
Jim Miller, lying in wait for his enemy Kels Nickell,
might have killed the boy by mistake. Then the frequent
battles between young Victor Miller and Willie Nickell
were recalled. Suspicion pointed to Victor, but in neither
case was sustaining evidence uncovered.

Tom Horn, too, was suspected—it would have been a
marvel if tongues had not wagged in that direction. But
here, also, there was no evidence and the youth of the
victim was a factor in Horn's favor. Few could credit
his guilt in such a case. So, the murder of Willie Nickell
seemed doomed to take its place among the many other
unsolved cases of Wyoming in general, that neighborhood in particular. Tom Horn continued to ride the
range.

In early August the excitement caused by Willie Nickell's murder was given a new fillip by a fresh quarrel between Miller and Nickell. Several hundreds of Nickell's sheep were driven across public land and into the pasture of Miller, the cowman. A shooting was expected, but the sheep were driven out and nothing happened—that day. The following day—August 4th—two men fired thirteen shots at Kels Nickell, wounding him twice.

Poor shooting! Those who in later days charged Horn with this bushwhacking overlooked his deadly accuracy with either Colt or long gun! *He* could hardly have fired a dozen times at any target and scored only two hits.

There was another peculiarity about this attempted assassination of Kels Nickell—the fact that two men were shooting at him. Horn was notorious for "lone wolfing it."

If we may trust the statements of Nickell's contemporaries, Nickell did not believe that Horn was the bushwhacker. He is reported to have said to his wife that he had recognized Jim Miller and one of the Miller boys. Later, when he and his wife were discussing the shooting with neighbors (a Mr. and Mrs. Joe Reid) he is alleged to have said:

"They will try to lay this on Tom Horn, but he never done it. It was the Millers!"

The coroner's inquest, meeting for its second session August 9th, brought out testimony (in connection with Kels Nickell's escape from death) of the younger Nickell children that they had seen two men ride off in the direction of the Millers', one riding a bay, the other a gray, horse. Miss Kimmell tells us, out of her intimate knowledge of the Miller household of which she was temporarily a member, that of the three Miller saddle horses, one was a bay, another a gray. Soon after this attempt at assassination, masked men came up to the Nickell sheep, ran off the herder and clubbed a bunch of the animals.

Apparently, this train of violent events broke Nickell's nerve. He was in the hospital at Cheyenne, recovering from the two gun-shot wounds. He wrote his family to come to him there. Then he advertised his ranch for sale.

All over Wyoming, complaints were being made about the authorities' failure to capture the murderer of Willie Nickell. Coming as it did at the tail-end of a long succession of unsolved killings, the murder of a young boy aroused popular indignation.

WE HAVE NOW to look very carefully at ''the pretty school teacher'' living in the Miller house. Glendolene Kimmell was a figure of extreme importance in subsequent events and, because her testimony was startling, her credibility becomes of vital importance to any inquiry into Horn's actions. That she was a close friend of the detective there is no doubt. Nor is there any doubt of her courage! Voluntarily, she came forward later on to wage battle with some of the most prominent men of the state and she told her story without (it seems to me) any thought of self. And I cannot find in her straightforward statement, any appearance of falsehood.

In a sworn statement, she asserts that shortly after the second inquest she overheard discussions between Victor Miller and his father. The tenor of the conversations she heard made it certain that Victor Miller had killed Willie Nickell. She states that, later, Jim Miller twice acknowledged to her that Victor had confessed Willie Nickell's murder. And she makes the definite assertion that, on October 10, 1901, Victor Miller himself confessed to her that he had murdered the boy.

She confesses that this admission put her in a quandary. On one hand, she was afraid that Horn or some other innocent person would be charged with the murder. On the other hand, it seems to her that both Victor Miller and little Willie Nickell were in large degree creatures of environment, hardly blamable for the savage, unjuvenile viewpoint both boys owned. She thought that on the shoulders of Jim Miller and Kels Nickell rested the real responsibility for Willie Nickell's death, Victor Miller's criminality.

Too, there was a personal angle: She had lived in the house, known Victor intimately. It was very hard to consider going to the authorities, to make a charge of murder against the boy. Apparently, she salved her conscience by telling Victor that she would not betray him, so long as Horn or any other innocent person was not charged with the crime.

In spite of the state-wide indignation, the summer passed, autumn came, then winter, without definite charge being lodged against anyone in the Willie Nickell case.

Horn "worked himself out of a job." There was little rustling now, an improvement due largely to Horn's ceaseless riding. But Horn had to look for a new connection.

Now enters one of the controversial figures of the case—Joe Lafors, who had been a stock-detective, like Horn, but who at this time was a deputy United States marshal, headquartering in Cheyenne. For some reason or other, Joe Lafors was bent on "breaking" the Willie Nickell case.

I pass no judgment on Lafors' motives, nor do I attempt any explanation of his great interest in a case which might be said to be none of his real business. The fact remains that Lafors intended to solve this mystery, and that he had his suspect *very* clearly in mind— Tom Horn.

Lafors and Horn knew each other well enough, though they had never worked together. They were what might be called "friendly acquaintances." So, when Lafors came to John Coble of the Iron Mountain Ranch and told Coble that he knew of a job Horn could fill, working for some Montana cowmen, both Coble and Horn regarded this as a very ordinary gesture of friendliness.

Horn accepted, writing a letter to Lafors in which he stated that he felt perfectly qualified to handle any rustler situation that might exist. He referred to cases he had worked on in the past, writing what amounted to a "sales letter."

Horn left to take the job. On the way he stopped at Omaha where he went on one of his "celebrations." No estimate of the man, or of the possibilities in any case in which he figured, can be made without remembering that at intervals he drank heavily. Nor was it an uncommon weakness in that day and place, among the cowboys and their employers. At work, Horn was temperate. But between jobs he drank heavily. Another characteristic must be noted and remembered—sober, Horn was noted for his taciturnity. Drunk, he—like many another—became very talkative, very boastful. He had the cowboy's keen, if crude, sense of humor. When under the influence of liquor it was his delight to tell the most outrageous stories that his vivid imagination could concoct and enjoy the reaction of his hearers. Every lurid deed that he had ever heard of, he claimed to have done. As an acquaintance said: "Drunk, Tom Horn would not have *admitted* that he shot Lincoln. He would have *sworn* that he did!"

Well, at Omaha, he got very drunk—so drunk that he lost his outfit. He had to go back to Coble's for another. While at Iron Mountain he had a letter from Lafors, asking him to come to Cheyenne. Lafors said that one of the Montana cowmen for whom Horn was to work would be in Cheyenne, to personally confer with the new detective. Also, Lafors added, he had a letter from Montana and he wanted Horn to read it.

Horn started for Cheyenne to meet Lafors, but at Laramie he got drunk again. When finally he arrived at Cheyenne he was "on a jag." He had been drinking so steadily that he must have "tapered off" gradually in any case. He continued to drink, in Cheyenne.

There is no questioning Lafors' intentions at this time. It seems obvious that he had used the Montana

job merely to get into Horn's confidence. Now, he had
Horn in Cheyenne—had him there for one purpose
alone. He wanted to get from him (to give Lafors credit
for complete honesty, even) admission that he had killed
Willie Nickell. The facts of the case permit no other
interpretation—not that I have ever encountered any
denial of Lafors' that this *was* the purpose of the interview with Horn.

Well—it seems that Horn was drunk enough to talk.
The trouble was, he was almost *too* drunk for Lafors'
purpose—almost too drunk to talk to the point Lafors
aimed at!

Horn was found in a saloon, very much intoxicated.
Lafors drew him out and to the office of the United
States marshal. Lafors had set the stage for what he
hoped would be a successful Last Act. Leslie Snow, a
deputy sheriff, and one Ohnhaus, a shorthand reporter,
were waiting for the men's arrival, concealed in an adjoining room. Lafors and Horn shut themselves in the
office. The reporter and Snow eavesdropped outside. The
stage was set. The famous "confession" was about to
be made!

THE PRIME essential was to get Horn to talking. So
Lafors began to yarn with Horn. They swapped gory
reminiscences. Then Lafors began to discuss the Montana
job. Horn was at pains, even in his drunken condition,
to assure Lafors that he need have no worry about his
ability to handle the job.

The deputy, Leslie Snow, with the reporter, Ohnhaus
were listening. Ohnhaus was taking down the conversation in shorthand. But not *all* the conversation, he admitted later on the witness stand.

Finally, Lafors said to Horn:

"Tom, I know you are a good man for the place.
You are the best man to cover your trail I ever saw. In
the Willie Nickell killing I could never find your trail
and I pride myself on being a trailer."

To which, Horn is reported to have replied:

"No, I left no trail. The only way to cover your trail is to go barefooted."

Lafors: "Where was your horse?" Horn: "He was a —— long ways off." Lafors: "I would be afraid to leave my horse so far away, you might get cut off from him." To which Horn replied: "You don't take much chances. These people are unorganized, and, anyway, I depend on this gun of mine. The only thing I was ever afraid of was that I would be compelled to kill an officer or a man I didn't want to. I would do everything to keep from being seen, but if he kept after me I would certainly kill him."

The conversation then continued as follows:

Lafors: "I never knew why Willie Nickell was killed. Was it because he was one of the victims named, or was it compulsory?"

Horn: "I think it was this way: Suppose a man was in the big draw to the right of the gate—you know where it is—the draw that comes into the creek below Nickell's house, where Nickell was shot. Well, suppose a man was in that and the kid came riding up on him from this way, and suppose the kid started to run for the house, and the fellow headed him off at the gate and killed him to keep him from going to the house and raising a hell of commotion. This is the way I think it occurred."

Lafors: "Tom, you had your boots on when you ran across there to cut the kid off, didn't you?"

Horn: No, I was barefooted."

Lafors: "You didn't run across there barefooted?"

Horn: "Yes, I did."

Lafors: "How did you get your boots on after cutting up your feet?"

Horn: "I generally have ten days to rest, after a job of that kind."

Lafors: "Tom, didn't Jim Dixon carry you grub?"

Horn: "No; no one carried me grub."

Lafors: "Tom, how can a man that weighs 204 pounds go without eating anything so long?"

Horn: "Well, I do. For some times I go for some days without a mouthful. Sometimes I have a little bacon along."

Lafors: "You must get terribly hungry, Tom."

Horn: "Yes, sometimes I get so hungry that I could kill my mother for some grub, but I never quit a job until I get my man."

Lafors: "What kind of a gun have you got?"

Horn: "I used a 30-30 Winchester."

Lafors: "Tom, do you think that will hold up as well as a 30-40?"

Horn: "No, but I like to get close to my man. The closer the better."

Lafors: "How far was Willie Nickell killed?"

Horn: "About 300 yards. It was the best shot that I ever made and the dirtiest trick I ever done. I thought at one time he would get away."

Lafors: "How about the shells? Did you carry them away?"

Horn: "You bet your —— life I did."

Lafors: "Tom, let us go down stairs and get a drink. I could always see your work clear, but I want you to tell me why you killed the kid. Was it a mistake?"

Horn: "Well, I will tell you all about that when I come back from Montana. It is too new yet."

Horn and Lafors then left the office, but they returned in the afternoon, when the conversation was continued (according to the "confession") as follows:

Horn: "Joe, we have only been together about fifteen minutes, and I will bet there is some people saying, 'What are these —— planning now, and who are they going to kill next?' We have come up here because there is no other place to go. If you go to the Inter Ocean (Hotel) to sit down and talk a few minutes, someone comes in and says, 'Let us have a drink,' and before you know it you are standing up talking, and my feet get so —— tired it almost kills me. I am 44 years, 3 months and 27 days old, and if I get killed now, I have the satisfaction of knowing I have lived about fifteen ordinary

lives. I would like to have had somebody who saw my
past, and could picture it to the public. It would be the
most —— interesting reading in the country; and if we
could describe to the author our feelings at different
times, it would be better still. The experience of my life,
or the first man I killed, was when I was only 26 years
old. He was a coarse ——."

Lafors: "How much did you get for killing these
fellows? In the Powell and Lewis case you got $600
apiece. You killed Lewis in the corral with a six-shooter.
I would like to have seen the expression on his face when
you shot him."

Horn: "He *was* the scaredest —— you ever saw. How
did you come to know that, Joe?"

Lafors: "I have known everything you have done,
Tom, for a great many years. I know where you were
paid this money."

Horn: "Yes, I was paid this money on the train between Cheyenne and Denver."

Lafors: "Why did you put the rock under the kid's
head after you killed him? That is one of your marks,
isn't it?"

Horn: "Yes, that is the way I hang out my sign to
collect my money for a job of this kind."

Lafors: "Have you got your money yet for the killing
of Nickell?"

Horn: "I got that before I did the job."

Lafors: "You got $500 for that. Why did you cut
the price?"

Horn: "I got $2,100."

Lafors: "How much is that a man?"

Horn: "That is for three dead men, and one man shot
at five times. Killing men is my specialty. I look at it as
a business proposition, and I think I have a corner on
the market."

This talk between Horn and Lafors occurred on
January 12, 1902.

Horn was arrested the next day and charged with the
murder of Willie Nickell. Of evidence connecting him

with the murder, there was none except that famous "confession." Stoll, the prosecuting attorney, had tried to connect Horn with the killing at the time of its occurrence, but had failed. Whether or not he had instructed Lafors to try the trick Lafors did execute, I have no means of knowing. Nor, possibly, has anyone else today except Lafors himself. For Stoll committed suicide at the end of a prolonged spree in June, 1911.

STOLL WORKED hard to build a case against Horn. He hunted up all the corroborative evidence he could. He brought in Frank Mulock and other witnesses from Denver, to testify that in a Denver saloon they had heard Horn boast of the murder of the Nickell boy. (After the trial Mulock repudiated his testimony, giving the weak excuse that he had seen a man who was Horn's double several times since the trial and was certain that Horn was innocent, that this "double" was the man he had heard boasting in the saloon.) Testimony was heard concerning Horn's movements at the time of the killing. Horn's own explanation of his presence in the vicinity at the time of Willie Nickell's killing was that he was merely making his rounds in accordance with his habit. He had heard that Nickell's sheep were trespassing on John Coble's range. He investigated, he said, and found the report to be untrue. The sheep were on Jim Miller's range, so he had no interest in them. But it was on the "confession" that the prosecution pinned its hope.

Apparently, Cheyenne in particular, Wyoming in general, thought that Stoll was due to be beat. Bets that Tom Horn would not be convicted found no takers on the streets. The Cheyenne *Leader*, October 16, 1902, summing up the evidence of five days of trial stated:

"The 'confession' standing alone would probably be given little credence." And again:

"Few people took his boasting seriously," it remarked—referring to his well-known habit of telling blood-curdling stories. And still again:

"If Horn was bragging, then the 'confession' of Horn, one of the principal facts on which the state relies, falls to the ground, *as there is insufficient other evidence to convict him of the killing of Willie Nickell*."

So, apparently, Wyoming hardly believed Tom Horn guilty. But, one must remember the conditions in the state at this time: Big cowman warring against little cowman, cowman against rustler, had made for bitter enmities, had forged strange and obscure alliances, financial and political. Tom Horn and his employers had many enemies. But, it is hard for me to understand how many *honest* men could be against Horn. He had always been in the employ of cowmen, hired to protect their property. What grievance could an *honest* man have, against the watchdog of property? A cowman said: "Show me a man who's against Horn and I'll show you a rustler!"

During the trial, Stoll pinned his hopes on that confession. Horn on the witness stand made an excellent impression on the courtroom and, in many cases, even on hostile newspapermen. They said of him, in effect, that he told a straightforward story that carried conviction to all who heard it.

He admitted the talk in the state house but denied, in general and in particular, confessing Willie Nickell's murder. For instance, he denied that he had made the assertion that he had left no trail because he went barefooted. He said that Lafors asked him how one could cover his trail and he replied: "Go barefooted."

He charged that the whole business was a "frame-up"; accused Ohnhaus of changing such *stenographic* notes as he had really made "at the instigation of someone."

He claimed that words were put into his mouth that he had never uttered, that other statements he had made had been twisted to make them mean guilt, admission, when they were really nothing but speculations concerning the case as it looked to an outsider. He said that the bulk of the "confession" had been written before he got to Cheyenne.

The jury listened. Wyoming waited for the verdict. During the trial the jury was taken out for its meals to a public restaurant. They heard much heated talk about the case. They could not have *helped* hearing the discussions of outsiders—and particularly the speculations as to whether or not the jury would find Horn guilty.

The head waitress of the hotel where the jury took their meals during the trial, later deposed that remarks were made by different people, to the effect that there would probably be a hung jury in the Horn case—that there were three men on the jury who were supposed to be particular friends of the defendant who would not convict him, and that a man would be more apt to tell the truth when drunk than when sober; that these statements were made by persons sitting at a table adjoining the one occupied by the jury.

Juror Payne deposed that he overheard similar remarks, and observed that he was pointed out as a friend of the defendant, which gave him the impression that people thought that he had been "bought or fixed." He further deposed that, while the jury were deliberating on their verdict, the argument was made in the jury room that, if they made a mistake, the trial court or the Supreme Court would grant defendant a new trial. A Denver newspaper reporter deposed to have heard remarks, similar to those referred to at the hotel while the jury were there.

As remarked before, it would seem that observers of the trial did not expect a conviction. Point by point, the defense seemed to score.

Stoll produced a .30-30 shell picked up in the vicinity of the Willie Nickell murder. He could only assert that he *believed* it to have been dropped by Horn in flight. And this in a country where half the riders carried rifles of that caliber!

His own doctor-witness failed him on the stand, when Stoll was attempting to establish the caliber of bullet which had killed Willie Nickell.

Mulock and the other Denver witness, testifying that Horn had boasted of Willie's murder in a Denver saloon, seem to have made a poor impression (and small wonder! when one keeps in mind Mulock's written retraction of his testimony as it applied to Horn).

Horn made accusations against Lafors that—if belived by the jury—must have thrown a mantle of suspicion over, not merely the "confession," but anything that Lafors had ever touched.

On the stand, Horn told of several talks he had with Lafors before that of January 12th in the state house. He claimed that Lafors was anxious to fix various crimes besides Willie Nickell's murder on Iron Mountain people. He charged that Lafors had attempted to get him "to throw in with him" in order to "cinch that damned outfit out there," and that his conversations outside of the state house with Lafors, were all along that line. Lafors denied having any such conversations with Horn.

Stoll in summing up for the jury, said, in part:

"Gentlemen of the jury, you do not have the ordinary man here to deal with; you have the criminal, a man of criminal mind and criminal instincts; an extraordinary man. . . . You need not fear imbruing your hands in the blood of the defendant; after you is the court, then the Supreme Court, and then the Governor. . . . The people are very much in earnest in this case; they have furnished the money necessary for the prosecution; the officers have done their duty, and now the people demand a verdict at your hands. . . . You do not wish to be placed in the position, and suffer the regrets, which a jury trying a case in this court at one time have suffered, where the nine who desired conviction yielded to the wishes of the three and acquitted the defendant, who shortly thereafter killed a whole family of six persons, some of which jurors you are undoubtedly acquainted with and have heard them express their regrets. . . ."

The jury retired to consider the case. They began to ballot. Five times the score stood ten for murder in the first degree, two for acquittal, the two voting for acquittal being Jurors Payne and Thomas. It looked like a deadlock.

Those of us familiar with the jury system, by which the will of the stubborn minority is often imposed upon a more pliant (or more impatient) majority, can easily picture the scene in that jury room. All were anxious to go home, to get this case off their minds, and the will of a majority was being blocked by two jurors.

One must believe that Payne and Thomas had as much reason for voting for Tom Horn's acquittal as the other ten had for demanding his conviction. They had heard the evidence, they had seen the witnesses. They must have made some decision concerning the credibility of the various men who testified, the worth of the evidence, pro and con. And here they sit, demanding that Tom Horn be set free, stating in effect that the state had not proved Tom Horn guilty of the murder of Willie Nickell. Five ballots. . . .

A sixth ballot was preparing when one of the jurors —Tolson by name—halted the proceeding. Tolson said that it might be advisable, before taking another ballot, to hear from the two dissenting jurymen their reasons for believing Tom Horn innocent. So, turning to the two stubborn ones, he asked them if they refused to accept the state's case because they believed that Horn had only been talking loosely and largely to Lafors at the time of the famous "confession."

Both men replied that they did not take the so-called confession seriously, and for that reason believed him to be innocent.

Tolson said (in an affidavit) that the whole case was then discussed and at the end of the discussion Payne and Thomas talked together and announced themselves ready to vote. When the sixth ballot was taken it stood twelve for conviction!

Consider this! Those two jurors sat in the courtroom and heard all the evidence. They were not convinced by Stoll's fervid oratory. They were not convinced by Lafors' manner, or that of Leslie Snow, the deputy sheriff who was Lafors' corroborating witness. Evidently, they did *not* believe that the famous "confession" was in fact a confession!

They went off to the jury room, their minds made up that Tom Horn was an innocent man. For five ballots they proved that belief. Then, they did an about-face!

Those who at this late date and often at a great distance—psychologically as well as geographically—claim that the defense of Tom Horn was a matter of ingenious quibbling, certainly should consider by what an exhibition of weakness Tom Horn was convicted!

In effect, we can say that Horn was not convicted in that courtroom by anything that Stoll and his array of witnesses had done. *He was convicted in the jury room by the arguments and the weight of dominating personalities, brought to bear upon two* (it seems to me) *weak and uncertain jurors.*

There can be no question that, left alone, Payne and Thomas would have stood out for a verdict of not guilty. But they were not so left alone! Around them gathered the other jurors, at close range, talking, arguing, attempting, not to make these two jurors see the truth—for they had already seen the truth according to their lights—but attempting to force upon them the will of the majority.

Many other cases have been settled in the jury room in precisely the same fashion. I have heard a juryman in another murder case tell how he was virtually forced by the opinion of the majority to subscribe to a verdict with which he did not agree. And so it appears to have been in this case.

Carried to the ultimate, the case must have ended in stalemate; the jury must have returned to the judge, to announce itself hopelessly dead-locked. Tom Horn would have received a new trial. Granted that we cannot foresee the outcome of that trial, had it been held, the fact remains that for all practical purposes, Jurors Payne and Thomas might just as well have been omitted from the trial. They served the purpose of a Greek Chorus and *only* the purpose of a Greek Chorus—to reflect the will of the other, stronger, ten.

It has been charged that on that jury sat men from whom Horn had recovered stolen stock. I have heard that story for years. This seems to me doubtful. It seems incredible that Horn's counsel would have permitted avowed enemies of Horn to sit on that jury. But that is one story that persists, even to this day.

But the verdict returned was "guilty of murder in the first degree." A Denver newspaper reporter, that same one who testified as to undue and improper influence being exercised upon the jury in the hotel dining room, wrote later that he talked over the verdict with Juror Payne. One gathers that Payne did not tell of the scene in the jury room at that time, that he gave an impression of civic virtue quite at variance with the facts as we know them. For he said to this reporter:

"It was hard to go against a man I have known and liked. But what could I do? The question was too hard to be dodged. I did my duty."

One George F. Walker also told of a conversation with Juror Payne, in which the latter said (in effect) that he had known Horn a long time, that he felt sorry for him, but he thought he was guilty and he *had* to bring in a guilty verdict.

Certainly, this hardly jibes with the affidavit of Juror Tolson, that Payne did *not* believe Horn guilty—until he learned in the jury room what he did believe!

Counsel for Horn immediately took an appeal, citing thirty-odd points of error. Months passed, during which Horn lay in Cheyenne jail, spending his time making rawhide and hair bridles and other odds and ends, in the fashion he had learned years before, down in the Apache country. He seems never to have believed that he would be hung. His letters were uniformly cheerful. Even when he remarked sardonically that if it would do anyone any good to see him hung, he would hate to disappoint them, still he could govern himself, cheer those friends who were not so optimistic.

And what of the little school teacher who, by her own testimony, knew very well that Horn was innocent, that Victor Miller had really killed the boy?

During the trial (she says) Horn's counsel had not admitted for a moment that there could be any doubt of his acquittal. She had written them, asking leading questions, but apparently *not* (one gathers) actually telling them what she had in the way of direct evidence in Horn's defense. She still hesitated to charge the boy whom she could not regard as more than technically guilty of murder, with the crime. She kept silence, hoping that it would not be necessary to incriminate Victor Miller in order to save Horn.

When the guilty verdict came in, she was determined to go to the proper authorities with what she knew. But, owing to a legal technicality, Horn's lawyers could not use her affidavit until the case was finally decided by the Supreme Court and placed in the Governor's hands.

In September, 1903, the Supreme Court of Wyoming ruled against Horn, sometimes—a layman thinks—rather straining themselves to justify everything done by the prosecution. Friday, November 20, 1903, was set by the Supreme Court for the execution of the death sentence pronounced by the trial court upon Tom Horn.

The Supreme Court pointed out that it was not authorized to pass upon the guilt or innocence of Horn, but only to say that he had or had not been given a fair trial, and if there had been sufficient evidence to warrant a verdict on the part of the jury.

Miss Kimmell's evidence, in the form of an affidavit, was placed before Governor Chatterton. Other evidence, including letters from Frank Mulock, one of the Denver witnesses, desirous of retracting his testimony insofar as it definitely connected Horn with the boastful man in the Denver saloon, was also given the Governor.

Chatterton was a politician. Apparently, he was very anxious to know the will of the majority in this case. He withheld his decision for a time.

Horn, meanwhile, steadfastly asserted his innocence, and wrote a letter to Ohnhaus, the reporter, which seems to me a model of straightforward and fearless pleading for a square deal. He pointed out various places in the alleged confession where statements were credited to him in the stenographic notes which were (he said) false. He accused Ohnhaus of altering the notes and begged him to make redress before it was too late. He spoke of "blood money" and of Ohnhaus's reputation as a "model, Christian young man."

Here is a point where one must believe Tom Horn, or believe Ohnhaus. I must admit that my leaning is toward Horn. If I am any authority on the written word, that letter could have been written only by an expert in literary construction—or by an innocent man. Nothing in Horn's record inclines me to believe that he was possessed of the literary skill to say enough to express innocence, and never a word too much; to voice his appeal in a manner that wakes in an unprejudiced reader the conviction that an innocent man speaks.

I have written and published some millions of words of calculated, planned fiction, in my day. Facing the task of composing such a letter as that—one intended to create the effect of innocence—I should expect trouble in doing the work. Yet we must believe that Horn, a self-educated cowboy, a man of action, not words, could sit down and do a job that would give a professional writer pause. We must believe it, if we are to consider that letter to Ohnhaus a studied composition intended to rouse sympathy for Horn. I cannot believe it.

Miss Kimmell had several conferences with Governor Chatterton. Also, she discussed Horn's case with members of the State Supreme Court. She tells us that Chief Justice Corn admitted to her that, even after the appeal had been refused, he had not made up his mind concerning Horn's guilt or innocence.

"In fact," he told her (by her account), "I am qualified to sit on a jury to try Tom Horn for murder."

Justice Knight told her that he had paid no attention to the case since its consideration by the Supreme Court.

"I might have," Miss Kimmell reports him as saying, "if they had not attacked my good friend Joe Lafors."

Which, as Miss Kimmell remarked aptly, is a statement rather hard to understand. It is difficult to see how counsel for Horn could make out a case for him without attacking Joe Lafors, whom they accused of writing the confession beforehand, of having it ready for Horn's appearance in Cheyenne on January 12th. They considered Lafors a shady and unscrupulous person, Leslie Snow the deputy and Ohnhaus the reporter creatures willing to perjure themselves, hang an innocent man, for $333 each. This is not to say that the defense counsel's accusations were true, but that they *had* to "attack Lafors."

Governor Chatterton refused to accept Miss Kimmell's statement as reason for interference with the sentence. Even the fact that Mulock, the Denver man, had obviously been a mistaken, if not a perjured, witness, did not matter, so far as Chatterton was concerned.

HORN'S TIME in Cheyenne jail was uneventful except for one incident. On August 6th he and a train robber imprisoned there escaped. They overpowered one of the guards and got out, snatching the sheriff's rifle and an automatic pistol. McCloud—the train robber—found him a horse when they got outside the jail. Horn tried to get away on foot. McCloud was carrying the rifle; Horn had the automatic pistol. Horn, weakened by his long imprisonment, was soon overtaken. After he had halted, surrounded by townsmen, Deputy Leslie Snow (Lafors' friend) ran up. He struck at Horn with his rifle. A policeman standing there jumped in between, throwing up his arm. So vicious was the blow that Snow aimed at Horn's head that the policeman's arm was broken.

When Horn was returned to jail much was made by his enemies of his attempt to escape. It was said that only his inability to work the then-new automatic pistol prevented his doing wholesale killing on the streets of Cheyenne. Speaking as something of a gun crank, this seems to me a weak tale. A man accustomed all his life to the use of firearms would have little difficulty in solving the simple mechanism of an automatic pistol. It seems to me that had Horn wished to shoot, he could have made that automatic a deadly weapon.

On the day before Horn's execution was to take place, the town was picketed with militia. The authorities were guarding against any attempt at rescue by the cowboys—who were outspoken in their liking for Horn. Courthouse Square was placed under martial law. Only those persons who lived on the square were permitted within the lines of sentries.

The town was crowded with people come to see the hanging. The jail itself was heavily-guarded. Some of the greatest gunfighters of that particular neighborhood and day had been drafted for the work. A man was posted over Horn's cot in the death cell. Tradition has it that he was ordered to kill Horn, in case the cowboys did break into the jail.

The day of the hanging dawned. Six o'clock came—November 20th, 1903. . . . Governor Chatterton refused for the last time to interfere. Horn wrote a letter to John Coble in which, for the last time, he described his movements on the day of Willie Nickell's killing, protested his innocence, spoke again of his friendship for Coble.

"This is the truth," he finished, "as I am to die in ten minutes."

Thereafter, he was the calmest man in the jail. He smoked a cigar. Most of his good-byes had been said. He had seen John Coble the day before. Charles and Frank Irwin were already in waiting. The time came for the death march. Horn was physically shaky from confinement. The procession moved slowly from jail to yard. The militiamen held back the crowds of morbidly curious congregated in streets nearby. Only the half-hundred invited witnesses were near the scaffold.

Horn stopped to shake hands with the Irwin brothers, old friends from the Iron Mountain region. They began shakily to sing, after a prayer had been said by a minister. The song was a favorite of Horn's—*Life's Railway to Heaven.*

The grim business on the scaffold platform went on without hitch, an undersheriff and assistant working under the eyes of Sheriff Ed Smalley. Horn said to Smalley as he looked over the witnesses—many of them peace officers from adjacent counties and states:

"Ed that's the *sickest* looking bunch of sheriffs I ever saw!"

Horn stood quietly while the straps, the noose, the black hood were adjusted. Before the hood was drawn over his head he smiled. He stood on the semi-automatic trap, that was sprung by letting water run from a vessel on a balanced beam. He stood very calmly. The seconds ticked off after his weight on the trap had opened a faucet. To the witnesses the interval seemed endless, before the water running out of the faucet tripped the beam, jerked the trap support from under the hinged doors, let Horn drop. It was only eleven seconds.

AND SO Tom Horn died. But his death only marked the beginning of a controversy that rages to this day. Was he guilty? Or was he innocent? Was Joe Lafors—anxious for a share of that thousand dollar reward offered in the Nickell case—merely the typical detective trying to break a murder mystery? Or was he so anxious for the reward that he—with the help of two tools, Leslie Snow and Ohnhaus—knowingly "framed" an innocent man, "railroaded" Tom Horn to the gallows?

There is no way of proving Horn's guilt. His *innocence* might be proved, if that Victor Miller who is alleged to have confessed the murder (if still alive) were to confess today.

All that one can do is look at the evidence carefully, as impartially as may be, then form his own opinion. My own belief is that Horn was not guilty. There are far too many discrepancies in the state's case! Going over the trial records carefully, with no bias in either direction, it seems to me that at least equal weight must be given to the testimony of Horn himself and his witnesses, concerning his movements on July 18th, 1901, the day of Willie Nickell's murder, as is given to the testimony of the state's witnesses.

Horn said that on the murder-day he was never closer than seven miles to the ranch of Kels Nickell. The prosecution attempted to show him on the ground very closely.

There is also the important question of motive. Horn hardly knew the Nickell boy. He had no grievance against any of the Nickell family—they were not bothering his employers. The only possible motive that could be assigned him would be one of financial gain—a price to be earned for the killing, not of Willie Nickell, but of Kels Nickell, the father.

The prosecution insinuated that Horn had killed Willie Nickell by mistake for Kels; implying that the boy was wearing his father's clothes. Willie's mother testified that the boy wore his own clothes, that day. Horn's eyesight was like an Indian's.

Stoll, the prosecuting attorney, dragged in testimony about the shooting of Kels Nickell after Willie's death. But the established circumstances of this attempted assassination do not fit what we know of Horn. He was—as I have said before—Indian-like in his solitary riding over the range. And, if he had intended to murder Nickell, it seems odd to incredible that he should go with another man when he could more easily, quietly, surely, do the killing by himself and have no witness. There was the poor shooting, too. Thirteen to seventeen shots fired (witnesses vary as to the number) and only two hits scored, neither in a fatal place! It is not like Horn.

I have seen the statement of a prominent Wyoming editor, bitterly assailing Horn, Coble, and all that the cowmen of the day stood for.

"Stock-detective! Horn was a stock-detective!" says this editor. "Infamous outlaws on salary were these stock-detectives! Eschewed by all decent people. . . ."

He then goes on to commend Joe Lafors—who had also been a stock-detective, one of the loathsome creatures he so despises! It is all very confusing to me.

The "confession" business I have pondered over many and many a time. I keep remembering how drunk Horn was. And I cannot forget that Ohnhaus and Snow only "peeped through a keyhole," but thereafter could state with certainty that his manner was that of a man intending to be believed. I see the stilted style of it, so unlike that of two men talking—yet it is called verbatim.

And the statements in the confession—so-called, do not jibe with the testimony of Mulock and the other Denver witnesses as to Horn's alleged statements in a Denver saloon. (Even without considering Mulock's letter of retraction, his feeling that Horn's "double" made those statements, I cannot take much stock in Mulock.)

In a sense, I have sat on that jury, listening to the testimony for the state and for the defense. I have considered the warring factions of Wyoming in that day, the hysteria that surrounded the trial. Like Payne and Thomas (before they blew about like weathervanes and reversed themselves), I have to vote "Not Guilty."

After Horn's death, a tale went the rounds in Cheyenne that a certain minister was saying that Horn had confessed to him. The knowing nodded wisely, triumphantly. So Horn *had* killed Willie Nickell. But when this preacher was run to earth, he admitted that he had spoken only in the most general sense—Horn had "confessed" that he was a worldly sinner. He had *not* said that Willie Nickell's death was by his hand.

Another tale that went the rounds was that Coble and other bloody-handed cowmen had hired Horn to commit so many atrocities that they dared not let him talk. So they hired the state's best lawyers, assured Tom Horn that he would never hang. And at the last, even, he believed that he wouldn't die.

But—if they "knew" that he would talk, why did he *not* talk, at the last? Why did he shake hands with Coble on the very day before his death, when Coble told him that he had to die? Why would a man with that bitter grievance against Coble write the letter that Horn did write, speaking of friendship?

The truth of the matter is, I am afraid, that Tom Horn was a dangerous man to certain ones, even after his death. And certain newspapers have painstakingly blackened his memory as much as possible. A hard man, yes! But a kindly man and one well-liked by his friends. A man who is remembered for many deeds of bravery and generosity.

My reader may not agree with me in my conclusions. But I have tried to consider Tom Horn's case as carefully and impartially as if fate still rested in my hands—and with no thought that, having formed my opinion, ten (or ten thousand) men could argue me to the other opinion and say, *that* would be "my duty."

CHAPTER XVII · *One Man Army Corps*
LEE CHRISTMAS

HE WOULD have been quite at home in medieval France or Italy, as a hell-roaring man-of-arms of old John Hawkwood's White Company. Or—to bring the figure down to a later date, a nearer—he was of the sort whom William Walker hunted for *La Falange Americana*, the "American Phalanx" that conquered Nicaragua in '56. Mighty drinker and mighty lover, he was also a mighty fighting man, this Lee Christmas.

His battleground was Central America, the troubled land of the Banana Flag, the republics of Guatemala, Honduras, Salvador, Nicaragua and Costa Rica. There, for thirty years, he was alternately a military leader "worth an army corps," and a private citizen hardly above the status of tropical tramp. In a sense, this alternation, this pendulum-swing of fortune, typed the whole amazing, blood-and-thunder career of the big-shouldered, swaggering, blue-eyed daredevil. There was never any middle ground for Lee Christmas. He was either up or down.

Knowing him well in his later years, having heard him voice his rough philosophy of life, having talked to a hundred men who knew him intimately in the days of his greatest activity, I am sure that for Christmas, as for any other bold gambler, he would have not have had it otherwise. *All or nothing* might have been his motto.

He was born February 22, 1863, in Livingston Parish near Baton Rouge, Louisiana. His father, until the War Between the States, was a well-to-do cotton planter and —more significant to us—a veteran of the Mexican War. But by the time Lee was old enough to look toward a career for himself, the Christmas family fortunes were at a low ebb—in fact, they might be said to have ebbed completely.

So the future commander of Central American armies spent his early manhood as a laborer, a locomotive fireman and finally as a full-fledged engineer on the Illinois Central. He married and children came. But he was not much of a family man. Already Lee Christmas had developed that enormous capacity for hard liquor that was to make him the marvel of many a tropical drinking bout. When he was twenty-eight, his life crashed around him. One day in 1891, he climbed into the cab dead drunk, fell asleep at the throttle and let his engine go into head-on collision with another train. He was injured and the railroad put him on the black list. For three or four years, then, he lived from hand to mouth, tramping, or bending his big, muscular body to labor of the hardest, commonest sort. It seemed that he was doomed to that life. Certainly no hint came to his rather slow mind, in those vagabond days, as he drifted boozily from one laborer's job to another, of the fascinating— the near-incredible—career that was to be his. And when, in 1894—almost three years after his accident— he had a chance for reëmployment as engineer, he found that the newly-instituted color test barred him perpetually from employment on any American railroad. For one of his oddities was color blindness.

"It looked like my luck had changed that day when I went into the car to take the test," he told me more than a quarter-century later, as we sat watching the opening of another revolution in Guatemala City. "Then they put out their damned little pieces of string— red and blue and green, you know. And I couldn't tell one from another."

He looked at the tie that I was wearing. A thick fore-finger stabbed out at it.

"I can't tell you now, if that's a red or a blue tie!" he said.

It chanced to be a solid green tie and the incident seemed perfect illustration of his point.

So—an accident of birth made a great soldier of fortune. In '94 Central America drew Lee Christmas— but not for any chance he saw of becoming a national figure in Banana Land. It was a far more prosaic lure. The railroad in Honduras was not concerned with small things like color blindness in its employes. Good crews were hard to get. Men were wanted who would stay in the tropics, to run the trains of the fruit railway.

So, Lee Christmas made his entry into Central American affairs by way of Port Cortez, Honduras, in the undramatic rôle of engineer on the narrow-gauge railway. He stayed there for several months, then, home-sick among those dark faces and that alien tongue, he went back to New Orleans. But chances for paying employment in the States were not good. Eventually, he drifted back to Honduras and his little engine.

Glory, reputation, a career, were just ahead. But when, April 14, 1897, he drove his tiny locomotive into the beginning of a new tropic revolt, he had no thought of any of these things. He smoked his *puro* and watched the track ahead as he neared Laguna. If he saw a small bunch of men beside the railway at the siding, it meant nothing to him, even though he knew that a revolt was being staged on the Atlantic Coast.

For, of all the things in which Engineer Christmas had no interest whatever, politics headed the roll. He knew, of course, that Policarpo Bonilla was president of Honduras; and that the allies of Bonilla were Manuel Bonilla and Terencio Sierra. But, so long as they made no trouble for him as he ran his trains and had his drinks and hunted his women in Port Cortez, they were none of his concern.

But others were vastly more interested. Chief among these was one Enrique Soto, who headquartered in Guatemala and received the sympathy, if not the actual assistance, of President Estrada Cabrera. Soto wished ardently to overthrow the government of Sierra and the two Bonillas. So in Port Barrios, Guatemala, Soto's revolutionary force embarked. It consisted of thirteen daredevils, two being Americans—Bill Jeffries and another who, in my time in Guatemala, was a familiar and respected figure on the capital's streets—General William Drummond.

Soto's expedition landed in Port Cortez and in a surprise attack captured the town. Cortez was a strategic point. A principal seaport, holding the end of a railroad and a customs house, it was a great capture. This blow struck, General Duron—in charge of the revolutionists —intended to march upon populous San Pedro Sula. And now Lee Christmas entered the play. He was captured at Laguna by the Sotoistas and ordered, under penalty of instant execution, to transport the revolutionists on his train.

"I made a kick to the American consul," Lee recalled grimly. "And that was all the good it did me. I didn't want any revolution, that time. But getting shot by the government troops was the next day, anyway, and these hairpins would have gunned me right then. Hah!"

He looked across our table in the Central at General Drummond's hawklike face. Drummond nodded, grinning.

"*Se fué guerra!*" he shrugged. "It was war!"

So, without enthusiasm, Lee Christmas proceeded to armor his train as well as the materials at hand permitted. Sandbags were piled up around the sides of a flat car, and three-quarter inch boiler iron, confiscated from the railroad yard, was added. A Hotckiss gun was mounted on the flat car and, when the revolutionists were ready to advance up the railroad towards San Pedro Sula, the flat car was put ahead of the engine, with a detachment of riflemen aboard it.

Many and various are the reports of that wild little battle at Laguna Trestle. As Lee Christmas recalled it— with General Drummond, another participant, sitting across from him—the Federals came down the railroad and attempted to cross the trestle to attack the revolutionists. Duron's men had made a breast-work of the only available material—great blocks of ice from the box cars which Christmas' train had pulled into the siding. The Federal leader ordered a charge. Heavy fire from behind the ice cakes broke the Federal ranks and killed the commander. The trestle was swarming with men when Christmas, something waking in him as wild yells shook the hot air and bullets whined past, felt his first war fervor. He pulled open the throttle of his engine and sent it as a deadly missile down upon the Federals on the trestle. He was a wild man, yelling hoarsely, firing his Winchester into the Federals, heedless of the lead that sang his way.

Christmas was immediately made a captain in the Sotoistas. He drove his train with the revolutionary party up the railroad towards San Pedro Sula. The Federal garrison there withdrew on orders from the capital and General Duron met no resistance as he occupied the town. But this was merely the calm before the storm. President Zelaya of Nicaragua, who had helped the three current leaders get into power in Honduras, was still a friend and ally of Sierra and the Bonillas. And—President Zelaya had a gunboat.

A message went from Tegucigalpa to Managua and Zelaya ordered his gunboat to steam up the coast and recapture Port Cortez for his friends. General Duron in San Pedro Sula heard of the arrival of the gunboat off the port. General Drummond was put aboard Captain Lee Christmas' train and sent down to drive off the invading vessel with the guns of the port.

Upon arrival in Cortez General Drummond took a long drink and looked out to sea where the Nicaraguan gunboat was steaming brazenly up and down. Drummond took charge of one of the ancient Spanish muzzleloaders which was trained "by-guess-and-by-God" out toward the Nicaraguan vessel. By his orders the cannoneer fired a shot or two from the Spanish gun. But Drummond was chagrined to see his cannon balls drop harmlessly short in the sea. He and Lee Christmas held conference over a bottle. It occurred to Drummond that

there was not enough powder in the charge they had
been using. It seemed a simple problem—if so much
powder drove a cannon ball so far, then three times that
much powder should drive the cannon ball three times
as far! He and Christmas gravely had another drink.
Then Drummond himself charged the fat belly of the
ancient Spanish piece. He yelled at the cannoneer.

"Now we'll put *two* cannon balls in her gut!"

The cannoneer, they told me, was a lanky Jamaican
negro. I fancy that he was a drafted man—one of
Central America's famous "volunteers of the rope" who
arrive in military camps under guard, tied together, and
bearing the classic note from the recruiting officer:
"Dear General: Herewith, twenty gallant and eager
volunteers for death on their country's battle-fields.
(Please return my rope.)"

The cannoneer watched Drummond's loading with
rolling eyes. Drummond straightened.

"*Now* whang away!" he told the negro.

The linstock was an iron rod, heated in a fire near the
cannon. The negro lifted it from its bed of embers. He
extended it—like a foil. He leaned toward the touch-
hole. But the red end of the rod was a yard from the
priming charge. He danced about, poking gingerly at the
touch-hole. Drummond watched solemnly, lifting bottle
to mouth occasionally—or frequently.

"Fire that cannon!" he bellowed, between drinks.

"Yes, General. Hi'll fire 'im, sah!" the cannoneer
assured him, dancing, poking.

But the linstock approached the powder no more
nearly and Drummond, flinging aside the empty bottle,
at last snatched the rod from his subordinate's hand.

"*Give* me that iron! You're scared—*that's* what's the
matter. You're *scared!*"

"No, sah. Hi'm not scared," the Jamaican replied
with dignity. "But that is gov'ment powder, sah. And
Hi'ates to se hit *wysted!*"

Drummond rammed the rod-end into the priming
charge, while Lee Christmas applauded from the side-

lines. But the rod had cooled. It would not ignite the priming charge. Drummond flung it aside and from his mouth snatched the *puro*—the finger-length cigar of Central America. He put the lighted end of it upon the touch-hole. But there was no satisfying explosion—the ash of the cigar insulated the powder. Drummond bent closely—and *blew!*

The resultant roar was all that Drummond could have hoped for. But he was in no condition to appreciate it. Out of the touch-hole spurted a fiery blast. He was hurled backward, with one eye blown—or burned—from the socket.

Lee Christmas bundled the little party on the train again. By his account, Drummond was liberally dosed all the way back to San Pedro Sula with the sovereign specific of the tropics—*guaro* or *aguardiente*, the colorless and terrifically potent sugar cane rum.

Sierra was leading a large army of Federal troops from Tegucigalpa to wipe out the *revolucionarios*. Zelaya's gunboat covered Port Cortez. The Soto party—including its latest recruit—borrowed mules from Charlie Jeffs and rode fast over the giddy mountain trails to Guatemala, where Manuel Estrada Cabrera was coming into power as Barrios' successor.

LEE CHRISTMAS "landed on his feet" in Guatemala. The tale of Laguna Trestle was known up and down Central America, now. "General" Christmas was a Figure. Cabrera made him an officer of the notorious secret police and he—in his own words—"lived the life Riley would have liked to lead." There was liquor for the General in every drinking place—free. There were women of high and low degree anxious to curry favor with the big *gringo* general—complaisant, sometimes, when a husband, a brother, a lover, cowered in Cabrera's cells.

Tropical tramps who were in Guatemala during Christmas' time tell a hundred stories of his exploits—which is to say, his escapades—each more incredible than the last. But there is no doubt that he was a privileged character, that he took whatever he wanted, whether money or women or liquor, and that Cabrera only shrugged and smiled when complaints were made. For he was a shrewd judge of men, and he recognized the value to him of this big fighting man.

There was a new revolution brewing and Christmas was sent by "The Party" to New Orleans to arrange for munitions. But he drank too heavily, talked too much. Not for him the stealth of secret conspiracy! He was a fighter. His "job in New Orleans blew up" and he went back to Honduras. It was safe to return—the books had been white-washed—the government had granted clear bills to the Soto revolutionaries.

FOR AWHILE it seemed that Lee Christmas was to settle down and prosper, with behind him no more than the one revolution allowed to any foreign settler in the land of revolutions. He had been divorced by his wife in Tennessee. He married again in Port Cortez and with a partner owned a store in Choloma. Marriage could never more than check the instinct to dalliance in Lee Christmas. He had flames in Choloma as in Port Cortez and the husband of one—according to the time-worn tale—ambushed himself and waited for his enemy with an ancient shotgun. A charge of buckshot tore into Christmas' breast and he dropped—dying, everyone believed. Dr. Waller, veteran physician of Honduras, saved his life; but Christmas' own grim will to live, his unwavering courage, made the good doctor's efforts availing. He lived—and as soon as he could walk shakily, he hunted up his attacker and nearly slew him with a rock!

The memory of his fighting at Laguna Trestle was very green. So were memories of other, personal battles. And he did various mysterious things for President Terencio Sierra—made journeys to Guatemala on governmental errands. He was known to be high in Sierra's favor.

So it was no surprise to the knowing when Sierra called the big *Americano* up to the capital, after he was once more upon his feet, and made him chief of police—a federal post, in Central America. Perhaps it was no surprise to Lee Christmas, either. Politics had become heated. The original alliance between Policarpo Bonilla, Manuel Bonilla (no relative of Policarpo) and Terencio Sierra had provided for alternation in the presidential chair. Policarpo had served his term. Sierra was finishing his in 1902, and Manuel expected frictionless elevation to office. But Sierra wanted to keep the presidency. A man like Christmas was very much an asset, when in command of a well-equipped, tolerable-drilled and loyal little army of nearly two hundred police. Christmas knew this as well as anyone.

But Sierra reckoned without due consideration of Manuel Bonilla—one of the outstanding figures of Central American history. Manuel was as much a fighting man as even Lee Christmas. He was a shrewd politician and a man of unimpeachable honesty. With the people at large he was tremendously popular. And he had no idea of being pushed aside by his former allies—Policarpo Bonilla and Terencio Sierra.

Sierra, one thinks, tried to be clever. He made Manuel Bonilla secretary of war and professed warm friendship for him. He pretended to favor his candidacy for the presidency—and then suddenly turned upon him, as if for cause, to support one Arias for the office.

But while Sierra professed friendship for Manuel, Lee Christmas had become a real friend of the dynamic, two-fisted little man. And Manuel warmly returned that feeling. When the election was held, Bonilla received a plurality of the vote, but Sierra refused to consider Manuel elected, since he had not got a majority. Manuel and his backers withdrew from Tegucigalpa. Lee Christmas did not hesitate. He led his policemen out to join Manuel, taking with him other Manuelistas down the San Lorenzo road to Amapala on the Pacific.

Arias was declared president in Tegucigalpa. Manuel
Bonilla was sworn in at Amapala. Sierra took the field
against Bonilla as army commander of Arias. Weeks
dragged by. February, 1903, passed. March came. Then
the Manuelistas fought Sierra and in a battle lasting
three days defeated the ex-president. But still Sierra refused to come to terms. Manuel Bonilla moved on the
capital—already enveloped by his forces.

LEE CHRISTMAS was in his glory. With a rifle under
his leg, twin Luger automatics holstered on his thighs,
bandoliers across his shoulders, he rode at the side of
General Medal. A *puro* cocked in the corner of his wide,
hard mouth, keen blue eyes glinting under his hatrim,
he was every inch the fighting man. His policemen
looked worshipfully at him. Presidents were one thing
—or another. But that big, heavy-handed, roaring man
was their commander. They "dressed on him."

He was the born soldier. Every trained veteran who
later came in contact with him conceded his instinct for
military tactics. On this first real campaign he was a
man finding himself. He was on the way to becoming
what he was called in later years—"a one-man army
corps."

At Lamaní Hill Sierra's force had mounted two
Gatling guns. In the level space below the Manuelistas
took cover and both sides fired desultorily as targets
showed. Christmas led fifty-odd of his police to wipe out
a charge of the Federals and General Medal made a
counter-charge that hurled Sierra's troops off Lamaní
and when the Manuelistas moved on toward the capital
they had the two Gatlings.

They fought again at Berrinche, a hill commanding
Tegucigalpa. Here they must face a six-point-five
mountain gun. And Christmas turned artilleryman. His
police had been dragging a seven-point-five Krupp rifle
along, all the way from Amapala. Now, he turned the
Krupp on the Federal gun and smashed it. Bonilla had
forced Sierra to fly to Salvador for his life. Now, his

army was swelling daily and his guns commanded Tegucigalpa from the heights. Arias gave in and was let go with his cabinet to Nicaragua. Manuel Bonilla assumed charge of the government of Honduras and Lee Christmas beside him had a new title—Brigadier General and Chief of Federal Police!

MANUEL BONILLA was now firmly established in the presidency. But that did not mean that his troubles were over—not in Honduras, "the Land of Depths and Revolutions." Terencio Sierra was against him. So was Policarpo Bonilla. So were various other malcontents. But Manuel was the man to ride the hurricane if any Hondureño could do it! With the help of Lee Christmas and the efficient Federal police force, Manuel made a fair stab at keeping control of governmental reins.

One of the outstanding events of Manuel's administration was a blow at Zelaya of Nicaragua. Nicaragua's president was helping the anti-administration forces in Honduras, because he felt that Manuel would never assist him in the matter of a strip of disputed territory lying between Nicaragua and Honduras. Zelaya had considered that disputed territory as his own for a long time. He had granted concessions in it and continued income from the concessionaires depended upon control of the strip.

Purely as a matter of political strategy, Manuel laid before King Alfonso of Spain the quarrel of Honduras and Nicaragua over this disputed strip of land. Bonilla's idea seems to have been very simple: If Alfonso ruled against Nicaragua, then Zelaya would fight. If Alfonso ruled against Honduras, Bonilla would fight. So an excellent war was insured, either way!

Lee Christmas had divorced his second wife in Port Cortez and remarried. But that was merely a small incident in a very busy career. Christmas ordered his resplendent uniforms from Paris, now, and the charger he rode was a magnificent Arab, presented by a lady very much enamored of the big American who, of all the Honduran governmental officials, was closest to the president. It was like Guatemala again—"the life that Riley would have *liked* to lead."

The rumblings of trouble with Nicaragua had no effect upon him. At most, according to his philosophy, it would be nothing but a fight, and man's chief aim is fighting, so—what would you?

The answer to Bonilla's expectations of trouble with Nicaragua came when, in 1906, the Spanish king ruled that the disputed territory was the rightful property of Honduras. Zelaya, of course, refused to abide by the decision of Alfonso. He started the army of Nicaragua north to Honduras, in 1907. Manuel Bonilla then organized two armies. Sotera Barahona, the minister of war, with Lee Christmas as his second-in-command, was given charge of what amounted to a home defense force. Barahona and Christmas occupied the plain of Maraita, to guard the capital in case the Nicaraguans got too far. Salamón Ordóñez, with the main army, marched to find the enemy, and was defeated in the first fight with Zelaya's troops. Manuel Bonilla then took the field with another force, but did not personally lead them into battle. Because of illness, he stayed behind them while his army went on. When the Hondurans met the Nicaraguans at Namasigüe, they were virtually wiped out. In fact, this defeat at Namasigüe established some sort of all-time record for proportionate losses of both sides. Something like 3,000 men were killed, within a few minutes. Which is something to be considered by those who think of all Central American warfare as comic opera!

Bonilla went to Amapala, on Tigre Island, while Sotera Barahona and Lee Christmas waited at Maraita for the Nicaraguans. Eventually, Bonilla made Guatemala, then British Honduras. But behind him Barahona and Christmas faced certain defeat. The Nicaraguan forces had been swelled by all the anti-Bonilla men in Honduras. In later years, Christmas was accustomed to say that, if he had been in supreme command, Bonilla's army would never have got into the trap that the invading forces set. It was his claim that he warned Barahona of the flanking moves of the enemy in ample time for withdrawal. The Barahona position was excellent, he said, for defense. But they could not get out of the hostile lines and there were enough of the enemy to sweep Maraita and overwhelm the Bonilla force.

This truth was quickly seen by the Bonilla leaders. A conference of officers was held. Lee Christmas listened for a while to Barahona's statement that the position of the army was hopeless. Then he interrupted, to voice his opinion very calmly.

"It's just a question of waiting here to be captured or killed—captured *and* killed—or taking a chance of getting killed in breaking through their lines. I'm going to try to break through. If I get killed it will be *doing* something."

Barahona himself, with Colonel Reyes and an American named Mills, agreed that it was better to go with Christmas in his charge against the enveloping line. After all, as Christmas had said, it was merely a question of which death they preferred.

The four desperate riders began their dash in the gray light before dawn. Riding at the gallop, they were greeted almost instantly by terrific rifle fire. Mills was killed, then Reyes. Barahona went down, "shot to dollrags," according to Lee Christmas. Christmas himself crashed under his dead horse with leg broken. He twisted his Luger around, for he saw a soldier running at him, bayonet ready. He shot his pistol empty, and then was made prisoner. He looked at the officer who came up to him, a boy-lieutenant. The *teniente* informed him calmly that he would of course be put before a firing squad. As calmly, Lee Christmas faced him.

He shrugged those big shoulders contemptuously. Firing squads had no terrors for him. His leg had been smashed by the bullet that killed his horse. The pain was terific. But he drew himself up, to stare the young *teniente* in the eye.

"But after I'm shot I have one request to make," he said haughtily. "Don't bury me."

"Don't bury you?" the young officer repeated, in a puzzled tone. "Why?"

"Because I don't want to be buried in this damn' country! What *I* want is to be thrown out on the field, so the *zopilotes* and the buzzards can eat me. Then I want 'em to fly up and scatter me over your dirty black faces!"

It was a gesture of defiance perfectly understandable to the men around him, officer and common soldier alike. This *gringo* was *un hombre valiente*—a man who had no fear of death. The defiance appealed to them. The young officer burst out laughing:

"You will not be shot at all—not here on the field," he assured Christmas. "You will be sent to the capital and there put in the hospital. After that—*quien sabe?* The authorities must say."

And so Lee Christmas, alone of the four desperate riders, survived Maraita. He was sent back to the capital and there put in a hospital.

"I lay in the hospital with my leg getting better," he said, "and a funny thing happened there. The beginning of it dated back to my time as chief of police. There was a man in town, a middle class native, who didn't like me. I don't recall what the trouble was about— maybe I stepped on his family bed some time. . . When I re-equipped the police force at Tegucigalpa, the salesman gave me a pair of little Browning-Colt automatics. I had holsters made for 'em and put my old guns away.

"One night, I was sitting on the sidewalk outside police headquarters. Usually, people walking on that side of the street stepped off the sidewalk when they neared headquarters or the police squad room on the right. They walked in the street until they got past us. Well, I was sitting there with my chair tilted back against the wall, when I noticed a man coming up the sidewalk toward me. I didn't pay any attention to him and he came on until he stood directly between me and the edge of the sidewalk.

"I didn't see him pull the gun. The first notice I got was when a bullet cut across my coat—I was sitting in my chair with my left side twisted toward the street. It tore off the left lapel and burned my arm. I started to get up and another bullet cut the brim off my hat.

"Well! I got up, pulling the one automatic I had on. I started shooting, walking toward the man as I shot. My first bullet knocked him down. I kept on shooting—seven or eight shots in all—till I got right up against him. He was shooting, too, but his bullets were going wide. I put the muzzle of the automatic against his head and pulled the trigger. But it didn't go off. I didn't realize until I had pulled the trigger a half-dozen times that I had shot it empty.

"There was a big Colt .45 hanging up inside headquarters. I ran in after that. When I got back with it the police had that fellow like a pack of hounds on a coon. You know—that fellow wasn't dead—didn't die at all! He had all my bullets in him, too! In his lungs, in his thigh, in his ankle. A bullet entered his breast and ranged down and came out below his kidney. When they undressed him in the hospital, this bullet fell out on the floor. It was lodged between his undershirt and his skin. That was the start of this funny business in the hospital...

"The American consul came to the hospital to see me, while I was wondering what Zelaya and my friends the Honduran revolutionists were going to do with me. The consul told me that Zelaya had given the word for me to be sent overland to Nicaragua. Hah! I knew what *that* meant! That was the way they used to give a fellow *ley fuga*—the law of flight. I'd be shot on the road and it would be reported that I had tried to escape. A friend of mine brought in an old Remington .41 caliber pistol—the kind that was made for cap-and-ball cartridge, then changed to straight fire. As soon as I was able to hobble a little I notified the authorities that I was ready to answer any charges pending and demanded release from parole.

"I had a crutch and a cane and I walked out of that hospital. I started for the consul's house with that old gun handy inside my waistband, for I expected someone to take a shot at me most any minute. Well, who should I meet, also hobbling along on crutches, but that fellow I'd shot up in front of police headquarters! We looked at each other for a minute, and we passed. I went along about twenty feet, then something made me turn and look at him. Hah! He had stopped, too. He was looking back at me. I made a fierce face at him—it was all I could do—and he went on pretty fast. But it worried me. I got to the consul's house as fast as I could and eventually got out of town on a mule that Charley Jeffs brought me."

Eventually, Christmas was back in Guatemala. This time he was raised to power greater than he had known before. He became the head of Cabrera's notorious secret police. His word was law in the capital; and every drifting foreigner who would fight found service quickly in what was known as Christmas' Foreign Legion. He got large sums of money easily, but it trickled through his hands as fast as it came in. Then, eventually, he quarreled with Cabrera. There is an interesting story told of the day that Christmas, well-liquored, swaggered into a telegraph station and demanded that the operator take a message for him.

"It's to the president!" he told the man—a government employe—and when the operator heard that message he almost fainted. It began—according to the story —"To Manuel Estrada Cabrera, Son of a Bitch, Cur of the Alleys, at the White Palace, Guatemala City—" It went on to enumerate the grievances which Christmas considered himself to have against the administration and it ended with his resignation from Cabrera's service.

Apocryphal or no, it was a message of typical Christmas type. Certainly, he was back on the trans-Guatemalan railroad soon afterward, pulling a throttle.

THE RAILWAY that connects Guatemala's Atlantic and Pacific coasts, between Port Barrios and San José, is narrow gauge and rather deliberate. Lee Christmas, in overalls again, sitting in the cab of the little engine, had plenty of time to think. As chief of the secret police, he had known all the devious ins and outs of Central American politics.

"A prominent man in Costa Rica couldn't kick the cat on Monday, but I'd know by Tuesday in Guatemala if the cat would live," he recalled that time, with a grim smile. "Hah!"

Among the bits of news and gossip that he had collected and which he mulled over, now, as his engine slid down the long slopes from Guatemala to Zacapa and the shops, and on to the palms of Port Barrios, were reports that Dávila, president of Honduras now, was exceedingly unpopular.

He wrote Manuel Bonilla again and again, urging a revolutionary attempt. But Bonilla was not ready. There was need for strong financial backing. A fruit company magnate was finally persuaded to furnish the sinews of war, but it was not until July, 1910, that Bonilla could write Christmas from Belize, commission him army commander of the revolt, and make an appointment with him for the meeting that was to inaugurate a revolution.

Glover's Reef was the rendezvous. Here the several vessels of Bonilla met. Arms and ammunition were sent ashore for General Moncada, the Bonilla man who was to march from Tela. Here it was that Lee Christmas— commanding Manuel Bonilla's army—met a young man who was to become one of his closest friends—Guy Molony of New Orleans. Molony had already behind him the Boer War, a hitch in the United States cavalry in the Philippines, and service in Nicaragua with the famous "Jew" Dreben, against Zelaya, that same year of 1910. Particularly, Molony was a genius with machine guns—their operation or their repair. By the time the Manuelista "fleet" had arrived at Port Cortez, Christmas and Molony understood each other thoroughly and liked each other immensely.

Disappointment awaited the Manuelistas at Cortez. The man in charge of Bonilla's affairs there had been shot and the plans of the revolution discovered. Other Manuelistas in and around Port Cortez were in custody— or dead.

"That damned fool, Marín—" so Lee Christmas told the story "—got cock-eyed drunk. He went howling down the street that he was Manuel Bonilla's right hand and the revolution had begun. They shot him—quick. That was all right with me! But they got all our plans and lists and were waiting for us—men enough to eat us. We skipped out, to land and join Moncada. The gunboat *Tatumbla* shelled our boat, but it was rotten shooting. Hah! They missed us. But when we found that Moncada had been licked, that was the end of the revolution—for the time being."

THEY WENT back to New Orleans. The fruit magnate still had faith in Bonilla. He bought for the second expedition the yacht *Hornet* and Christmas, Bonilla and other Manuelistas spent money liberally around New Orleans while preparations went on. They were shadowed constantly by Federal men alert to prevent violation of neutrality laws. But the *Hornet* cleared for Nicaragua and still Bonilla's party was seen around the red light district.

But not for long were they there! In the cruiser of a friend of their backer, with the magnate himself deckhand and cook, Bonilla, Christmas and Guy Molony were taken down the Mississippi into the Gulf to meet the *Hornet*. Here the fruit company man said "goodbye and good luck!" And—seeing that Bonilla had no overcoat—he pulled off his own and put it on the little man.

"Hell, Manuel! I've shot the roll on you. I might as well shoot the coat!" he said, grinning.

That was Christmas Eve, 1910. Four days later, the *Hornet* was receiving thirty veterans of Bonilla campaigns, and taking aboard the guns and ammunition hidden after the disastrous summer attempt. Coxin's Hole on Roatan Island was their first objective. The village was taken and more men joined Bonilla—some hundred of recruits.

Lee Christmas, with Guy Molony and a half-dozen men, then captured Utila and its garrison of twenty-odd men. That conquest saw the New Year in. Next was Trujillo. Christmas' force captured the ancient sea port, captured Iriona. The Bonilla cause was prosperous, now. For the North Coast makes most of Honduras' money —from the customs houses. La Ceiba was next on the schedule—and Ceiba was a hard nut to crack. .

It was not so much the military forces facing Christmas, that made La Ceiba difficult of capture. It was politics! Warships of the United States and England lay off the port. President Dávila of Honduras was at the moment the white-haired child of the Taft administration. For he was about to sign and force through the Congress of Honduras a treaty which Wall Street very much wanted. In exchange for approval of this treaty the United States agreed not to recognize any government which came into power in Honduras by force of arms. In other words—any government such as Manuel Bonilla was about to establish.

Time was "the essence of the contract," now. For Bonilla, it meant that he must complete his sway over the North Coast by capture of La Ceiba and Port Cortez. For the various foreign elements represented by those warships at La Ceiba it meant that Bonilla's attack must be delayed, if possible, until Dávila could get that treaty approved. A move in this direction was the capture of Bonilla's "navy," the *Hornet*, by men from the American cruiser *Tacoma*.

Christmas—with Colonel Guy Molony leading the Bonilla army through chill, slanting January rain toward La Ceiba—was assaulted by a very barrage of correspondence. Notes came from the commanding officers of the warships, and from the consuls at La

Ceiba. Christmas and Molony looked at the notes and Christmas—never long of temper—roared furiously. For the various foreigners in La Ceiba had drawn up the rules and regulations by which he must fight at La Ceiba, and published them without any consideration whatever of Manuel Bonilla's provisional government and his interest in the affair. As a matter of fact, the neutral zone which had been established by the commanding officers of the warships, acting in conjunction with the consuls and various foreigners ashore, worked only to the advantage of the Federal garrison. As Lee Christmas put it, the Dávilists could shoot *him* at will. But if he shot at *them*, his bullets were apt to go into the neutral zone and the *Tacoma* would open fire on the beach. But Lee Christmas was not to be checked by this very obvious partiality of the policing warships for the Dávilists. He snarled and growled at the message-bearers—and told them that he was going to attack.

So, January 25, 1911, he divided his army and gave the order to advance on the town. There were two avenues of approach: The road from the back country to the sea-coast crossed the Cangrejal River well inland. From the mouth of the Cangrejal the town might be gained by going along the beach. Both the ford and the beach had been covered by the Dávilists. In trenches at the ford between three hundred and four hundred men guarded the "*vado*"—the "wade," as Central Americans name a ford. From the swamp that comes down to the beach, out into the sea, several barbed wire fences had been built and here General Guerrero, commanding the garrison, had posted a strong force, entrenched.

Christmas assigned to General Leiva two-thirds of the Manuelistas for the attack on the Cangrejal ford while he, with Colonel Guy Molony and other infantry, took the beach road when once across the Cangrejal's mouth. Molony and the advance guard met heavy fire and dead Manuelistas began to dot the sand. Molony quieted the Dávilist firing with machine gun bursts and drew his Hotchkiss gun forward to wreck the Dávilist trench behind the barbed wire with a few rounds.

Young Pedro Gonzales, veteran of other campaigns of Manuel Bonilla, and a wild man in battle, now scouted ahead and reported it quite possible to wade out to sea around the ends of the barbed wire entanglements. Molony's handful made the charge. Christmas followed at the double with his infantry. There was no more opposition here; the fire from the Hotchkiss gun had routed General Guerrero's men.

Christmas' force got into town and found the Dávilists sheltered in a trench near the neutral zone. Molony, firing low to keep his bullets out of neutral territory, drove the Dávilists out to surrender to the naval guards in the zone.

Still, Leiva was on the far side of the Congrejal. His machine guns had jammed, his Krupp gun's crew had been wiped out. He could not cross the river in the face of the murderous Dávilist fire. But Lee Christmas, conferring with the commanders of American and British warships, calmly informed them that he had La Ceiba in his hand. He wanted to avoid further bloodshed. If they would persuade the Federals to surrender he would be spared the necessity of wiping them out. They were sufficiently impressed to carry the message and the Dávilists laid down their guns. Then, only, was it apparent that Christmas' heavy losses in dead and wounded had reduced his force well below the strength of the surrendering Dávilists!

OF THE IMPORTANT towns, only Port Cortez remained to be taken, to complete Manuel Bonilla's grasp of the North Coast. Lee Christmas advanced on Cortez but the Dávilists retired and the triumphant Manuelistas marched in without the firing of a shot.

Dávila, thoroughly discredited, retired from office. Dr. Bertrand was named provisional president and in the election of October, 1911, Manuel Bonilla became president, elected by the largest vote a Honduran candidate had ever received.

Bonilla, as I have said elsewhere, was one of the outstanding figures of Central America. Not, it seems to me, merely in his own time, but from my study of Central American affairs at long distance and on the ground, of all time. But that is a mere matter of opinion, and of no particular importance. The important thing, and the indisputable thing, is that Manuel Bonilla was a generous enemy and a staunch friend. And between the little revolutionist now seated in Honduras' capital and that swaggering man of battle, Lee Christmas, existed the warmest friendship. So, it was natural that now began the time of Lee Christmas' greatest power and prosperity. Not even in Guatemala, as the right hand of Estrada Cabrera, had he been so much the personage. Bonilla made him commanding general of the army, *comandante* of Port Cortez, inspector general of the North Coast. Money came to him—money or its equivalent, property—so fast that he hardly knew what to do with it. For he was still the fighting man, whose idea of the proper enjoyment of prosperity was a spree. He gave prodigally to relatives and friends, he entertained on a baronial scale. He made triumphant tours of the States. There was no more familiar, no more feared and respected, figure in all Honduras than the big red-faced *Americano* with his deadly Luger automatic on his hip—the automatic with which he could ruin a silver half-dollar at almost incredible distances. For Lee Christmas was the modern gunman. Not for him the slow, old single-action of the Western gunfighter, but he was as proficient in weapon-play as most of the tall figures of an earlier day pictured in this gallery. Then—

Manuel Bonilla died of Bright's disease, March 21, 1913. It was a great blow for Honduras. For Christmas, though he did not see it then, it was Tragedy! For Bonilla's death marked the beginning of the end.

He had never got on well with anyone in governmental circles, except Manuel. His wealth had trickled through his fingers, vanished. The new government was not disposed to be prodigal in its treatment of him, as Manuel had been. In fact, it was not even generous. When, in 1917, the United States entered the World War, a graying Lee Christmas resigned the small position he held under the Honduran government and went to Washington. He applied to Woodrow Wilson for a commission as general officer in the United States Army. He actually got an interview with President Wilson, but received no encouragement.

From his scrap book I copied the clipping from a Washington paper mentioning his visit:

"General Lee Christmas, soldier of fortune, prominent figure in many Central American revolutions, offered his services yesterday to President Wilson. The President told him that he would like to talk to him later."

That, according to Christmas, was not quite accurate. The President informed him that appointments to the army were in the hands of a board and Christmas went before medical examiners and was rejected. His big body was scarred by many a wound and hard living, harder pleasuring, had debilitated his magnificent constitution. He waited vainly for any appointment of importance in keeping with the figure he felt he was. Then he went back to Central America—and found that in Honduras, also, he had no influential friends.

Between 1917 and the spring of 1920, when I came out of El Salvador to Guatemala, Christmas drifted back and forth, from the States to Guatemala, on various commissions for interests wanting contracts or concessions in Banana Land. I found him in the room adjoining mine in the Hotel Gran Central. He was no longer the swaggering, hard-drinking soldier of many light loves, who had moved about these very streets possessed of almost limitless powers in the land. But still the twin Lugers sagged upon his hips and he sat habitually with back to something solid, and suspected efforts to poison him.

His rough sense of humor had not deserted him. When upon return to my room one day I found a large, black thumb print on my every clean collar, he roared amusedly and tossed over a wad of Guatemalan *billetes*.

"The secret police have been investigating you. I watched 'em through a crack. I told 'em you were an American army officer in disguise, spying. I'll pay for the laundry bill."

And when I told him later of being shot at on a dark street, again he roared. *He* had been shot at so many times that the incident seemed unimportant. He was only interested in learning if I had shot the man who shot at me.

"You can go kick to the American minister, if you want to. He'll tell you to stay off the streets."

He was promised certain valuable concessions by President Cabrera and I had my own private axe to grind. So for a while our interests were parallel and he drew upon his store of knowledge to sketch for me the current political situation. Estrada Cabrera was ill and his iron grip was laxing on the country he had ruled since '98. Christmas, the old war horse, sniffed the battle from afar as the Unionista Party gained strength and boldness. Cabrera was striking out at his enemies with the desperation of weakness.

"It's a question," Christmas said, "whether the Old Man can ride out this one. Hah! He's like me—he's getting old."

But, old or no, his name had not lost its power. Agents of the Unionistas came with all the mysterious airs proper to conspirators, to the man whose name alone was "worth an army corps." They wanted him to command the Unionista army. They told him that Cabrera was doomed—and he had confessed that he began to believe the Old Man was toppling. His interests demanded an intimate friendly relation with the administration in power. But Cabrera men, too, were coming to him. They admitted the gravity of the situation, but—The Old Man would win again! He had always won.

Christmas hesitated. One day he was warning the young son of an old friend not to join the Unionistas and get his family on Cabrera's black list. The next:

"Know anything about machine guns?" he asked me. My trailmate and I nodded, mentioning navy training on the Colt.

"Fine! Colts'd be what you'd have to handle." Then, drawlingly, he said: "You can be a couple of majors if you want to. Looks like I'm going to have to get into this. . . . Unionista side, too."

Those were tense and highly interesting days, preceding March 11th, when the Unionistas staged an enormous parade through the streets and Secret Police trailed known leaders. Excitement waxed when in front of the Military Academy—temporarily the Hall of Congress—the crowd was fired on by soldiers acting under orders of Captain Anguiano (later to be mobbed and killed in the street). Through it all, the old soldier of fortune moved restlessly with us, stopping frequently to talk to old acquaintances like William Drummond, with whom he had smelled his first powder burning at Laguna Trestle. Eventually, he decided to take no active part in the revolution.

When, in April, Cabrera was deposed and imprisoned and Carlos Herrera came in as president, Christmas continued to work for his backers until counter-revolution overthrew Herrera. Christmas' health was very bad—as bad as the state of his personal fortunes. He came back to New Orleans, suffering from tropical sprue and attendant pernicious anemia. He was only the gray shadow of that big-bodied, full-blooded fighting man who—second only to William Walker—types the foreign warrior of tropic battles. In January, 1924, he died, and Guy Molony, staunch friend, paid his funeral expenses.

Whatever stone, whatever inscription, may mark his grave, his real epitaph is not found in the States. It is heard in the Land of the Banana Flag, when a man turns to another and says:

"That reminds me of Lee Christmas—"

CHAPTER XVIII · *Triggernometry*

"CURLY BILL" Graham and a bunch of wild cowboys were amusing themselves by shooting up the thriving village of Tombstone. They whirled their pistols in the single and double rolls and the .45s, cocked by their own weight as they spun, roared and slung lead into the Arizona sky and the Arizona sand and the walls and the windows of Tombstone's buildings.

Marshal Fred White had been the town's boss-policeman for ten months, to the day. For this was November 6, 1880. He was a veteran officer, by now. He leaped out upon the street with six-shooter drawn. The first man he saw was Virgil Earp, brother of the more notorious Wyatt. White yelled to Virgil to come along and help put the hobbles on these leather-pounders. Virgil nodded and sided White as he ran toward the yelling, shooting celebrants.

But the cowboys did not wait to be arrested. A large part of their amusement was sight of the marshal panting out to stop their shooting. So they scattered like quail, whooping enthusiastically. Curly Bill streaked it down an alley, with White and Virgil Earp on his heels. He stopped at their command, turned to face them.

"Give me that six-shooter!" White snapped—so an old-time Tombstone citizen told me, years ago. "Hand it over—butt first!"

Curly Bill grinned. Meekly he extended the pistol as ordered. As the marshal reached for it the muzzle of his own weapon sagged a tiny bit. The .45 in Curly Bill's brown paw performed a maneuver new to White. It whirled, the butt slapping into Curly Bill's palm. The big hammer was thumbed back. Before White could more than gasp, Virgil Earp snatched at Curly. The .45 bellowed—and Fred White was dead in the alley—first

414

recorded victim of "the spin," which is often particularized in the West as the "Curly Bill" or "road-agent's spin."

It is recorded that Curly Bill surrendered his .45 to Virgil Earp and claimed that, as he had handed over his weapon to White, Earp seized him from behind, and his six-shooter, being a hair-trigger, was accidentally fired. For various reasons this story hath an odor like that of ancient fish. It would have breathed forth a queer aroma under the torrid Arizona sun, even though vouched for by other than a member of the notorious Earps—for whose veracity, I admit freely herewith, nothing in the record gives me admiration. Old Hard Rock Urch, who told me of the matter, was neither a Clanton nor a White-and Earp factionist. Said he:

"That was just a stall, that tale. Curly Bill said his gun was awful light-triggered. Hell! What difference did that make—unless he was handin' Fred White a cocked pistol, with the muzzle pointing at Fred's dinner. And d' you think White was *that* short a shorthorn? That he'd disarm a man with Curly Bill's rep' that way? *Nunca! Jamás!* 'T was the road-agent's spin killed White."

And he demonstrated the spin. It is simplicity itself and, therefore, the more easy to learn and to practise— the more deadly against a man unfamiliar with it, expecting nothing but a pistol meekly surrendered.

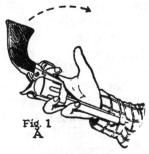

Fig. 1
A

The pistol is held as shown in Figure 1. The forefinger is hooked in the trigger-guard, the butt toward the "other fellow," and the barrel is gripped lightly with the remaining fingers of the gun-hand. The spin is started by a slight jerk upward of the hand, accompanied by release of the barrel. The forefinger is a pivot, and so perfectly balanced is the Colt Single Action Army—better known as the Frontier Model—that the butt comes upward from horizontal, describes a half-circle as indicated by the dotted line and arrow, and smacks into the waiting palm.

The lifted thumb drops to the hammer, cocks it while the forefinger holds back the trigger in firing position (Figure 2), and—Marshal White lies dead in the Tombstone alley of half a century ago; Curly Bill Graham (alias Bill Brocius) holds a .45 from the hot muzzle of which drifts a tiny wisp of pungent smoke; Virgil Earp gapes down at the dying man, then lifts his eyes to Curly Bill.

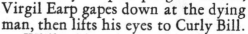

Fig. 2 B

While this spin is often credited to Curly Bill, it is hardly possible that he invented it. He may have figured it out, independently, against a time of need, or it may have been shown him. I have heard that the Plummer gang used it, in Montana, in '63. And it was known to at least one other famous gunfighter—that champion killer whose name still stands in Texas very high in the Gallery of Gunfighters, the forty notches on his guns unapproached by the tally of any other I know, even the fabulous Wild Bill Hickok. Gentlemen! John Wesley Hardin, a gunfighter from the Hard Water Fork of Bitter Creek!

Hardin claims to have used "the spin" on Wild Bill in Abilene in 1871—or nine years before Curly Bill demonstrated it to Fred White. Said he:

"Wild Bill whirled around and met me. He asked: 'What are you howling about, and what are you doing with those pistols on?'

" 'I'm just taking in the town,' I said.

"He pulled his pistol and said: 'Take those pistols off! I arrest you.'

"I said 'all right', and pulled them out of the scabbards, but while he was reaching for them I reversed them and whirled them over on him with the muzzles in his face, springing back at the same time. I told him to put his pistol up, which he did."

BEFORE discussing any more of the tricks performed by the old gunfighters, it may be worth while to have a look at the old fellows, contrasted with target-pistol champions of today.

Every month or so, it seems to me, some writer breaks into print to explain how over-rated the old-time Westerner was, as a gun-shark. It has been claimed very recently that most of them couldn't hit a barn a-wing; that any recruit cop of an Eastern force, given an hour and twenty minutes of pistol practise, can perform shooting which would make the old-timers turn green with envy. Not only in the matter of accuracy, but in the speed of delivery.

One such amazing declaration of recent date compared the "fanning" of a single-action .45 by a Western sheriff with the target shooting of a novice policeman. It was stated that the policeman made five bull's eyes at 40 feet and nicked the sixth. But the Westerner's score at 25 feet was—no bulls, two in the target, and four in the roof and sides of the range. More! The chronicler claimed that the sheriff required nine seconds to loose his six shots by fanning the gun, against the policeman's five and a half seconds time for straight shooting with regular trigger pull.

Well—in the first place, fanning is a pistol stunt so rarely practised in real life that some old-time Rangers and peace officers of my acquaintance—veterans of dozens of duels; men who could notch their guns if they were the ostentatious sort—have never seen it used in a fight. Consider Figure 3.

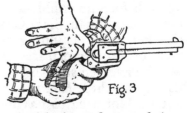

Fig. 3

The pistol is held at hip-level, the inside of the forearm jammed hard against the hip-bone for steadying. The muzzle is pointed in the general direction of the target, trigger held back in firing position. Taking it for granted that the "fanner" is right-handed, the stiffly-open left hand slaps the big single-action hammer rapidly, cocking and firing the pistol.

Regardless of that alleged nine seconds required by this unnamed Westerner on the Eastern target range, fanning is the most rapid method known to any of us in the West for "shaking the loads out of a gun" and spraying lead—*in a general direction*. I have fanned an empty gun six times in one second and emptied five chambers (all that any sane person ever loads in a pistol!) in less than three seconds. This time of mine is called just average fast by the famous modern expert, Ed Mc-Givern of Lewistown, Montana, who takes the old-style Colt and duplicates the old-timers' feats—when he doesn't better them.

But the point I make here is that, in such comparisons as this—made all too often by writers wholly incompetent to speak—the fundamental facts behind the old-timers' "triggernometry" are completely ignored. Yesterday I asked an old *buscadero* who does sheer, twinkling magic with the sixes, what he conceived to be the difference between target shooting and the ancient business of gunplay. He hesitated not a split second in answering:

"State of mind! Even if your target shot could make Clay Allison, or Harvey Logan, or John Wesley Hardin, or Billy the Kid, look like a bunch of amateurs—not that I believe he could—ary one of them could walk off that range where they'd been beat and kill the Target Expert before he could say Jack Robinson—or a heap shorter name than that! Chances are, he couldn't give Saint Peter the beginning of an idee about what happened, or why—much less how!

"The average shooting-gallery shot is used to doing this—doing that. And used to having plenty of time to do it in. Not used to having the split part of a second make the difference between his living and his dying. The gunfighter was schooled to kill. He was not a man whose nerves bothered him in a tight minute. He could hold tight to the one idea of killing the other man—

and he could figger out lots and lots of ways to do it. If he wasn't an apt scholar at the business, he got killed in the early beginning and never was heard of."

This sums up the difference well enough. Wes Hardin, for an example, killed men who were mechanically his equals, men whose speed on the draw was as amazing as his own; whose target-shooting was as good as his. He killed them because his temperament was different. He could stand covered by the other fellow's gun, his life trembling on the other man's trigger-finger or hammer-thumb, without being in the least panicky. Instead of thinking about being killed, he thought of killing the man who covered him! He focussed his thoughts on ways of beating the drop.

Between amazing speed and hair-line accuracy, naturally the gunman chose to perfect his speed. What use to be the International Pistol Champ', able to shoot a cigarette out from under the harelipped lady's mustache, if the other fellow was going to get his hogleg out and smoking and, out of five shots at twelve or fifteen feet, land two bullets in a 22-inch segment of your intimate personality? So the old-time six-slinger practised the draws, perfected hide-outs, thought of nerve-racking tricks.

He had one other advantage over the average pistol shot, this gunfighter. Another advantage which must also come under the label "state of mind." *He was always ready to shoot!* When he dropped hand to pistol butt and she came out, there was no pondering, none of the hesitation which a peace officer of the stamp of, say, Jim Gillett, or Captain Hughes, would feel in a similar situation. No! When the gunfighter's pistol came out, the hammer dropped! That made for blazing speed.

JUMPING BACK to the act of fanning . . . Captain Bill McDonald, the famous Texas Ranger of whom I have written in earlier pages, once explained to me its mechanics and—more important!—its psychology. He said that one man, facing in a saloon or other room a

bunch of hostile men, could whip out his pistol, fan
five shots at the crowd, certainly hit two or three of
them, and by the blaze of his fire disconcert the others
so as to give him the psychological edge on them.

Akin to this in purpose is what I have heard the *Old
Buscadero* call the "hat trick." He was up against a bad
Mexican in a *plazita* south of the border. The Mexican
was not only a robber chieftain; he was a gunman,
faster than most of the American "high-line riders"
just then hanging out in that tiny settlement. He
caught my acquaintance off-guard in a *cantina*. He had
his pistol half out of a holster, and the old *buscadero*
might have been pardoned for believing that the slight
breeze on his face came from the pearly gates slatting
gently back and forth under Saint Peter's ready hand.

"I was all ready to grab a pitchfork. He had that
split-second advantage because he seen me before I
seen him. I had an idee, and it was my only chance. I
caught hold of my John B. with the left hand. I flipped
it off my head and across the three yards between us. I
was goin' for my gun all time, of course. And he flinched!
He drove a bullet into the ceilin' and had to take aim
ag'in. Me, I was in no such fix. It was the hat killed
him!"

An old ex-town marshal used to tell us about going
into a saloon at Henrietta, Texas, to corral a smilingly
ferocious young man of the Billy the Kid order. Being a
cautious soul, who never posed as a gunman, the marshal
drew his pistol at the door and walked inside holding
the "Peacemaker" beside his thigh. The young fellow
at the bar turned at the command to surrender. Guile-
lessly he eyed the marshal.

What? He was under arrest? How strange! But if the
marshal insisted, why—'*sta bueno!* The marshal didn't
mind his having one more snort? Fine! Thanks!

"He turned around, an' I watched him hawk-eyed,
I tell you, in the bar-mirror. He poured out another
drink and told the bartender it was good liquor. He
held his glass up—me watching that free hand—and

turned around to me, grinning. Then he flung that whisky into my face and slapped down my cutter in the same minute. Say! I thought somebody had sneaked in and blowed up the saloon! And by the time I could see, he'd hightailed! Run right out the door and jumped on his horse and busted down the timber!''

For the most part, when two men got "on the prod" and came hunting each other, they depended on speed on the draw, though neither was apt to overlook an opportunity to get the edge on his opponent by some trick or ferocious acting. And since the straight draw from a belt holster was the chief method of getting a pistol into action, right here is a good place to look at its technique.

There are two methods of drawing, whether from waistband, belt or shoulder holster. You can play safe with Method One, in which you drop gun hand to pistol butt, draw the pistol from the holster and, when it is pointing generally at the target, cock it. But this is not the fast way—not the gunman's way! For any one wishing to become fast on the draw, Method Two is the thing.

Belt on the pistol and, whether it be on the left side with butt front for a cross draw (the proper method of carrying a pistol when riding) or on the right side, butt to rear, check the height of it to be sure that the hand falls naturally to the butt, with elbow only slightly bent. A gun too high-hung means a muzzle caught on holster top and—what flowers are your favorites?

Now, load the gun with exploded shells. Let your hands fall loosely to the sides. At a mental word of command, or a mark on a watch, whip the gun hand up to the pistol butt, catching the hammer of the single-action under the thumb and sliding the forefinger into the trigger-guard. Draw the gun, pulling back the hammer as it comes. Tighten the fingers on the butt as the gun clears the holster. Accustom yourself to whang away as the muzzle comes to level. But not until you have developed skill should the pistol be loaded, for the practiser will be clumsy at first.

This is the old gunfighter's method and is illustrated in Figures 4 and 5. To mention the list of those who were like sleight-of-hand artists in its use is to call the roll of the Gallery of Gunfighters. Out of the Colt-smoked past, what a procession comes—Wild Bill Hickok, with his hawk's nose and cold blue eyes and shoulder-long golden hair; tall Clay Allison of the Washita, Allison

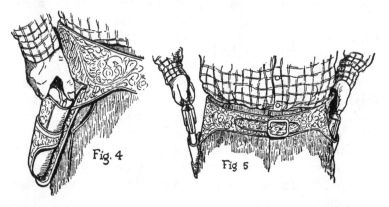

Fig. 4

Fig 5

the Wolf-Killer, another blond type with a slight limp; John Wesley Hardin and Ben Thompson, dark-haired and blue-eyed, both men of middle height, powerfully muscled but with hands as supple-fingered as any pianist's; Big Bill Longley; Mellish and Comstock; little Bass Outlaw; Billy the Kid, with his perpetual grin; John Ringo; John Slaughter; Long-Haired Jim Courtright, and many another.

These men were all quick-draw artists such as an Eastern target shot will hardly become, because he has no such impelling motive for practise and experiment. And whatever he could do on an orthodox pistol range, in a battle with such as they he would be killed before he knew exactly what was happening!

Long-haired Jim Courtright rarely gets the credit due him as expert with the Colts, as I have commented be-

fore in these pages. But the old-timers do not forget
him! They still puzzle over the mystery of Luke Short
killing him.

"Short?" Jim Gillett once said, in answer to a question. "Oh, yes, Luke was pretty fast with a six-shooter.
But Jim Courtright—Short just wasn't in his class."

In my chapter on Courtright, I said that there was
no backing down to Short. This dapper, smooth-faced
little friend of Bat Masterson and Doc Holliday and

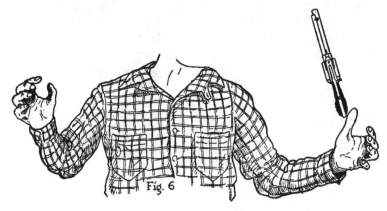

Fig. 6

Charley Bassett and the brothers Earp had run gambling
houses in the tough trail-herd towns like Dodge City.
Leadville, Colorado, too, had heard the staccato bark
of his guns. He was salty!

But when Jim Courtright of the T. I. C. Agency
tangled ropes with Luke Short, Fort Worth nodded:
Short would pay—or else. On that evening of February
8, 1887, when Courtright met Short outside the White
Elephant, they came to shooting very quickly, and a
lucky bullet from Short's double action tore off Courtright's hammer thumb.

Lightning-fast, Courtright tried desperately to perform that evolution known as the "border shift"
(Figure 6); but before the pistol could hurtle from right
hand to left hand and explode, Courtright was shot to
pieces. The border shift had failed Courtright!

Pink Simms of Lewistown, Montana, old Lincoln County cowboy who worked all over the West and served his time as peace officer, was yarning with me not long ago, about old-time gunfighters. We came to mention Courtright and Luke Short and Simms was reminded of hearing a contemporary of Short's tell how the little gambler always crowded in close during a shooting scrape.

"That way, he got the effect of the muzzle blast. It knocked the other man off balance. The .45 burned terribly at close range. It was impossible to face it—as I once discovered for myself! It will even set your clothes on fire. So, the man who got to shooting first when only a few feet away, he had a big advantage even if he missed his first shot."

Fig. 7

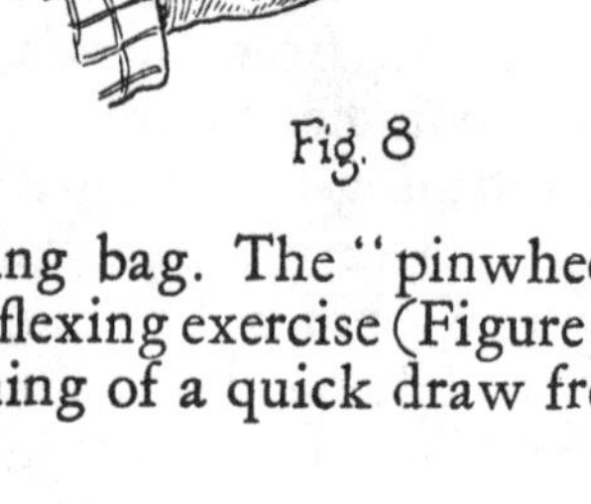

THE OLD-TIMERS were always practising the quick draw. They used such gymnastics as the "rolls" (Figure 7) to limber up their fingers and give them rhythm and balance and timing, just as the boxer training for a fight

Fig. 8

will work out on the punching bag. The "pinwheel" is another eye-training, finger-flexing exercise (Figure 8).

Figure 9 shows the beginning of a quick draw from the waistband.

The rolling of a gun is performed somewhat like the "road agent's spin," but the motion is reversed. The gun is grasped by the butt with forefinger in the trigger-guard—virtual firing position. The butt is released as a downward jerk of the muzzle spins the gun end-over-end on the forefinger. The thumb catches the hammer, and the pistol is cocked by its own weight.

In "pinwheeling" pure juggling is done. (Better stand at the side of a bed while practising this!) The gun

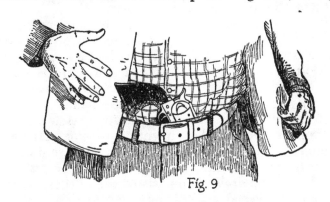

Fig. 9

is flipped into the air, to revolve so that the butt drops naturally into the palm. It is splendid legerdemain, especially when performed with two guns which cross —left-hand gun pinwheeling to right hand; right-hand gun to left hand.

John Wesley Hardin was adept at all gunology, triggernometry. Born at Bonham, Texas, in '53, he killed his first man—an insolent freed negro—at the age of fifteen. When soldiers came hunting him, he killed three of them in one battle. Ben Thompson was ten years his senior, but by the time Wes Hardin was eighteen their names were being coupled together as outstanding six-shooterologists.

Those forty killings he is credited with between November, 1868, and May, 1874, ended with the shooting of Deputy Sheriff Charley Webb at Comanche. Hardin got away, but was arrested in 1877 in Florida and returned to Texas. During his transfer from one jail to another in the custody of Ranger Lieutenant N. O. Reynolds, the Ranger guards were very curious, as men of arms, to see what this wizard of the sixes could do. With Lieutenant Reynolds' grudging consent, they handed Hardin empty pistols, and told him to show his stunts. Jim Gillett says that nothing he had ever dreamed of compared with Hardin's speed and skill. The quick draw, the spin, the rolls, pinwheeling, border shift—he did them all with magical precision.

Wes Hardin was not addicted to any particular fashion in gun-harness. When he was captured on a Florida train by Texas Rangers, he had a .44 cap-and-ball Colt between under shirt and shirt, in his waist-band. But he is credited with designing a unique "holster vest" which was given his name. It was a skeleton-vest of soft calf-skin and upon its front were two holster pockets slanting outward from center to hip-bones. He carried his six-shooters in these holsters, the butts pointing inward. To draw, the arms were crossed, and the drawn guns passed each other, coming out. But not everyone liked the "Hardin Vest" . . .

When James B. Gillett succeeded Dallas Stoudenmire as chief of police of old El Paso, he had to ride herd on what was, in '82, just about as wild a frontier town as any fictionist could construct. The building-in of four grand trunk lines simultaneously had brought countless sporting characters and restless belligerents, to add their unsettling influence to a simmering political warfare between local Democrats and Republicans who still burned with the bad feeling of Reconstruction days.

Beneky and Pierce, pioneer hardware merchants of El Paso Street, located opposite Uncle Ben Dowell's famous saloon, congratulated the 25-year-old marshal. They presented him with a beautiful pair of white-handled double-action six-shooters, holstered in a John Wesley Hardin vest. Captain Gillett relates with much enthusiasm his pride in the outfit. He went back to his office and exhibited the vest and pistols to his deputies.

They were impressed by the elegance of the rigout. They asked for a demonstration of Wes Hardin's cross-arm draw.

Gillett says he lifted his hands to shoulder-level, then snapped them down, crossing each other, to the butts of the new weapons. His hands interfered with each other. The pistols, coming out, clashed together. He tried it again and again, with little more success.

Deputy Marshal Scotten said gravely: "Jim, that's a tony rig-out. The stitching on that vest is as fine as I've ever seen. And look at the six-shooters! Why, they're as good an article as Colonel Colt ever turned out. Yes, sir; they are! We'll bury you, later in the week, in that vest."

"And I was having the same idea!" Captain Gillett told me. "I had always worn a pistol in a belt holster, and I was used to drawing fast from that position. This was no time for me to be changing my style of drawing! I got out of that vest, and later it was raffled off. A little later, I put on a belt which carried two Colts without holster. I like that belt better than anything I've ever used on the ground." (The Gillett belt and fittings is shown in Figures 10, 11 and 12.)

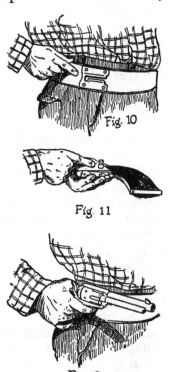

Fig. 10

Fig. 11

Fig. 12

This belt to which the famous old Ranger and peace officer refers was then and subsequently a hand-made affair. King Fisher wore one of them. Chief of Police Jenkins, who followed Gillett by nearly thirty years as chief of El Paso's police, wore a replica of it.

On the belt is riveted a plate (Figure 10) slotted to receive the hand-made pin-headed screw (Figure 11) which replaces the regular hammer-screw of the single-action Colt. To carry the pistol, the pin is entered in the slot and the pistol pushed back until the pin drops into the slight depression at the rear end of the slot. It hangs there, swinging easily.

"I used to have to watch the gambling games," Captain Gillett says. "So I'd sit on the edge of a table, or on the bar in a saloon. I could swing the gun muzzles up or down, and they were out of the way and at the same time ready for instant use. I could shoot the pistols—though I never had to—without drawing them, just as one shoots out of an open-toed swivel holster."

Figure 12 shows the gun in position on the belt, if it were being fired from the bracket.

WHEN THEIR lives hung as hung their pistols, small wonder that the gunfighters—whether peace officers or the sort who gave the peace officers their work—were always looking for new and better ways of hanging a holster! Sam Myres has been making gun harness for some forty years. In that time, many a quiet, grim-faced, alert-eyed man has come to him for expert advice on a new type of holster or belt. I know of nobody in the United States so familiar with both gun harness and the men who designed and used it as Myres. Some of the items in his collection probably have no duplicates anywhere. From the State Police at Albany, to the Border Patrol at El Paso, technical questions come regularly to his El Paso shop.

Captain John R. Hughes was directly responsible for what Myres calls the "Buscadero" belt. Back in the days when he was a cowboy and a wild-horse hunter and scout, Captain Hughes had a meeting with a six-shooterful gentleman. It resulted in a funeral and a shift, by Hughes, from right-hand to left-hand shooting.

In spite of the fact that he is one of those big, ever-courteous, soft-speaking Westerners who look anything but gun experts, Captain Hughes' change of shooting hands only increased his reputation. And the man who wears a gun develops ideas about its carrying.

His favorite gun harness was designed by Hughes himself to make the quick draw quicker still. Upon a plain leather belt he had stitched diagonally a short strap with buckle-stub to engage it. This strap slipped through the top of the holster and was buckled. It permitted quick disengagement of the weapon and, being a studied degree off horizontal, canted the pistol butt forward, the holster toe backward.

Sam Myres achieved this effect in his "Buscadero" belt. It is merely another of his small alterations which make for tiny but all-important quickening of the draw. He got the idea from Captain John R. Hughes' gun harness.

The swivel-holster is one of those things we have all heard much about—and almost never see. The military holster has a leather tab above the holster proper. The holster is attached to this by a swiveling rivet. Thus the holster, strapped by its toe to the thigh, moves with the leg, backward and forward.

In the gunman's variation of this, a hole was made in the holster and a twisted piece of rawhide set in it, then passed through a hole in the belt. The stiff rawhide served as a swivel. Since the holster was open at the toe, the wearer could easily drop hand to pistol-butt, push backward and down, bring the weapon's barrel to horizontal—and fire without drawing. For close range shooting it was an excellent harness.

I once saw an Indian Territory officer who had his holster fastened by a single copper rivet to his belt. He could swivel the holster very deftly on the rivet.

So much for wearing the weapons openly. But as the Western towns annexed peace officers, ordinances were passed requiring all but travelers passing straight through to take off their guns and hang them up when within the corporate limits of the municipality. This ruling quite naturally produced in a suspicious and belligerent population what the West called a "hideout."

The hide-outs were various. A man rammed his six-gun into the leg of his boot—just in case something came up, in which he'd want to gain what was lost in the deal by what he could do on the draw. Or he rammed the pistol into the waistband of his pants, behind. Or in front (Figure 9). Even a 5½ inch barrel, .45 caliber frame, when slid skilfully into the waistband with a buttoned vest pulled over it, becomes highly inconspicuous.

WHEN SAM BASS, the notorious Texas train robber, with Sebe Barnes and Frank Jackson walked into Copprel's store at Round Rock (July 19, 1878), Sam had his .45 in his holster. Barnes and Jackson were more cautious; their pistols were "hide-outs"—carried in the saddle-pockets which they bore in their hands. You will recall that they had come professionally, to look over the Round Rock bank. While the Rangers were warned and on the way there in force, and the adjutant general and a couple of Rangers were already in town, the outcome of the visit might have been different had Sam Bass' coat not whipped back. There ensued the gunfight which ended with Bass, Barnes and Deputy Sheriff Grimes dead.

Wild Bill Hickok seldom or never used holsters. He usually carried two pistols in his waistband, their butts pointing inward for a cross-arm draw. Dallas Stoudenmire—who in '81 ran to the scene of a murder, whipped out his pistols and killed three men in about as many seconds, and later under fire of a double-barreled shotgun again did the quick-draw, got the shotgun user, and put to flight the man's numerous backers—was another of our Gallery of Gunfighters who had little use for gun-scabbards. He had leather-lined hip-pockets tailored into his pants, in which to carry his lethal six-shooters. From those low pockets he could produce the guns with prestidigital speed.

Ben Thompson, gambling ex-Confederate soldier, ex-marshal of Austin, all-round *hombre malo*, was lightning-fast on the draw from either holster or waistband—or from a pocket or whatever other place he chose to conceal his pistol. As we have shown elsewhere! Nobody but Thompson himself knew the actual tally of his killings, but I can check nine.

Tradition credits Ben with the invention of the shoulder-holster which, of all the hide-outs, is the most practical for extended use. The original shoulder-holster (**Figure 13**) was merely a modified belt-holster, the principal modification consisting of a shoulder-loop cut to assure perfect hang of the holster and addition of a back-strap. While this old-style holster carries the gun handily, it is by no means a fast-draw harness.

Fig. 13

Far better is the spring shoulder-holster (Figure 14) which is but the skeleton of a holster—the under half, to which is sewed a toe in which rests the muzzle and a spring which fits lightly but firmly around the cylinder. The draw from the spring shoulder-holster is, of course, a cross-draw. The forefinger slips into the trigger-guard; the thumb

Fig. 14

pulls back the hammer as three fingers tighten on the butt and pull the pistol sidewise and out against the spring's tension. (Figure 15). This is a very fast holster. Chicago and New York gunmen, today, like many of our modern Westerners, prefer it to all others.

The half-breed spring-holster is similar, except that it is a complete holster, with open side, the spring being covered by the holster-front.

Sam Myres likes to shove into my Gallery of Gunfighters Colonel Higdon, a gentleman well-known not so many years ago in Central Texas and who "infested" the Myres establishment in Sweetwater. Higdon, says Myres, was a courteous, calm-eyed figure, commonly seen with a carbine contiguous to his large and firm right hand.

Fig. 15

"He toted that rifle more or less as a blind," Myres recalls. "Knowing it was against the law to carry a belt gun, and appreciating perfectly that the idea of Colonel Higdon appearing naked would have been regarded by the informed as Pure Absurdity, he always wore the carbine to draw the officers' thoughts away from what might possibly be concealed by a clean, starched shirt. I don't know whether the carbine was ever loaded, even!

"One day Captain Ransom of the Rangers (later killed in Sweetwater) passed Higdon in my door. The Captain came on in and was moved to meditate aloud about my good friend Higdon, as he called him. He said that Higdon was without doubt the most dangerous man in the State of Texas that morning. I was surprised. I knew that Higdon had killed some people. But he had had such a wide, frank blue eye, and such pleasant manners, that the idea of his being terrible rather surprised me.

" 'Oh, Yes!' Captain Ransom agreed. 'He smiles pleasantly. Even if you throw down on him, and he sees the hammer of your six-shooter going back, he'll never lose that smile. He hasn't a nerve in his body, in the ordinary sense of the term. All he lacks is opportunity to become as notorious as Wes Hardin and Ben Thompson and Billy the Kid. He's off the same bolt. He can face a cocked pistol and virtual certainty of death and keep his smile—and decide just how he'll turn the tables and kill you!'

"The next time Higdon came into the shop, I brought the talk around to gun-play. He smiled, as usual. He was standing perhaps a yard away with his hands loosely at his sides. He leaned a little toward me and said: 'Mr. Myres, you've often wondered about the speed of the shoulder-holster as compared to the speed of the fast-draw belt-holster. You've wondered, too, about my six-shooter; if I carried one, and where. So I'll settle both questions for you with one answer.'

"And his hand came up and slid under the coat, precisely like a snake flashing into a hole. With what seemed nothing but the back-lash of that same movement, his hand reappeared. Something round and hard pressed my navel.

" 'You wouldn't give a poor old fellow away, now, would you?' he whispered, looking pleadingly into my popped-out eyes.

" 'Colonel,' I told him, 'if you like, we'll go out and borrow a Bible—two Bibles—a dozen Bibles! And I'll swear on all the stack that I wouldn't dream of discussing your personal affairs!' "

IT WAS QUITE a way from Sweetwater that the rain was slanting down upon a little Texas cow-town. A cowboy, hunched in the saddle so that slicker collar was high under his Stetson rim, jogged up the middle of Main Street. He pulled in before the gray front of a saloon as the lights were coming on. Swinging down, he tied his horse to the rack.

Another cowboy came out of the saloon and looked through the dusk at the new arrival. He stiffened, and his head jerked back toward the swinging doors. Then he slid across the warped planks of the awninged porch.

"He's in there!" he whispered without preface. "Talkin' war!"

The cowboy at the rack nodded, staring at the saloon door. He nodded again and turned back toward the horse. His friend stared narrowly. But the slickered man was not untying his horse. He was fishing in a saddle pocket. He had something bright in his hand when he faced the porch again.

"No use this goin' on," he said. "He's mighty fast. I been studying that. But what you can't go around you climb over."

He slipped out of the yellow slicker and methodically tied it behind the cantle. The cowboy on the porch watched curiously while the newcomer tied a piece of strong white cord to the trigger-guard of a short .38 double-action. He watched the gun vanish under the shabby coat, poked into the right sleeve; saw it re-appear in the cowboy's right hand, where the butt was grasped.

"Now tie the end o' the string to my suspender," the gun-holder grunted tonelessly. "Not too tight! Just take up the slack. Fine!"

He lifted right hand to shoulder-level and let go the butt of the little "stingy" gun. It disappeared in his sleeve. He took out tobacco and brown saddle-blanket papers. He made a cigarette and lighted it. He held it in the fingers of his right hand, near his lips, as he crossed the porch and pushed through the swinging door of the saloon.

A big, red-haired, red-faced man stood at the bar, round, cold blue eyes steady on the newcomer. Other drinkers—townsmen, freighters, cowboys—looked from one principal to the other and moved instantly out of the line of fire. There came a silence to the shabby bar-room that caught the bartender's attention, where he stacked glasses on the backbar. He turned around and saw the cowboy walking along the bar. His heavy face turned fish-belly white.

"Oh—my God!" he said despairingly and sank, precisely like a swimmer, to the floor behind the bar.

The red-haired man's eyes roved over the cowboy, studying particularly the region about the waist. His eyes narrowed abruptly; into them came a light from behind.

"So you aim to kill me, do you?" he snarled at the cowboy. Then, "Don't you pull no gun on me!" he finished in a shout.

His hand flashed up to where his shirt was unbuttoned at the throat; slid inside. The cowboy dropped the hand holding the cigarette. As it came to waist-level the stingy gun slid down his sleeve into his hand. Across three yards of floor, he fired as fast as he could pull trigger.

The red-faced man gaped at him amazedly, rocking a little, cocked pistol in his hand. Then he swayed, neck, waist, knees, all going limp at once. The gun in his hand roared under a slipped thumb. The .45 slug tore into the floor at his own feet. The cowboy stared at him dumbly, then shook his head and reached up to untie the string from his suspender.

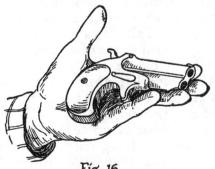

Fig. 16

"A blamed good stunt. Evened us up like trimmin' with a sharp butcher-knife."

The pet hide-out weapon of them all was that "wicked little gun with the big, bad bite"—the .41 double-barreled derringer (Figure 16). It was no uncommon thing, not so long ago, to see a man reach into pants-pocket and pull out a handful of silver, some matches, a keyring and a derringer. And the soft-nosed slugs its superposed barrels flung were terrible missiles at seven to ten feet, which was the normal range at which the gun was used.

Just the other day, here in El Paso, a derringer dropped from an officer's pocket and exploded. The vicious slug struck a bystander in the leg and mangled it so badly that amputation above the knee was necessary. The officer's badge was Number 13, incidentally! They are deadly—these stubby pistols—out of all proportion to their small size!

When Wild Bill Hickok was marshal of Abilene, Kansas, in '71, Phil Coe of Texas was partner in the famous old Bull's Head Saloon with Ben Thompson, the gambler-gunman. Wild Bill and Thompson were like two champion boxers. Each had a hefty rep' and a thorough respect for the other's prowess. There can be no argument about this, for both gentlemen bore permanent shoulder-callouses from chip-carrying, Thompson being the more belligerent, Hickok the craftier. In their respective roles of chief of police and Protector-of-Texasmen, Hickok and Thompson were natural antagonists. But they managed to avoid open friction.

Phil Coe, however, was no Ben Thompson. It is always amusing to hear him referred to as a gunman. In his native Austin, Texas, he almost never carried a weapon. Tall, always immaculately dressed, he was a magnificent figure of a man. So was Wild Bill. And they fell out over a lovely painted lady of the town. Ben Thompson left Abilene to get his wife and family. Coe went on a spree and shot his six-shooter off in Texas Street. Out popped Wild Bill and—there are two tales as to what happened. The story that came to Ben Thompson, lying with an injured leg in a Kansas City hotel, was that Wild Bill took advantage of Coe— waited until he turned his head away, then whipped out two derringers, and fired them at pointblank range into Coe. True or not, this is the story which was generally believed in Texas in my own childhood.

Ten years ago, on an El Paso street, two of us saw a man shot down at short range by a derringer. We looked incredulously at the holes made by the .41 slugs. I told the other man then that I could at last understand how Phil Coe, pistol in hand, failed to get Wild Bill after being shot. The numbing force of those mushrooming projectiles is tremendous.

Sleeve-draws are like swivel-holsters—more talked about than used. Actually, most so-called sleeve-draws are productions, rather than draws. I have heard of cunningly contrived mechanisms, similar to the gamblers' card-holders, used for derringers in the sleeve, but for me they remain in that hazy region where lives the hoop-snake.

However, one derringer-producer appears on very good authority—no less authority than the word of that famous Plainview ranchman, J. Frank Norfleet, who trailed the swindlers who had bilked him back and forth across the continent until he put the cuffs on them.

Norfleet had walked into a hotel room upon two of his men. He "threw down" on them and snapped his command:

"Up with 'em!"

One of the men snapped up his hands with a jerk that somehow roused Norfleet's suspicion. He stared hard at the fellow's right hand, and it seemed to him that there was an odd lump showing on the crook's fingers. Very cautiously he investigated and found that a derringer was suspended from the elbow by a length of elastic webbing. Normally it hung with the muzzle just above the heel of the palm. That jerk had snapped it into the fellow's palm. So he stood, ostensibly helpless, with a deadly weapon which would have escaped the notice of one less keen-eyed than this ranchman.

But it remained for a gambler on a steamship, Central America bound, to show me the neatest derringer hide-out of them all. He had not figured it out for himself, he admitted. In his roving life he had seen a tiny sleeve spring holster and had it duplicated. (Sam Myres tells me he has made several of these in the past forty years, besides the one I illustrate as Figure 17.)

When strapped to the wrist, the coat sleeve hoods the derringer butt which, as shown, is at the wrist, the muzzles pointing up the arm. This holster differs from the regular full-sized spring holster, in that the pistol is slid under the holding spring loop with butt pointing away from the owner.

Doubtless, there are still other hide-outs. But the ones described and illustrated in my text and pictures are

those tested, proven maneuvers commonly used by the gun-fighters—the stunts so often encountered in the pages of Western fact and fiction.

Fig. 17

By way of farewell to the fascinating topic of Triggernometry, I bring forward Dutch Henry Ziplinsky, old Hashknife and Carlisle man, whose ancestors' legs have been bowed to the shape of a horse's ribs and their hands curved to fit the handles of weapons for a thousand years. He is the son of a Cossack officer who came to Mexico with the ill-fated Maximilian and barely escaped the Emperor's fate. Henry has known many of the old gunmen; has watched them perform their sleight-of-hand; has perfected himself in the tricks of each. He says:

"For practice, there's nothing better than the so-called poker chip draw. Hang your gun to fit your arm. Now, take a poker chip and put it on the back of your gun-hand. Hold the gun-hand out at shoulder-level. Turn the wrist deliberately, to let the poker chip drop—and go for your gun as if somebody was pulling to kill you! See if you can get it out, cocked, up to horizontal, and pointed—as you'd point your forefinger—at the target, and a shot loosed, all before the chip hits the floor.

"It will be some time before you can loose one shot ahead of the rap of the chip on the floor. But practice will make you amazingly fast and accurate. Harvey Logan (Kid Curry) of Butch Cassidy's Wild Bunch could click out three shots, to beat the chip. Whatever luck you have with the stunt, your draw will be improved marvelously. That falling chip is something to compete with. It keeps you at high tension."

Henry talks of Logan's speed. But I have seen him do as well as Logan's record.

Pink Simms is always "monkeying around" with his fellow-Lewistowner, Ed McGivern, the famous pistol expert. Simms and McGivern have recently put a stop-watch on the poker chip trick. Three-tenths of a second is Simms' time for one shot ahead of the dropping chip, but he will do faster drawing than that, with practice.

McGivern has done more to check the *possibilities* of gunplay than any other man I know. With electric timing and firing devices created by himself, he has definitely exploded many a Wild Bill myth, by demonstrating that the feat mentioned by hero-worshipping chroniclers is beyond the physical capabilities of arm or ammunition.

On January 24, 1934, McGivern made a world's record for fast shooting and one which (I think) none of the old-timers could have approached. Checked by electric timers, he put five shots into a target, grouped to be covered by a hand, *in 2/5ths of a second!*

Photographs and descriptions of this and other well-nigh incredible, but always authenticated, feats will appear in McGivern's forthcoming book.

TRIGGERNOMETRY · *Bibliography*

EUGENE Cunningham described his bibliography as "good, bad and indifferent," and many of the books were added to his list as each edition appeared, with no attempt to present them alphabetically. Therefore, they have now been alphabetized and updated to include the name of the publisher, the year of publication, and any subsequent reprints.

Bowers, Claude G. *Tragic Era: The Revolution after Lincoln.* Cambridge: Houghton Mifflin, 1929.

Breakenridge, William M. *Helldorado: Bringing the Law to the Mesquite.* Boston: Houghton Mifflin, 1928. Reprint, Glorieta, N.M.: Rio Grande Press, 1970.

Burns, Walter Noble. *The Saga of Billy the Kid.* N.Y.: Doubleday, Page, 1926, 1951.

Bush, Dr. I. J. *Gringo Doctor.* Caldwell, Idaho.: Caxton Printers, 1939.

Chapel, Charles Edward. *Gun Collecting.* N.Y.: Coward-McCann, 1939.

Cowan, Robert Ellsworth ("Bud"). *Range Rider.* N.Y.: Doubleday, Doran, 1930.

Deutsch, Hermann B. *The Incredible Yanqui: The Career of Lee Christmas.* London: Longmans, Green, 1931.

Dixon, Mrs. Olive K. *The Life of Billy Dixon.* Dallas, Tex.: P. L. Turner, 1914; rev. ed. 1927.

El Paso Times. El Paso, Tex.

Frontier Times Magazine. Bandera, Tex.

Fuller, Henry Clay. *Adventures of Bill Longley.* Nacogdoches, Tex.: Baker Printing, [1878?].

Garrett, Pat F. *Authentic Life of Billy the Kid.* Ed. Maurice Garland Fulton. N.Y.: Macmillan, 1927. Reprint, Norman: Univ. of Oklahoma Press, 1954.

Gillett, James B. *Six Years with the Texas Rangers.* New Haven, Conn.: Yale Univ. Press, 1925.

441

Hardin, John Wesley. *The Life of John Wesley Hardin As Written by Himself.* Seguin, Tex.: Smith and Moore, 1896. Reprint, Bandera, Tex.: Frontier Times, 1926; Norman: Univ. of Oklahoma Press, 1961.

Henry, Stuart. *Conquering Our Great American Plains.* N.Y.: E. P. Dutton, 1930.

Hogg, Thomas E. *Authentic History of Sam Bass and His Gang.* Denton, Tex.: Monitor Job Office, 1878. Reprint, Bandera, Tex.: Frontier Times, 1926.

Hough, Emerson. *The Story of the Outlaw.* N.Y.: Grosset and Dunlap, 1907.

Hoyt, Henry Franklin. *A Frontier Doctor.* Boston: Houghton Mifflin, 1929.

James, Marquis. *The Raven: A Biography of Sam Houston.* Indianapolis, Ind.: Bobbs-Merrill, 1929.

Jennings, Napoleon Augustus. *A Texas Ranger.* N.Y.: Charles Scribner's Sons, 1899. Reprint, Dallas, Tex.: Southwest Press, 1930; Ruidoso, N.M.; Frontier Book, 1960; Norman, Univ. of Oklahoma Press, 1997.

Lake, Stuart N. *Wyatt Earp: Frontier Marshal.* Boston: Houghton Mifflin, 1931.

Langford, Nathaniel Pitt. *Vigilante Days and Ways.* Boston: J. G. Cupples, 1890. Reprint, Missoula: Montana State Univ. Press, 1957.

McGivern, Ed. *Ed McGivern's Book on Fast and Fancy Revolver Shooting and Police Training.* Springfield, Mass.: King-Richardson, 1938.

McIntire, James. *Early Days in Texas: A Trip to Hell and Heaven.* Kansas City, Mo.: McIntire Publishing, 1902. Reprint, Norman: Univ. of Oklahoma Press, 1992.

Mills, William W. *Forty Years at El Paso (1858–1898).* Chicago: W. B. Conkey, 1901. Reprint, El Paso, Tex.: Carl Hertzog, 1962.

Poe, John W. *The True Story of the Death of "Billy the Kid" (Notorious New Mexico Outlaw), As Detailed . . . to E. A. Brininstool.* Los Angeles, Calif.: privately printed by E. A. Brininstool, 1922. Reprint, Houston, Tex.: Frontier Press of Texas, 1958.

Poe, Sophie (Mrs. John W. Poe). *Buckboard Days.* Ed. Eugene Cunningham. Caldwell, Idaho: Caxton Printers, 1936.

Raine, William MacLeod, and Will C. Barnes. *Cattle.* N.Y.: Doubleday, Doran, 1930.

Reports of the Adjutant General, Texas. Austin, Tex.: Adjutant General's Office, [various years].

Ridings, Samuel P. *The Chisholm Trail: A History of the World's Greatest Cattle Trail.* Guthrie, Okla.: Co-operative Publishing, 1936. Reprint, Medford, Okla.: Grant County Historical Society, 1975.

Shipman, Mrs. O. L. *Taming the Big Bend: A History of the Extreme Western Portion of Texas from Fort Clark to El Paso*. Austin, Tex.: von Boeckmann-Jones, 1926.

Siringo, Charles A. *A Cowboy Detective*. Chicago: W. B. Conkey, 1912.

———. *Riata and Spurs: The Story of a Lifetime Spent in the Saddle As Cowboy and Detective*. Boston: Houghton Mifflin, 1927.

Smith and Wesson. *Burning Powder*. Springfield, Mass.: Smith and Wesson, n.d.

Sullivan, W. John L. *Twelve Years in the Saddle for Law and Order on the Frontiers of Texas*. Austin, Tex.: von Boeckmann-Jones, 1909. Reprint, N.Y.: Buffalo-Head Press, 1966.

Train, Arthur. *True Stores of Crime from the District Attorney's Office*. N.Y.: Charles Scribner's Sons, 1908.

Further Reading

Most of the following volumes are still in print or are easily obtainable and reflect current opinion and up-to-date research.

Adams, Ramon F. *Six-Guns and Saddle Leather: A Bibliography of Books and Pamphlets on Western Outlaws and Gunmen*. Norman: Univ. of Oklahoma Press, 1954; rev. ed. 1969.

Bell, Bob Boze. *The Illustrated Life and Times of Billy the Kid*. Cave Creek, Ariz.: Boze Books, 1992.

———. *The Illustrated Life and Times of Doc Holliday*. Cave Creek, Ariz.: Boze Books, 1994.

———. *The Illustrated Life and Times of Wyatt Earp*. Cave Creek, Ariz.: Boze Books, 1994.

Betenson, Lula Parker (as told to Dora Flack). *Butch Cassidy: My Brother*. Provo, Utah: Brigham Young Univ. Press, 1975.

Boessenecker, John. *Badge and Buckshot: Lawlessness in Old California*. Norman: Univ. of Oklahoma Press, 1988.

Burton, Art. *Black, Red, and Deadly: Black and Indian Gunfighters of the Indian Territory, 1870–1907*. Austin, Tex.: Eakin Press, 1991.

DeArment, Robert K. *Bat Masterson: The Man and the Legend*. Norman: Univ. of Oklahoma Press, 1979.

———. *George Scarborough: The Life and Death of a Lawman on the Closing Frontier*. Norman: Univ. of Oklahoma Press, 1992.

DeMattos, Jack. *Mysterious Gunfighter: The Story of Dave Mather.* College Station, Tex.: Creative Publishing, 1992.

Dimsdale, Thomas. *The Vigilantes of Montana.* Virginia City, Mont.: T. E. Castle and C. W. Bank, 1921. Reprint, Norman: Univ. of Oklahoma Press, 1953.

Dugan, Mark. *Tales Never Told Around the Campfire: True Stories of Frontier America.* Athens, Ohio: Swallow Press/Univ. of Ohio Press, 1992.

Dykstra, Robert R. *The Cattle Towns.* N.Y.: Alfred A. Knopf, 1968.

Egloff, Fred R. *El Paso Lawman: G. W. Campbell.* College Station, Tex.: Creative Publishing, 1982.

Freeman, G.D. *Midnight and Noonday: Or the Incidental History of Southern Kansas and the Indian Territory, 1871–1890.* Ed. and annot. by Richard Lane. Norman: Univ. of Oklahoma Press, 1984.

Gard, Wayne. *Frontier Justice.* Norman: Univ. of Oklahoma Press, 1949.

Hendricks, George D. *The Bad Man of the West.* San Antonio, Tex.: Naylor Company, 1950.

Horn, Tom. *Life of Tom Horn, Government Scout and Interpreter, Written by Himself, Together with His Letters and Statements by His Friends: A Vindication.* Denver, Colo.: Louthan Book, 1904. Reprint, Norman: Univ. of Oklahoma Press, 1964.

Knight, Oliver. *Fort Worth: Outpost on the Trinity.* Norman: Univ. of Oklahoma Press, 1953.

Krakel, Dean F. *The Saga of Tom Horn.* Laramie, Wyo.: Powder River Publishers, 1954.

Lamar, Howard R., ed. *The Reader's Encyclopedia of the American West.* N.Y.: Thomas Y. Crowell, 1977.

McGivern, Edward. *Fast and Fancy Revolver Shooting.* Chicago: Follett Publishing, 1975.

Marohn, Richard C. *The Last Gunfighter: John Wesley Hardin.* College Station, Tex.: Creative Publishing, 1995.

Martin, Charles L. *A Sketch of Sam Bass, the Bandit.* Dallas, Tex.: Worley, 1880. Reprint, Norman: Univ. of Oklahoma Press, 1956.

Masterson, William B. *Famous Gun Fighters of the Western Frontier.* 1907. Reprint, annot. and illus. by Jack DeMattos. Monroe, Wash.: Weatherford Press, 1982.

Metz, Leon C. *Dallas Stoudenmire: El Paso Marshal.* Austin, Tex.: Pemberton Publishing, 1969. Reprint, Norman: Univ. of Oklahoma Press, 1979.

———. *John Selman: Texas Gunfighter.* N.Y.: Hastings House, 1966. Reprint, Norman: Univ. of Oklahoma Press, 1980.

————. *Pat Garrett: The Story of a Western Lawman.* Norman: Univ. of Oklahoma Press, 1974.

Miller, Nyle H. and Joseph W. Snell. *Why the West Was Wild.* Topeka: Kansas State Historical Society, 1963. Republished in an abridged form as *Great Gunfighters of the Kansas Cowtowns, 1867–1886.* Lincoln: Univ. of Nebraska Press, 1966.

Nolan, Frederick. *The Lincoln County War: A Documentary History.* Norman: Univ. of Oklahoma Press, 1992.

O'Neal, Bill. *Encyclopedia of Western Gunfighters.* Norman: Univ. of Oklahoma Press, 1979.

Pointer, Larry. *In Search of Butch Cassidy.* Norman: Univ. of Oklahoma Press, 1977.

Prassel, Frank R. *The Great American Outlaw: A Legacy of Fact and Fiction.* Norman: Univ. of Oklahoma Press, 1993.

————. *The Western Peace Officer: A Legacy of Law and Order.* Norman: Univ. of Oklahoma Press, 1977.

Rosa, Joseph G. *Age of the Gunfighter: Men and Weapons on the Frontier 1840–1900.* London: Salamander Books, 1993; Norman: Univ. of Oklahoma Press, 1995.

————. *The Gunfighter: Man or Myth?* Norman: Univ. of Oklahoma Press, 1969.

————. *Guns of the American West.* London: Arms and Armour Press, 1985.

————. *They Called Him Wild Bill: The Life and Adventures of James Butler Hickok.* Norman: Univ. of Oklahoma Press, 1964; 2nd ed. 1974.

————. *The West of Wild Bill Hickok.* Norman: Univ. of Oklahoma Press, 1982.

Rosa, Joseph G., and Waldo E. Koop. *Rowdy Joe Lowe: Gambler with a Gun.* Norman: Univ. of Oklahoma Press, 1989.

Rosa, Joseph G., and Robin May. *Gunsmoke: A Study of Violence in The Wild West.* London: New English Library, 1977. Published in the United States as *Gun Law: A Study of Violence in the Wild West.* Chicago: Contemporary Books, 1977.

Secrest, William B. *Dangerous Men: Gunfighters, Lawmen and Outlaws of Old California.* Fresno, Cal.: Saga-West Publishing, 1976.

————. *Lawmen and Desperadoes: A Compendium of Noted, Early California Peace Officers, Badmen and Outlaws (1850–1900).* Spokane, Wash.: Arthur H. Clark, 1994.

Shillingberg, William B. *Wyatt Earp and the "Buntline Special" Myth.* Tucson, Ariz.: Blaine Publishing, 1976.

Steckmesser, Kent L. *The Western Hero in History and Legend*. Norman: Univ. of Oklahoma Press, 1965.

Streeter, Floyd Benjamin. *Ben Thompson: Man with a Gun*. Intro. by William F. Kelleher. N.Y.: Frederick Fell, 1957.

Tuska, Jon. *Billy the Kid: His Life and Legend*. Westport, Conn.: Greenwood Press, 1994.

Utley, Robert M. *Billy the Kid: A Short and Violent Life*. Lincoln: Univ. of Nebraska Press, 1989.

Webb, Walter Prescott. *The Texas Rangers: A Century of Frontier Defense*. Austin: Univ. of Texas Press, 1965.